Migration in the Mediterranean

Migration in the Mediterranean region is a widely debated and much studied topic. This is due to the present refugee crisis, consequences of Arab revolutions, the proximity with emigration and transit countries, but also to the involvement of Southern European countries and the mass arrival of migrants. The management of border controls, migration, development, human trafficking, human rights and the clash or convergence of civilizations has generated a great deal of controversy and media attention.

Migration in the Mediterranean offers a unique multidisciplinary theoretical and methodological framework, bringing together scholars from different subject areas. This book aims to address the following research questions: What are the main characteristics of migration movements in this region? What are the most important theoretical challenges? What are the perspectives for the future? This book begins with an overview of the economic perspective of the Mediterranean migration model, with a particular focus on labour market outcomes of migrants. It then presents the original results of field studies on the unintended effects of the EU's external border controls on migration and integration in the Euro-Mediterranean region, before addressing the themes of mobility, migration and transnationalism.

This volume focuses on migration with a multidisciplinary approach, with scholars from various areas including sociology, economics, geography, political science and history. This book is well suited for those who study international economics, migration and political sociology.

Elena Ambrosetti is Assistant Professor in Demography at the Faculty of Economics and affiliated to the Department of Methods and Models for Economics, Territory and Finance, Sapienza University of Rome, Italy.

Donatella Strangio is Associate Professor of Economic History at the Faculty of Economics and affiliated to the Department of Methods and Models for Economics, Territory and Finance, Sapienza University of Rome, Italy.

Catherine Wihtol de Wenden is Director of Research at CNRS (CERI), Paris, France.

Routledge Studies in the European Economy

Migration in the Mediterranean
Socio-economic perspectives

**Edited by Elena Ambrosetti,
Donatella Strangio and
Catherine Wihtol de Wenden**

Routledge
Taylor & Francis Group

LONDON AND NEW YORK

First published 2016
by Routledge

2 Park Square, Milton Park, Abingdon, Oxfordshire OX14 4RN
52 Vanderbilt Avenue, New York, NY 10017

Routledge is an imprint of the Taylor & Francis Group, an informa business

First issued in paperback 2020

British Library Cataloguing in Publication Data
A catalogue record for this book is available from the British Library

Library of Congress Cataloging in Publication Data
Names: Ambrosetti, Elena, editor. | Strangio, Donatella, editor. | Wihtol de
Wenden, Catherine, editor.
Title: Migration in the Mediterranean : socio-economic perspectives / edited
by Elena Ambrosetti, Donatella Strangio and Catherine Wihtol de Wenden.
Description: Abingdon, Oxon ; New York, NY : Routledge, 2016. | Includes
bibliographical references.
Identifiers: LCCN 2015048451| ISBN 9781138642492 (hardback) | ISBN
9781315629957 (ebook)
Subjects: LCSH: Mediterranean Region–Emigration and immigration. |
European Union countries–Emigration and immigration–Government
policy.
Classification: LCC JV7590 .M486 2016 | DDC 304.809182/2–dc23
LC record available at http://lccn.loc.gov/2015048451

ISBN: 978-1-138-64249-2 (hbk)
ISBN: 978-0-367-66833-4 (pbk)

Typeset in Times New Roman
by Cenveo Publisher Services

Contents

Figures

Tables

Foreword

Raimondo Cagiano de Azevedo

During the past 30 years, migration flows from the Mediterranean countries towards Western Europe have changed in content, nature and purposes: from a European internal phenomenon, they have acquired an intercontinental dimension due to underdevelopment, overpopulation, political instability and wars.

How should Europe, now facing an enduring population ageing process, react to such migratory pressure? Should it endeavour to absorb and integrate such flows or should it discourage them through repressive measures? Alternatively, should Europe cooperate with the countries of origin to endorse development, stability and thus prevent emigration?

Too quickly neglected, the Neighbourhood Policy of the European Union aimed at maintaining an 'understanding' approach in respect to all neighbours, centred on the idea of sharing 'everything but institutions'. In this regard, it referred specifically to a model, based on a single market and a single *acquis communautaire* (that is, the set of rights and duties that the Europeans have given themselves over the past 60 years), which linked EFTA countries with the EU 'under the same roof'. This model, which did not necessarily involve membership as a compulsory condition, has acquired its importance nowadays considering the fact that countries bordering the Mediterranean have suggested the creation and development of a common Euro-Mediterranean area. Therefore, the *acquis communautaire* appears as a real boundary, since it represents a qualitative and quantitative parameter for the implementation of new policies in the EU. The *acquis communautaire* represents the sedimentation of treaties, agreements, laws, regulations and procedures that the EU has adopted over the last 60 years.

Which are Europe's borders? Which boundaries define its limits? In the past, European borders were defined by geographical and political demarcations and straits (Gibraltar). While many people see boundaries in religion and others in human rights, nevertheless, more likely, Europe's borders correspond to the boundaries of the *acquis communautaire*.

The *acquis communautaire* is, by its very nature, closely linked to the above-mentioned legal principles. However, it is also embedded in the 'society of knowledge' which consists firstly of rules and rights and secondly of technological and technical-scientific progress, implemented through academic exchanges and research. Finally the *acquis communautaire* is, more in general, curiosity and openness towards one another. This last should lead to social cohesion and integration in our society.

The various aspects of immigration and asylum policies are restricted to national boundaries especially with regard to the admission of third-country nationals in the territory of each member state; and today we can add the very difficult issue of asylum seekers.

The predominant approach to migration remains the national one, or even the local, despite the ongoing interconnections among territories and policies, and are perceived as such by a growing number of people who wish to access them.

At a time when all factors are moving in a globalized world, it is now impossible for the European Union, which is a strong pole of attraction for those who are outside it, to further delay the overcoming of this still partial vision. To implement such policies, it is necessary to develop a common and integrated governance for all aspects of migration. This would be, indeed, the only possible response to a fragmentation of opposite ideological positions creating situations of exclusion that, far from guaranteeing security, often produce the opposite result.

The European approach to migration policy as a whole – based upon the principle of subsidiarity – should handle the problems of integration and multiculturalism locally, the migratory flows and the settlements nationally, and should preserve on a supranational level (EU) the political directions of migration, including relations with the regions of origin.

The studies included in this volume are a clear and positive contribution to the academic analysis of these issues and a very pertinent way of thinking and facing the current concerns in the Mediterranean region.

Contributors

Elena Ambrosetti is Assistant Professor in Demography at the Faculty of Economics and affiliated to the Department of Methods and Models for Economics, Territory and Finance, Sapienza University of Rome. She holds a doctorate in Demography and Economics (2006) from the Institut d'Etudes Politiques in Paris. She is regularly visiting research fellow at INED (France), Université Aix-Marseille (France), Institut d'Etudes Politiques de Paris (France). Her main fields of interest are: the demography of the Mediterranean countries, fertility transition, gender issues and migration in the Mediterranean area.

Maurizio Ambrosini, PhD in Sociology (1989), is Professor of Sociology of Migrations at the university of Milan and Chargé d'enseignement at the University of Nice (France). He is the editor of the journal *Mondi migranti*, one of the most cited Italian sociological journals, and the Director of the Summer School of Sociology of Migrations of Genoa. He is the author of more than 200 articles, chapters and books in this field, published in different languages, among them, *Irregular Migrations and Invisible Welfare* (Palgrave, 2013) and *Sociologia delle migrazioni* (Il Mulino, 2011), adopted as textbook in many Italian universities.

Raimondo Cagiano de Azevedo is full Professor of Demography and Director of a Unesco Chair on 'Population, Migrations and Development' at Sapienza University of Rome. He has been Director of CUIA (Italian University Consortium for Argentina) and Deputy Rector for international affairs of Sapienza University. He was President of the European Committee for the Population of the Council of Europe (Strasbourg). He was also Scientific Secretary of the National Committee on Population at the Premier's Cabinet of the Italian Government, Department of Social Affairs. He is member of the Editorial Board of the Reviews *Affari Sociali Internazionali*, *L'Europe en Formation*, *Studi Emigrazione*, *GENUS*, *Welfare papers*.

Giovanna Campani is Professor of Intercultural Pedagogy and Gender Anthropology at the University of Florence. Her main research field comprises intercultural education, comparative pedagogy, female migrations, migrations and gender, social inclusion/exclusion, refugee protection, trafficking in human beings, migrants' labour integration, and unaccompanied minor migrants. Professor Campani has operated in the field of international multilevel research beginning from 1988–89 with a project on self-employed women, entitled 'Immigrant Women and Social Promotion', and directed by Mirjana Morokvasic (Commission for Equal Opportunities), and another one on 'Women's Education in Italy', directed by Professor Margaret Sutherland for the Council of Comparative Education.

Anna Di Bartolomeo holds a PhD in Demography from the Sapienza University of Rome and the European Research Master of Demography, obtained at the European Doctoral School of Demography. She is currently Research Fellow at the Migration Policy Centre, European University Institute. Her research interests include international migration and demographic determinants, migration in Arab and CIS countries, immigrants' children and education, migrants' integration. Her recent publications include *The Geography of Arab Highly-Skilled Migration* (with P. Fargues), IB Tauris, London, 2015; 'Calling into Question the Link between Educational Achievement and Migrant Background' (with S. Bonfanti), EUI, San Domenico di Fiesole, 44: 2014.

Francesca Fauri has extensively published on issues concerning the history of European economic integration, Italy's post-war economic and business history and the history of European and Italian migration movements. Her last book in English (edited with Routledge) was on the History of Migration in Europe. She holds a Jean Monnet Chair in European Economic and Migration History, she is an Associate Professor of Economic History at the Department of Economics of the University of Bologna and teaches European Economic History at the School of Political Sciences (Forlì Campus) and Economic History at the School of Economics in Bologna.

Ivana Fellini is Assistant Professor in Economic Sociology at the University of Milan-Bicocca where she teaches Sociology of Work. With a degree in Economics and PhD in Economic Sociology, her main interests cover the labour market structure and trends, with focus on immigration, gender, flexibility and social inclusion issues. She contributed to national and international projects on migration and to several research and evaluation activities in the field of labour policy both for the EC and the European Parliament, and for national and regional institutions. She is coordinating the Italian team of an international research project on migration (GEMM – Growth Equal Opportunities, Migration and Markets) funded by the European Commission (started in 2015).

Giovanna Fullin is Associate Professor in Economic Sociology at the University of Milan-Bicocca with a degree in Economics and PhD in Economic

Sociology. Her main interests cover the labour market structure and trends, with focus on immigrants, work conditions in the service sector and non-standard jobs. She participated to several international research projects on migrations issues. Recently, together with Emilio Reyneri, she coordinated two international research groups on integration of immigrants in the labour market (part of Network of Excellence EQUALSOC) and was guest editor of two special issues on migration (*International Migration* and *International Journal of Comparative Sociology*). She is involved in an international research project on migration (GEMM – Growth Equal Opportunities, Migration and Markets) funded by the European Commission (started in 2015).

Giuseppe Gabrielli is Assistant Professor in Demography at the University of Naples, Federico II. He teaches Economic Demography and Applied Demography at the Department of Political Sciences. He is general secretary of the Italian Association for Population Studies (AISP). His research topics focus on the dynamics of immigrant populations in Europe, in Italy and its regions; the family formation and the reproductive behaviour of autochthonous and immigrants, according to their different origins; the different levels of integration, in order to individuate intervention policies. In addition, his research interests concern immigrants' occupational condition, the integration of second generations and transnational couples.

Thomas Lacroix is CNRS Research Fellow and Deputy Director of Migrinter, University of Poitiers. His work focuses on the nexus between transnational-ism, development and integration. He has extensively published in journals such as *International Migration Review*, *Journal of Ethnic and Migration Studies* and *Journal of Intercultural Studies*. He os the author of two books: *Les Réseaux Marocains du Développement* (Presses de Science Po, 2005) and *Hometown Transnationalism: Long Distance Villageness among North African Berbers and Indian Punjabis* (Palgrave, 2015).

Zoran Lapov, PhD. Formed in a multidisciplinary and interdisciplinary environ-ment, Lapov's scientific profile involves contributions from anthropology, linguistics, pedagogy and intercultural studies. His research work focuses on socio-cultural and linguistic diversity, identity dynamics, intercultural relations and mechanisms of social inclusion/exclusion in relation to minorities and migrations. Lapov's research activity is best reflected in his numerous publica-tions. Along with academic activities (lectures/seminars, participation in local, national and international research projects), Lapov has a long-standing experi-ence with foreign and minority (especially Roma) children both in terms of research and teaching.

Guillaume Le Roux, geographer and statistician, is a post-doctoral fellow at Migrinter, University of Poitiers, France. His doctoral work provides an analysis of recent urban changes in Bogotá through the study of migration and residential trajectories of the inhabitants. He contributed to several chapters of the book *Mobilités et changement urbain: Bogotá, Santiago et São Paulo* (Dureau *et al.* 2014) and presented papers in various international seminars: in Lyon (France, MSFS, November 2015); in Bogotá (Colombia, ACIUR, September 2012); in Belo Horizonte (Brazil, RII, October 2012).

Lea Müller-Funk is a joint PhD candidate in Political Science and Arabic Studies at Sciences Po Paris and the University of Vienna. She holds an MA in Comparative Politics in the Middle East from Sciences Paris, an MA in Arabic Studies and a BA in Political Science from the University of Vienna. Between 2011 and 2015, she worked as a researcher and lecturer at the Department for Near Eastern Studies at the University of Vienna.

Angela Paparusso is a PhD candidate in Demography at the Doctoral School in Statistical Sciences at Sapienza University of Rome, with a research project on Italian immigration and integration policies. She graduated with honours in International Cooperation and Development, with a thesis on borders and migration in Europe that has been awarded by the Foundation Roma Sapienza for the 'best master's degree in the discipline of Social Sciences'. She recently finished the European Master in Demography degree of the European Doctoral School of Demography (EDSD) – at the Autonomous University of Barcelona. She has been also visiting doctoral student at CERI Sciences Po.

Enza Roberta Petrillo is a Post-Doctoral Researcher at EuroSapienza, the Centre for European, International and Development Studies of the Sapienza University of Rome. Her research interests include national and EU migration policy, forced migration, EU borderlands, trans-border smuggling and Eastern European politics and geopolitics. Graduated with mention in Political Science (2003) and PhD in Geopolitics (2009), she has ten years of progressive professional experience in policy-oriented analysis including service for international organizations, NGOs, think-tanks, and governmental institutions. She has extensive experience in field research in Eastern European countries and in analysing complex political and social settings, using qualitative research methodology.

Roberta Ricucci is Associate Professor at the University of Turin in the Department of Culture, Politics and Society, where she teaches Sociology of Inter-ethnic Relations and Sociology of Islam. She is also senior researcher at the International and European Forum of Migration Research and member of the international networks IMISCOE (International Migration, Integration and Social Cohesion). She has wide and varied experience of research on immigration issues, both at national and international levels, also as visiting research fellow at the University of Princeton (NJ, US), Melbourne (Australia), Notre Dame (IN, US). Her recent research has generally been focused on immigrant children and second generations, investigating, especially among Muslims, their identity-building process and religiousness.

Donatella Strangio is Associate Professor of Economic History at the Faculty of Economics and affiliated to the Department of Methods and Models for Economics, Territory and Finance, Sapienza University of Rome. She has a PhD in Economic History and was a Research Fellow at the London School of Economics (UK), the Maison des Sciences de l'Homme, Paris, France and the University of Adelaide (AU). She is regular visiting professor on immigration issues at the University of Buenos Aires (UBA) and the University of Caxias do Sul (BRA). Among her main research interests are international migration, public finance, and long-term economic growth.

Salvatore Strozza is full Professor in Demography at the University of Naples Federico II, Vice-Director of the Department of Political Sciences. He is currently President of the Italian Association for Population Studies (AISP-SIS) and is on the editorial board of two international journals: *Genus and Studi Emigrazione/Migration Studies*. His main area of research is international migration and, in particular, foreign immigration in Italy. Major contributions concern the sources and methods of measurement and estimates of the phenomenon; demographic consequences of international migration; immigration and labour markets in the receiving country; measures and determinants of immigrant integration; the second generation and the Italian school system.

Emanuela Trevisan Semi is Associate Professor in Modern Hebrew and Jewish Studies at University Ca' Foscari of Venice. She is European Coordinator of a EMJMD programme Erasmus plus 'Crossing the Mediterranean: Cultural Mediation Towards Investment and Integration' (with UAB in Barcelona and UPVM in Montpellier). She has published books and articles on Karaites, Jews of Ethiopia, Judaizing movements and on issues related to memory and perception of Jews in Morocco. She is currently working on life-writing of Morocco Jewish diaspora.

Catherine Wihtol de Wenden is Director of Research at CNRS (CERI). For 30 years she has been a researcher on international migration, from a Political Science and Public Law approach. She studied in Sciences-Po Paris and University Paris I (Panthéon-Sorbonne). She got her PhD in Political Science in 1986. She has published 20 books, alone or as co-writer, and around 150 articles. She is also teaching at Sciences-Po, at the University La Sapienza in an EU Socrates Programme. She has been President of the Research Committee Migration of ISA (International Sociological Association) (2002–08) and expert for several international organizations (UNHCR, Council of Europe and European Commission).

Introduction

Elena Ambrosetti and Donatella Strangio

The richness of the Mediterranean is the fruit of diversity. Many attempts have been made in the past to find some common element that distinguishes the Mediterranean countries from other areas of the world, defining a distinctive character.

Often this common element was identified in the physical conditions, for example the orography, characterized by regions facing the inland sea; other times in some aspects of flora and wildlife; finally in the common cultural roots that sink in ancient civilization. In reality all these attempts to identify the specificity of the Mediterranean were and are doomed to fail.

Mediterranean regions have, in fact, sharp diversities. The physical characteristics are quite different from area to area; there are various productive and economic specializations; differences between cultures are difficult to reconcile; there are also strong inequalities in social forms and in the political organization. However these differences were the main cause of the wealth of the Mediterranean region in its long history. Since the inland sea (Malanima 2005) enables easier and cheaper communications than the land does, these differences have been turned into a source of wealth. From the economic point of view, it has allowed the existence of exchanges of different goods: from raw materials industry (silk, wool, leather, metallic) to food (wheat) and manufactured goods.

If we Google 'Migration in the Mediterranean' the first ten results are as follows: security, a boat full of migrants, the numbers of illegal migrants detected, a map of 'the encampments' in Europe and around the Mediterranean Sea, a map of African and Mediterranean irregular migration routes … and so on. This is not surprising because, paradoxically, this important world region is one of the most closed to migration movements when it comes to South–North migration, as border control has been the *leitmotiv* of European migration policies for more than two decades. Migration in the Mediterranean region is a widely debated and much studied topic. Border controls and management, migration and development, human trafficking and human rights and the clash or convergence of civilizations are among the themes presented daily in local and international newspapers and on television news.

This book aims, starting from the recent history of migration movements in the Mediterranean, to shed light on the characteristics of contemporary migration in this region. It questions the economic and social dynamics that migration can stimulate in the local contexts of origin and destination and the possible role of migrants in the challenge of the Euro-Mediterranean integration.

The book is organized in three parts. Part 1 brings together economics, demography and sociology. It is dedicated to theoretical debate and the advancement of the topic of Mediterranean migrations. In Chapter 1, Ambrosetti and Strangio deal with the theoretical framework of the book: is the Mediterranean a migration space? Could a migration system be identified? Or more realistically, is there a migratory 'régime'? The following chapters are organized so as to give an overview of the economic perspective of the Mediterranean migration model, with a particular focus on labour market outcomes of migrants. Chapter 2 deals with Italian migrations to North Africa during Italy's mass migration movement (1890–1914). This chapter by Francesca Fauri offers a good example of the migration system existing at that time because African Mediterranean countries allowed quite a free circulation of goods and men, as no documents were requested on arrival and registration with the local consulate was often disregarded. In Chapter 3 Fellini and Fullin explore the South-European model for the incorporation of immigrants into the labour market with particular regard to Italy, Spain and Portugal and with a special focus on people from Eastern Europe, North Africa and Latin America, taking into account the role of the recent economic crisis: the new features of the 'model' of Southern European immigration proposed by Russell King in 2000 are presented further on. In Chapter 4 Di Bartolomeo, Gabrielli and Strozza deal with the analysis of the evolution of the different characteristics of migration flows in Italy, Spain and the United Kingdom (three of the EU member states with the largest net immigration in the last decade) in order to test how these differences impact upon the occupational conditions of immigrants. In particular, after considering employment conditions, the authors focus on the mismatch between the professional and educational levels of workers by comparing immigrants and natives. The results confirm the different patterns existing between Mediterranean countries and the UK. In contrast to the UK, the overqualification of migrants is much more evident in Italy and Spain, and this is one of the main characteristics of the Southern European model of immigration.

Part 2 of the book presents the original results of field studies on the unintended effects of the EU's external border controls on migration and integration in the Euro-Mediterranean region. In particular Ambrosini in Chapter 5 provides an interesting and innovative theoretical perspective on illegal migration, showing how the fight against illegal immigration proclaimed by governments is counteracted by diverse interests and social representations of the phenomenon that tend to redefine it selectively. In order to do that the chapter examines two main topics: the first is the selective treatment of irregular immigration by receiving societies; the second is the easier transition to a legal status of a part of irregular migrants. In Chapter 6 Petrillo deals with an analysis of the EU's Integrated Border Management Strategy using the paradigmatic case study of unaccompanied Afghan minors smuggled along the Eastern Mediterranean route. Through an analysis of this case study, the research scrutinizes the nature, scope and humanitarian implications of the EU approach to irregular migration. In Chapter 7 Campani and Lapov analyse the gender dimension in the process of border-crossing. It focuses on the case of sub-Saharan African women as border-crossers in the panorama of Africa-to-Europe migrations in three Mediterranean countries, namely Italy, Greece and Turkey. On one side, the contents of this chapter are based upon reports and studies addressing the policies aimed at border hardening and control; on the other, it resorts to findings emerging from the European LeFamSol Project developed in the said Mediterranean countries with women native to the sub-Saharan region who experience migration paths from Africa to Europe and concomitant border crossings. Chapter 8 offers an overview of civic integration policies, using both legal texts and literature references. Angela Paparusso argues that the European convergence towards civic integration is underpinned by a philosophy based on migration control and selection. This philosophy is coherent with the EU policy ideology, which appears to be marked by a 'securitization' approach towards migration.

Part 3 deals with the themes of mobility, migration and transnationalism in the Mediterranean region. Chapter 9 is based on a statistical analysis of the INED survey *Trajectoires et Origines*, on field research and interviews with policy-makers, and it seeks to understand the passage from private to public transnationalism. The study of Lacroix and Le Roux compares the Algerian and Moroccan cases. Specific attention is paid to the influence of the right to vote (present in the Algerian case, but not the Moroccan one) on public transnational practices. In Chapter 10 Müller-Funk examines homeland politics in the aftermath of the Arab Spring revolution in Egypt focusing on networks in Vienna and Paris as case studies. The chapter analyses the differences between the two networks on the basis of two main axes: first, the respective structure and characteristics of Egyptian migration to France and Austria, and second, the interplay between Egyptian state policies governing Egyptians abroad and the political opportunity structure in France and Austria shaping homeland politics. In Chapter 11 Trevisan Semi reconsiders the discourse on diasporas in general and in particular on the Jewish diaspora according to which migration can be distinguished from a diaspora because of the desire to return to the country of origin (real or virtual). In Chapter 12 Ricucci examines generational differences in the ethno-religious identity of Muslim Italians, and places its findings within the larger literature on second generation, acculturation and religiosity.

Several disciplines and scholars meet at the crossroads between the three parts of this volume: demography, sociology, anthropology, economic history, ethnography, political science, geography and literature. As far as the methodological framework is concerned we may classify the chapters of this volume according to three broad approaches: quantitative (Chapters 1, 2, 3, 4 and 9), qualitative (Chapters 6, 7, 9, 10, 11 and 12) and theoretical (Chapters 5 and 8). In Chapter 2 the author built an original dataset using Yearbooks of Statistics from the Italian National Statistics Institute and from the Italian Ministry of Foreign Affairs in order to present Italian migration stocks and flows. In Chapter 3 the authors provide an exploratory cross-national analysis of the Eurostat Labour

Force Survey (LFS) microdata for 2007 and 2012. In Chapter 4 a multidimensional data analysis is performed, on both aggregate and individual data, using micro data from the EU Labour Force Survey carried out in 2008. Chapter 9 is based on a mixed methodology (qualitative and quantitative) provided through the statistical analysis of the INED survey *Trajectoires et Origines* dataset (2008–09) and on field research and interviews with policy-makers. Chapter 6 is based on in-depth semi-structured interviews performed (in 2014) with unaccompanied migrant minors living in Rome. Chapter 7 contains an analysis based on the collection of ten life histories in three countries (Turkey, Greece and Italy). Chapter 10 is based on data collected between March 2012 and July 2014 among political networks of Egyptian migrants living in Paris and Vienna. Qualitative interviews were conducted with people active in these networks, and an analysis was made on the use of social media for political protest. Chapter 11 uses narratives of writers who emigrated to Israel and of Jewish Moroccan origin who emigrated to France, Canada or the United States as its main source. Chapter 12 is based on the data of semi-structured qualitative interviews, on the one hand with 40 Muslims living in Turin, and with civil servants and local administrators on the other.

Part 1

Labour migration movements in the Mediterranean

Past and present

1 Migration in the Mediterranean across disciplines

Elena Ambrosetti and Donatella Strangio

Introduction

Migration in the Mediterranean region is a widely debated and much studied topic. Border controls and management, migration and development, human trafficking and human rights and the clash or convergence of civilizations are among the themes presented daily in local and international newspapers and on television news. The Mediterranean migration area is the largest in the world together with the border between the US and Mexico. The total population of the countries around the Mediterranean coast was 470 million (6.8 per cent of the world population) in 2010 (UN). In the same year the Mediterranean countries hosted 32.7 million migrants, while the total number of emigrants from these countries was 17 million (8 per cent of all international migrants); a significant proportion of these flows are within the region, as nearly 7 million emigrants left home to live in another Mediterranean country.

The Mediterranean region

What is the Mediterranean?

> A thousand things together. Not a landscape, but many landscapes. Not one sea, but a succession of seas. Not one civilization, but a series of civilizations stacked on top of each other … Both in physical and human landscapes, the Mediterranean as a crossroads, a heterogeneous Mediterranean, is presented to our memory as a coherent image, a system where everything is melted and is re-composed in an original unity. (Braudel 1977)

The Mediterranean may be seen as a border but also as a window; undoubtedly it joins together three continents. A great deal of effort is needed to explain the profound essence of the Mediterranean.

The striking feature of the Mediterranean is its diversity: in this region, there are sharp differences both in terms of productions and economic specializations and in terms of cultures and forms of social and political organizations. Since the inland sea (Malanima 2005) enables easier and cheaper communications than the land does, these differences have been turned into a source of wealth. From the economic point of view, it has allowed the existence of exchanges of different goods: from raw materials industry (silk, wool, leather, metals) to food (wheat) and manufactured goods.

Over the last two centuries, in the Mediterranean countries, the differences in terms of regional economic conditions have increased. Moreover, industrialization and modernization have transformed them in inequalities: as a result, nowadays in the region, there is a clear distinction between development and underdevelopment, with an additional clear division between north and south. While the gross domestic product per capita and consumptions has grown in the northern regions of the Mediterranean, in the southern and the eastern areas they have remained unchanged or have grown at a lesser pace. Economic inequality is accompanied by numerous inequalities in the political organization. In conclusion there have been processes of economic and political divergence. These divergences are still there: they emerge in the demography of the region, in the public sector, in the environment, in the consumer sector and in the sector of energy production.

From the demographic point of view, the countries of the northern shore of the Mediterranean – with the exception of Albania – are characterized by low natural population growth, and in some cases by negative growth (Italy, Portugal, Croatia). The southern and eastern shores are characterized by high rates of natural growth. The different rate of population growth is basically the consequence of the process of *demographic transition*. The countries of the Mediterranean are at different stages of this process: while the countries of the northern shore have ended their demographic transition, most countries of the southern and eastern shores are still in the third stage of the transition. That stage is characterized by a sustained population growth because of the delay of the decline in the birth rate, which occurs after a certain time of the decline in mortality. The results of these differences between the two regions is a quite unequal population age structure: while the median age in most of the ageing countries of the north of the Mediterranean is over 40 years (except Albania and Montenegro), in the southern and eastern shores the median age is less than 30 years, confirming a younger age structure.

These inequalities are also confirmed by the character of the flow of goods and capital but also of people (see below).

In terms of human migration, at present, the Mediterranean is the result of three great migrations developed over more than three millennia (Aymard 1977). The first, the longest and the most conspicuous migration, corresponds to the arrival of the Indo-Europeans, who from the second millennium BC to the end of the barbarian invasion populated the peninsula and the coasts of the north. The other two migratory movements affected two groups: the Arabs and the Turks. The Mediterranean, apart from striking examples, has been animated from a regular circulation of people.

The migration involves a huge number of people and affects not only the countries of origin and destination but also transit countries. To explain the contemporary migration there are several interwoven reasons: cultural, political, natural disasters, armed conflicts, the new consumerist needs and aspirations of migrants, the situation of the labour market and the reception conditions. The deep changes that affected the society and an increasingly globalized economic system, the quantitative and qualitative dimensions of the migration process, as well as its dynamics, make it difficult to limit the analysis of migration to interpretations built on a single discipline. Migratory movements have always existed in this geographic area: in order to understand and to consider those movements and their essence it is necessary to bring together the theoretical and empirical tools of various disciplines.

Theoretical foundation of the dialogue across disciplines

Therefore in this volume we adopt a multidisciplinary theoretical and methodological framework. We are convinced that one single discipline cannot perfectly depict migration in the Mediterranean and international migrations in general. We are not in search of a unique answer or a unified theory but rather a dialogue between theories, disciplines and methodologies, in order to offer new insights into migration in the Mediterranean that go beyond the existing literature. Previous studies during the last 20 years on this topic have helped to disentangle a very complex research field; however, they have often looked at Mediterranean migration from a single disciplinary side and are mostly dedicated to one or two specific topics on migration in the Mediterranean (e.g. labour market and integration).

Among the most important and quoted studies dedicated to migration in the Mediterranean we should mention the following, listed according to the main topic analysed: population policies and demographic dynamics (Courbage and Todd 2011; de Haas 2010; Eljim and Parant 2014; Fargues and Le Bras 2009; Fargues 2003); migration policies (Arango 2012; Carling and Hernandez-Carretero 2011; Cassarino 2005a, 2005b; Wihtol de Wenden 2009, 2010, 2013); gender and migration (Blangiardo 2012); migration after the Arab Spring (Fargues and Fandrich 2012; Schmoll *et al.* 2015); return and circular migration (Cassarino 2007, 2010, 2014; Triandafyllidou 2013); migrations and territories of mobility in the Mediterranean, transit migration, temporary migration, the role of migrant remittances in development and Irregular migration (Carling 2007; de Haas 2010; Triandafyllidou and Maroukis 2012); migration statistics, migrants' integration, history of migration and transnationalism (Beauchemin *et al.* 2011; Peraldi 2001, 2002; Lacroix 2014); legal and juridical aspects, labour migration and the informal economy and migration (Baldwin-Edwards and Arango 1999; Peixoto *et al.* 2012; Reyneri and Fullin 2008, 2011; Reyneri 1998, 2001, 2003); return migration and the Southern European model of migration (King *et al.* 2000; King and Thompson 2008; King and DeBono 2013); and unaccompanied minors (Peraldi 2014).

We argue that although several disciplines across social sciences have studied international migration in the Mediterranean, the dialogue between them is still in the early stages. The need for a multidisciplinary approach while studying international migration has been underlined more than once by some of the most important scholars on international migration (Brettell and Hollifield 2008). To mention just one, in 1994 Douglas Massey *et al.* pointed out that:

> Social scientists do not approach the study of immigration from a shared paradigm, but from a variety of competing theoretical viewpoints fragmented across disciplines, regions and ideologies. As a result, research on the subject tends to be narrow, often inefficient, and characterized by duplication, miscommunication, reinvention, and bickering around fundamentals and terminology. Only when researchers accept common theories, concepts, tools, and standard will knowledge begin to accumulate. (1994: 700–1)

Therefore, each contribution included in this volume is based on an effort to address the specific questions with the different methodologies and tools available within the individual disciplinary approach and in the intersection between disciplines. In this volume we aim to address the study of migration in the Mediterranean following the indication made by Castles in 1993 that it should be 'strongly multidisciplinary in its theory and methodology' (1993: 30). The three main research questions addressed are: What are the main characteristics of migration movements in this region? What are the most important theoretical challenges? What are the prospects for the future? Following the theoretical background set by Brettell and Hollifield (2008) in their seminal volume on migration theories across disciplines, we aim to answer our questions by using a multidisciplinary approach. Even though borders and barriers may be raised on both sides of the Mediterranean, borders between disciplines need to come down in order to contribute to the understanding of this phenomenon and to address future research and policies.

Migration systems in the Mediterranean

The so-called globalization of migration has led to great changes in the last 40 years, not only in the number of migrants worldwide but also in the number of countries affected by migration and in the types of migrants (Wihtol de Wenden 2010). In terms of geographical areas, globalization has resulted in major changes in the routes used by migrants, the distances travelled and the countries of origin and destination. Some areas of the world constituted the major poles of attraction for migrants in the last century and continue to do so today: consider, for example, North America and Europe. However, the origins of migrants going to these areas are not the same as in the past few decades. For instance, in Europe in the past there was a large influx of migrants from former colonies; this has nowadays been replaced by flows coming from Eastern Europe (Czaika and de Haas 2014). The same applies to many other regions of the world. Therefore we can identify a supposed paradox of globalization: the regionalization of migration.

Regionalization is nothing but the creation of complex migration systems built around a well-defined region: within that region migration flows are favoured by geographical, cultural and linguistic proximity, by historical ties, by transnational networks of migrants and by a formal or informal circulation space, regulated or not by an institutionalized system that regulates the flows (Massey *et al.* 1993; Wihtol de Wenden 2013: 15). This means that there are a number of migration systems worldwide: North America and South America, Europe, the Mediterranean and sub-Saharan Africa, Russia, the Persian Gulf, Southeast Asia, Australia and New Zealand.

But is the Mediterranean a migration space? Could a migration system be identified? Or more realistically, is there a migratory 'regime'?

Europe forms a *migration space* with the south shore of the Mediterranean: this is a concept that was first defined by geographers such as Gildas Simon (1979) indicating persistent and continuous relationships developed between zones of departure and arrival. According to Simon, there are constant relationships between a sending area or emigration space (and its social, demographic and economic context) and a destination area or immigration space (and its social, demographic and economic context). Indeed, the majority of migration flows to Europe are from the southern shore of the Mediterranean, given the historical and neighbourhood ties it has with this region and the population and economic complementarities offered by the two spaces. Amid this fairly well-defined territory which justifies the term *Euro-Mediterranean migration space*, the Mediterranean is also one of the largest dividing lines in the world, creating divisions from an economic, political, social, cultural and demographic point of view, despite dialogues and proximities. Is the Mediterranean a unity or is it a divided space? A juncture or a fault line? Is it central or peripheral? Much of the history of the Mediterranean can be condensed in the oscillation between such extremes, and these very polarities emerge when we focus specifically on the recent history of the Mediterranean as a space for migration and an arena of migratory policies. From the post-Second World War period until the 1970s, the Mediterranean as a whole played a crucial role as a recruitment basin for the economic core of Europe, badly in need of manpower for reconstruction and industrial growth. Between the early 1980s and the end of the 1990s, the boundary between European sending and receiving countries shifted south, from the Alps and Pyrenees to the Mediterranean shores. Italy first, followed by Spain, Portugal and Greece turned into large-scale immigration destinations.

The historical dependencies, the reciprocal presence and the complementarities, passions and hatreds could make this space a *migration system*. The idea of migration systems was originally developed in the field of international migration by Akin Mabogunje and defined as:

> formal and informal subsystems that operate to perpetuate and reinforce the systematic nature of international flows by encouraging migration along certain pathways, and discouraging it along others. The end result is a set of

relatively stable exchanges ... yielding an identifiable geographical structure that persists across space and time'. (1970: 12)

A migration systems theory was later conceptualized by Massey *et al.*: 'An international migration system generally includes a core receiving region, which may be a country or a group of countries, and a set of specific sending countries linked to it by unusually large flows of immigrants' (1993: 454). The definition of a migratory system was developed by Massey *et al.* regarding the relationship between the United States and Mexico, which they defined as a regional migration system, which was then extended to other parts of the world. The conditions for forming a system are as follows: the countries in the system do not need to be geographically close, but should have strong economic and political links; generally sending countries may belong to more than one system; systems are not fixed over time as economic and political situations may evolve; and finally, there could be multi-polar systems. The Mediterranean is one of the most exclusive areas in the world in terms of border controls, since it constitutes the outer edge of Europe to the south. Furthermore, the migratory space does not mean a migration system, because the European Union is turning its back on migration from the south since it is built on freedom of movement, residence and work within the enlarged Europe, thus closing its borders to the south of the Mediterranean while opening its eastern borders. There is therefore a gap between the reality of flows to Europe and the institutional apparatus supposed to manage them.

In the mix of institutions and administrative practices, of bargaining, agreements and stop policies, we can speak of a Euro-Mediterranean migration régime, made by rules but also by discretionary provisions, such as the recent closure of the border in Ventimiglia in June 2015, a decision already implemented in the spring 2011 in the aftermath of the Arab revolutions. The concept of a 'migratory régime' was introduced by Guidecoq in 2012 for the analysis of migration in the United States. According to Guidecoq, this concept makes it possible to characterize each set of principles and rules that have historically existed and are legally institutionalized in the United States to regulate the arrival and the conditions of residence of foreigners. This component determines the numbers and composition of immigration, in conjunction with other factors. It can be viewed as a system of principles and rules of admission for aliens that is resilient to changes in economic conditions and other exogenous shocks.

Overview of population movements across the Mediterranean

By focusing on the most recent period we can argue that migration in the Mediterranean has undergone important changes between 1950 and 2015: these changes are largely due to economic and political factors (de Haas 2010: S60). Using a chronological approach to migration in the Mediterranean the evolution of migration in the region can be divided in four periods.

The first period (1948–63) is characterized by the reconstruction after the war in the countries of Northern and Western Europe. At that time, the labour-exporting

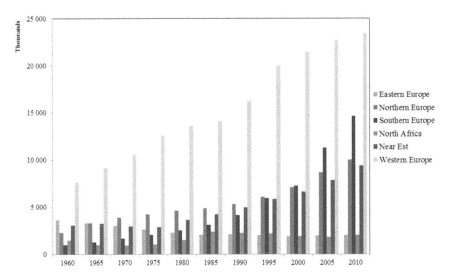

Figure 1.1 Stock of migrants resident in Europe, North Africa and Near East, 1960–2010

Source: authors' elaboration on United Nations, Trends in International Migrant Stock: The 2008 Revision

countries are the countries of southern Europe. In the early 1960, stocks of migrants in Western Europe represent 7.6 million (Figure 1.1). At the same time, population movement in the southern and eastern shores of the Mediterranean are mostly internal.

The next period (1963–73) is characterized by reduced mobility from South-east Europe to the countries of Western Europe and an increase in migration from the countries of the southern and eastern shores of the Mediterranean to France, Germany, Switzerland, Belgium and Austria. France and Germany during this phase are the main receiving countries in Europe: France is characterized by a strong presence of migrants from the Maghreb, while Germany shows a strong increase in the presence of Turkish migrants who replace migrants from the countries of Southern Europe, in particular Italy.

In the early 1970s, the oil crisis of 1973 was a breaking point for international migration trends in the Mediterranean and the start of the third period (1973–95). Changes during this period were largely influenced by the globalization process (Castles *et al.* 2014). A major consequence of this process has been the growth of inequalities within regional groups and between regions, as we already stressed above.

The European countries that were traditionally receiving countries of migration adopted restrictive migration policies, hoping for the massive return of migrants to their country of origin. As a consequence there was a change in the nature and destination of migratory flows. From the 1980s onwards the flow of refugees and asylum seekers to Europe increased significantly. In addition the countries of Southern Europe become in the early 1970s receiving countries of migration flows from countries of the southern shore of the Mediterranean, sub-Saharan Africa, Latin America, and, after the fall of the Berlin Wall, Eastern Europe.

The late 1990s and early 2000s marked a new phase of migration in the Mediterranean region (1996–present): this period opens a new migration sequence, strongly influenced by positive economic conditions. In the northern Mediterranean shore, Spain and Italy are confirmed as focal points of labour for unskilled migrants from countries of the southern shores (see Figures 1.2 and 1.3). These migrants are employed in agriculture, family care services, food services, small retail businesses and the construction sector.

More recent migration flows in Europe are characterized by the highly skilled migration. A common legislation on that kind of migration was adopted by the European Council with the Directive on the EU Blue Card (Directive 2009/50/EC of 25 May 2009). The Directive aims at facilitating entry and mobility of highly skilled migrants and members of their families and to harmonize procedures for entry and residence in the member countries. Highly skilled migration has decreased in all EU countries since 2010 (Figure 1.4). The countries of the northern shore of the Mediterranean do not attract many skilled migrants: among them only France is attractive for the category of researchers. However, there are countries of Northern Europe, including the Netherlands, Denmark, Sweden and the United Kingdom that are able to attract qualified labour. Highly skilled migrants are mainly of Chinese, Indian, American and Russian origin.

Illegal migration is a widespread phenomenon and subject of debate in the Mediterranean region. Estimates of illegal migration are complicated by its very nature; at European level the definitions and categories are not uniform. Given the growing interest of the media and public opinion by this type of migration, accompanied by the use of 'imaginary' figures, the European Commission funded

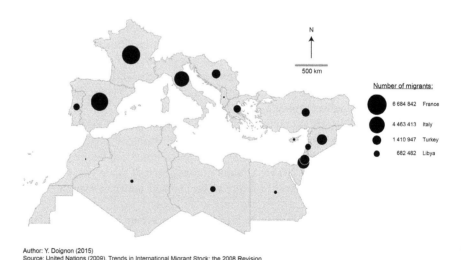

Author: Y. Doignon (2015)
Source: United Nations (2009). Trends in International Migrant Stock: the 2008 Revision

Figure 1.2 Stock of migrants resident in the Mediterranean countries, 2010

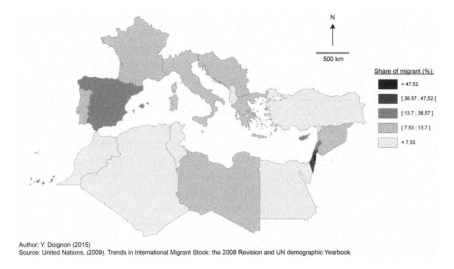

Author: Y. Doignon (2015)
Source: United Nations, (2009). Trends in International Migrant Stock: the 2008 Revision and UN demographic Yearbook

Figure 1.3 Migrant stock as percentage of the total population of the Mediterranean, 2010

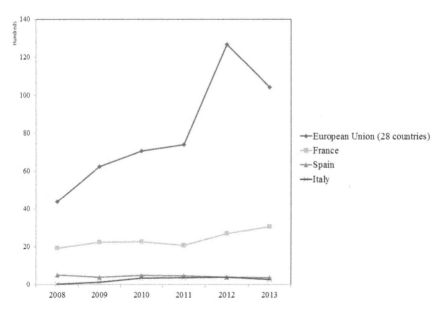

Figure 1.4 Flows of highly skilled migrants (EU, France, Italy and Spain), 2008–13

Source: Authors' elaboration on Eurostat database

between 2007 and 2009 the Clandestino project (Vogel 2009). The project aimed to harmonize data sources and methodology used to study illegal migration, to build a database on illegal migration and to guide policies on that topic in Europe.

One of the characteristics of the 'Southern European model of migration' (King 2000) is the presence of a large illegal component. The estimate of the scale of illegal migration is made on several bases of information, including number of applications for regularization.

The borders of Europe are greatly affected by the threat of illegal migration; therefore the Frontex Agency (the European Agency for the Management of Operational Cooperation at the External Borders of the Member States of the European Union) was created in 2004 by the European Council and has been operational since October 2005. The Frontex Agency has the tasks to promote, coordinate and develop European border management. Frontex collects data on the flow of illegal crossings of external borders and illegal migrant detections reported within European borders. Illegal crossings of external borders have been stable between 2009 and 2013 (around 100,000 passages). In 2014, because of the worsening of the Syrian crisis, approximately 283,000 illegal crossings were spotted by Frontex; 60 per cent (170,000) crossed the maritime border of the central Mediterranean (Italy and Malta) (Frontex 2015).

References

Arango, J. 2012. 'Early starters and latecomers: comparing countries of immigration and immigration regimes in Europe'. In M. Okólski, ed., *European Immigrations: Trends, Structures and Policy Implications*, 45–63. Amsterdam: Amsterdam University Press.

Aymard, M. 1977. 'Migrations'. In F. Braudel, ed., *La Méditerranée, l'espace et l'histoire*, 219–42. Paris: Flammarion.

Baldwin-Edwards, M. and Arango, J., eds. 1999. *Immigration and the Informal Economy in Southern Europe*. London: Frank Cass.

Beauchemin, C., Lagrange, H. and Safi, M. 2011. 'Transnationalism and immigrant assimilation in France: between here and there?' INED: Document de Travail, no. 172: 42.

Blangiardo, G. C. 2012. *Gender and Migration in Southern and Eastern Mediterranean and Sub-Saharan African countries*. San Domenico di Fiesole: European University Institute, Robert Schuman Centre for advanced studies (Carim Research Report 2012/01).

Braudel, F., ed., 1977. *La Méditerranée, l'espace et l'histoire*, Paris: Flammarion.

Brettell, C. B. and Hollifield, J. F. 2008. *Migration Theory: Talking Across Disciplines*. New York/London: Routledge.

Carling, J. 2007. 'Unauthorised migration from Africa to Spain', *International Migration* 45(4): 3–37.

Carling, J. and Hernandez-Carretero, M. 2011. 'Protecting Europe and protecting migrants? Strategies for managing unauthorised migration from Africa'. *British Journal of Politics and International Relations* 13: 42–58.

Cassarino, J.-P. 2005a. *Migration and Border Management in the Euro-Mediterranean Area: Heading Towards New Forms of Interconnectedness*. www.cadmus.eui.eu/bitstream/handle/1814/6283/med_2005_cassarino.pdf?sequence.

Cassarino, J.-P. 2005b. *Europe's Migration Policy in the Mediterranean: An Overview*. Carim AS 10, Robert Schuman Center for Advanced Studies, San Domenico di Fiesole, Florence.

Cassarino, J.-P. 2007. 'Informalising Readmission Agreements in the EU Neighbourhood'. *International Spectator* 42(2): 179–96.

Cassarino, J.-P. 2010. *Readmission Policy in the European Union*. Strasbourg: European Parliament Publications Office.

Cassarino, J.-P. 2014. 'A Reappraisal of the EU's Expanding Readmission System'. *International Spectator* 49(4): 130–45.

Castles, S. 1993. 'Migrations and minorities in Europe. Perspectives for the 1990s: eleven hypotheses'. In J. Wrench and J. Solomos, eds, *Racism and Migration in Western Europe*, 17–34. Oxford: Berg.

Castles, S., de Haas, H. and Miller, M. J. 2014. *The Age of Migration*, 5th edn. London: Palgrave Macmillan.

Courbage, Y. and Todd, E. 2011. *A Convergence of Civilizations: The Transformation of Muslim Societies Around the World*. New York: Columbia University Press.

Czaika M. and de Haas, H. 2014. 'The globalization of migration: has the world become more migratory?' *International Migration Review* 48(2): 283–323.

de Haas, H. 2010. 'Mediterranean migration futures: patterns, drivers and scenarios'. *Global Environmental Change* 21(Supplement 1): S59–S69.

Eljim, K. and Parant, A. 2014. 'Migration of Mediterranean nationals within the Mediterranean region'. *South-East European Journal of Political Science* 2(3): 97–109.

Eurostat online database: http://ec.europa.eu/eurostat/data/database.

Fargues, P. 2003. *The Mediterranean, A Gulf or Bridge? Population and Migration in the Euro-Med Process*. Center for Western European Studies working paper series 10. Kalamazoo, MI: Kalamazoo College, Center for Western European Studies.

Fargues, P. and Fandrich, C. 2012. *Migration after the Arab Spring*. MPC research report 2012/09. Florence: European University Institute, Robert Schuman Centre for Advanced Studies: www.migrationpolicycentre.eu/docs/MPC%202012%20EN%2009.pdf.

Fargues, P. and Le Bras, H. 2009. *Migrants et migrations dans le bassin de la Méditerranée*. Paris: Institut de prospective économique du monde méditerranéen (Ipemed), Les notes Ipemed. Etudes & analyses. www.ipemed.coop/IMG/pdf/LesNotesIPEMED_1_migrant-setmigrations.pdf.

Frontex. 2015. *Annual Risk Analysis 2015*. Warsaw: European Agency for the Management of Operational Cooperation at the External Borders of the Member States of the European Union.

Guidecoq, S. 2012. *L'économie politique du système d'immigration américain: une analyse des échecs des réformes de la politique d'immigration des Etats-Unis, 1994–2010*. PhD thesis in Political Science, Universitée de Grenoble (in French).

King, R. 2000. 'Southern Europe in the changing global map of migration'. In R. King, G. Lazaridis and C. Tsardanidis, eds, *Eldorado or Fortress? Migration in Southern Europe*, 1–26. Basingtoke: Macmillan.

King R. and DeBono, D. 2013. 'Irregular migration and the "Southern European Model" of migration'. *Journal of Mediterranean Studies* 22(1): 1–31.

King, R. and Thompson, M. 2008. 'The Southern European model of immigration: do the cases of Malta, Cyprus and Slovenia fit?' *Journal of Southern Europe and the Balkans* 10(3): 265–91.

King, R., Lazaridis, G. and Tsardanidis, C., eds. 2000. *Eldorado or Fortress? Migration in Southern Europe*. Basingstoke: Macmillan; New York: St Martin's Press.

Lacroix, T. 2014. 'Conceptualizing transnational engagements: a structure and agency perspective on (hometown) transnationalism'. *International Migration Review* 48(3): 643–79. doi:10.1111/imre.12105.

Mabogunje, A. L. 1970. 'Systems approach to a theory of rural-urban migration'. *Geographical Analysis* 2: 1–18.

Malanima, P., ed. 2005. *Rapporto sulle economie del mediterraneo*, Bologna: il Mulino.

Massey D. S., Arango, J., Hugo, G., Kouaouci, A., Pellegrino, A. and Edward Taylor, J. 1993. 'Theories of international migration: a review and appraisal'. *Population and Development Review* 19(3): 431–66.

Massey D. S., Arango, J., Hugo, G., Kouaouci, A., Pellegrino, A. and Edward Taylor, J. 1994. 'An evaluation of international migration theory: the North American case'. *Population and Development Review* 20(4): 699–751.

Peixoto, J. 2009. 'Back to the South: social and political aspects of Latin American migration to Southern Europe'. *International Migration* 50(6): 58–81.

Peixoto, J., Arango, J., Bonifazi, C., Finotelli, C., Sabino, C., Strozza, S. and Triandafyllidou, A. 2012. 'Immigrants, markets and policies in Southern Europe: the making of an immigration model?' In M. Okólski, ed., *European Immigrations: Trends, Structures and Policy Implications*, 107–47. Amsterdam: Amsterdam University Press.

Peraldi, M. 2001. *Cabas et containers: Activités marchandes informelles et réseaux migrants transfrontaliers*. Paris: Maison méditerranéenne des sciences de l'homme.

Peraldi, M. 2002. *La fin des norias? Réseaux migrants dans les économies marchandes en méditerranée*. Paris: Maisonneuve et Larose.

Peraldi, M. 2014. *Les mineurs migrants non accompagnés: Un défi pour les pays européens*. Paris: Karthala.

Reyneri, E. 1998. 'The role of the underground economy in irregular migration to Italy: cause or effect?' *Journal of Ethnic and Migration Studies* 24(2): 313–31.

Reyneri, E. 2001. *Migrants' Involvement in Irregular Employment in the Mediterranean Countries of the European Union*. ILO International Migration Papers 39.

Reyneri, E. 2003. 'Immigration and the underground economy in new receiving South European countries: manifold negative effects, manifold deep-rooted causes'. *International Review of Sociology* 13(1): 117–43.

Reyneri, E. and Fullin, G. 2008. 'New immigration and labour markets in Western Europe: a trade-off between employment and job quality?' *Transfer* 14(4): 573–88.

Reyneri, E. and Fullin, G. 2011. 'Labour market penalties of new immigrants in new and old receiving West European countries'. *International Migration* 49: 31–57.

Schmoll, C., Thiollet, H. and Wihtol de Wenden, C., eds. 2015. *Migrations en Méditérranée*. Paris: CNRS éditions.

Simon, G. 1979. *L'espace des travailleurs tunisiens en France structures et fonctionnement d'un champ migratoire international*, PhD thesis, Poitiers University (in French).

Triandafyllidou, A., ed. 2013. *Circular Migration between Europe and its Neighbourhood: Choice or Necessity?* Oxford: Oxford University Press.

Triandafyllidou, A. and Maroukis, T. 2012. *Migrant Smuggling: Irregular Migration from Asia and Africa to Europe*. London: Palgrave.

United Nations, Department of Economic and Social Affairs, Population Division (2009) *Trends in International Migrant Stock: The 2008 Revision* (United Nations database, POP/DB/MIG/Stock/Rev.2008).

Vogel, D. 2009. *Size and Development of Irregular Migration to the EU*. Comparative Policy brief, Clandestino Project. http://clandestino.eliamep.gr/wp-content/uploads/2009/12/clandestino_policy_brief_comparative_size-of-irregular-migration.pdf.

Wihtol de Wenden, C. 2009. *La globalisation humaine*. Paris: Presses Universitaires de France.

Wihtol de Wenden, C. 2010. *La question migratoire au XXIe siècle. Migrants, réfugiés et relations internationales*. Paris: Presses de la Fondation Nationale de Sciences Politiques.

Wihtol de Wenden, C. 2013. *Pour accompagner les migrations en Méditerranée*. Paris: l'Harmattan (La bibliothèque de l'Iremmo 11).

2 A provincial level analysis of Italian emigration to Africa in mass migration years

Who left and why

Francesca Fauri

During Italy's mass migration movement (1890–1914), Italians went all over the world, the United States, Argentina and Brazil being the main destination countries and income differentials being one of the basic push factors (Fauri 2015a). In the case of Italian emigration to Africa, also historical, cultural and geographical reasons made the Mediterranean African countries (in particular Egypt, Algeria and Tunisia) the natural destination shores of Italian labourers, a movement which had started and developed many decades before the Italian state was born (1861). The Italian community in Africa had grown steadily (manual workers but also merchants, engineers, doctors and accountants poured into the Mediterranean African countries) and it was often the link with the post-unification immigration fluxes. The historical role of migration chains is beyond doubt: it directed the flows and had a multiplier effect: a web of links which joined in every direction, branching out to increasingly distant relatives, to cousins of cousins and even further.

Sardinia and Sicily, and in particular the cities of Cagliari, Trapani, Siracusa and Napoli, were among the regions and towns that developed the strongest links with Africa: during mass migration years emigrants from these provinces were typically young farmers or fishermen, but also artisans and carpenters, either with no or limited formal schooling. As this chapter will show, the provincial level analysis of Italian emigration to Africa will be able to tell us who left and why. Many left on a temporary basis in search of a job, better salaries and the possibility to come back to Italy with some savings; some decided to stay and after a few years as daily agricultural workers invested the savings in the land and became small landowners (Sori 1979: 32; Labanca 1997; Paris 1976; Filesi 1978; Natili 2009; Rassegna Bibliografica 1989; Clancy-Smith 2011).

Quite interestingly, this chapter will also show that many females (in comparative terms) emigrated to Africa from southern towns, which can be considered a first step towards emancipation through work, a temporary step that was agreed upon by the whole family and whose sole objective was to increase the family's earnings. Southern women left as dressmakers and wet-nurses and sometimes stayed on as prostitutes (although the data for the latter category are unavailable and inferred only by contemporary writers' reports).

This chapter concentrates on free migration movements and does not deal with the fascist government assisted or induced migration to the Italian colonial empire, which have already been considered by a vast literature on the subject (Del Boca 1992; Labanca 1993). Finally, in comparative terms, Africa indeed attracted feeble fluxes in mass migration years – 1 to 3 per cent of total Italian emigrants – yet for Sardinians in particular and a few other Italian provinces the Mediterranean countries have represented an often temporary way out of a harsh life and hunger and an important source of income in an open and familiar environment.

The Italian diaspora

Italy was overall a poor country at unification; the interregional economic differences were present, yet, as Vecchi as recently demonstrated, mild at the level of GNP per capita and life expectancy. The south had major problems at the level of literacy (only from 12 to 20 per cent of the population was able to read and write, while half of the population of Piedmont and Lombardy was literate already at unification), public infrastructure (the Kingdom of the Two Sicilies had invested very little in building roads, only 99 km of tracks, almost inexistent banking facilities and what we call today 'social overhead capital') and uneven distribution of land. The large majority of people worked as day labourers in the southern latifundia, were employed mainly during the harvest season and spent most winter months unemployed.[1] Thus, given an average daily wage of 2.10 lire in 1911 Vera Zamagni has calculated that 280 days of work a year would have been necessary in order to guarantee an income above the subsistence level (solely in terms of food). However, 'We know that day labourers never worked more than 180–200 days a year and this figure was often lower in heavily populated areas or in areas where there was extensive farming' (Zamagni 1978, 1993).

This backlog of poor socio-economic legacies, together with the increased population growth, frustrated the successive development of the south.[2] As a matter of fact, with the progressive decrease of the mortality rate (and rise in life expectancy), the enlarged labour force resulted in a labour market slack and relatively higher migration, as Easterlin correctly predicted (1961: 337). He argued that past demographic events had an indirect influence on present emigration through the home labour supply. Cohen and Federico speak accordingly of excess of population relative to available resources: 'Too many people chasing too little good land' due to a lack of compelling alternatives, except for emigration (2001: 109).

Figure 2.1 illustrates the growth of the Italian exodus: from the first available data we can see how Italian emigration soared to almost 400,000 with the 1887/88 crisis and kept on growing thereafter.

What should be underlined from the beginning is that, despite the north–south divide and a late start of the southern propensity to leave, Italy's migration movement concerned all Italian regions, with different intensities yet not correlated to

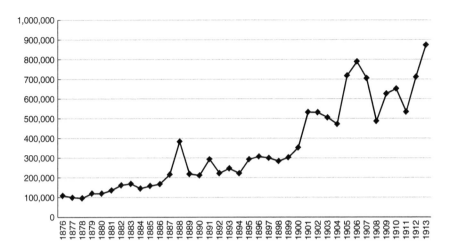

Figure 2.1 The growth of Italian emigration, 1876–1913

Source: Istat, *Annuario dell'Emigrazione*, various issues. Thank you to Andrea Gentili for sharing the collected data.

a north–south differential. What is beyond doubt is that in the 30 years before the war Italian emigration amazingly raised from 100,000 to almost 900,000 people a year and that people left from southern and northern villages alike. In many instances, a similar pattern can be traced among farmers living in hilly or mountain zones, with poor incomes and a long-established tradition of seasonal migrant labour force (Lucassen 2014).

What we will analyse here is a very small but increasing percentage of this mass migration movement (from 1 to 3 per cent of the total) that was directed to Africa and mainly to three countries in Africa: Egypt, Tunisia and Algeria, which absorbed more than 90 per cent of Italians moving to Africa in the period under consideration.

As a matter of fact, the data don't capture the whole extension of the migration movement to Africa, since, as reported by the Italian consulates in Africa, many emigrants from the south left the Italian coasts without a passport on small private sailing boats and their entrance was never recorded. The Italian consul in Tunis estimated for instance that probably 8,205 immigrants a year landed in Tunisia without any formal control or possibility to record the extension of the influx (Ministero Affari Esteri 1893). So probably the amounts shown by ISTAT significantly underestimate the phenomenon.

The data only show gross migration, not taking account of the returns. Thus a more trustworthy picture of the Italian presence in northern Africa can be inferred by the numbers of Italians living in Africa according to Italian census data. As shown in Figure 2.4 they increased the most in the case of Tunisia, which shows a steady growth of Italian residents from 1871 to 1927, a path followed by

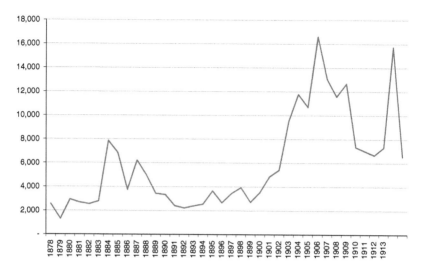

Figure 2.2 Italian emigration to Africa

Source: Istat, *Annuario dell'Emigrazione*, various issues. Thank you to Andrea Gentili for sharing the collected data.

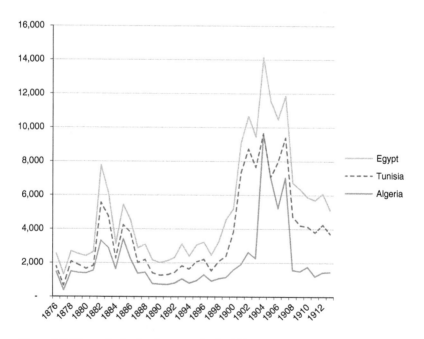

Figure 2.3 The main destination countries in Africa

Source: Istat, *Annuario dell'Emigrazione*, various issues. Thank you to Andrea Gentili for sharing the collected data.

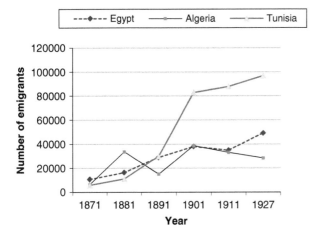

Figure 2.4 Number of Italian residents in Tunisia, Algeria and Egypt

Source: *MAE, Censimenti degli italiani all'estero*, various issues.

Egypt too, albeit at a slower pace. Algeria, on the other hand, shows a more stable presence of Italian migrants, whose community, except for the fall of 1891, stabilized around 30,000 individuals.

But why were Italians attracted to the African Mediterranean countries in particular? The answers can be found in both the history of the long-term relations with Italy of each of these three countries and the economic opportunities available there (Fauri 2015b, 2015c). In economic terms, we should briefly bear in mind the following reasons for Africa's attractiveness: low-cost tickets, reasonable distance from southern ports, more and better paid job opportunities in various sectors – surely the onset of substantial public works was a key factor in all three cases – and last but not least, the concrete possibility of becoming small landowners especially in Tunisia.

The African attraction: regions and provinces of departure

Between 1876 and 1914 more than 230,000 Italians landed on African shores. Sardinia stands out as the main region as far as migration to Africa is concerned with a noteworthy share of 31 per cent of total emigrants moving to north African countries throughout these years, followed by Sicily (4.5 per cent), Apulia (2.6 per cent), Calabria (2.3 per cent), and Tuscany (2.3 per cent), as Table 2.1 shows. Africa was the favourite destination continent of Sardinians (followed by Europe and Latin America) who, it is worth remembering, were the people in Italy who showed the lowest emigration propensity for the period under consideration. It is still a puzzle why Sardinians did not emigrate. Against all standard economic models, people from Sardinia, with similar living and

Table 2.1 Regional Italian emigration to main destination countries, 1884–1913[*]

Region	In %					
	Europe	*Africa*	*USA*	*America*	*Asia*	*Oceania*
Piedmont	58.2	1.1	12.3	28.1	0.2	0.1
Liguria	17.7	1.5	25.8	54.7	0.1	0.1
Lombardy	66.7	0.6	7.2	24.5	0.1	0.9
Veneto	82.7	0.3	2.8	14.2	0.0	0.0
Emilia-Romagna	69.6	1.6	13.0	15.7	0.1	0.0
Tuscany	60.7	2.3	18.2	18.6	0.1	0.1
Marche	32.8	0.5	20.5	46.0	0.0	0.0
Umbria	69.0	0.4	19.0	11.5	0.0	0.0
Lazio	13.7	1.2	70.3	14.5	0.2	0.0
Abruzzo	12.9	0.4	58.8	27.9	0.0	0.0
Campania	7.0	1.4	65.8	25.8	0.0	0.0
Apulia	14.7	2.6	58.8	23.5	0.3	0.1
Basilicata	4.9	0.5	55.2	39.4	0.0	0.1
Calabria	2.8	2.3	50.3	44.6	0.0	0.0
Sicily	2.4	4.5	72.3	20.4	0.1	0.2
Sardinia	27.7	31.5	12.2	28.5	0.1	0.0
Total	41.4	1.6	32.4	24.3	0.1	0.1

[*] No available data for 1888, 1890, 1892.

Source: Istat, *Annuario dell'Emigrazione*, various issues. Thank you to Andrea Gentili for sharing the collected data.

poor economic conditions of many high-emigration southern areas, were not attracted by moving abroad. The weight of emigrants on resident population in 1901 only reached 2.7 per cent in the case of Sardinia, while the average rate for the Italian Meridione was 17.2 per cent. Coletti, an economist of the time, commenting on the low migration propensity of Sardinia, said: 'Sardinians are just too savage to emigrate.' Among the possible less simplistic explanations, we should remember that in Sardinia a strong and traditional culture of mobility closely linked to fishing had survived, which entailed long months spent in the sea, but this was always a temporary experience that ended with the boat returning to its harbour. Besides, many isolated villages were governed by archaic and proudly closed communities where the patriarchal authority still had the power to forbid emigration, only allowing temporary working trips abroad. Return was not a choice, but an obligatory common practice (Gentileschi 1995: 20). Therefore, Sardinian emigration was first of all a choice driven by geographical proximity and the buoyant demand for temporary jobs (just like the emigrants from Veneto going to Austria or Germany for seasonal jobs). All the other regions show a remarkably lower propensity to emigrate towards Africa, which remained a niche solution for a few areas within each region and over a certain period of time.

Indeed, the propensity of Italy's emigration to Africa changed over time. That's why it is very interesting at this point to perform a provincial level analysis

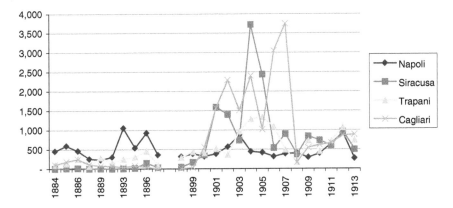

Figure 2.5 Emigration to Africa from the four most important provinces, 1884–1914

Source: Istat, *Annuario dell'Emigrazione*, various issues. Thank you to Andrea Gentili for sharing the collected data.

and look at the towns that sent the highest number of emigrants to the African continent. Italians who left for Africa came mainly from four provinces: Cagliari (Sardinia), Trapani and Siracusa (Sicily), and Napoli (Campania). Between 1884 and 1914 gross emigration to Africa per province reached 20,844 emigrants from Cagliari, 16,100 from Siracusa, 13,181 from Trapani and 12,443 from Napoli. As Figure 2.5 shows, Africa gained and lost importance according to the province of origin (and international economic downturns; the 1907–08 crisis halted all emigration flows): quite a small but steady flow from Naples, while the numbers from Trapani and Siracusa, after reaching top level in the first half of the 1910s, rapidly slowed down in successive years. At the turn of the century, emigrants from Siracusa, Trapani and Napoli started massively to leave for southern and mostly northern American destinations.

However, despite mass emigration flows to the United States, the African emigration pattern never died out completely before the First World War and remained a well-known niche opportunity. In the case of Cagliari, Africa kept representing the major continent of destination, despite a slowing down of the flows after the 1907 crisis. In the other cases the emigration boom towards the United States soon obfuscated the traditional Mediterranean links (see Figure 2.6).

The following analysis will deal with these four cases, plus Catanzaro and Livorno, which enjoyed the strongest links with Africa in the decades or even centuries before the beginning of the great African exodus started from the 1890s. However, they are worth remembering since in the case of Catanzaro the relevant male fluxes were matched by important female emigration flows, while for Livorno the links built throughout history with the north Mediterranean countries were peculiar in two ways: the city provided highly skilled professionals and built stable links and chains between the near continent and Tuscany.

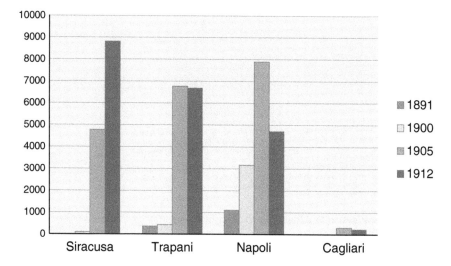

Figure 2.6 Emigration trend to the US from Siracusa, Trapani, Napoli and Cagliari

Source: Istat, *Annuario dell'Emigrazione*, various issues. Thank you to Andrea Gentili for sharing the collected data.

Cagliari

Sardinians enjoyed a long tradition of stable relationship with African Mediterranean countries; Egypt, Algeria and Tunisia were close countries of destination of an increasing influx of temporary workers. The shipping company Raffaele Rubattino set up a new bi-monthly maritime connection between Cagliari and Tunis in 1852, further stimulating emigration from Sardinia towards Tunisia and slowly diverting the usual flow towards Algeria. In the case of Sardinians, two important factors must be underlined. First, they despised emigration to the Americas and preferred the usual pre-unity route of close temporary African destinations. As the data from Cagliari clearly show there has been little or no outward migration towards North or South America in the years under consideration but a constant preference for the near Mediterranean sea towns (1,565 moved to Africa in 1901). Second, despite being illiterate, they were often skilled workers who brought their expertise in the fishing, mines and forestry fields to the North African coast (MAIC 1913). From Cagliari 500–600 Sardinians disembarked on the Tunisian coast each May and went to work in the forests (where for instance they knew how to remove the bark of cork-oaks). Temporary specialized emigrants earned from 3.50 to 4 francs a day and never stayed longer than three months. During the summer months about 400 Sardinians from Iglesias also traditionally moved to Tunisia to work in the mines. They were renowned for their technical knowledge about minerals, which was often matched by their ability in the construction of galleries and in the triage of minerals. They were the best-paid specialized category of workers earning from 5 to 9 francs a day (given also the fact that their type of job was particularly dangerous, fatiguing and illness-prone). Unspecialized workers in the mines were often indigenous and earned 30–40 per cent less compared to European workers – according to Loth, they earned less because they worked less, being physically weaker (Marilotti 2006; Loth 1905: 146). The emigration peak was reached in 1907 when 3,047 workers from Cagliari moved to Africa, it was also the beginning of a downturn trend which ceased almost completely when the war broke out.

Trapani and Siracusa

Despite the undisputable fact that many Sicilians started to move massively to the US by the last decades of the nineteenth century, the North African route remained the favourite one for Siracusa and Trapani until the beginning of the twentieth century, as Figure 2.7 shows.

In particular, the two cities showed a clear propensity to move to Tunisia, which steadily grew over time as the main African country of destination, outdoing Egypt already in the last decade of the nineteenth century. It is worth remembering that in 1868 the Italian government, in order to protect the growing Italian community in Tunisia, negotiated and signed a treaty granting Italian settlers the possibility to set up firms and buy land properties. In 1870 a weekly connection from Palermo and Tunis started to operate: for 5 francs on a steamer Sicilians could reach Tunis overnight (Ganiage 1959). When in 1881 France established its protectorate over Tunisia there were 20,000 Europeans in Tunisia, only 500 of whom were French, while 11,000 were Italian.

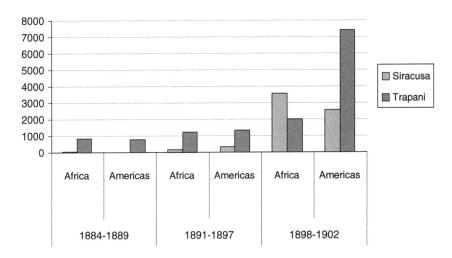

Figure 2.7 Siracusa and Trapani's continents of destination, 1884–1902

Source: Istat, *Annuario dell'Emigrazione*, various issues. Thank you to Andrea Gentili for sharing the collected data.

A more permanent form of emigration was composed of farmers coming from Sicily and the island of Pantelleria: a well-integrated group speaking the same language (dialect) and with the same cultural background. The trade with Sicily was well developed and carried forward by small sailing boats which daily connected Trapani with La Goletta. In the words of the Italian Consul in Tunis: 'Sicilian peasants are not influenced by emigration agents to move to Tunisia since they are certain of finding a second homeland in Tunis and increased material wellbeing' (MAIC 1882: 205). According to French contemporary observers: 'Sicily willingly offered its labour force ousted from their home country by hunger, malaria, heavy taxes and mafia ... Italians moved to Tunisia because their country, Sicily in particular, is overpopulated and the existing bad social and land organization does not allow them to nourish their large families' (Sayous 1927: 69). The Italian population of Tunisia mushroomed, increasing by 88 per cent during the first decade of the protectorate, and it outnumbered French citizens by a ratio of five to one by 1896. In the first years of the new century, Sicilians reached 60,000 out of a foreign population of 80,000 (MAE 1904: 334). As the Sicilian agricultural community increased, migration chains attracted daily labourers from the same area also on a temporary basis to work in the harvest period or during summer months.

One of the most interesting aspects of Sicilian emigration to Tunisia is that Sicilians increasingly became small landowners. Indeed, as the parliamentary inquiry on southern farmers underlined, 'Sicilians are not so much attracted by higher salaries, but by the mirage of becoming land owners, something that it would be crazy to hope for in their region where latifundia dominated' (*Inchiesta parlamentare* 1911: 743).

Likewise, Coletti described Sicilian emigration to Tunisia as determined by 'special circumstances', not only the fact that it was close, easily accessible and with similar climatic and soil characteristics, but there existed the concrete possibility to become a small landowner (1911: 134). Or again, one of the leading Italian newspapers of the time (*Il Corriere della Sera*) stated in 1900: 'The Sicilian immigrant has got one and only aim: buy a little piece of land to support his family even if it means to mortgage his future work for many years ahead.'

Sicilian emigration flows from Siracusa to Africa went up from 438 in 1899 to 1,587 units in 1901 and reached the peak of 3,720 in 1904, while Trapani increased from 966 in 1903 to the top level of 1,332 people leaving in 1905, rapidly decreasing thereafter.

Napoli

According to the Prefect of Napoli in 1880, the poorest farmers leaving from the province of Naples chose Africa and Egypt in particular because of the low cost of the journey (MAIC 1882: 50–2). As a matter of fact, geographical proximity to the southern coasts greatly eased the poverty trap: the very low cost of the boat passage allowed the poorest to leave, who in many cases chose Africa over the

Americas for this very reason. For the most part, Italians were able to reach the African shore on small sailing boats (*bilancelle*) for only 10–25 lire. They did not have a passport, there were no formal controls, immigration was free, and in most cases they never registered at the Italian Consulate.

However, even though unquestionably underestimated, the data that we have tell us that in the 1870s Egypt was the African country with the greatest numbers of Italians, given the generous financing of a great amount of public works. A large part of workers came from the province of Naples (but also from Sicily and Calabria), worked as masons or stonecutters at the construction of the Suez Canal, as canal-makers, helped to build the barrage across the Nile, an open weir half a mile long (1888–1902). They also worked at the Assam dam, on the bridges across the Nile at Kafr-el-Zaiat and Behna, the latter a part of the railway route from Cairo to Alexandria (Foerster 1919: 212). Emigrants leaving from Naples went to Egypt but also to Algeria, where from 1879, besides passages on small inexpensive boats, workers could embark on a national steamship called *Principe di Napoli* (Prince of Naples), which regularly connected Naples and the Algerian ports, carrying 100 passengers per way. They settled in the northern coast of Algeria, in Costantina, Philippeville, Bona and La Calle. In the latter town, out of a population of 4,000, 2,500 were Italians in 1881. Italian emigrants to Algeria were mainly fishermen, especially coral, but they were also agricultural daily workers, shoemakers, mine workers, marble workers, brickmakers, plasterers and masons who were often attracted and engaged in public works. The latter usually repatriated when the works were over.

The peak for Naples was reached in 1893 when 1,050 emigrants left for Africa; after that the outflow stabilized around 500 people per year until the First World War.

Catanzaro

As to Catanzaro, it was the lack of job opportunities and the wish to earn higher salaries abroad, compared to the local miserable wage level that pushed farmers to leave. In 1881, still only a few left for America, while the majority embarked for Alessandria in Egypt (see Figure 2.8). Thus, Africa was chosen because it was close, it was a low-cost trip, it offered better paid even though often temporary jobs and the migration chains established in the past (in a few cases before unification) apparently worked very well as emigration agents, advising when job opportunities opened and closed.

Female emigration from Catanzaro (and also Reggio Calabria) is a very interesting case in point. Unfortunately, ISTAT data do not specify the emigration destination of women, but knowing that very few people moved to the Americas from Catanzaro before 1896, it is very likely that the majority of the 71 women who emigrated from this province in 1884 and the annual drain of 250–300 females in the following ten years was temporarily directed to Africa. It was one of the first times that female emigration became a possible solution to improve the family budget. The women from the little Commune of Bagnara were well

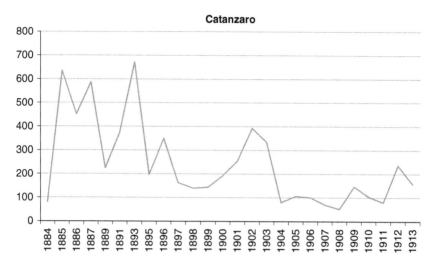

Figure 2.8 Emigration from Catanzaro to Africa

Source: Istat, *Annuario dell'Emigrazione*, various issues. Thank you to Andrea Gentili for sharing the collected data.

known to emigrate to Alessandria as dressmakers, but many also moved as wet-nurses (lured by very good remunerations) and probably prostitutes. In the latter case, apparently, when demand for wet-nurses started decreasing, many women made due with another occupation and became prostitutes. This is what can be inferred by a contemporary writer's report:

> Women took the African route from many Communes in Calabria: Marcellinara, Miglierina, Tiriolo, Settingiano, Amato and Nicastro, the most beautiful women of the region live in these towns and wear gorgeous costumes which make them look even more stunning. These small working tribes moved in great numbers towards Alessandria since many foreign ladies embarked on an incessant search for wet nurses. Rich in money but not in milk or simply not willing to bother with breastfeeding, these wealthy foreign mothers paid 80–100 lire per month, including food, housing and precious fabric for clothes. The husbands of the wet-nurses, who were well aware of the fact that in Calabria the most generous salary would be 10 lire per month, moved heaven and earth to make it happen. They found local wet-nurses for their babies and sent the wives to Alessandria. It was a lucky speculation, rumours spread like wildfire and women were caught up in this business of selling their milk for 5 lire per litre. Not only the married puerperal women were swift in organizing their leave, but also the unmarried ones. The good looking young women decided not to turn away from love and the boat to Egypt represented the security valve in

response to an unfaithful lover or the anger of the family upon which she had brought disgrace. Many women made a fortune with milk, but when the need for wet nurses slowed down, the newcomers, with their beauty and charm, found other temporary and enjoyable occupations which in international trade are worth plenty of gold coins (*Luigi d'oro*). (Marincola S. Floro 1896: 172–3)

These episodes are often disregarded in the general literature on emigration; it is true that women in southern Italy rarely took individual employment outside the home or family business and almost never travelled alone, yet they positively responded to the African labour market opportunities and people's mentality gradually started to change. With the new century, the migration propensity of Catanzaro and the other small Communes in Calabria changed massively in favour of North America. An increasing percentage of women, in most cases, left to reach the husbands or fathers already working in the United States, where they 'broke with tradition by working in factories, especially as garment workers and textile factory operatives' (Macdonald and Macdonald 1964: 89). The relative freedom to move and work abroad should be somehow linked with the past experience of African emancipation.

Livorno

In 1700 Italian emigration to Tunisia started to grow when a group of well-educated Italian Jews from Livorno settled in Tunis. Most of them were bankers and merchants who made use of the linkages to Mediterranean commercial networks to assume important roles in Tunis, as agents for the corsairs and their financial backers. Their contacts and wealth enabled them to join the circle of the ruling elite, where they served as advisors, business representatives or physicians to several Beys. They developed thriving trade relations with Tuscany and Sardinia, to which cereals, oil, olives, almonds and dates were exported in great quantities, in exchange for manufactures and finished European goods (Vernassa 2002: 434–6; Perkins 2004: 20). Tuscan interests in Tunisia grew and vice-consulates multiplied, testifying to the interest of the Granducato in a widespread diplomatic presence in order to defend and protect its citizens. After unification, migrants from Livorno built Italian schools and the first Italian hospital (1893) where all doctors but one (who was French) were Italian. Tuscans in Tunisia also included professionals such as lawyers, engineers and architects, the latter greatly contributed to the architectural revival of Tunis (El Houssi 2012: 167).

Conclusion

The African flow of Italian emigration must be considered in the general context of Italy's mass exodus of those years. Why were people from these towns attracted to Africa? As the analysis has shown, for a few common motives and other very different reasons, which varied according to the emigrants' geographical origin and according to the historical period analysed. Common push factors included: first, its proximity to the Italian south, the northern African coast was close and easy to reach even on small sailing boats (*bilancelle*). Six hours and an outlay of a few lire sufficed for the journey from Palermo to Tunis. Second, Mediterranean African countries allowed a fairly free circulation of goods and men, no documents were requested on arrival and registration with the local consulate was often disregarded. Third, long-established migrant communities before unification helped in generating new influxes and developing migrant networks. Fourth, the wage differential represented an important push factor, as migration theory has consistently demonstrated. However, income differential was not always the sole push factor: the farmers coming from the provinces of Trapani and Siracusa were increasingly attracted by the possibility of becoming small landowners. Tunisia, in particular, made their dream come true in the face of the impossibility of obtaining a more equal land distribution in Sicily. The African country was seen as 'a promised land' where everyone could aspire to improve its position through hard work: 'the mason can become the boss and the day labourer the owner of the land' (Melfa 2008: 72). This was so true in practical terms that despite a tradition of good enough relations with France, Italian migration and land acquisition fomented the psychosis of the '*invasion sicilienne*'. As a matter of fact, after the First World War, Italian immigration to Tunisia started to slow down; many had repatriated at the outbreak of the war, many chose the Americas by virtue of much higher salaries, and others preferred not to go back to Tunisia due to the relative saturation of the labour market in agriculture, where the land was just enough to support the first migrant family and its (numerous) descendants. However, for those who had already settled in Tunisia, even French observers had to admit that it was prosperity that character-ized Italian colonial farming: a prosperity that had quickly increased on the solid basis of relentless work and good final prices for wine. Sicilians were by far the major component of the Italian colony in Tunisia; they had turned into permanent inhabitants of Tunisia and would only 'shortly go back to Sicily on occasion of traditionally important religious feasts such as *La Madonna di Trapani*' (Sayous 1927: 69–71). Finally, Africa represents an interesting destination continent because it also attracted a considerable influx of single female migrants, thus representing for many women an uneasy and sometimes heartbreaking (wet-nurses had to leave their newborn babies behind) yet emancipating experi-ence (though initially agreed upon within the family context).

Africa's appeal waned considerably as North American destinations became well known, more profitable and soon the major destination choice of migrants from southern Italy. With the sole and significant exception of Sardinians: not only were their propensity to migrate and absolute migration figures the lowest among all Italian regions, but when the massive exodus to the United States started, they did not join in, preferring their temporary African jobs.

As clearly emerges from this analysis, no standard emigration theory applies to the multi-form Italian experience. The province level analysis of the African migration route has shown how the flows, in many aspects, differed from town to town. Some provinces preferred certain African Mediterranean countries over others, depending on the occupations sought out; some emigrants were willing to accept only temporary jobs (as masons in public works but also as daily labourers in agriculture during the harvest season); others were farmers and aimed for permanent settlement and tended to bring the family along. Most emigrants were young males, but a few small towns in the province of Catanzaro supplied women to cover a sudden, lucrative increase in demand for female labour. Some specialized workers from Cagliari travelled on a seasonal basis in order to work in mines or in the forest; fishermen from Pantelleria were requested for their ability with coral. If no macro-theory applies, it is the sum of local micro-stories that helps explain Italian flows towards Africa. What historians underline is that most of the young people who left had a well-planned earning target which was agreed upon with their families of origin and usually entailed a stay lasting only a few months (even though, as we have seen, a share of Sicilians decided to permanently settle in Africa).

No general rule applies to Italian emigration to Africa. In many cases, the emigration experience was most likely part of a temporary strategy to increase the well-being of the family at home, and the African migration route was chosen since it involved a nearby, profitable and low-cost destination. It is also true that the African path was swiftly abandoned when Italian families realized that better opportunities were offered in North America, but, again, this did not apply to the four provinces under consideration, which showed increasing flows to Africa as well during mass migration years. Last but not least, not only did the North American appeal not apply to Sardinians, but their African path has represented one of the very few cases in which poor and illiterate Italian emigrants moved to a foreign continent to earn more than native workers.

Notes

1 That strategy maintained people on the land (at barely tolerable levels of subsistence) economized on capital and depressed output per worker. The poverty of the rural population before 1914 may be also attributed to the fact that Italy's industrial and urban economy had not developed enough to pull under-employed labour from the countryside (see O'Brien and Toniolo 1994).

2 The annual growth rate of agricultural production over the first 35 years was only 0.4 per cent and could not keep up with a demographic increase around 0.7 per cent. Thus, Italian agriculture absorbed more labour than it could employ (see Toniolo 1990: 4–5.) Hatton and Williamson found that between 1985 and 1905 lagged natural increase raised the emigration rate by 1 per thousand in Sweden, by 1.3 in Norway and by 0.3 per thousand in Denmark (Hatton and Williamson 1998: 104).

References

Clancy-Smith, J. A. *2011. North Africa and Europe in an Age of Migration, 1800–1900.* Berkeley and Los Angeles: University of California Press.

Cohen, J. and Federico, G. 2001. *The Growth of the Italian Economy 1820–1960.* Cambridge: Cambridge University Press, 2001.

Coletti, F. 1911. *Dell'Emigrazione Italiana, Cinquant'anni di vita italiana*. Milano: Accademia dei Lincei.

Del Boca, A. 1992. *Gli Italiani in Africa Orientale*. Vols I–V. Milano: Mondadori.

Easterlin, R. A. 1961. 'Influences in European overseas migration before World War I'. *Economic Development and Cultural Change* 9: 33–51.

El Houssi, L. 2012. 'Italians in Tunisia: between regional organisation, cultural adaptation and political division 1860s–1940'. *European Review of History* 19(1): 163–81.

Fauri, F. 2015a. *Storia economica delle migrazioni italiane*. Bologna: Il Mulino.

Fauri, F. 2015b. 'L'emigrazione italiana nell'Africa mediterranea 1876–1914'. *Italia Contemporanea* 277(4): 34–62.

Fauri, F. 2015c. 'Italians in Africa (1870s–1914) or how to escape poverty and become a landowner'. *International History Review* 37(2): 324–41.

Filesi, T. 1978. 'Significato e portata della presenza italiana in Africa dalla fine del XVIII secolo ai nostri giorni'. In F. Assante, ed., *Il movimento migratorio italiano dall'unità nazionale ai giorni nostri*. Ginevra: Librairie Droz.

Foerster, R. F. 1919. *The Italian Emigration of our Time*. Cambridge, MA: Harvard University Press.

Ganiage, J. 1959. *Les origines du protectorat français en Tunisie (1861–1881)*. Paris: Presse Universitaire de France.

Gaston, L. 1905. *Le Peuplement Italien en Tunisie & en Algérie*. Paris: Librairie Armand Colin.

Gentileschi, M. L. 1995. 'Il bilancio migratorio'. In M. L. Gentileschi, ed., *Sardegna Emigrazione*. Cagliari: Edizioni della Torre.

Hatton, T. and Williamson, J. G. 1998. *The Age of Mass Migration: Causes and Economic Impact*. New York: Oxford University Press.

Inchiesta parlamentare sulle condizioni dei contadini nelle province meridionali e nella Sicilia, Vol. VI. 1911. Roma: Tip. nazionale G. Bertero.

Labanca, N. 1993. *In marcia verso Adua*. Torino: Einaudi.

Labanca, N. 1997. 'Italiani d'Africa'. In A. Del Boca, ed., *Adua Le ragioni di una sconfitta*, 193–229. Bari: Laterza.

Lucassen, L. and Lucassen, J. 2014. 'Cross-cultural migrations in Europe since 1500: a plea for a broader view'. In F. Fauri, ed., *The History of Migration in Europe Perspectives from Economics, Politics and Sociology*, 13–38. London: Routledge.

Macdonald, J. S. and Macdonald, L. D. 1964. 'Chain migration ethnic neighborhood formation and social networks'. *Milbank Memorial Fund Quarterly* 42(1): 82–97.

MAE (Ministero Affari Esteri). 1893. *Emigrazione e colonie. Rapporti di Agenti diplomatici e consolari*. Roma: Tipografia nazionale di G. Bertero.

MAE. 1904. *Emigrazione e colonie, Tunisia*. Roma: Tipografia Nazionale G. Bertero.

MAIC (Ministero di agricoltura, industria e commercio. 1882. Direzione della statistica generale, *Statistica della emigrazione italiana all'estero nel 1881*. Roma: Tipografia Bodoniana.

MAIC. 1913. *Statistica della emigrazione italiana per l'estero con una appendice di confronti internazionali*. Roma: Tipografia Bodoniana.

Marilotti, G. 2006. 'La comunità italiana in Tunisia: società lavoro e emigrazione. Il caso dei sardi'. In G. Marilotti, ed., *L'Italia e il Nord Africa*. Firenze: Carocci.

Marincola S. Floro, F. 1896. *Le forze economiche della provincia di Catanzaro*. Catanzaro: Tipografia Giuseppe Dastoli.

Melfa, D. 2008. *Migrando a sud Coloni italiani in Tunisia (1881–1939)*. Roma: Aracne.

Natili, D. 2009. *Una parabola migratoria: fisionomie e percorsi delle collettività italiane in Africa.* Viterbo: Sette Città.

O'Brien, P. K. and Toniolo, G. 1994. 'The poverty of Italy and the backwardness of its agriculture before 1914'. In G. Federico, ed., *The Economic Development of Italy since 1870*, 346–70. Aldershot: Edward Elgar.

Paris, R. 1976. 'L'Italia fuori d'Italia'. In *Storia d'Italia*, vol. IV, t.1. Torino: Einaudi.

Perkins K. J. 2004. *A History of Modern Tunisia.* Cambridge, Cambridge University Press.

'Rassegna bibliografica sull'emigrazione e sulle comunità italiane all'estero dal 1975 ad oggi'. 1989. *Studi Emigrazione* XXVI: 464–596.

Sayous, A.-E. 1927. 'Les italiens en Tunisie'. *Revue Economique international* 2(7): 61–99.

Sori, E. 1979. *L'emigrazione Italiana dall'unità alla seconda Guerra mondiale.* Bologna: Il Mulino.

Toniolo, G. 1990. *An Economic History of Liberal Italy 1850–1918.* London: Routledge.

Vernassa, M. 2002. 'Presenze toscane nella reggenza di Tunisi (1843–1851)'. In V. A. Salvadorini, ed., *In Tunisia e Toscana.* Pisa: Edistudio.

Zamagni, V. 1978. *Industrializzazione e squilibri regionali in Italia.* Bologna: Il Mulino.

Zamagni, V. 1993. *The Economic History of Italy 1860–1990.* Oxford: Oxford University Press.

3 The South-European model of immigration

Cross-national differences by sending area in labour-market outcomes and the crisis

Ivana Fellini and Giovanna Fullin

Despite some recent dissenting opinions, the sociological literature agrees on the definition of a South-European model of immigration. Migratory inflows to Italy, Portugal, Spain and also to Greece in the past 30 years, as well as the incorporation of immigrants in the receiving labour markets, share several notable similarities. In particular, according to this literature, in the South-European labour markets immigrants are at relatively little risk of unemployment, but they are strongly penalized in access to highly skilled jobs.

In this chapter, we explore the South-European model of integration of immigrants into the labour market with particular regard to Italy, Spain and Portugal, and with a special focus on people from Eastern Europe (mainly Romanians), North Africa (mainly Moroccans) and Latin America. We have adopted this research design because the hypothesis of the South-European model is usually grounded on studies that consider immigrants as a whole, without any distinction by sending country, although this might instead reveal some differences. Cross-national differences by sending area in immigrants' labour-market outcomes may be important even though they are not necessarily the same in the three receiving areas. For this reason, the chapter focuses on immigrants from specific sending countries who represent large pools of the immigrant population in Italy, Spain and Portugal. Given the current severe economic crisis, the chapter also explores what has occurred to the disadvantage pattern that immigrants experience in the South-European countries, the purpose being to provide evidence on the persistence, or rather the differentiation, of the so-called South-European model.

The chapter is based on an exploratory cross-national analysis of the Eurostat Labour Force Survey (LFS) microdata for 2007 and 2012 which enable us to evaluate the impact of the economic crisis. We consider two dimensions of the incorporation of immigrants into Southern European labour markets: *the risk of unemployment*, and the *chances of accessing high-skilled non-manual jobs*. The chapter is organized as follows. In the first section, we briefly outline the main features of the South-European model of immigration. In the second, we show the main characteristics of Latin American, North African and East European immigrants in Italy, Spain and Portugal. In the third section, we provide evidence of the common pattern of labour-market insertion of the different groups of immigrants in the three countries, and in the fourth we discuss the impact of the crisis.

Is the South-European model of immigration still well founded?

Despite a recent dissenting opinion (Baldwin-Edwards 2012), research agrees that immigration into Italy, Portugal, Spain (and also Greece) has largely the same features (Baganha 1997, Arango 2012, Peixoto *et al.* 2012). The South-European model of immigration has three main dimensions: (a) the timing and the size of inflows; (b) the reasons for and the modes of entry; and (c) the distinctive pattern of incorporation into the receiving labour market.

As for the timing and the size of inflows, all three countries were formerly out-migration countries, at least until the mid-1970s – and Portugal even afterwards – and only in the early 1990s started to receive mass immigration, which since 2008 has stopped in Portugal and Spain and greatly slackened in Italy due to the economic crisis. Moreover, the three countries represent the most important receiving areas in Europe in the past 30 years, and they have experienced very rapid increases in their foreign populations. From 1991 to 2006, 10 million foreigners entered the EU-15, over 57 per cent of them entering Spain, Italy, Portugal and Greece, a group of countries that account for only 32 per cent of the European population. This has meant a very rapid increase in the share of foreigners in the total population, which rose from 1.6 per cent to 8.4 per cent in Italy, from 1 per cent to over 10 per cent in Spain – despite the very recent decline due to the crisis – and from 1.3 per cent to 2.4 per cent in Portugal, which had recorded a peak of 3.4 per cent before the crisis.

As for the reasons for and modes of entry, one may speak of back-door entry in search of a job, given that in all the three countries both asylum seekers and immigrants possessing stay permits for work reasons before they enter the country are very few in number. The reason for this is that Italy, Spain and Portugal provide scant welfare for refugees and have adopted a strict migratory policy (the so-called quota system). All the three South-European countries have instead a very large and consolidated underground economy offering numerous work opportunities to immigrants even when they are unauthorized or undocumented. The composition of the migratory inflows that enter Southern Europe is consequently very different from those that enter Northern European countries, where refugees are numerous. But it also significantly differs from those entering either Continental Europe or the English-speaking countries, where labour migration prevails but most (selected) immigrants find jobs before entering the country (Table 3.1).

In the Southern European countries, when mass migration began most immigrants were clandestine ('boat people') without stay permits. Thereafter, most of them were over-stayers (holding short-term visas, many of them issued by either Germany or France); almost all of them managed to obtain (temporary) stay permits for working reasons by applying during one of the frequent regularization

Table 3.1 Reasons for and modes of entry: a typology of the most significant migratory inflows in Europe

Refugees	*Job found before entry*	*Job not found before entry*
Sweden	Germany	Italy
Norway	Belgium	Spain
Denmark	Great Britain	Portugal
	Ireland	Greece

Source: ELFS, ad hoc module 2008

drives. Beginning in the early 1990s, Italy had eight regularizations, Spain six, and Portugal three. Regularization drives were accompanied by the quota system for yearly entries that *de facto* regularized immigrant workers already in the country (Reyneri 2003).

In Southern Europe, unauthorized immigrants found shelter in a huge black labour market. If it were not for the widespread irregular economy and labour, unauthorized immigrants would have soon been forced back to their home countries. The attractiveness of Southern European countries to immigrants, in fact, can be explained on considering that they enter countries where it is easy to live even without a stay permit for work reasons (Baganha 1998; Reyneri 1998, 2001; Baldwin-Edwards and Arango 1999). The 'pull effect' of irregular work went along with the increasing incorporation of immigrant workers into the regular economy. In fact, most regularized migrants managed to retain registered jobs and permanently entered the regular economy because, for demographic and social reasons, the latter was in need of additional labour willing to take low-skilled jobs (OECD 2005). The process of settlement started, and so did inflows for family reunification reasons.

As for the incorporation of immigrants into Southern European receiving labour markets, recent research has emphasized a distinctive pattern (Reyneri and Fullin 2008, 2011). According to these studies account must be taken, on the one hand, of a quantitative dimension, i.e. the different risks of unemployment for natives and immigrants, and on the other, of a qualitative dimension, i.e. the different access to highly skilled occupations. A trade-off between the two dimensions is evident in Europe. Southern European countries – the 'new' destinations for immigrants – combine a somewhat low disadvantage for immigrants as regards the risk of unemployment with a huge disadvantage as regards access to highly qualified jobs. Conversely, the European 'old' receiving countries are more likely to combine a very high disadvantage for the risk of unemployment with a much lower disadvantage[1] for occupational segregation in low-skilled jobs, even for new immigrants (Reyneri and Fullin 2008; Fullin and Reyneri 2011). The reason is that the economic and social fabric is similar among the Southern European countries but different from that of the Central and North European ones. In the former, the demand for immigrant labour is strictly connected to (unsatisfied) occupational needs for unskilled jobs in an institutional frame comprising no explicit economic immigration policies. Rather, the usual option is an ex-post management of immigrant inflows through regularization (Kogan 2014), which works as an 'implicit' policy to control migration flows (Ambrosini 1999; Sciortino 2004).

East Europeans, North Africans and Latin Americans in Italy, Spain and Portugal: same country of origin, similar socio-demographic profile, but different relations with the receiving countries

Cross-national research has already attempted to provide a framework within which to compare the labour-market outcomes of immigrants. Two main approaches can be identified: the first considers people from various countries of origin in a single host country, while the second tracks a single immigrant group across two or more receiving societies. Some studies have combined both approaches. For instance, Kesler (2006) analysed the labour-market outcomes relative to those of natives for many immigrant groups in three old receiving European countries. Kogan (2007) focused on the performance of immigrants in 14 countries, breaking down very broad categories of immigrants. Tubergen *et al.* (2004) considered a large number of both immigrant groups and receiving countries, also non-European, even though they only very partially conducted comparison with the labour-market outcomes of natives. These studies have certainly increased our understanding of the mechanisms behind the incorporation of immigrants into receiving labour markets.

Following this approach we have selected three sending areas that account for large and significant pools of immigrant population in all the three destination countries. They also well represent the different migration waves that have occurred in the Mediterranean area since the late 1980s. On the basis of Eurostat LFS data, which give information on 15 broad areas of origin and do not provide more detailed information on countries of origin,[2] we focused on immigrants from three sending areas: (1) the East European countries of Romania and Bulgaria (which entered the European Union in 2007); (2) the North African countries; and (3) the Latin American countries.[3] Two other groups were defined in order to assess the labour-markets outcomes of the three target ones in comparison with natives: a group of foreign-born in all the other sending countries, and a group of people from the so-called 'more economically developed countries' (USA, Canada, Japan, etc.).[4]

East Europeans, North Africans and Latin Americans show many similarities in the three receiving countries, but also notable differences, especially due to a colonial past which established different previous political, economic and cultural connections.[5] By referring to available data on foreign-born population stocks (OECD 2013), we can provide a more detailed picture of the three groups, highlighting that the group from Eastern European countries that became EU members in 2007 includes nearly exclusively Romanians in all the three destination countries, but also a few Bulgarians in Spain. In all the three countries, the group of North Africans consists mostly of Moroccans, even though in Italy there are also some Tunisians and Algerians. Unfortunately, we could not distinguish this group for Portugal because the Eurostat LFS sample is too small.[6] East Europeans and North Africans are then representatives of very specific nationalities in all the three countries: for this reason, in the rest of the chapter we will refer to data on East Europeans and North Africans as indicators of the labour-market outcomes of Romanians and Moroccans. Romanians have the same (null) relationships with the three South European receiving countries because they speak a different language (although of Latin origin) and have no previous cultural or political connections with them, while Moroccans have previous colonial ties with Spain, but not with Italy (Table 3.2).

Latin Americans show other and even more important differences. In Spain, Ecuadoreans, Colombians and Argentines are the most significant in quantity (followed by Peruvians, Bolivians and Venezuelans), while Latin Americans in Portugal are exclusively Brazilians. In Italy, similarly to Spain, Ecuadoreans and Peruvians dominate the group (Table 3.2). As regards Latin Americans, it is useful to distinguish people with citizenship of the destination country from others, due to the very large numbers for this group. Indeed, the colonial pasts of Spain and Portugal make migrant flows from Spanish-speaking countries to Spain and from Brazil to Portugal not only particularly large but also quite distinctive (Peixoto 2009). In Spain and Portugal, many Latin Americans hold citizenship and are well integrated in the country. Unlike what happens in Italy, where immigrants from Latin America do not speak the language of the natives (except for a few Argentineans), Latin Americans are Spanish-speakers in Spain and Portuguese-speakers in Portugal. Also in Italy they represent a special group of immigrants, because they have relatively easier access to the spoken language and many of them hold Italian citizenship.

Table 3.2 Foreign-born areas included in Eurostat LFS codes and actual origin according to migration statistics

ELFS area of origin	Spain	Italy	Portugal
New EU member states	Romanians (= 85%) Bulgarians (= 15%)	Romanians (= 95%) Bulgarians (= 5%)	Romanians (= 95%)
North Africa	Moroccans (= 95%)	Moroccans (= 60%) Tunisians (= 20%)	–
Central–South America	Spanish-speaking countries (= 100%)	Spanish-speaking countries (= 100%)	Brazilians (= 80%)
Other areas	'New emigration countries' (China, India, etc.)	'New emigration countries' (China, India, Ukraine, etc.)	PALOP (African former colonies, Angola, Mozambique, etc.)

Source: Own elaboration on OECD data 2013

The group of foreign-born from other sending areas, which includes all the other foreign-born except for those from 'more economically developed countries', exhibits even more marked differences indicating some country-specific aspects of migration processes. In Portugal, people from the former African colonies – the so-called PALOP (Portuguese-speaking African countries[7]) – dominate this group (above all Angolans, Mozambicans, but also people from Cape Verde, Guinea-Bissau, Sao Tomé and Principe), and the past colonial connection makes them immigrants of a very special type. In Italy and Spain, this group instead comprises Chinese immigrants, people from the Philippines, India or other non-EU countries (i.e. Ukraine and Moldavia in Italy): that is, migrants from countries with no or very weak previous connections with the destination country.

Romanians, Moroccans and Latin Americans represent a significant share of the working-age population in all the three countries. Immigration from Latin America (7 per cent of the working-age population) and North Africa (2.8 per cent) is especially notable in Spain, due the country's colonial past, but Romanians too are important in amount (2.4 per cent). In Portugal, there is a large pool of people from the PALOP (4.8 per cent), who dominate the group of foreign-born from other areas, followed by Brazilians (1.6 per cent); while in Italy, although migrants from Romania represent an important share of the working-age population (2.6 per cent), the sending areas are more differentiated, as the dominance of the group from other areas shows (5.2 per cent). Moroccans nevertheless account for a significant 1.3 per cent, while Latin Americans account for another 1.3 per cent.

According to data for 2007, the groups of foreign-born in working age have socio-demographic features distinct from those for the native population (Table 3.3). Differences are especially significant as far as age and family status are concerned, because in all the foreign-born groups the share of young adults (aged 25–34) and the share of people living with a partner and children is much larger than for natives. The groups of foreign-born show distinctive features, also distinct one from the other. Among Romanians, women are somewhat more numerous than men, and young adults prevail in comparison not only with natives but also the other groups of foreign-born. Moroccans are the least feminized and the lowest educated group in both Italy and Spain. In both countries, the adult group (35–44) of Moroccans is larger, and so too is the share of those living in a couple with children. The reason for this is that Moroccans were part of the first wave of immigrants into Southern Europe and are more settled in the destination countries.

Foreign-born from Latin America without citizenship are the most feminized group in all the three countries, and their educational attainment is intermediate: it is not as low as that of Romanians and Moroccans, but it is lower than that of Latin Americans. Also among these immigrants, the share of young adults and of those living with a partner and with children is very significant.

In all the three countries, foreign-born from Latin America with citizenship show notable differences from those without, being more similar to the natives. They are more educated than Latin Americans without citizenship and, most of all, they much more often live with their parents.

Table 3.3 Natives and foreign-born (aged 15–64) in Italy, Spain and Portugal by socio-demographic features, 2007

	Natives	East Europeans	North Africans	Latin Americans (non-citizen)	Latin Americans (citizen)	From other areas
Italy						
% women (15–64)	49.8	54.8	35.9	61.9	59.5	50.0
% tertiary education	12.1	8.8	7.0	10.0	18.0	10.0
% upper secondary	39.3	61.6	27.4	47.3	44.2	31.9
% lower secondary	36.0	23.8	39.6	33.7	33.1	41.7
% no or primary school	12.7	5.9	26.0	9.1	4.7	16.4
% 15–24	15.7	12.8	13.3	16.2	17.1	16.2
% 25–34	20.2	41.4	28.4	35.2	19.6	30.9
% 35–44	24.0	28.6	35.0	29.4	28.3	31.3
% over 45	40.1	17.2	23.3	19.2	35.0	21.6
% living alone	7.9	15.7	23.2	17.6	8.1	19.1
% living with partner and children	37.1	38.6	48.4	42.4	46.8	45.6
% living with partner, no children	27.9	32.3	13.6	16.2	23.5	18.0
% youth living with parents	22.9	5.3	7.1	9.2	14.5	8.6
% other	4.2	8.1	7.7	14.7	7.1	8.7
Spain						
% women (15–64)	49.0	51.7	42.4	58.4	52.5	47.8
% tertiary education	27.9	17.9	7.9	16.7	31.7	31.1
% upper secondary	31.8	20.8	22.5	23.4	24.3	15.9
% lower secondary	21.5	50.1	21.1	40.2	35.4	27.6
% no or primary school	18.8	11.3	48.5	19.8	8.6	25.4
% 15–24	16.5	19.7	15.9	19.4	14.6	15.8
% 25–34	22.6	44.4	38.9	39.3	20.3	37.5
% 35–44	22.9	23.2	29.8	25.4	34.1	27.4
over 45%	38.0	12.7	15.4	15.9	31.0	19.3
% living alone	4.7	4.0	7.1	4.6	3.4	7.2
% living with partner and children	36.5	43.4	44.0	39.8	43.7	45.8
% living with partner, no children	29.8	27.9	22.1	19.2	25.8	16.7
% youth living with parents	23.8	8.3	8.4	12.0	17.5	11.3
% other	5.2	16.5	18.4	24.4	9.6	19.0
Portugal						
% women (15–64)	50.4	50.5	60.7	51.8	48.9	49.9
% tertiary education	11.3	23.8	–	15.0	21.7	19.6
% upper secondary	15.9	45.5	–	35.3	29.3	21.5

(*Continued*)

Table 3.3 Natives and foreign-born (aged 15–64) in Italy, Spain and Portugal by socio-demographic features, 2007 (*Continued*)

	Natives	East Europeans	North Africans	Latin Americans (non-citizen)	Latin Americans (citizen)	From other areas
% lower secondary	20.3	19.1	–	28.7	24.2	24.3
% no or primary school	52.5	11.6	–	21.1	24.8	34.7
% 15–24	17.6	17.8	–	17.7	23.7	9.9
% 25–34	22.3	54.8	–	40.8	34.0	25.4
% 35–44	21.4	19.0	–	28.2	25.6	33.8
% over 45	38.7	8.4	–	13.3	16.7	30.9
% living alone	3.8	8.0	–	9.2	2.2	8.1
% living with partner and children	27.8	29.9	–	25.5	19.2	22.2
% living with partner, no children	39.2	50.3	–	41.4	34.0	45.7
% youth living with parents	22.9	0.8	–	10.1	35.2	12.5
parents % Other	6.3	11.0	–	13.8	9.4	11.5

The common pattern of labour-market disadvantage of Romanians, Moroccans and Latin Americans in Southern Europe

According to the South-European model, in Italy, Spain and Portugal immigrants experience a relatively low risk of unemployment, but are hugely disadvantaged as regards access to highly skilled occupations. In comparison with natives, their risk of being unemployed is only slightly higher, while their concentration in low-skilled positions is very much greater. As said, this finding emerges from cross-country studies that do not differentiate immigrants by area of origin. To find more subtle distinctions in the South-European model, we can inquire whether the pattern of the disadvantage is the same for Romanians, Moroccans and Latin Americans, and whether it is the same in all the three Southern Europe countries. Moreover, in the next section the comparison between 2007 and 2012 will highlight the impact of the crisis on this pattern.

We take two main indicators into account: (1) the *unemployment rates* of the different groups of foreign-born and that of the natives; and (2) the *share of those employed in highly-skilled occupations* among the various groups of foreign-born and natives. In particular, the highly skilled jobs include managers, professionals and technicians, i.e. the first three groups of the ISCO classification (International Standard Classification of Occupations).

With the important exception of Moroccans, before the crisis, in all the three countries the unemployment rate of foreign-born was only a few points higher than that of natives, indicating a very limited disadvantage (Table 3.4). In 2007, in Italy the gap ranged from around 1.6 percentage points for Romanians and

Table 3.4 Unemployment rates and percentage of employed in non-manual skilled jobs (ISCO 1–3) by sending area, 2007

	Italy	*Spain*	*Portugal*
Unemployment rate			
Natives	5.9	7.9	7.8
East Europeans	7.5	9.2	6.2
North Africans	10.8	16.1	–
Latin Americans (non-citizen)	8.7	9.3	9.4
Latin Americans (citizen)	7.6	7.1	5.4
% in medium & highly-skilled non-manual occupations (ISCO 1–3)			
Natives	54.4	45.9	33.2
East Europeans	14.4	4.9	4.1
North Africans	13.8	12.0	–
Latin Americans (non-citizen)	13.0	13.2	19.7
Latin Americans (citizen)	48.7	40.8	51.0

Latin Americans to 2.8 percentage points for the foreign-born from other areas. In Spain, the difference between natives and foreign-born from other areas was larger (over 5.5 percentage points), but it was less than in Italy for Romanians and Latin Americans (1.3–1.4 percentage points) and it was even negative for national Latin Americans. In Portugal, natives were even disadvantaged, because their unemployment rate was higher than that of Romanians and that of Latin Americans without citizenship, while the gap with respect to that of national Latin Americans was only 1.5 percentage points, and that with foreign-born from other areas was around 3 percentage points.

Before the crisis, the pattern of disadvantage in terms of unemployment rates was not the same for the different groups of foreign-born *within* Italy, Spain and Portugal, but it was largely the same in the cross-national comparison. Romanians were only slightly disadvantaged, while the disadvantage of Moroccans was substantial. Also, Latin Americans were only slightly disadvantaged compared with natives and other groups of immigrants; but, more interestingly, in all the three destination countries those with citizenship were less disadvantaged than those without it.

The concentration of immigrants in low-skilled jobs is the 'other side of the coin' of the relatively low disadvantage in unemployment risk (Table 3.4). Also in this case, before the crisis, the overall under-representation of the various groups of foreign-born in non-manual skilled occupations (ISCO 1–3) showed some differences among the groups of foreign-born and across countries, although we may say that the pattern was common to all the three receiving countries. Romanians were concentrated in manual or low-skilled non-manual jobs – especially in Spain and Portugal – and the same held for Moroccans in Italy and Spain. Latin Americans without citizenship were also concentrated in low-skilled jobs in all the three countries, while those with citizenship had greater chances of accessing highly skilled jobs. Portugal showed a specific pattern as regards Latin Americans (Brazilians) with citizenship, who entered highly skilled non-manual occupations much more often than natives.[8]

In this frame, which highlights subtler differences within South-European model, gender differences are important. In the three Southern European countries, the female disadvantage as regards the unemployment risk is a structural feature that involves both natives and immigrants (Reyneri and Fullin 2011). Indeed, before the crisis, most groups of foreign-born women showed a marked disadvantage when compared both to men from the same area of origin and to native females.[9] The pattern of the female disadvantage was the same in the three destination countries: Moroccan women were the most disadvantaged, while Romanians and Latin Americans – especially those with citizenship – were only slightly disadvantaged. Country specificities are anyway interesting: in Italy, for instance, the male disadvantage was more limited than in the other two countries, while the female gap was larger.

Before the crisis, the concentration of immigrants in low-skilled jobs affected both men and women; and, overall, female employment was slightly more qualified for both natives and foreign-born. However, there were some differences by area of origin and receiving country. In all the countries, almost no Romanians had highly skilled occupations, with the partial exception of women in Italy. Moroccans and Latin Americans without citizenship – both men and women – were very much under-represented in skilled jobs, while Latin Americans with citizenship showed only some under-representation, with the exception of Portugal, where many men and the majority of women were employed in highly qualified jobs.

One could argue that this pattern of immigrants' disadvantage depends on compositional effects: that is, on the distinctive features of the various groups of foreign-born, for instance their lower educational attainment with respect to natives. However, if we focus only on the population with at least secondary education (Table 3.5), the situation does not change, and the picture of a segmented labour market even strengthens. Indeed, the small disadvantage for immigrants as regards unemployment either does not change or slightly increases in Italy and Spain, indicating that, paradoxically, higher educational attainment widens the gap with natives. Relatively unchanged is also the huge under-representation of the more educated foreign-born in skilled occupations, which higher educational attainment should instead temper. This under-representation decreases only for Latin Americans with citizenship and partly for Moroccans, while for Romanians and Latin Americans with citizenship the situation is only marginally better. Hence, in South-European countries also the more educated immigrants are much more likely to have low-skilled occupations than natives, and the educational attainment does not reduce, but even increases, the disadvantage compared with natives.

Also the role played by the family status strengthens the picture of a labour market segmented between natives and immigrants. People living with a partner and children, which is the typical socio-demographic profile of immigrants, are especially compelled to look for work and to accept any job opportunity, due to the family burden in countries where welfare provisions for the unemployed are not generous (Esping-Andersen 1990; Gallie and Paugam 2000). One might argue that the limited disadvantage of immigrants as regards unemployment can be explained by the different distribution by family status of natives and migrants. Therefore we focus only on people living with a partner and children, in order to

Table 3.5 Unemployment rates and percentage of employed in non-manual skilled jobs (ISCO 1-3) by sending area, 2007

	People with at least secondary education[*]		
	Italy	*Spain*	*Portugal*
Unemployment rate			
Natives	5.1	5.9	7.8
East Europeans	6.8	6.7	8.7
North Africans	10.7	15.7	–
Latin Americans (non-citizen)	8.3	8.1	8.0
Latin Americans (citizen)	6.1	7.4	6.8
% in medium and highly skilled non-manual occupations (ISCO 1–3)			
Natives	73.9	66.7	79.1
East Europeans	16.8	6.4	6.3
North Africans	24.3	28.2	–
Latin Americans (non-citizen)	16.0	18.3	28.8
Latin Americans (citizen)	59.3	52.3	78.0

[*]At least the third level of the ISCED – International Standard Classification of Education corresponding to the upper secondary education.

highlight whether and to what extent the small unemployment gap between natives and the three immigrant groups persists (Table 3.6). The data show that the unemployment gap, given the same family status, increases a little because the unemployment rates of natives living with a partner and children are markedly lower than the average (over 2 percentage points in Italy and Spain) whereas this is not the case of immigrants, whose unemployment rates are aligned with the overall averages. Romanians, Moroccans and Latin Americans living with a partner and children show an unemployment rate similar to the average of their group; only Latin Americans with citizenship in Italy record an unemployment rate significantly lower than that of Latin Americans with citizenship as a whole.

Therefore, the pattern of immigrants' insertion in the South-European labour markets does not seem to depend on compositional effects, because higher educational attainments and family burden do not change the overall pattern. The educational level indicates an even stronger disadvantage of all the groups of immigrants, while family status only slightly increases the scant disadvantage in terms of unemployment. Only Latin Americans with citizenship, who are the least disadvantaged in the general pattern, show some impact of educational attainment and the family status, thus resulting closer to the situation of natives (or are even advantaged, as in the case of Portugal).[10]

The advantage of Latin Americans with citizenship of the destination countries compared with the other groups of immigrants, and above all Latin Americans without citizenship, suggests that thorough analysis should be made of the South-European model of immigrants' insertion in the labour market. In economic and social systems like those of Italy, Spain and Portugal, where all immigrants are hugely segregated in low-skilled jobs, cultural proximity and language skills seem to give immigrants very little advantage as far as some labour-market

Table 3.6 Unemployment rates by sending area, 2007

	People living with a partner and children		
	Italy	*Spain*	*Portugal*
Natives	3.6	5.8	6.3
East Europeans	7.7	9.9	10.3
North Africans	10.9	16.7	–
Latin Americans (non-citizen)	7.9	8.4	11.6
Latin Americans (citizen)	5.0	6.6	5.3

outcomes are concerned. The dual structure of the labour market in these countries restricts immigrants to specific sectors and occupations, those that are less appealing to natives, where command of the country's language is not at all important for finding a job. General labourers in construction and agriculture, manual workers in personal or social services do not need a good knowledge of the language to find jobs; rather, language skills become important in improving the chances of accessing non-manual semi-skilled or skilled occupations.

The data suggest that citizenship of the receiving country instead matters, because it goes along with lower unemployment rates and above all much higher chances of accessing highly skilled positions. The literature has already shown that citizenship is associated with better labour-market outcomes for immigrant workers (Bevelander and Veenman 2006; Bratsberg *et al.* 2002; Chiswick 1978; Fougère and Safi 2009; Kogan 2003; Scott 2008; Steinhardt 2008). Citizenship may be important for many reasons: it affects job search behaviour because it intertwines with the legal status of immigrants; it fosters investment by immigrants in education, language and country-specific skills; it may act as a signal of integration to employers; and it removes barriers to some jobs like those in the public sector. However, the relation may go in the opposite direction, because all these factors may affect the probability of applying for and obtaining citizenship. Research often fails to consider that immigrants who obtain citizenship in the host country are likely to be a self-selected group, with characteristics that influence the probability of both being naturalized and finding a good job (Corluy *et al.* 2011). Among the observable characteristics (i.e. information available in survey data), years since migration are the most important as in many receiving countries foreigners are entitled to apply for citizenship only after a more or less long period of continuous residence.

As this is the case of Italy, Spain and Portugal, we statistically controlled the labour-market outcomes of foreign-born by years since immigration.[11] It emerged that the pattern of the differences between those with citizenship and those without was significant, indicating that citizenship does indeed matter. Of course, we cannot say anything about the causal relation between citizenship and access to skilled jobs because we know nothing about other unobservable characteristics of people applying for naturalization that might account for the differences. We can nevertheless argue that if a 'naturalization premium' exists in the Southern European dual labour markets, it affects the chances of accessing skilled jobs much more than the unemployment risk.

The impact of the crisis

The effects of the crisis are evident in the sharp rise in unemployment rates from 2007 to 2012 (Table 3.7 compared to Table 3.4). Spain is among the European countries that suffered most, with an unemployment rate three times that of 2007, but also in Italy and in Portugal the unemployment rate of natives nearly doubled in the five-year period.

As regards the disadvantage of the various groups of foreign-born, all the three countries show a marked increase in the gap with natives; but its magnitude is exceptional in Spain, where the gap for North Africans exceeds 30 percentage points, and the gap with national Latin Americans is becoming positive and quite significant (over 10 percentage points). In Portugal, the pre-crisis advantage of Romanians and Latin Americans without citizenship turned into a significant disadvantage with the crisis (10 and 1.6 percentage points respectively) and over-all the position of the foreign-born worsened quite significantly. In Italy, the unemployment risk for Romanians, North Africans and Latin Americans increased significantly between 2007 and 2012, but the gap with respect to natives increased much less than in the other two countries: indeed, the increase in unemployment rates was quite uniform across the various groups of immigrants (Table 3.7 and Figure 3.1).

To furnish an overview of what has occurred with the crisis to foreign-born in comparison with natives, Figures 3.1 and 3.2 show the data for 2007 and 2012 on the unemployment rates for natives and foreign-born and on the percentage share of persons employed in highly skilled non-manual occupations. In both figures the lighter line represents the situation of natives in 2007, and the darker line represents the situation of natives in 2012. The situation of the various groups of immigrants is instead represented by the pale small squares for 2007 and by the dark small squares for 2012. In this way, it is easy to compare the situation before and after the crisis for immigrants with respect to natives.

Table 3.7 Unemployment rates and percentage of employed in non-manual skilled jobs (ISCO 1–3) by sending country, 2012

	Italy	Spain	Portugal
Unemployment rate			
Natives	10.2	22.8	15.3
East Europeans	13.4	38.9	25.3
North Africans	19.8	54.2	–
Latin Americans (non-citizen)	14.1	33.2	22.3
Latin Americans (citizen)	16.9	32.6	16.9
% in medium and highly skilled non-manual occupations (ISCO 1–3)			
Natives	52.2	47.2	38.6
East Europeans	8.0	9.7	11.0
North Africans	8.6	11.3	–
Latin Americans (non-citizen)	10.6	13.7	13.4
Latin Americans (citizen)	42.3	29.9	55.2

As regards the occupational structure, the crisis caused a stronger concentration of Romanians, North Africans and Latin Americans without citizenship in low-skilled jobs only in Italy, where also the share of natives with high-skilled jobs decreased (Table 3.7). This trend did not occur in Spain, where not only natives but also Romanians and national Latin Americans seem to have slightly upgraded their occupational positions. With the exception of Latin Americans without citizenship, also in Portugal a slight upgrading of the employment structure occurred not only for natives but also for foreign-born.

As can be seen from Figures 3.1 and 3.2, before the crisis, the three countries shared a common pattern, albeit with country specificities. On the one hand, well evident is the relatively low disadvantage in unemployment rates for the various groups of foreign-born (Figure 3.1: pale small squares quite close to the lighter line), apart from Moroccans. On the other hand, well evident is the huge concentration of foreign-born in low-skilled occupations (Figure 3.2: pale small squares much below the lighter line), with the exception of Latin Americans with citizenship of the destination countries.

The crisis has partially changed the picture of immigrants' incorporation into Southern European labour markets. As Figure 3.1 shows, the small disadvantage of immigrants in regard to the risk of unemployment has become substantial, especially in Spain and Portugal, also considering the significant worsening in the position of the native labour force (the line for natives rises, but the small squares rise much more). In Italy instead, the gap only slightly increases.

The ethnic dualism of the employment structure remains a distinctive feature of all the three receiving destination countries also with the crisis, although in different country-specific frames (Figure 3.2). Italy exhibits a downgrading trend involving both natives and immigrants, while Spain and Portugal register an upgrading of the employment structure for natives, which also involves some groups of immigrants. In both countries, however, there is an evident downgrading trend for Latin Americans with Spanish and Portuguese citizenship.[12]

To understand these outcomes of the crisis, it should be considered that the impact of the crisis on employment has not been the same in the three countries (European Commission 2012; Eurofound 2013), in the frame of different employment structure. Between 2007 and 2012 job losses in Italy, Spain and Portugal were different (Table 3.8): after years of exceptional growth, in Spain the employment rate fell by over 15 per cent, with a peak of over 20 per cent among men. In Portugal, too, job losses were dramatic: they amounted to over 10 per cent, although they were less selective by gender. By contrast, in Italy the employment reduction did not exceed 1.4 per cent[13] and affected only men (−4.4 per cent), whereas female employment even increased (+3.2 per cent).

Job losses were not uniform across ethnic groups in the three countries. In Spain, all groups of foreign-born were severely affected by the crisis, with the exception of female Moroccans and national Latin Americans, whose employment even increased. Moreover, job losses were greater for foreign-born than for natives. Quite the opposite occurred in Italy, where the crisis affected mainly native men, and native women to only a partial extent, while for all the groups of

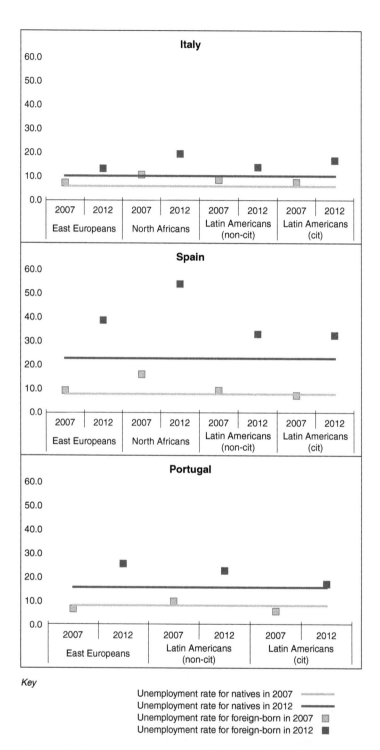

Figure 3.1 Unemployment rates by sending area and destination country: the trends in the crisis

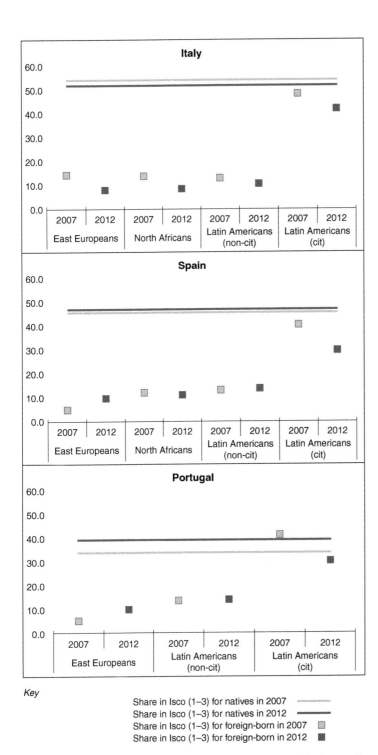

Share in Isco (1–3) for natives in 2007
Share in Isco (1–3) for natives in 2012
Share in Isco (1–3) for foreign-born in 2007
Share in Isco (1–3) for foreign-born in 2012

Figure 3.2 Percentage of employed in non-manual skilled jobs by sending area and destination country: the trends in the crisis

Table 3.8 Employment growth rates (%) by gender and sending area, 2012/2007

	Italy			Spain			Portugal		
	Male	Female	Total	Male	Female	Total	Male	Female	Total
Natives	−8.0	−2.3	−5.8	−20.3	−5.2	−14.2	−13.4	−9.4	−11.6
East Europeans	119.7	177.3	146.2	−32.5	−8.5	−21.8	−12.1	31.7	6.3
North Africans	9.6	44.9	14.9	−41.2	3.5	−31.6	–	–	–
Latin Americans (non-citizen)	26.8	29.0	28.0	−39.1	−32.7	−35.7	−51.2	−19.7	−36.2
Latin Americans (citizen)	3.0	29.7	16.1	1.9	37.3	18.7	69.2	69.7	69.5
From other areas	38.0	57.4	45.4	−11.8	−11.9	−11.8	−4.0	−0.3	−2.2
Total employment	−4.4	3.2	−1.4	−21.2	−6.4	−15.1	−12.4	−8.0	−10.4

foreign-born – and especially for females – the trend in employment was positive, with a marked increase for Romanians. In Portugal, native men, Romanian men, and Latin Americans without Portuguese citizenship were the most affected by the crisis, whereas for Romanian women and national Latin Americans the employment trend was even very positive.

Those trends can be explained by considering the different dynamics of sectors over the crisis period[14] (Table 3.9) and the composition of employment by sector of foreign-born workers (Table 3.10). All the manufacturing branches and the majority of service activities suffered job losses, but the trends were different in the three countries. Job losses in construction and manufacturing were dramatic in Spain, followed by the negative trends in 'trade and hotels' and in 'transport and communications'. These, in fact, are the sectors where foreign-born workers are hugely concentrated, mainly in low-skilled jobs; and this is the likely reason why,

Table 3.9 Absolute employment growth and employment growth rates (%) by sector, 2012/2008

	Absolute growth (000)			Growth rate (%)		
	Italy	Spain	Portugal	Italy	Spain	Portugal
Agriculture	−18	−85	−94	−2.1	−10.2	−16.0
Manufacturing	−393	−753	−143	−7.9	−23.3	−15.2
Construction	−233	−1299	−197	−11.7	−52.8	−36.4
Trade and hotels	−32	−483	−131	−0.7	−10.3	−12.3
Transport and communications	−11	−157	−16	−0.7	−10.2	−6.0
Finance, real estate, business services	−97	−148	−19	−4.3	−9.6	−6.6
Public administration, education, health	−181	58	−7	−4.6	1.7	−0.9
Social and personal services	458	29	37	15.0	1.1	6.1

Table 3.10 Employment by sector and area of origin (%), 2012

	Natives	East Europeans	North Africans	Latin Americans (non-citizen)	Latin Americans (citizen)	From other areas
Spain						
Agriculture	3.9	10.1	20.5	6.1	2.1	5.8
Manufacturing	15.2	8.9	10.5	5.8	11.6	10.4
Construction	6.1	20.1	5.4	4.8	6.5	6.2
Trade and hotels	22.9	20.3	38.5	29.7	31.6	47.4
Transport and communications	8.0	5.4	4.8	6.4	6.9	5.4
Finance, real estate, business services	13.1	9.2	6.6	8.1	16.3	6.0
Public administration, education, health	25.1	4.7	6.7	7.0	15.8	2.9
Social and personal services	5.7	21.4	7.0	32.2	9.2	15.9
Total	100.00	100.00	100.00	100.00	100.00	100.00
Italy						
Agriculture	3.6	7.2	6.3	0.7	0.7	4.4
Manufacturing	20.2	14.1	25.5	10.4	17.9	21.9
Construction	6.9	19.9	16.2	8.7	5.2	11.7
Trade and hotels	20.5	14.0	26.5	14.3	25.6	19.0
Transport and communications	7.4	4.8	5.6	6.3	3.6	4.2
Finance, real estate, business services	14.0	5.6	7.9	10.3	15.6	6.3
Public administration, education, health	22.2	5.8	4.1	8.5	19.8	4.1
Social and personal services	5.2	28.6	7.9	40.9	11.6	28.6
Total	100.00	100.00	100.00	100.00	100.00	100.00
Portugal						
Agriculture	11.3	8.1	–	3.0	5.1	1.6
Manufacturing	18.5	11.0	–	4.0	9.7	11.1
Construction	7.7	10.6	–	12.5	8.1	8.0
Trade and hotels	20.3	32.0	–	33.0	24.4	22.3
Transport and communications	5.4	0.8	–	2.0	7.8	7.4
Finance, real estate, business services	8.8	11.4	–	9.0	10.9	14.9
Public administration, education, health	22.3	13.3	–	8.4	27.3	25.7
Social and personal services	5.7	12.9	–	28.1	6.8	9.0
Total	100.00	100.00	100.00	100.00	100.00	100.00

with the crisis, the employment structure by occupation of Romanians and Latin Americans slightly upgraded. Such upgrading was not due to a stronger demand for skilled labour addressed to immigrants; rather, it was the outcome of the collapse of employment in low-skilled jobs, where immigrants are most concentrated.

In Italy, job losses were significant in manufacturing and construction, and also in public administration, education and health. Impressive and distinctive in Italy was the employment growth in social and personal services, where an increase of over 450,000 persons employed explains the important growth in the number of Romanian and Latin American female workers.[15] Contrary to what occurred in Spain, the demand for unskilled labour in Italy did not diminish with the crisis, but increased because of the unsatisfied domestic and care needs of households. Thus, immigrants – especially Romanian and Latin American women – found numerous job opportunities in the secondary labour market even during the crisis. Contrary to Spain, in Italy the fall in employment was mainly due to job losses among skilled labour in manufacturing, business services, public administration, education and health, mainly addressed to natives, whereas the trend of the most unskilled labour, which mainly concerned immigrants, remained somewhat positive. Portugal was in an intermediate position, although its overall outcome was that of an upgrading trend in the employment structure as in Spain. Job losses mainly affected construction, where many Romanian men were employed in low-skilled occupations, whereas 'social and personal services' increased even during the crisis, providing Romanian and non-national Latin American women with work opportunities that supported their employment levels.

The different adjustment patterns undergone by the three countries during the crisis entailed different impacts on immigrants due to their different involvement in low-skilled jobs connected to the sectoral trends. As a recent analysis shows (Eurofound 2014), an upgrading trend occurred in Spain and Portugal, even though it was due to the employment collapse of low-skilled jobs, whereas a downgrading trend occurred in Italy due to the decrease in highly skilled jobs and the growth of low-skilled ones (Figure 3.3).

Conclusion: is the South-European model of migration creaking?

In this chapter, we have explored the South-European model of immigration through a cross-national comparison of the incorporation of immigrants into the Italian, Spanish and Portuguese labour markets. We have done so with an especial focus on Romanians, Moroccans and Latin Americans – important pools of immigrants in all the three countries – and considering the impact of the crisis. The analysis has followed the stream of literature that seeks to determine the labour-market outcomes of immigrants by taking into account, on the one hand, people from different countries of origin and, on the other, the various receiving societies. The analysis has been carried out along the two main dimensions that characterize the South-European model of immigrant labour-market inclusion: relatively low unemployment risk, and extremely difficult access to highly skilled jobs.

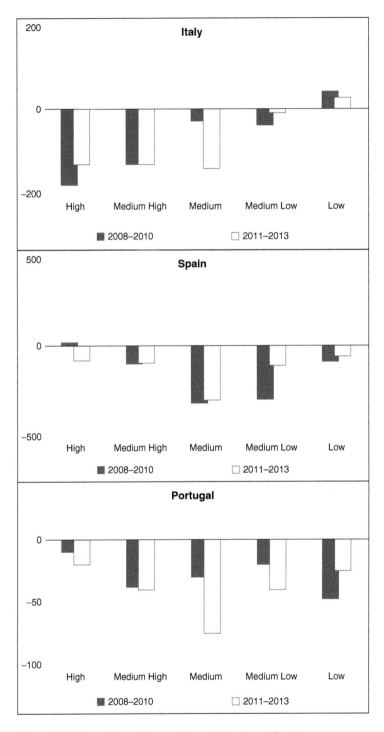

Figure 3.3 Change in employment by quintile of qualification

Source: Adapted from Eurofound (2014)

The analysis has shown that before the crisis the three South-European countries not only shared this overall pattern differentiating the immigrant and native labour forces – albeit with country specificities – but also showed a common structure of disadvantage for Romanians, Moroccans and Latin Americans. Indeed, in all the three countries, not all the groups of immigrants are disadvantaged in the same way, although the structure of the disadvantage is quite similar in the three national contexts. For some immigrant workers, such as Moroccans, their concentration in low-skilled jobs is combined with a higher risk of unemployment, producing a situation of very great disadvantage. By contrast, for some others, such as Latin Americans with citizenship, a lower concentration in low-skilled jobs is not combined with a higher risk of unemployment. Romanians are those to whom the trade-off hypothesis seems to apply most closely, even in Portugal.

Interestingly, and supporting the idea of the South-European model, in all the three countries, and with some exceptions in Portugal, the 'hierarchy' of the disadvantage is the same. Moroccans are in the weakest position (especially when they are female), followed by Romanians and Latin Americans without citizenship of the host country, who are more or less aligned with the group of migrants from other areas, but disadvantaged compared with those holding the citizenship, especially as regards access to skilled jobs.

Closer study of the South-European model showed some differences that seem to bear out the hypothesis of a common underlying pattern. The similar differences that immigrants from the same sending areas exhibit in the three countries confirm the importance of migratory systems and of the previous migratory connections among countries. At the same time, they provide new evidence for the hypothesis of a common model of labour-market inclusion of immigrants in the southern European countries.

The hypothesis of the South-European model is also supported by the results showing that the pattern of immigrant disadvantage does not seem to depend on compositional effects, such as the lower educational profile of the various groups of immigrants or their family status. We have shown that, on the one hand, the pattern of disadvantage for Romanians, Moroccans and Latin Americans compared with natives does not change, and becomes even stronger when the focus is only on the highly educated. On the other hand, we have shown that the low risk of unemployment is not a distinctive feature of immigrants with a family burden and consequently more active in searching for work and more willing to accept a job of any kind.

In Spain and Portugal, the case of Latin Americans is of especial interest: it shows that in segmented labour markets like those of the Southern European countries, command of the language is not crucial for finding a job, but it is important in determining what kind of job is found. In these labour markets, immigrants are in a subordinate position and mainly employed in the secondary labour market, so that cultural proximity and language skills do not give immigrants from Latin America the clear advantages over immigrants from other areas that one would expect. Citizenship instead plays a role, although we cannot know if it is mediated by years since immigration and other unobservable features: Latin Americans with citizenship of the host country are more similar to natives in all the three countries, in terms of both socio-demographic characters and labour-market outcomes. However, if a 'naturalization premium' exists in Southern European dual labour markets, it would affect more the chances of accessing skilled jobs than those of avoiding unemployment.

However, with the crisis, some evident differences have emerged in the three countries. The 'low unemployment risk – no access to skilled jobs' pattern seems to be more persistent in Italy than in the other two countries, where the disadvantage as regards the unemployment rate has significantly increased and segregation in low-skilled jobs has not changed, or for some groups has slightly weakened. Not surprisingly, in all the three countries, labour-market outcomes have worsened for both natives and immigrants, and immigrants have everywhere been hit harder than natives by the crisis. But the features of the South-European model weaken in Spain and Portugal, whereas they are even reinforced in Italy.

As regards the differences among the three immigrant groups studied, the 'hierarchy' of disadvantage among them is unchanged in the three countries. Moroccans are still at greatest disadvantage with respect to both the risk of unemployment and employment segregation. Hence we cannot detect any compensation between the two aspects. Romanians and Latin Americans significantly worsen their position in regard to unemployment risk, while segregation in low-skilled jobs did not increase and in Italy even increased.

The changes in the relative disadvantage of immigrants in the three labour markets seem to be more the outcomes of the different overall employment adjustments in the three countries than of a structural change in the positions of immigrants in the Italian, Spanish and Portuguese labour markets. More specifically, with the crisis, the main driver of differentiation among the three countries seems to have been the change in the skills composition of the employment structure. In Spain and Portugal, the dramatic collapse of low-skilled jobs affected more the increase in the disadvantage of immigrants as regards the unemployment risk, while leaving unchanged disadvantage in access to skilled occupations. In situations where employment dramatically fell, and unskilled jobs were those most destroyed, a slight upgrading of the employment structure occurred. This was not the case of Italy, where the employment decrease was not as dramatic as in Spain and Portugal, but where skilled jobs were significantly affected by employment downsizing and, above all, the demand for unskilled labour addressed to immigrants due to households' domestic and care needs continued to grow significantly even during the crisis.

This exploratory analysis has provided a general framework in which to examine the South-European model of the incorporation of immigrants into the labour market and its recent trends. Given that the history, features and peculiarities of immigrant groups and their migratory experiences in the destination countries are important explanatory factors of their labour-market outcomes, our cross-national analysis by sending areas should provide the basis for further research. In particular, an in-depth look at national groups in each destination country could be the next step towards better understanding of the common patterns and differences that we have identified through analysis of Eurostat LFS statistical data.

Acknowledgements

We are thankful to Professor Emilio Reyneri for his very useful comments and suggestions.

Notes

1 Previous research has suggested that a distinction should be drawn between ethnic disadvantage and ethnic penalization when analysing the differences between natives and immigrants. The 'ethnic penalty' should be considered as the residual disadvantage that remains after controlling for as many personal characteristics as possible (Heath and McMahon 1997; Berthoud 2000; Heath and Cheung 2007). The ethnic penalty tells us, for instance, whether immigrants from a particular country have poorer chances of securing employment or higher-level jobs than natives with the same gender, age, education, and living in the same region (in the case of larger countries). Of course, the 'ethnic penalty' approach that goes beyond the simpler and grosser assessment of disadvantages cannot tell us anything about both unobservable reasons for such a disadvantage (i.e. fluency in the language of the host country) and/or discriminatory behaviours (i.e. ethnic prejudice of employers).

2 The Eurostat LFS variable 'country of birth' aggregates countries in areas of birth. The variable identifies people born in countries different from the responding country of the survey and we use it to identify immigrants. For this reason in the text we will use indifferently the words 'immigrant' and 'foreign-born'.

3 We built this group by considering people from Central and South America. In the text, we use 'Latin Americans' with this specific meaning.

4 Countries with a high level of GDP per capita.

5 In this exploratory analysis it was not possible to take specific account of the literature focused on the migration of Romanians, North Africans and Latin Americans into the three receiving countries that would have helped us in referring to specificities of their history and main features.

6 Thus, the few North Africans in Portugal included the group of foreign-born from other countries.

7 Países Africanos de Língua Oficial Portuguesa.

8 In Portugal, differently from the other two South-European countries, also the 'other group of foreign-born' was more concentrated than natives in highly skilled jobs. In this case, it is necessary to consider the distinctive composition of the group in Portugal, which includes especially Angolans, who have a special connection with the destination country because Angola was a Portuguese colony until 1975. Many of them have a Portuguese passport, are highly educated, and have easy access to good and skilled jobs.

9 Data are not shown but are available on request.

10 These results are confirmed also by multivariate analysis with regression models that take the interplay of all these variables into account.

11 We estimated the probability of being unemployed and the probability of accessing highly skilled occupations for the non-native groups.

12 Multivariate analysis would allow more in-depth analysis of the impact of the crisis. Some preliminary results are available on request.

13 Job losses were limited in Italy (especially in manufacturing) also due to the temporary lay-off scheme that keeps the worker formally employed in the firm for the entire period that s/he receives the benefit, even if s/he has no chance of returning to work.

14 Because of changes in the NACE Classification (Nomenclature of Economic Activities) since 2008, data show the employment growth over the period 2008–2012 according to aggregate data available from the Eurostat online database instead of over the period 2007–2012 according to microdata.

15 Some overestimation is probably due to the regularization drive for domestic and care workers in 2009 and to the special quota devoted to domestic and care workers in 2010/2011, which regularized many immigrants already present and working in the country.

References

Ambrosini, M. 1999. *Utili invasori*. Milano: Franco Angeli.

Arango, J. 2012. 'Early starters and latecomers: comparing countries of immigration and immigration regimes in Europe'. In M. Okólski, ed., *European Immigrations: Trends, Structures and Policy Implications*, 45–63. Amsterdam: Amsterdam University Press.

Baganha, M. I., ed. 1997. *Immigration in Southern Europe*. Oeiras: Celta.

Baganha, M. I. 1998. 'Immigrant involvement in the informal economy: the Portuguese case'. *Journal of Ethnic and Migration Studies* 24(2): 367–85.

Baldwin-Edwards, M. 2012. 'The Southern European' model of immigration: a sceptical view'. In M. Okólski, ed., *European Immigrations: Trends, Structures and Policy Implications*, 149–57. Amsterdam: Amsterdam University Press.

Baldwin-Edwards, M. and Arango, J., eds. 1999. *Immigration and the Informal Economy in Southern Europe*. London: Frank Cass.

Berthoud, R. 2000. 'Ethnic employment penalties in Britain'. *Journal of Ethnic and Migration Studies* 26(3): 389–416.

Bevelander, P. and Veenman, J. 2006. 'Naturalization and employment integration of Turkish and Moroccan immigrants in the Netherlands'. *Journal of international migration and integration* 7(3): 327–49.

Bratsberg, B., Ragan, J. F. Jr and Nasir, Z. M. 2002. 'The effect of naturalization on wage growth: a panel study of young male immigrants'. *Journal of Labor Economics* 20(3): 568–97.

Chiswick, B. R. 1978. 'The effect of Americanization on the earnings of foreign-born men'. *Journal of Political Economy* 86(5): 897–921.

Corluy, V. and Marx, I. and Verbist, G. 2011. 'Employment chances and changes of immigrants in Belgium: the impact of citizenship'. *International Journal of Comparative Sociology* 52(4): 350–68.

Esping-Andersen, G.1990. *The Three Worlds of Welfare Capitalism*. Cambridge: Cambridge University Press.

Eurofound. 2013. *Employment Polarisation and Job Quality in the Crisis: European Jobs Monitor 2013*. Dublin: Eurofound.

Eurofound. 2014. *Drivers of Recent Job Polarisation and Upgrading in Europe. European Jobs Monitor 2013*. Luxembourg: Publications Office of the European Union.

European Commission. 2012. *Employment and Social Developments in Europe 2012*. Luxembourg: Publications Office of the European Union.

Fougère, D. and Safi, M. 2009. 'Naturalization and employment of immigrants in France (1968–1999)'. *International Journal of Manpower* 30(1/2): 83–96.

Fullin, G. and Reyneri, E. 2011. 'Low unemployment and bad jobs for new immigrants in Italy'. *International Migration* 49: 118–47.

Gallie, D. and Paugam, S., eds. 2000. *Welfare Regimes and the Experience of Unemployment in Europe*. Oxford: Oxford University Press.

Heath, A. F. and Cheung, S. Y., eds. 2007. *Unequal Chances: Ethnic Minorities in Western Labour Markets*. Oxford: Oxford University Press.

Heath, A. F. and McMahon, D. 1997. 'Education and occupational attainments: the impact of ethnic origins'. In V. Karn, ed., *Ethnicity in the 1991 Census, Vol. 4: Education, Employment and Housing*, 91–113. London: HMSO.

Kesler, C. 2006. 'Social policy and immigrant joblessness in Britain, Germany and Sweden'. *Social Forces* 85(2): 743–70.

Kogan, I. 2003. 'Ex-Yugoslavs in the Austrian and Swedish labour markets: the signifi-cance of the period of migration and the effect of citizenship acquisition'. *Journal of Ethnic and Migration Studies* 29(4): 595–622.

Kogan, I. 2007. *Working Through Barriers. Host Countries Institutions and Immigrant Labour Market Performance in Europe*. Dordrecht: Springer.

Kogan, I. 2014. 'Politiche migratorie, processi di selezione e inserimento occupazionale degli immigrati'. In P. Barbieri and G. Fullin, eds, *Lavoro, istituzioni, diseguaglianze*, 271–89. Bologna: Il Mulino.

OECD. 2005. *International Migration Outlook 2006*. Paris: OECD.

OECD. 2013. *International Migration Outlook 2013*. Paris: OECD.

Peixoto, J. 2009. 'Back to the South: social and political aspects of Latin American migra-tion to Southern Europe'. *International Migration* 50(6): 58–81.

Peixoto, J., Arango, J., Bonifazi, C., Finotelli, C., Sabino, C., Strozza, S. and Triandafyllidou, A. 2012. 'Immigrants, markets and policies in Southern Europe: the making of an immi-gration model?' In M. Okólski, ed., *European Immigrations: Trends, Structures and Policy Implications*, 107–47. Amsterdam: Amsterdam University Press.

Reyneri, E. 1998. 'The role of the underground economy in irregular migration to Italy: cause of effect?' *Journal of Ethnic and Migration Studies* 24(2): 313–31.

Reyneri, E. 2001. 'Migrants' involvement in irregular employment in the Mediterranean countries of the European Union'. *ILO International Migration Papers* 39.

Reyneri, E. 2003. 'Immigration and the underground economy in new receiving South European countries: manifold negative effects, manifold deep-rooted causes'. *International Review of Sociology* 13(1): 117–43.

Reyneri, E. and Fullin, G. 2008. 'New immigration and labour markets in Western Europe: a trade-off between employment and job quality?' *Transfer* 14(4): 573–88.

Reyneri, E. and Fullin, G. 2011. 'Labour market penalties of new immigrants in new and old receiving West European countries'. *International Migration* 49: 31–57.

Sciortino, G. 2004. 'Immigration in a Mediterranean welfare state: the Italian experience in comparative perspective'. *Journal of Comparative Policy Analysis* 6(2): 111–29.

Scott, K. 2008. 'The economics of citizenship: is there a naturalization effect?'. In P. Bevelander and D. J. Devoretz, eds, *The Economics of Citizenship*, 105–26. Malmö: Holmbergs.

Steinhardt, M. F. 2008. 'Does citizenship matter? The economic impact of naturalizations in Germany'. *HWWI Research Paper* 3–13. Hamburg: HWWI.

Van Tubergen, F., Maas, I. and Flap, H. 2004. 'The economic incorporation of immigrants in 18 western societies: origin, destination and community effect'. *American Sociological Review* 69(4): 704–27.

4 The labour market insertion of immigrants into Italy, Spain and the United Kingdom

Similarities and differences and the Southern European model of migration

Anna Di Bartolomeo, Giuseppe Gabrielli and Salvatore Strozza

Introduction

The 'Southern European model' of migration was first elaborated by Russell King and his co-authors (King and Rybaczuk 1993; King *et al.* 1997; King and DeBono 2013), and further discussed by other authors (Baldwin-Edwards and Arango 1999; Ribas-Mateos 2004; Peixoto *et al.* 2012), who sometimes criticized its heuristic value (Baldwin-Edwards 2012). The model is based on important and empirically grounded similarities between Italy, Spain, Greece and Portugal, in terms of country socio-economic features; migration histories and policies; types of immigration and migrant characteristics; migrant labour market access and integration in the receiving society.

Essentially, these countries all evolved from being mass emigration producers into mass immigration receivers. This changeover occurred in the 1970s and 1980s in concomitance with a significant inflow of national returnees. The absence or lack of effectiveness of migration policies has boosted irregular migration or, at least, made irregular migration more prevalent that in the countries of Western and Northern Europe. Irregular migration is thus considered a characteristic of the Southern European migration regime. Another feature is the spontaneity and unpredictability of its immigration flows. International immigration has long been (un)managed by explicit or implicit large-scale and periodically repeated *ad hoc* regularization campaigns. The presence of a larger informal economy than is found in other Western European countries has facilitated the arrival and employment of irregular immigrants, but it has also provided employment to a number of immigrants with residence permits. In addition, the welfare system, and in particular the care regime, where the family takes on much of the burden of care, has encouraged migrants capable of meeting the growing demand for care services and domestic assistance to families. Domestic service for women and agriculture and construction for men have been the main entry points into the labour market for irregular migrants arriving in Southern Europe (King and DeBono 2013).

Another element characterizing the Southern European model is the variety of countries of origin of immigrants. This is mostly linked to the globalization of migration, and 'gender' models, deriving from the specialization of certain migrant groups in gender-specific labour niches, such as care-work, construction or ambulatory selling on streets and beaches. As a matter of fact, immigrants work in a wide variety of labour-market segments (King and DeBono 2013), and a complex segmentation of the labour market has been achieved along gender and ethnic lines (Bettio *et al.* 2006; Strozza *et al.* 2009). Recently, some of these characteristics have been called into question (Baldwin-Edwards 2012), as they are not true of all the countries classed in this model: in short, they work better for Italy and Spain, as opposed to Greece and Portugal. Baldwin-Edwards (2012) went so far as to question the validity of the Southern European model of migration. Some of its characteristics (for example, migration policies) would indeed emerge only when compared with other European immigration countries, or in contrast with long-standing European receiving societies (Baldwin-Edwards 2012), characterized by the so-called 'continental model of migration' (Strozza *et al.* 2009; Istat 2009).

Reyneri and Fullin (2011) have shown that in long-standing receiving countries (they considered Denmark, Germany, the Netherlands and the UK) immigrants are much less frequently in employment, and they are more likely to be unemployed than natives. On the contrary, in the 'new' receiving states (Italy and Spain) they are more frequently employed than natives and they are only slightly penalized in unemployment terms. At the same time, Reyneri and Fullin have pointed out that

> if we look at the qualification of jobs, immigrants perform worse in the two Southern European countries than in all the other countries. […] In Spain and Italy the proportion of new immigrants who are over-educated for their jobs (i.e. highly or medium educated immigrants working in manual jobs) is much higher than in the other countries. (2011: 43)

This may be another characteristic of the Southern European model of migration. Immigrants need employment in order to stay in the receiving country, though they find it hard to find a job corresponding to their level of education and labour experience. This likely depends on the type of immigration (short vs medium to long-term migration) and local labour demand (high demand of low-skilled profiles and a parallel low demand of highly qualified ones). All of this makes upward professional mobility more difficult than in other host countries.

This chapter aims at asking whether we can still speak of a Southern European model of *labour* migration. It does so by adopting a different approach. To judge the specificities of labour migration in the Southern European model of migration, Southern European countries can usefully be compared with another major receiver of labour migration that does not belong to the Mediterranean sphere. We have chosen the UK for this purpose. The typical approach of comparing Southern and Western European immigration societies is thus abandoned here: western countries being mostly governed by family migration dynamics.

The aim of this chapter is to analyse the evolution of the differential characteristics of migration flows in three European countries: Italy, Spain and the United Kingdom. We will test how these differences affect the occupational conditions of immigrants. In particular, we focus on two different aspects of labour insertion: first, the access of migrants to the labour market (in terms of employment); and second, their job conditions once they enter the labour market in terms of the mismatch between professional and educational levels. Their relative position compared with natives is taken into account.

Though these three countries are the European leaders in attracting labour migrants, different labour market structures, approaches and admission policies have certainly affected migrant workers' performances. By looking at labour market access and integration, we aim to verify whether a Southern European model of *labour* migration still stands, in contrast with the UK's selective and managed migration model.

Figures and demographic characteristics for born-abroad net migration

The focus on Italy, Spain and the UK is also justified by European immigration trends in the last decades. In order to take in the magnitude, demographic characteristics and origin of European international migration flows, net migration balances of the born-abroad population were estimated for the last decade by gender, age and macro-region of birth. Net migration estimates of the total resident population had already been proposed (for example, Zimmermann 2005; Jennissen *et al*. 2006; Bonifazi 2008; Strozza 2010). Our estimates focus on the born-abroad population classified by macro-region of birth. The born-abroad population gives an estimate of the immigrant population (Dumont and Lemaître 2008), even if these data have to be taken with extreme caution because they also include the children of returned national emigrants who happened to be born abroad; these, of course, are significant in countries with recent significant emigration. Estimates were performed for EU15 countries, for Norway and Switzerland in the 2002–11 period, corresponding to the interval between the last two census rounds.

The methodology is taken from Hill (1987) and based on the equations for general population age distributions developed by Preston and Coale (1982) and particularly on the further formulations of Coale (1985).

To this end, the following Eurostat data were used: the stock of the born-abroad population by gender, age group and macro-region of birth in the 2001 and 2011 census rounds; number of deaths of individuals born-abroad and life tables of the resident population in the selected countries.[1]

In 2011, nearly 50 million born-abroad persons resided in the 17 selected countries. Higher numbers are registered in Germany (fewer than 14 million), the United Kingdom (just under 8 million), France (over 7.3 million), Spain (nearly 5.7 million) and Italy (4.8 million). The biggest numbers of the born-abroad as a percentage of total resident population are to be found in: Luxembourg

(40 per cent), Switzerland (almost 26 per cent), Germany (17.4 per cent), Ireland and Austria (both just under 16 per cent) (Table 4.1). Overall, the proportion of individuals born abroad has remained significantly larger in Western EU15 countries, though it has notably increased in Northern and Southern countries.

The estimates for 2002–11 confirmed the significant absolute net immigration of individuals born abroad to Germany (4.3 million), Spain, the UK (both about 3.6 million), Italy (almost 2.7 million) and France (2 million). In the first five positions of net immigration we find the countries that have the highest stock of born-abroad population, though not quite in the same order. It should be noted, however, that Spain and Italy record the highest annual average migration rate equal, respectively, to almost 103 and exactly 82 immigrants every year *per* 1,000 born-abroad residents. Fairly high rates are also recorded in Northern European countries, in descending order Norway, Ireland, Finland and the UK, while all other countries show much lower rates.

Table 4.1 Stock of born-abroad population around 2011 and estimated 2002–11 net migration of born-abroad population residing in EU15 countries, Norway and Switzerland. Absolute values (thousands), percentages and annual rates (per 1,000 born-abroad population)

Country of residence	Born-abroad population (around 2011)		Estimated net migration (period 2002–2011)		
	Absolute values (thousand)	% of total population	Absolute values (thousand)	Rates (per 1,000 born-abroad)	% women
Denmark	518	9.3	181	42.2	53.2
Finland	248	4.6	117	63.9	48.3
Ireland[a]	726	15.8	345	64.0	52.8
Sweden	1,427	15.1	506	42.3	49.7
United Kingdom	7,993	12.7	3,602	58.2	49.7
Austria	1,316	15.7	402	35.0	53.8
Belgium	1,629	14.8	634	47.4	49.9
France	7,326	11.3	2,003	30.6	53.0
Germany[b]	13,895	17.4	4,317	36.2	...
Luxemburg	206	40.2	71	41.5	48.3
Netherlands[a]	1,906	11.4	390	22.2	57.7
Greece	1,286	11.9	217	18.1	60.9
Italy	4,804	8.1	2,688	82.0	56.8
Portugal	872	8.3	253	33.5	58.4
Spain	5,662	12.1	3,609	102.9	48.9
Norway	612	12.3	313	71.7	46.3
Switzerland[a]	2,034	25.6	307	15.9	48.8
EU-15	49,814	12.5	19,336	47.8	51.9

Notes:
(a) The figure refers to the beginning of 2012 and not the census data.
(b) For 2001 only the number of born-abroad population published by the OECD is available. This estimate is a raw evaluation without distinction by gender, age group and area of birth.
Sources: our elaboration from Eurostat data coming from national statistics collected in the 2001 and 2011 census rounds and in continuous recording of deaths.

Given these dynamics, it was decided to focus on immigration in Italy, Spain and the UK. First, they are the three countries with the largest net immigration in the past decade (apart from Germany), with net migration rates that are particularly high or at least among the highest. Second, starting from the 1990s and especially from the 2000s, they have evolved into the main poles of attraction for labour migrants. Growing economies, specific labour market needs and related admission policies have all contributed to make them the major poles of attraction for migrants seeking job opportunities. Third, in these countries East European immigration, especially from the new-EU member countries, was consistent: though note that the actual country of birth differs somewhat. Migration to Spain and the UK is still affected by the colonial histories of these countries. Spain continues to attract predominantly Latino immigrants and, in particular, people coming from South American countries (more than 40 per cent). The net immigration to the UK originated, meanwhile, in, for the most part, two macro-regions, Central and Eastern Asia and the neo-EU countries; on a minor level there has also been immigration from sub-Saharan Africa. Italy has attracted, in the past decade, migrants from Central and Eastern Europe, especially from neo-EU countries, but also migrants from the Balkans and from the former Soviet republics in Europe.

UK migrant populations, from traditional UK immigrant countries, have been basically balanced in age and gender terms. Even in Spain, the gender composition in net immigration appears relatively balanced within the largest migrant groups: a clear male predominance is only observed among immigrants born in more developed countries. Italy is different. Women dominate net immigration from East European EU states, the former Soviet European republics, south-eastern European and Latin American states. A male-dominated model is instead observed in net immigration from African and Asian states. The overall prevalence of women in net immigration to Italy is therefore the result of the different weight assumed by the distinct migratory flows, in particular strong East European net immigration.[2]

Looking at distribution by age group, some interesting general conclusions can be drawn in terms of migration type and, ultimately, the potential migrants' labour market participation. For example, net immigration to the UK is clearly younger than that directed towards Italy and Spain.

For Euro-Mediterranean inflows, two migration models seem to coexist. North African flows represent the traditional model. It is made of young men searching for a job and better conditions of life, who later bring their wives and children to the country. A second model is represented by migration from the East, characterized by middle-aged women, with high levels of education who have no ambition to bring their family and children. These are not the only existing models but certainly they are the most interesting ones, in terms of the occupational conditions and migrants characteristics.

In the next sections we discuss how such differentials may affect immigrant access in the host labour market and their occupational conditions. We do so to answer the following questions. How do immigrants perform with respect to natives in terms of employment access and education–job matching dynamics? What is the role played by gender, origin and destination dynamics? And can we still speak about a Southern European model of migration?

Previous research and reference literature on over-education

As the core of our analysis, over-education is an indicator of labour-market performance, along with employment prospects, unemployment rate and job quality (Dell'Aringa and Pagani 2011). A worker is generally defined as over-educated if he or she has obtained more education than his or her job requires. Aleksynska and Tritah (2013) reviewed the following theoretical and empirical explanations of over-education: (a) the imperfect 'screening' of workers' education by employers (Spence 1973); (b) the incorrect temporary matching due to imperfect information in the labour market (Groot and Van Der Brink 2000); (c) career building or conscious over-education to aid promotion (Sicherman and Galor 1990); (d) the trade-off between, and hence a substitution of, different types of human capital, such as education and experience (Sicherman 1991). Many relatively recent studies have found that over-education rates are higher among immigrants than among the native-born populations in some receiving countries including European ones (Weiss *et al.* 2003; Chiswick and Miller 2009; Aleksynska and Tritah 2013). Over-education is especially common among immigrants with non-Western qualifications in Western nations (Green *et al.* 2007; Hardoy and Schøne 2014). Different explanations depend, of course, on different hypotheses and theoretical references. According to the synthesis proposed by Dell'Aringa and Pagani (2011) the following hypotheses may be advanced.

1   Foreign and domestic human capital are not necessarily equivalent. Human capital obtained abroad may be less valued than domestically obtained human capital because it provides less country-specific skills or because the quality of foreign schooling is lower (*skill transferability*). The portability of the human capital of immigrants may, though, increase following the acquisition of country-specific skills and through work experience: these make a better adaptation of their human capital in the country of destination possible. Inadequate language skills are an obvious and important reason that immigrants find it difficult to obtain a job consistent with their educational level. Improvement in language proficiency will often favour skill transferability (*assimilation theory*). Several studies find that immigrants are less likely to be overeducated the greater their experience in the host country, but human capital earned prior to migration is not fully transferable to the host labour market (Green *et al.* 2007; Chiswick and Miller 2009; Aleksynska and Tritah 2013).

2   Foreign workers have fewer networks and less country-specific labour market information than natives. This makes the job search more difficult for them and hampers a good education–job match (*imperfect and asymmetric*

information). It has also been suggested that immigrants are more willing than natives to accept poor working conditions; educational mismatch does not induce immigrants to search for new jobs appropriate to their education, favouring their segregation in low-quality occupations (Dell'Aringa and Pagani 2011).

3   Education obtained abroad is less a signal of unobserved ability than education acquired in the host country because employers do not know foreign educational systems (Chiswick and Miller 2009).

4   *Discrimination* towards foreign nationals in the form of *segregation* into low-quality and low-paid jobs may play an important role in explaining their higher over-education (*segmented assimilation theory*). This situation is particularly evident in countries that are characterized by strong labour market segmentation or restrictive citizenship laws (see, among others, Portes and Zhou 1993; Kalter and Kogan 2006; Kogan 2011). A classic scheme divides the production system and the labour market into two sectors: a primary or capital-intensive sector with national skilled workers and a secondary or labour-intensive sector with mostly unskilled and immigrant workers who are assigned to menial jobs. If first-generation immigrants remain segregated in the secondary sector, it is unlikely that over-education will decrease over time. More generally, differences in schooling and non-recognition of diplomas, different technologies and barriers to entry into specific occupations, and discrimination against immigrants makes skill transferability across labour markets less than perfect (Dell'Aringa and Pagani 2011).

In search of determinants of over-education, we paid, of course, close attention to individual characteristics: demographic (gender, age, marital status, number of household members, or number of children, presence of cohabiting partner, etc.); migratory (age at arrival, immigration cohort, reason for migration, years since migration, country of origin, language skills, etc.) and professional (work experience abroad and in the host country, etc.). But we also looked at determinants relating to the employment (type of contract, full or part-time work, work hours, etc.) and the company where they work (firm size, sector, etc.). Among these variables, the length of stay of migrants in host countries is particularly important: it should favour the reduction of over-education in the absence of either discrimination in the labour market or significant differences in the educational systems of the origin and destination countries. Another extremely important variable is the country or region of origin of immigrants. Educational mismatch varies, after all, across immigrant ethnic/national groups. This is not only because of differential educational background, but also because of ethnic differences in immigrant incorporation into the labour market and, indeed, the host society. Some immigrant national groups are concentrated in specific niches of the labour market. Here they find work fairly easily, but they also find it difficult to escape from these niches, making professional mobility very difficult. Gender differences are extremely important: women are more likely to be over-educated than men; however, the difference is sometimes very small and the reverse has also been found (Faini *et al.* 2009; Quintini 2011).

Another important point that emerged in the literature is the way in which the rates of over-education vary between receiving countries.

This depends, of course, on host country institutions in the educational arena and the labour market, and policies that facilitate immigrant incorporation (Aleksynska and Tritah 2013; Prokic-Breier and McManus 2014). Over-education is determined, to a great extent, by destination country economic conditions and labour market institutions. In addition, immigration policy may implicitly or explicitly select immigrants with characteristics that are associated with over-education (Altorjai 2013).

Data and methods

Our micro data comes from the *EU Labour Force Survey* (hereafter EU-LFS) carried out in 2008. The great advantage of this data is that it draws on a large sample, allowing for detailed comparative analyses of occupational status of interviewees by different socio-economic, demographic and territorial characteristics. EU-LFS provides annual and quarterly data on the labour participation of residents aged 15 and over and on persons outside the labour force. It covers residents in private households according to labour status: employment, unemployment and inactivity. The EU-LFS has, however, one important limitation for our analysis: the survey is limited to legally resident immigrants, not irregular or illegal migrants or those who have a permit of stay but no legal residency. As a consequence, the estimates based on the EU-LFS sample significantly underestimate the true presence of immigrants in the labour market. Most importantly, the EU-LFS 'observes' a segment of the labour market which is selected for being more stable (as far as residence and employment are concerned). This narrow approach – particularly important in economic sectors characterized by high irregularity like agriculture, construction and household services – must be taken into consideration when interpreting these data. Despite the aforementioned limitations, the EU-LFS survey remains one of the most reliable sources of information for comparative studies into European migrant labour forces.

EU-LFS data in 2008 (EU-LFS 2008) are supplemented with the *ad hoc* module on the labour market situation of migrants. For the first time, a comprehensive and comparable data set on the labour market situation of migrants and their immediate descendants has been collected in order to monitor the phenomenon. The use of such data helps the researcher better consider the factors affecting access and participation of migrants in the labour market.

The analyses concern natives and first-generation immigrants (from now on, 'migrants'). We consider the country of birth of respondents and the country of birth of their parents in order to define 'migrants' within the EU-LFS sample.[3] We confine our analyses to respondents aged 20–64 with lower secondary or better education who are resident in Italy, Spain and the United Kingdom (see Table 4.2). These restrictive sample characteristics have been chosen in

Table 4.2 Respondents aged 20–64 with lower secondary or better education by country of residence and employment status

Country	Total sample	Employed persons	of whom: migrants
		Men	
Italy	41,311	31,932	1,458
Spain	24,191	19,594	1,073
United Kingdom	30,328	24,787	2,324
		Women	
Italy	40,485	22,722	1,141
Spain	24,485	15,577	1,053
United Kingdom	33,159	22,815	1,777

Source: our elaboration on EU-LFS data, 2008.

order to provide a wider homogeneity within countries and comparability between countries. Moreover, they allow us to maintain a sufficient sample size (mostly among migrants) according to specific dimensions.

Following the International Labour Organization's guidelines, we consider separately employed, unemployed and inactive people. Employed people are aged 15 and over and conducted at least one hour of paid work in the week of the interview or had a job or business from which they were temporarily absent. Unemployed people are persons who have looked for work at least once in the four weeks preceding the interview and who are available for work within the next two weeks. The inactive population includes children, students, pensioners and housewives or house-husbands, provided that they are not working and not available or looking for work. This definition is applicable to employees, self-employed persons and family workers.

To determine over-education we must measure differences between the profession and the educational level of workers. To this end we crossed information on individual professional levels according to the International Standard Classification of Occupations (ISCO-88) and individual educational levels according to the International Standard Classification on Education (ISCED-97). The major groups from 2 to 9 of the ISCO-88 classification are arranged with ISCED-97 classification. In particular, group 2 (intellectual professions, scientific and highly specialized) corresponds to the Bachelor's degree or postgraduate; while group 9 (unqualified occupations) corresponds to basic literacy (primary school). In the end, group 1 (legislators, executives and entrepreneurs) and group 9 (military professions) are not associated with any level of education. For this reason they are excluded from the analysis. The mismatch between the characteristics of the labour force (with particular reference to higher educational qualifications) and professions serves to identify the inefficient use of labour input in the production process and shows a disconnect between the education system and labour demand.

In order to disentangle the causes of the differences in over-education by country of residence, we use the two-step Heckman procedure. This fits a maximum-likelihood probit model with sample selection (Heckman 1976; Winship and Mare 1992):

$$y_j^{select} = (Z_j\gamma + u_{2j} > 0) \qquad\qquad y_j^{probit} = (x_j\beta + u_{1j} > 0)$$

The procedure estimates a selection equation (that should contain at least one variable that is not in the outcome equation) to analyse whether the sub-sample of persons in employment is selected and, in that case, to compute an 'adding covariate' to correct the existing distortion of this selection. In particular, the selection equation has a dummy dependent variable that assumes value 1 in case of employed respondents and 0 otherwise. The outcome equation has over-education as a dependent dummy variable (over-educated vs not over-educated) and includes the 'adding covariate'.

We run two sets of models by country of residence considering both the whole sample (native and migrants) and the sub-sample of migrants by gender.

We include in all estimated models only one different predictor in the selection equation: the educational level. As this variable has been used to define the over-education of respondents, there is no theoretical reason to include it in the outcome model and the fundamental assumption of the Heckman procedure has been respected.

Some covariates are included in both equations (selection and outcome models), such as the interaction between gender and area of birth or, alternatively, the area of birth when running separate models by gender; the age groups at interview; the presence of a cohabiting partner; and the number of cohabiting children.

Others are included only in the outcome model such as: the type of employment (self-employed vs employee); the occupational sector; and holding a part-time job.

In the end, considering the specific questions of the *ad hoc* module of EU-LFS 2008, we added covariates in the set of models restricted to migrant respondents (both in selection and outcome models), such as years since migration; facilities for equating diploma in the destination country; main reason for migrating; and need to improve language skills.

We controlled for other covariates (such as the macro-region of residence; holding host citizenship; host country help in finding the current job; holding a temporary job), but we have decided to exclude them from the analyses because they are not statistically significant.

Immigrants in the labour markets: a descriptive glance

This section describes labour market indicators including employment and over-education rates of natives and migrants in our three countries of interest according to gender and area of birth. Employment rates of migrants are very high in all three countries (Figure 4.1). They range from 79 per cent in the UK to 88 per cent in Italy among men and from 56 per cent in Italy and the UK to 67 per cent in Spain among women (compared with a EU15 average of respectively 74 per cent and 55 per cent for men and women). This is the result of admission policies which, for the last 20 years, have attracted workers to these countries.

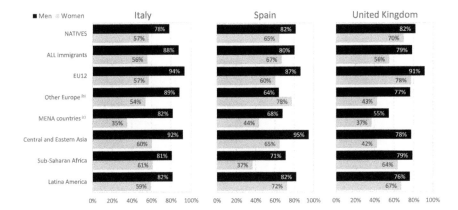

Figure 4.1 Employment rate of native and immigrant populations[a] by gender, country of residence and area of birth, 2008

Notes: (a) immigrants are defined according to the country of birth criterion; (b) Other Europe comprises East Europe and South-East Europe; (c) The term MENA refers to the Middle East and North Africa countries.

Source: our elaboration on EU-Labour Force Survey, ad hoc-module.

In Italy and Spain, these values are even larger than (or very similar to) those of natives (Figure 4.1). Indeed, the weak welfare systems of these two countries make it difficult for unemployed migrants to remain in the country: immigrants must work or leave. Accordingly – and especially at the beginning – they accept any kind of jobs regardless of conditions, future prospects and their own qualifications. These are among the reasons why migrants tend also to be much more over-educated than natives (Reyneri and Fullin 2011; Fernández and Ortega 2008). In Italy, the differentials between migrants and natives' over-education rates equal +13 and +35 percentage points respectively for men and women. The same values in Spain stand at +11 and +24 percentage points (Figure 4.2).

Another shared characteristic of Italy and Spain is found in the very difficult employment position of female migrants. Unlike other EU countries, female migrants to Spain and Italy are largely there for work. But, more than half of them (53 per cent in Italy and 57 per cent in Spain) are over-educated compared with 'only' 18 per cent and 33 per cent of their native counterparts and 26 per cent and 37 per cent of male migrants.

Why have Italy and Spain attracted such a large number of working women who, however, tend to be so over-educated? The scarcity of public welfare facilities and the parallel growing need for services for aged people and children give a partial answer. This combination has gradually generated a structural demand for household care-giving services, which have long been filled by immigrant women. Increasing levels of female education at home (Fargues 2011) has done the rest.

For instance, the high levels of education among migrant women from 'other European countries' and their strong concentration in low-skilled jobs (especially

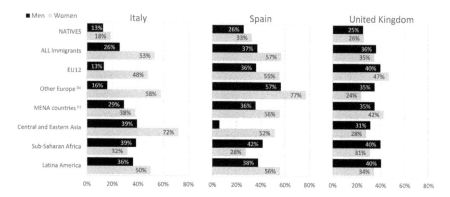

Figure 4.2 Over-education rate of native and immigrant populations[a] by gender, country of residence and area of birth, 2008

Notes: (a) immigrants are defined according to the country of birth criterion; (b) Other Europe comprises Eastern Europe and South-Eastern Europe; (c) The term MENA refers to the Middle East and North Africa countries.

Source: our elaboration on EU-Labour Force Survey, *ad hoc*-module.

in household services where 26 per cent and 28 per cent of female migrants living respectively in Spain and Italy are employed – see Tables 4.3 and 4.4) make them the first and the second over-educated group in Spain and Italy (Figure 4.2). Their over-education rates stand at 77 per cent in Spain and 53 per cent in Italy.

Furthermore, in Italy, Central and Eastern Asian women have a skill–job mismatch that reaches as high as 72 per cent. Here, their over-concentration in the 'secondary sector' and especially in household care activities is again impressive: more than one out of two (52 per cent) are employed in care-giving activities (Table 4.3).

The UK has lower differences between native and migrant over-education (Figure 4.2). A notable exception is that of migrants born in EU12 countries. Their over-education rates equal 40 per cent for men, respectively, 4 and 15 percentage points higher than those of all men migrants and natives. Among women, it stands at 47 per cent, or +12 and +21 percentage points with respect to all women migrants and natives.

These high values are the result of a 'cohort effect' as the vast majority of them arrived after 2004 (78 per cent of men and 69 per cent of women) when the EU8 countries gained non-restricted access to the UK labour market. As a result, most of them arrived for work reasons (82 per cent of men and 57 per cent of women) and they were open to any kind of job offer – at least temporarily – requiring lower qualifications than their own.

This situation is exacerbated by a number of factors. Having recently arrived, the vast majority of them have little experience in the host labour market and their 'country-specific' skills are scarcely transferable to the UK. They also have a very young age structure (56 per cent are aged 20–29), giving some backing to the *matching theory*, according to which younger labour market entrants are more likely to be over-educated since skill–job matching dynamics take time (Jovanovic 1979;

Table 4.3 Occupational characteristics of employed native and immigrant populations[a] residing in Italy by gender and area of birth, 2008

	Natives	All immigrants	EU12	Other Europe[b]	MENA countries[c]	Sub-Saharan Africa	Cen. & East. Asia	Latina America
Men								
Self-employment rate	28.2	16.9	16.4	19.9	22.9	11.2	11.9	16.2
Part time (%)	4.6	8.1	3.0	4.6	6.5	6.9	16.6	15.5
Temporary job (%)	7.8	11.3	9.1	10.2	11.5	20.6	11.3	12.0
% by sector								
Agriculture	3.4	2.4	2.3	1.8	3.5	0.5	3.6	0.7
Mining and quarrying	41.1	35.5	24.3	32.6	40.3	56.1	44.3	25.8
Construction	10.9	28.2	50.5	42.0	22.7	7.8	3.5	16.5
Transport, pub. admin., etc.	27.5	10.1	13.3	9.4	9.1	15.4	5.9	10.7
Accom. and food ser. activ.	4.0	7.0	1.9	7.0	10.5	5.2	10.3	8.4
Other tertiary services	13.0	11.1	7.7	6.5	11.9	12.3	15.0	20.9
Household services	0.1	5.7	0.0	0.7	2.0	2.7	17.4	17.0
Women								
Self-employment rate	16.7	9.8	10.4	9.1	7.4	14.9	11.4	7.0
Part time (%)	26.3	39.6	38.4	39.0	46.2	37.2	32.0	48.8
Temporary job (%)	12.9	15.1	16.6	18.0	17.3	16.2	10.7	10.9
% by sector								
Agriculture	2.1	1.0	2.3	0.6	0.1	2.2	0.1	0.1
Mining and quarrying	30.5	20.3	21.1	20.9	34.2	28.9	16.8	13.8
Construction	1.2	0.7	0.4	1.6	0.1	0.0	0.0	1.0
Transport, pub. admin., etc.	41.2	13.2	13.3	13.4	8.7	20.6	7.4	17
Accom. and food ser. activ.	5.9	11.1	12.4	12.2	15.1	5.9	9.5	9.5
Other tertiary services	18.0	20.0	19.4	22.9	17.5	21.5	13.9	22.5
Household services	1.1	33.7	31.1	28.4	24.3	20.9	52.3	36.1

Notes:
(a) Immigrants are defined according to the country of birth criterion;
(b) Other Europe comprises East Europe and South-Eastern Europe;
(c) The term MENA refers to the Middle East and North African countries.

Source: our elaboration on EU-Labour Force Survey, ad-hoc-module.

Table 4.4 Occupational characteristics of employed native and immigrant populations[a] residing in Spain by gender and area of birth, 2008

	Natives	All immigrants	EU12	Other Europe[b]	MENA countries[c]	Sub-Saharan Africa	Cen. & East. Asia	Latina America
Men								
Self-employment rate	20.7	11.5	14.4	11.8	10.5	5.5	40.6	9.5
Part time (%)	3.7	6.3	4.2	9.6	7.9	0.0	10.5	6.7
Temporary job (%)	16.4	43.3	44.5	41.7	49.4	50.2	5.8	43.2
% by sector								
agriculture	3.5	4.8	8.3	10.2	8.5	5.3	0.0	2.7
mining and quarrying	35.9	25.9	20.7	15.0	33.1	31.8	55.6	25.1
construction	15.1	35.5	49.2	45.0	22.7	28.6	3.4	34.4
transport., pub. admin., etc.	29.4	11.1	8.9	18.4	12.1	16.5	8.6	11.3
accom. and food ser. activ.	4.5	10.2	5.8	4.8	15.5	12.6	29.1	10.1
other tertiary services	11.4	10.8	7.0	0.0	7.6	5.2	0.9	14.1
household services	0.2	1.7	0.1	6.6	0.5	0.0	2.4	2.3
Women								
Self-employment rate	11.6	6.7	2.3	6.8	5.0	10.5	26.6	7.3
Part time (%)	19.9	28.2	23.5	35.3	24.0	59.1	40.3	28.3
Temporary job (%)	24.1	39.0	46.3	37.1	38.0	45.0	24.5	37.7
% by sector								
agriculture	1.8	2.3	5.1	3.6	0.0	0.0	0.0	1.8
mining and quarrying	28.2	19.8	18.9	13.0	16.0	19.1	17.2	21.0
construction	2.3	1.0	0.8	0.0	0.3	0.0	0.0	1.2
transport., pub. admin., etc.	40.9	10.0	3.5	7.6	11.9	24.4	14.0	11.5
accom. and food ser. activ.	6.9	21.4	29.6	29.2	24.7	31.5	33.0	17.6
other tertiary services	17.2	16.0	9.6	21.1	27.8	25.0	10.8	16.5
household services	2.7	29.5	32.5	25.5	19.3	0.0	25.0	30.4

Notes:
(a) Immigrants are defined according to the country of birth criterion;
(b) Other Europe comprises East Europe and South-Eastern Europe;
(c) The term MENA refers to the Middle East and North African countries.

Source: our elaboration on EU-Labour Force Survey, *ad-hoc*-module.

Table 4.5 Occupational characteristics of employed native and immigrant populations[a] residing in the UK by gender and area of birth, 2008

	Natives	All immigrants	EU12	Other Europe (b)	MENA countries (c)	Sub-Saharan Africa	Cen. & East. Asia	Latina America
Men								
Self-employment rate	17.1	17.1	16.7	19.0	17.2	14.0	18.6	19.1
Part time (%)	7.3	12.6	5.4	19.1	12.1	11.1	17.5	9.7
Temporary job (%)	3.0	7.1	6.3	5.2	4.3	7.5	8.0	7.1
% by sector								
agriculture	1.4	0.6	2.6	0.0	0.0	0.3	0.0	0.0
mining and quarrying	32.2	30.5	37.1	28.8	29.8	26.5	31.1	17.7
construction	14.9	9.1	19.8	17.5	6.7	6.5	3.2	12.6
transport., pub. admin.., etc.	34.6	34.5	19.1	23.6	32.4	42.9	40.2	34.4
accom. and food ser. activ.	2.1	11.1	10.5	20.8	13.9	5.6	13.5	8.7
other tertiary services	14.4	13.8	10.8	9.3	17.1	17.9	11.4	25.8
household services	0.4	0.4	0.1	0.0	0.1	0.3	0.6	0.8
Women								
Self-employment rate	7.7	7.3	7.1	25.6	13.8	7.0	5.6	5.7
Part time (%)	41.7	29.3	23.2	29.2	35.9	28.9	32.7	33.1
Temporary job (%)	4.8	7.0	7.4	2.0	7.0	5.8	7.8	8.5
% by sector								
agriculture	0.7	0.7	2.1	0.0	0.0	0.6	0.0	0.0
mining and quarrying	20.9	22.6	31.4	33.6	31.6	16.5	20.5	15.8
construction	2.7	2.5	2.6	2.8	4.7	3.3	1.3	3.1
transport., pub. admin., etc.	55.5	47.7	27.3	20.2	39.6	58.9	55.5	59.4
accom. and food scr. activ.	3.8	8.8	14.9	9.1	7.2	3.6	9.2	6.4
other tertiary services	15.8	16.2	18.8	34.3	16.9	16.5	12.4	13.6
household services	0.6	1.5	2.9	0.0	0.0	0.6	1.1	1.7

Notes:
(a) Immigrants are defined according to the country of birth criterion;
(b) Other Europe comprises Eastern Europe and South-Eastern Europe;
(c) The term MENA refers to the Middle East and North African countries.

Source: our elaboration on EU-Labour Force Survey, ad-hoc-module.

Sloane *et al.* 1999; Rubb 2006). In addition, they often declare major difficulties with the host country language. 'Only' 78 per cent of EU12 men and women declare sufficient language skills at work, compared to 86 per cent and 85 per cent respectively of all men and women migrants.

In the end, it seems that these three countries are, today, the main poles of attraction for work-seeking migrants in the EU. Favourable employment entry channels are here guaranteed to all migrants as confirmed by their very high rates of employment, especially in Italy and Spain.

However, once established in the labour market, their integration trajectories are very different depending on destination. The Italian and Spanish experiences of migrants show a great deal of over-education, suggesting that the Southern European model of *labour* migration still holds up. Not only are migrants dispro-portionally hit by over-education dynamics but female migrants are particularly at risk.

It seems, then, that though admission policies prioritizing labour migration are effective in all three countries and guarantee migrants relatively easy entrance into the labour market, the different nature of these policies means varied labour market integration processes. In the UK, selective policies tend to diminish the risk of over-education (with the notable exception of EU12 migrants). On the other hand, lax and unselective Italian and Spanish policies make it hard for migrants to match their qualifications in a highly segmented labour market where migrants tend still to occupy low-skilled jobs with scarce possibility of career advancement.

Over-education of immigrants: multidimensional analysis

National trends and determinants are here deepened through a multidimensional analysis. The interplay of gender, age, migratory and occupational dynamics is expected to have an important effect on our results. Specifically, the core results of the probit model with sample selection are presented here. Overall, the Heckman procedure shows in all the models that the selection equation is signifi-cant ($p<0.01$ both for ρ and for LR test[4]) and negative ($\rho<0$), thus the coefficients would be under-estimated without the correction.

Gender and area of birth. A first set of models considers the whole sample (natives and migrants) of EU-LFS. Table 4.6 shows the effect of the interaction between gender and area of birth within the selection equation (for employment status) and the outcome equation (for over-educated employment status). It allows a comparison of all the estimate coefficients within each observed destina-tion country, controlling for many other covariates listed below the table.

Our multidimensional results somehow confirm the descriptive analyses presented above. But in many cases they also show different patterns by gender and by area of birth. Such discrepancies can easily be explained by the strong relationship between the origin country and the specific socio-demographic and occupational characteristics of migrant groups. The effect of the origin country, in fact, is partially 'statistically reduced' (or explained) by the other control vari-ables included in the models.

Table 4.6 Coefficients of the interaction variable between gender and area of birth by country of destination. Heckman two-step procedure: employment (selection model) and over-education (outcome model). Natives and migrants aged 20–64

Interaction variable between gender and area of birth	Italy			Spain			United Kingdom		
	Coef.	(S.E.)	p-value	Coef.	(S.E.)	p-value	Coef.	(S.E.)	p-value
				Outcome model (overeducated vs not overeducated)					
Reference: Native men	0.000			0.000			0.000		
Native women	0.527	(0.02)	***	0.123	(0.08)		0.114	(0.07)	
Men									
of EU12	0.351	(0.10)	***	0.227	(0.08)	***	0.012	(0.07)	
of other Europe	0.161	(0.09)	*	0.623	(0.22)	***	0.234	(0.17)	
of MENA countries	0.370	(0.10)	***	0.295	(0.12)	**	0.556	(0.14)	***
of sub-Saharan Africa	0.459	(0.14)	***	0.344	(0.21)	*	0.229	(0.10)	**
of Central-Eastern Asia	0.151	(0.10)		-1.223	(0.36)	***	0.071	(0.09)	
of Latin America	0.208	(0.14)		0.057	(0.09)		0.280	(0.14)	**
Women									
of EU12	0.767	(0.07)	***	0.405	(0.11)	***	0.309	(0.10)	***
of other Europe	1.002	(0.08)	***	0.801	(0.20)	***	0.537	(0.19)	***
of MENA countries	1.093	(0.15)	***	0.719	(0.15)	***	0.804	(0.18)	***
of Sub-Saharan Africa	0.498	(0.15)	***	0.702	(0.28)	**	0.169	(0.10)	*
of Central-Eastern Asia	1.038	(0.12)	***	0.310	(0.24)		0.541	(0.09)	***
of Latin America	0.738	(0.10)	***	0.253	(0.09)	***	0.204	(0.13)	
Constant term	-0.661	(0.03)	***	-0.162	(0.08)		-0.121	(0.08)	***

(Continued)

Table 4.6 Coefficients of the interaction variable between gender and area of birth by country of destination. Heckman two-step procedure: employment (selection model) and over-education (outcome model). Natives and migrants aged 20-64 (Continued)

Interaction variable between gender and area of birth	Italy			Spain			United Kingdom		
	Coef.	(S.E.)	p-value	Coef.	(S.E.)	p-value	Coef.	(S.E.)	p-value
	Selection model (employed vs otherwise)								
Reference: Native men	0.000			0.000			0.000		
Native women	−0.663	(0.02)	***	−0.180	(0.10)	*	−0.526	(0.10)	***
Men									
of EU12	0.699	(0.13)	***	−0.670	(0.10)	***	−0.902	(0.10)	***
of other Europe	0.412	(0.11)	***	−0.976	(0.22)	***	−0.702	(0.19)	***
of MENA countries	−0.030	(0.11)		−0.539	(0.13)	***	−1.444	(0.15)	***
of sub-Saharan Africa	0.022	(0.16)		−0.520	(0.22)	**	−0.766	(0.13)	***
of Central-Eastern Asia	0.602	(0.13)	***	0.697	(0.39)	*	−0.732	(0.11)	***
of Latin America	0.217	(0.16)		−0.098	(0.11)		−0.622	(0.17)	***
Women									
of EU12	−0.690	(0.07)	***	−0.703	(0.12)	***	−0.657	(0.13)	***
of other Europe	−0.759	(0.07)	***	−0.486	(0.19)	**	−1.653	(0.19)	***
of MENA countries	−1.097	(0.13)	***	−1.124	(0.15)	***	−1.914	(0.17)	***
of sub-Saharan Africa	−0.523	(0.15)	***	−1.216	(0.27)	***	−1.080	(0.12)	***
of Central-Eastern Asia	−0.620	(0.10)	***	−0.726	(0.23)	***	−1.631	(0.11)	***
of Latin America	−0.593	(0.09)	***	−0.393	(0.10)	***	−0.984	(0.15)	***
Constant term	0.911	(0.02)	***	0.921	(0.10)	***	1.089	(0.10)	***
/athrho	−2.708	(0.15)	***	−2.578	(0.12)	***	−2.024	(0.10)	***
rho	−0.991	(0.00)		−0.989	(0.00)		−0.966	(0.01)	

Note:
*p-value < .1; **p-value < .05; ***p-value < .01.
Control variables: Age groups at interview; Education; The presence of a cohabiting partner; The number of cohabiting children; Type of employment; Occupational sector; Holding a part time job.
Source: our data processing on dataset EU-LFS 2008.

The most striking result is observed in the selection model. Only migrant men in Italy have systematically (regardless of origin) positive employment coefficients in respect to natives. The same result is found for migrant women in Italy (in comparison with native women) coming from Asia, Central-South America and sub-Saharan states. In Spain and in the UK, the coefficients by area of birth are systematically lower than the native referent counterpart by gender (the only exception is the one for men from other parts of Asia in Spain). The specific socio-demographic and occupational characteristics of migrant groups explain, especially for Spain, the higher employment rates observed in the descriptive analyses.

Also in the UK, immigrants born in EU12 countries are no longer the group with the highest level of employment and the highest levels of over-education, regardless of gender, once age structure, educational level and occupational sector have been controlled for. In fact, MENA migrants (both men and women) assume the most disadvantaged positions in terms of employment level (selection model) and over-education (outcome model) in the UK. Women in the UK from Eastern Europe and Asia have the second worst values in both models.

Confining our attention to over-education, we observe that all groups regardless of gender and of destination country (the only exception is represented by Asian men in Spain) have higher levels of over-education than the reference group (native men). Moreover, migrant women assume the worst over-educated positions in all three countries of residence. The highest coefficient values are assumed in Italy by female migrant groups coming from MENA countries, Central and Eastern Asia and Eastern Europe. In Spain they are those coming from Africa and East European countries. In all the observed destination countries men have lower disparities of over-education.

Does a Southern European model of migration still exist? Generally speaking and according to the multi-dimensional results we can confirm that Italy and the UK have different patterns. In Italy migrant groups assume higher employment levels than natives while the opposite is observed in the UK. Moreover, the over-education of migrants is much more evident in Italy than in the UK and migrant women assume disadvantaged occupational positions more often in Italy than in the UK. Spain is instead much more affected by socio-demographic and occupational characteristics of migrant groups. Nevertheless, over-education and the positions of women in Spain are more similar to the ones observed in Italy than in the UK. Once more, we underline the occupational position of MENA migrants (especially women) that have, net of control variables, the worst conditions in the three destination countries.

Other predictors. Restricting the observed sub-sample to migrants, the other covariates included in our analyses give us the characteristics of migrants of the *ad hoc* module.[5] The models have been estimated separately by gender and destination country. They can provide useful information and comparisons of the effect of predictors on employment (selection models in Table 4.7) and on over-education (outcome models in Table 4.8). We confine our comments to the variables that can help us to define or deny the existence of a Southern European model of migration.

Table 4.7 Determinants of the employment (selection model) by gender and country of destination. Heckman two-step procedure. Migrants aged 20–64

Variables	Italy				Spain				United Kingdom			
	Men		Women		Men		Women		Men		Women	
	Coef.	p	Coef.	p	Coef.	p	Coef.	p	Coef.	p	Coef.	p
Area of birth (ref. EU12)												
Other Europe	-0.162		0.015		-0.684	***	0.397	*	-0.460	**	-0.781	**
MENA countries	-0.519	**	0.047		-0.582	***	-0.398	**	-1.111	***	-1.035	**
Sub-Saharan Africa	-0.411	*	0.164		-0.591	**	-0.422	**	-0.514	***	-0.286	**
Central-Eastern Asia	-0.004		0.499	***	–		-0.181		-0.498	***	-0.767	**
Latin America	-0.272		0.014		-0.203		0.249	**	-0.295		-0.250	
Age (ref. 30-39)												
20-29	-0.003		-0.176		-0.257	**	0.120		-0.268	**	-0.094	
40-49	-0.349	**	-0.079		-0.143		-0.036		-0.018		0.321	**
50-64	-0.613	***	-0.085		-0.515	***	-0.087		-0.501	***	-0.296	**
Highest level of education (ref. Low secondary school)												
High secondary school	0.134		0.164	*	0.043		0.057		0.100		0.323	**
Post secondary school	1.218	***	0.612	***	0.691	***	0.592	***	0.758	***	1.001	**
Cohabiting partner (ref. No)												
Yes	0.332	*	-0.612	***	0.079		-0.380	***	0.585	***	0.158	**
Number of cohabiting children (ref. None)												
One child	-0.198		-0.255	**	-0.241	**	-0.084		-0.105		-0.124	
Two children	-0.029		-0.393	***	-0.100		-0.153		-0.234	*	-0.356	**
Three or more	-0.364		-0.706	***	-0.397	**	-0.361	**	-0.374	***	-0.703	**

Adding variables with the ad-hoc module

Years since migration (ref. 4 yrs or less)											
5-9	0.534	***	0.431	***	0.044		0.160	*	0.251	**	0.122
10-19	0.489	**	0.523	***	0.045		0.603	***	0.130		0.098
20+	0.277		0.518	**	0.710	**	0.282		-0.053		0.027
Facilities for equating diploma (ref. No)											
Yes	-0.305		-0.115		-0.040		–		–		–
Diploma in the destin. country	-0.485	**	-0.380	*	-0.565	**	–		–		–
Need to improve language skills (ref. No)											
Yes	0.250		0.478	***	0.033		0.074		–		–
Reason for migration (ref. Employment)											
Family	-0.494	***	-0.274	**	-0.162		-0.451	***	-0.687	***	-0.960	**
Other	-0.516	**	-0.475	**	-0.105		-0.349	***	-0.897	***	-0.845	**
Constant term	1.145	***	0.927	***	1.592	***	0.701	***	1.324	***	0.851	**
/athrho	-2.115	*	-2.232	***	-2.247	**	-3.491	***	-1.817	***	-1.663	**
rho	-0.971	***	-0.977	***	-0.978	***	-0.998	***	-0.949	***	-0.931	**

Note:
*p-value < .1; **p-value < .05; ***p-value < .01.
Source: our data processing on dataset EU-LFS 2008.

Table 4.8 Determinants of the over-education (outcome model) by gender and country of destination. Heckman two-step procedure. Migrants aged 20–64

Variables	Italy				Spain				United Kingdom			
	Men		Women		Men		Women		Men		Women	
	Coef.	p	Coef.	p	Coef.	p	Coef.	p	Coef.	p	Coef.	p
Area of birth (ref. EU12)												
Other Europe	0.138		0.274	***	0.137		0.347		0.098		0.058	
MENA countries	0.582	***	0.174		0.111		0.302		0.385	**	0.387	*
Sub-Saharan Africa	0.556	***	0.222		0.166		0.268		0.057		0.233	*
Central-Eastern Asia	0.298	*	0.230		–		0.104		0.096		0.036	
Latin America	0.419	**	0.027		0.038		0.108		0.095		0.094	
Age (ref. 30-39)												
20-29	0.108		0.031		-0.442	***	-0.457	***	0.141		-0.050	
40-49	0.182		0.079		0.064		-0.157		-0.075		-0.149	
50-64	0.511	***	0.286		-0.277	*	-0.059		0.298	**	0.072	
Cohabiting partner (ref. No)												
Yes	-0.230	*	0.354	***	-0.090		0.262	***	-0.473	***	0.132	
Number of cohabiting children (ref. None)												
One child	0.117		0.086		-0.205	**	0.016		0.094		0.019	
Two children	0.142		0.087		-0.390	***	-0.204	**	0.186	*	0.127	
Three or more	0.173		0.248		-0.618	***	-0.378	**	0.336	**	0.536	**
Adding variables with the ad-hoc module:												
Years since migration (ref. 4 yrs or less)												
5-9	-0.176		-0.324	**	-0.096		0.112		-0.337	***	-0.166	
10-19	-0.173		-0.539	***	-0.374	**	0.019		-0.103		-0.135	
20+	-0.291		-0.793	***	-0.369		-0.111		-0.060		-0.073	
Facilities for equating diploma (ref. No)												
Yes	-0.189		-0.185		-0.174	*	-0.167	***	–		–	
Diploma in the destin. country	-0.043		-0.020		-0.431		-0.082		–		–	

Need to improve language skills (ref. No)

Yes	0.400 ***	0.406 ***	0.025	0.052	—	0.625 **

Reason for migration (ref. Employment)

Family	0.438 ***	0.063	0.007	0.123	0.529 ***	0.625 **
Other	0.210	0.061	0.087	0.107	0.557 ***	0.377 **

Adding variables about employment in the output model:

Part time job (ref. No)

Yes	0.290 *	0.081	0.144	0.043	0.200 **	0.193 **

Type of employment (ref. Employee)

Self-employed	-0.055	-0.026	-0.406 **	-0.352 **	-0.255 ***	-0.054

Occupational sector (ref. Transport., inform., public admin., education, health and social work activities)

Agriculture	0.455	0.586 ***	1.237 ***	1.054 ***	0.799 ***	0.172
Household services	1.201 ***	1.165 ***	1.296 ***	1.648 ***	0.076	0.176
Accom. and food ser. activities	-0.287	-0.264 ***	0.225	0.006	-0.001	0.305 **
Other tertiary services	0.059	0.495 ***	0.254	0.647 ***	0.364 ***	0.293 **
Mining and Quarrying	-0.327 **	-0.051	0.304 **	0.227 *	-0.067	0.029
Construction	-0.514 ***	-0.213 ***	0.203	0.128	-0.065	0.044
Constant term	-0.293 ***	-0.048 ***	-0.454 ***	-0.124 ***	-0.107 ***	-0.107 **
/athrho	-2.115 *	-2.232 ***	-2.247 **	-3.491 *	-1.817 ***	-1.663 **
rho	-0.971 ***	-0.977 ***	-0.978 ***	-0.998 ***	-0.949 ***	-0.931 **

Note:
*p-value < .1; **p-value < .05; *** p-value < .01.
Source: our data processing on dataset EU-LFS 2008.

In Table 4.7, not considering area of birth variables (widely described above), we observe in all destination countries a ∩-shape of the risk of being employed around the referent *age* group (30–39 years old). Interestingly the largest negative effect occurs among men rather than women. This result confirms the general model of mostly young migrant men working, above all, in manual unskilled sectors and of older migrant women employed in the tertiary sector.

Cohabitation with partner shows a different picture among destination countries. In Spain and in Italy it increases the risk of being employed among men, while it decreases the same risk among women. This is typical of the male bread-winner model and of the Southern European model of migration, generally. In the UK, both sexes assume a positive risk of being employed once they cohabit with their partner (dual earner model). The number of cohabiting children negatively affects the employment status of respondents, particularly women. In large families women are most likely to stop working.

Also looking at the over-education effect (outcome models in Table 4.8), *cohabitation with the partner* in the destination country assumes a typical gender role effect in all destination countries, though at different levels of significance: men have a lower risk of being over-educated once they cohabit with their partner, and the opposite is true for women. Such result confirms the 'traditional' migratory model where the breadwinner is more frequently male and occupies more advantaged occupational positions.

Another interesting variable, which helps us to define the existence of a Southern European model of migration, concerns the *occupational sector*. Results show different scenarios according to sex and destination country. Agriculture (especially in Spain) and household services (in particular in Italy and Spain) have, too, it might be noted, the highest risk of over-education. The structural demand of manual workers and care-giving services, which have been filled by immigrant men and women, tend to increase over-educated positions. In the UK, over-educated employment among immigrants does not involve particular household services, but rather the other tertiary occupational sectors. In particular, immigrant women enrolled in accommodation and food services assume the highest risk of being over-educated in the UK. Interestingly, in Italy the lowest risk of over-education is among migrant men in the mining, quarrying and construction sectors. This is not true of the other two countries.

Conclusion

In this chapter we asked whether it still makes sense to speak of a Southern European model of migration. To this end, we compared the major receivers of labour migrants in the EU, namely Italy, Spain and the UK. In particular, two aspects of labour insertion were considered: (a) the access to the labour market; and (b) job conditions. While the former is analysed in terms of employment outcomes, the latter is approached by looking at over-education dynamics.

Looking at the results of labour market access, Italy, Spain and the UK have very high employment rates. This is likely the result of formal and *de facto* admission policies, which have long preferred labour migrants over other categories. Migrants arrive in these countries to work. A first trait which seems to characterize the Southern European model of migration is that in Italy and Spain migrants have higher employment rates than their native counterparts. The weak welfare systems of these two countries make it difficult for unemployed migrants to remain in the country: immigrants must work or leave. The multivariate analysis confirms that there is a different pattern of work in Italy and the UK, while the Spanish case is more ambiguous. In Spain, migrant employment outcomes seem much more affected by socio-demographic and occupational characteristics.

In the labour market, clear patterns emerge. In Southern European countries, the over-education of migrants is much more evident than in the UK. More often, migrant women occupy disadvantaged positions. Again, the family welfare model which characterizes these two countries, as well as a rise in the level of education among migrants, seems largely to explain this pattern. The scarcity of welfare services and the parallel growing need for long-term care services for both the elderly and children has generated a structural demand for care-giving services which have been long filled by immigrant women. Here, high educational levels – and more generally specific skilled competencies – are not required. Working conditions are, also, notably difficult.

On this evidence, it still makes sense to talk and write about a Southern European model of migration. What are its characteristics? Extremely high employment outcomes – better than native outcomes – feature. But this is counterbalanced by very difficult labour market insertion in terms of over-education dynamics and by the dramatic condition of women migrants. Though admission policies prioritizing labour migration are effective in all three countries and guarantee migrants easy employment entry, the different nature of these policies makes for differences in labour market integration. In the UK, selective policies tend to diminish the risk of over-education. Lax and unselective Italian and Spanish policies make it, instead, hard for migrants – and especially for women migrants – to match their qualifications in a labour market, which is highly segmented along ethnic and gender line. In Italy and Spain migrants tend, then, still to occupy low-skilled jobs with little hope of career advancement.

Notes

1 Detailed estimates of net migration (by sex, age group and macro-region of birth) were not computed for Germany due to the lack of information on the born-abroad population, broken down according to the required characteristics in 2001. To this date only the number of born-abroad residents is available, a figure which, moreover, is only indicative: there have been doubts about its reliability. For the other three countries (Ireland, the Netherlands and Switzerland) it was necessary to use Eurostat data on population calculated at the beginning of 2012 due to the unavailability of data on the 2011 population census broken down by gender, age group and macro-region of birth. In all three cases, the total born-abroad population calculated at the beginning of 2012 was, however, consistent with that derived from the census counts.

2 Detailed results of the estimates are reported in Strozza (2015). They are also all available upon request.

3 The country of birth of respondents allows us to focus in on the migrant population, avoiding any consideration of the acquisition of citizenship in different countries. The parents' country of birth allows us to exclude from the analysis second generation migrants and those born abroad to native parents.
4 This takes the significant difference between the model without selection (ρ=0) and the estimated model.
5 We avoid two variables in the UK models because of excessive missing data. We do not consider Asian men in Spain because of their small sample and their large standard error (fewer than 20 cases).

References

Aleksynska, M. and Ahmed, T. 2013. 'Occupation–education mismatch of immigrant workers in Europe: context and policies'. *Economics of Education Review* 36: 229–44.
Altorjai, S. 2013. *Over-qualification of Immigrants in the UK*. Institute for Social & Economic Research, No. 2013–11.
Baldwin-Edwards, M. 2012. 'The Southern European "model of immigration": a sceptical view'. In M. Okólski, ed., *European Immigrations: Trends, Structures and Policy Implications*, 149–57. Amsterdam: Amsterdam University Press.
Baldwin-Edwards, M. and Arango, J., eds. 1999. *Immigrants and the Informal Economy in Southern Europe*. London: Routledge.
Bettio, F., Simonazzi, A. and Villa, P. 2006. 'Change in care and female migration: the "care drain" in the Mediterranean'. *Journal of European Social Policy* 16(3): 271–85.
Bonifazi, C. 2008. 'Evolution of regional patterns of international migration in Europe'. In C. Bonifazi, M. Okólski, J. Schoorl and P. Simon, eds, *International Migration in Europe: New Trends and New Methods of Analysis*, 107–28. Amsterdam: Amsterdam University Press.
Chiswick, B. R. and Miller, P. W. 2009. 'The international transferability of immigrants' human capital'. *Economics of Education Review* 28: 162–9.
Coale, A. J. 1985. 'An extension and simplification of a new synthesis of age structure and growth'. *Asian and Pacific Census Forum* 12(1).
Dell'Arringa, C. and Pagani, L. 2011. 'Labour market assimilation and over-education: the case of immigrant workers in Italy'. *Economia Politica* 28(2): 219–40.
Dumont, J.-C. and Lemaître, G. 2008. 'Counting foreign-born and expatriates in OECD countries: a new prospective'. In J. Raymer and F. Willekens, eds, *International Migration in Europe: Data, Models and Estimates*, 11–40. West Sussex: Wiley & Sons Ltd.
Faini, R., Strom, S., Venturini, A. and Villosio, C. 2009. *Are Foreign Migrants More Assimilated Than Native Ones?* IZA Discussion Paper No. 4639.
Fargues, P. 2011. 'International migration and the demographic transition: a two-way interaction'. *International Migration Review* 45(3): 588–614.
Fernández, C. and Ortega, C. 2008. 'Labor market assimilation of immigrants in Spain: employment at the expense of bad job-matches?' *Spanish Economic Review* 10(2): 83–107.
Green, C., Kler, P. and Leeves, G. 2007. 'Immigrant overeducation: evidence from recent arrivals to Australia', *Economics of Education Review* 26: 420–32.
Groot, W. and van den Brink, H. M. 2000. 'Overeducation in the labor market: a meta-analysis'. *Economics of Education Review* 19(2): 149–58.
Hardoy, I. and Schøne, P. 2014. 'Returns to pre-immigration education for non-western immigrants: why so low?' *Education Economics* 22(1): 48–72.

Heckman, J. J. 1976. 'Simultaneous equation model with continuous and discrete endogenous variables and structural shift'. In S. M. Goldfeld and R. E. Quandt, eds, *Studies in Non-linear Estimation*. Cambridge, MA: Ballinger.

Hill, K. 1987. 'New approaches to the estimation of migration flows from census and administrative data'. *International Migration Review* 21(4): 1279–303.

Istat. 2009. 'Gli stranieri nel mercato del lavoro', Rome: Istat.

Jennissen, R., Van Der Gaag, N. and Van Wissen, L. 2006. 'Searching for similar international trends across countries in Europe'. *Genus* 62(2): 37–64.

Jovanovic, B. 1979. 'Job matching and the theory of turnover'. *Journal of Political Economy* 87(5): 972–90.

Kalter, F. and Kogan, I. 2006. 'Ethnic inequalities at the transition from school to work in Belgium and Spain: discrimination or self-Exclusion?' *Research in Social Stratification and Mobility* 24(3): 259–74.

King, R. and DeBono, D. 2013. 'Irregular migration and the "Southern European Model" of Migration'. *Journal of Mediterranean Studies* 22(1): 1–31.

King, R. and Rybaczuk, K. 1993. 'Southern Europe and the international division of labour: from mass migration to mass immigration'. In R. King, ed., *The New Geography of European Migrations*, 175–206. London: Belhaven Press.

King, R., Fielding, A. and Black, R. 1997. 'The international migration turnaround in Southern Europe'. In R. King and R. Black, eds, *Southern Europe and the New Immigrations*, 1–25. Brighton: Sussex Academic Press.

Kogan, I. 2011. 'New immigrants – old disadvantage patterns? Labour market integration of recent immigrants into Germany'. *International Migration* 49(1): 91–116.

Peixoto, J., Arango, J., Bonifazi, C., Finotelli, C., Sabino, C., Strozza, C. and Triandafyllidou, A. 2012. 'Immigrants, markets and policies in Southern Europe: the making of an immigration model?' In M. Okólski, ed., *European Immigrations: Trends, Structures and Policy Implications*, 107–46. Amsterdam: Amsterdam University Press.

Portes, A. and Zhou, M. 1993. 'The new second generation: segmented assimilation and its variants'. *Annals of the American Academy of Political and Social Sciences*, 530: 74–96.

Preston, S. H. and Coale, A. J. 1982. 'Age structure, growth, attrition, and accession: a new synthesis'. *Population Index*, 48(2): 217–59.

Prokic-Breier, T. and McManus, P. 2014. 'Immigrant qualification mismatch 13 developed countries, apparent or real?' mimeo.

Quintini, G. 2011. *Over-qualified or Under-skilled: A Review of Existing Literature*, OECD Social, Employment and Migration Working Papers 121, OECD Publishing. www.oecd.org/els/workingpapers.

Reyneri, E. and Fullin, G. 2011. 'Labour market penalties of new immigrants in new and old receiving West European countries'. *International Migration* 49(1): 31–57.

Ribas-Mateos, N. 2004. 'How can we understand immigration in Southern Europe?' *Journal of Ethnic and Migration Studies* 30(6): 1045–63.

Rubb, S. 2006. 'Educational mismatches and earnings: extensions of occupational mobility theory and evidence of human capital depreciation'. *Education Economics* 14(2): 135–54.

Sicherman, N. 1991. '"Overeducation" in the labor market'. *Journal of Labor Economics* 9(2): 101–22.

Sicherman, N. and Galor, O. 1990. 'A theory of career mobility'. *Journal of Political Economy* 98(1): 169–92.

Sloane, P. J., Battu, H. and Seaman, P. T. 1999. 'Overeducation, undereducation and the British labour market'. *Applied Economics* 31(11): 1437–53.

Spence, M. 1973. 'Job market signaling'. *Quarterly Journal of Economics* 87(3): 355–74.

Strozza, S. 2010. 'International migration in Europe in the first decade of the 21st century'. *Rivista Italiana di Economia Demografia e Statistica* 64(3): 7–43.

Strozza, S. 2015. 'A re-examination of net migration in European countries in the period 2002–2011: estimates by gender, age and region of birth'. *Rivista Italiana di Economia Demografia e Statistica* 69(3–4).

Strozza, S., Paterno, A., Bernardi, L. and Gabrielli, G. 2009. 'Migrants in the Italian labour market: gender differences and regional disparities'. In H. Stalford, S. Currie and S. Velluti, eds, *Gender and Migration in 21st Century Europe*, 131–60. Farnham and Burlington: Ashgate.

Weiss, Y., Sauer, R. M. and Gotlibovski, M. 2003. 'Immigration, search, and loss of skill'. *Journal of Labor Economics* 21(3): 557–92.

Winship, C. and Mare, R. D. 1992. 'Models for sample selection bias'. *Annual Review of Sociology* 18: 327–50.

Zimmermann, K. F., ed. 2005. *European Migration. What Do We Know?* Oxford and New York: Oxford University Press.

Part 2

The unintended effect of the EU's external borders securitization

5 Illegal immigration beyond stereotypes

Processes of selection, tolerance, regularization of irregular immigrants

Maurizio Ambrosini

Illegal immigration is a typical area where the dominant representations differ from social phenomena. This chapter concerns two topics. The first one is the selective treatment of irregular immigration by receiving societies. The second, related one, is the easier transition to a legal status of a part of irregular migrants.

Starting from the Italian setting, I will begin discussing how some immigrants are labelled as illegal and thus stigmatized, while other immigrants, even if they live in the receiving society without the necessary authorization, are neither perceived nor treated as 'illegal'. I will then discuss the passage to a legal status, in particular through regularization processes. I will focus on actors that enable immigrants' survival and progression, and in particular on the intermediaries between the receiving societies and irregular immigrants.

Regarding it, I will examine in particular the role of civil society organizations and 'street level bureaucracies' (Lipsky 1980).

Formal authorization and social recognition

Despite official statements and declared policies, host societies in fact distinguish and classify various categories of irregular immigrants (Menjívar 2006; Sciortino 2011; Van der Leun and Ilies 2012): women attract less attention than men, unless they perform sex work in public spaces; irregular immigrants in work are less subject to control than unemployed ones; those who have somewhere to sleep are less targeted than the homeless; those who harass passers-by are more likely to be detained than those who try to remain unnoticed. In fact, there are many grey and blurred areas between illegal migration (to be repressed) and authorized migration.

Moreover, situations of uncertainty also arise in the legal system (Wihtol de Wenden 2010). They concern, for instance, irregular immigrants for whom employers have applied for regularization but have not yet received a reply; asylum seekers whose claims have been rejected but who have appealed and are awaiting the outcome; women who have escaped prostitution networks and have applied for state protection but still do not know if their application has been accepted.

On the other hand, immigrants develop forms of 'irregularity negotiation' with both the networks of compatriots and the receiving societies (McIlwaine 2014). They invent practices of survival (Bloch *et al.* 2014), seeking to develop some sort of 'moral economy of migrant illegality' (Chauvin and Garcés-Mascareñas 2012). If irregular immigrants are often too weak to develop true 'coping strategies' to overcome the hardships of their condition of non-citizens, they adopt a 'range of tactics' in their efforts to carve a life for themselves in receiving societies (Datta *et al.* 2007).

In Italy, they mostly try to find employers willing to regularize or sponsor them by representing and defending them towards the authorities (Ambrosini 2013a). Elsewhere, they accumulate evidence of good conduct, or documents evidencing their duration of residence and their social integration. Sometimes, especially where there are no other opportunities, they look for a marriage partner, either real or sham. Unauthorized immigrants may instead try to avoid identification and to satisfy their needs without being intercepted by government institutions (Engbersen and Broeders 2009): in this way, they gain time and increase their chances of subsequent legalization.

The outcome of distinctions and categorizations by receiving societies and their institutions, and efforts by irregular immigrants to be accepted or at least tolerated, is a landscape of different living conditions, access to work and services, exposure to detention and deportation, and opportunities to acquire a legal status.

Developing a suggestion by Saskia Sassen (2008), it is possible to identify two dimensions of the relationship among the receiving society, public institutions, and foreign or minority groups perceived as 'aliens'. The first is the *authorization* of entry and residence, which regards the formal aspects governed by institutional arrangements. The second refers to *recognition*, which concerns the broader phenomena of social acceptance, resistance, or rejection of people or groups considered as strangers. There are clearly links and mutual influences between these two dimensions: once a group has been strongly stigmatized by public opinion, the media are often willing to give voice to social prejudice, and some political actors will try to translate negative feelings into political arguments and, possibly, into norms. Also the institutions in charge of control of law and order are affected by these dynamics and strengthen the surveillance of, and restrictions on, the groups involved. Consider the prejudices that affect Roma and Sinti minorities, including those with Italian citizenship (Ambrosini and Tosi 2007, 2008). Conversely, the alarm raised by political leaders, as well as the strengthening of formal rules, have an influence on the media, which are ready to propagate their claims in public opinion. Consider, for example, the definition of 'illegal immigrants', or even 'clandestine', which was widely applied to migrants landing on the Italian coasts until the tragedies of October 2013.

However, there may be a considerable distance between authorization and recognition. The typical case is that of the thousands of immigrant women delivering crucial care in Italian families, which I have extensively discussed elsewhere (Ambrosini 2014). Many of them have gone through a period of irregularity, but in political discourse, as well in the media and public opinion, these figures (childminders, housekeepers, and mainly care workers with the elderly) are rarely described as 'illegal' (which, on the contrary, is the adjective often applied to males). Their illegal status is often discovered when an amnesty has allowed the transition of immigrants of this kind from illegal to authorized status.

Table 5.1 cross-references the two dimensions of authorization and recognition to identify four ideal-typical cases, which are considered separately below.

Exclusion

Where the lack of legal authorization is strengthened by the lack of social recognition, or even more so with a negative representation, a situation of marked hostility towards foreigners arises. This category includes those immigrants commonly referred to as 'clandestine' and perceived as threats to security and public order, and now also as an undue burden on the welfare system. They are especially subject to the overlap between immigration and crime expressed by the concept of 'crimmigration' (Coutin 2011). Expulsion is therefore the measure demanded by society and promised by politicians, even though the actual implementation is more complicated and expensive. Social exclusion is its internal projection in social relations. An emblematic example concerns the volunteer groups along the border between the US and Mexico. Actively involved in border surveillance, they report unauthorized crossings to the police, in a sort of competition with the associations which, on the contrary, work to support them (Eastman 2012).

Stigmatization

This category includes the minority groups with formal authorization of residence – and sometimes even with citizenship rights – but that are substantially rejected by the majority. In several countries this is the case of refugees and asylum seekers, despite the ambiguities noted by Ellerman (2006): when asylum seekers are considered in abstract terms, social closure and prejudice are very strong; on the other hand, when people experience actual relations with real persons with faces and names, established in the local community, and perhaps

Table 5.1 Authorization and recognition of immigrants in receiving society

	Formal authorization	
	–	+
– social recognition	*Exclusion* ('illegal migrants', threatening invaders)	*Stigmatization* (asylum seekers, socially undesirable minorities)
+	*Tolerance* (irregular 'deserving' workers)	*Integration* (socially accepted regular immigrants)

accompanied by children who attend local schools, groups of citizens often rise to their defence.

Also in Italy there is a growing intolerance of refugees fuelled by certain political parties and rhetorically justified by the economic crisis. But the most striking and paradoxical gap between formal approval and social recognition concerns the Roma and Sinti minorities: even when they are nationals of a European Union country, and even when they have Italian citizenship, they are usually perceived as alien and dangerous.

Tolerance

This is the opposite case, where the absence of formal authorization is offset, and even substituted, by widespread social recognition. A clear example is provided by the already mentioned immigrant women employed in the domestic care sector (Boccagni and Ambrosini 2012; Catanzaro and Colombo 2009). While this phenomenon is widespread in Southern Europe, which has created a sort of 'invisible' (or parallel) welfare system (Ambrosini and Cominelli 2005; Tognetti Bordogna 2010), it also regards countries with more public services and more rigorous policies, where it assumes other forms and features: the improper use of au pairs in UK and elsewhere (Anderson 2011), the on-call cleaners employed in Sweden (Gavanas 2010[1]), the childminders employed without formal contracts that have got some public figures in the United States into trouble, and the 'tourists', mainly from Eastern European countries, in Germany where they take turns to clean houses or care for the elderly (Lutz and Palenga-Möllenbeck 2010). The most interesting aspect of this dynamic is the fact that, especially in Italy, these immigrants are free to move with (Italian) elderly and children in public spaces, from parks to supermarkets, without having to fear checks on their legal status.

More generally, the category of 'deserving' irregular migrants (Chauvin and Garcés-Mascareñas 2014) impacts on social experience, especially when they legitimize their presence with their work in the service of the majority, avoiding forms of social conflict or rebellion. For instance, in the south of Italy and in other agricultural regions the use of immigrant irregular labour is considered a normal practice tolerated and in some way institutionalized by various local authorities, which often, for example, provide shelters and toilets for immigrant agricultural workers.[2]

This does not mean that 'tolerated' immigrants have no problems. In my research I have identified two main issues: the first is what De Genova (2002) has called 'deportability', i.e. the 'Sword of Damocles' of possible interception and deportation. The second is the suffering of these immigrants due to their being 'prisoners' in the receiving country, deprived of the opportunity to return home to visit their families for fear of revealing their situation and seeing their re-entry blocked (Ambrosini 2013a).

Moreover, the tolerance related to work cannot be easily transferred outside the work sphere. If immigrants without appropriate documents do not live with their employers, as in the case of family care-workers, they are perceived as a problem when they leave the workplace and become visible in urban areas. Hence, tolerance and deservingness can be contingent and spatialized.

Especially when irregular immigrants work for other immigrants, another version of tolerance can appear: protest against their exploitation and consequent victimization. Immigrants deserve protection because they are subject to serious violations of human rights. I will return to this aspect later.

Integration

When formal authorization is combined with sufficient social recognition, the foundations for the inclusion of migrants in the receiving society are laid. But this is neither a linear nor an obvious process: the integration practised by the receiving society is a 'subordinate integration'. It is based on a tacit agreement that immigrants will adapt to occupations rejected by national workers without claiming social advancement or social rights (Ambrosini 2011; Calavita 2005). In times of prolonged economic crisis, when the economic basis of the integration becomes weaker, formal authorization may be lost and social acceptance can become more uncertain: indicative of this is the desire expressed by many immigrants to return to their home countries.

Transition processes

The typology described above may appear static, as if immigrants classified in a particular category are bound to remain in it. From a constructivist point of view, the issue of illegal immigration is instead a dynamic concept (Van Meeteren 2010). The market, the public institutions and local societies tend to incorporate segments of the unauthorized immigrant population in the gradual normalization of their situations in different ways, both in fact and in law. Indeed, few irregular immigrants are actually deported compared with the total volume of the phenomenon (Chauvin and Garcés-Mascareñas 2014): not even in the United States, where deportations have exceeded 300,000 units per year. This is an effort that hardly offsets the amount of new unauthorized sojourners and is unable to abate the huge phenomenon of irregular migration, estimated at over 11 million people. The Immigration Reform proposed by President Obama (November 2014) is a clear admission of the need to find other ways to deal with the problem. Europe is far below these numbers, but also below an equally large commitment of resources. The most conservative estimate of the 'Clandestino' Project is that there are around 1.9 million undocumented residents in the European Union (Vogel *et al.* 2011), but the places available in the detention centres that should be used to identify and remove them are around 32,000: a rate of 1.68 per cent.

In the Italian case, the government has fewer than 2,000 places in the Centres for Identification and Expulsion (hereafter, CIE) that are crucial for the identification and repatriation of unwanted migrants: to be exact, data for 2013 report 13 facilities with a total capacity of about 1,901 people; some of these facilities, however, are currently unusable or undergoing restructuring due to fire, damage or management problems. It should also be noted that the CIEs cost at least 55 million euros per year. Today, as a result of the spending review of 2011, the daily expenditure per capita has diminished to 30 euros plus VAT. This has worsened the living conditions of the inmates; but at the same time it has confirmed that the lack of financial means is a serious constraint on more rigorous repression. Above all, the CIEs are far from achieving the objectives for which they were established: out of 169,071 people detained in the centres between 1998 and 2012, those repatriated amounted to only 78,045, i.e. 46.2 per cent of the total (www.lunaria.org). Moreover, this is a very small fraction of all irregular immigrants (estimated at 400,000–500,000), while in same period more than a million were regularized (Ambrosini 2013a).

The transition to legal status is a crucial juncture in their 'careers' (Glytsos 2005), so far: 'the dichotomous distinction between regular and irregular is not only blurred but shifts through processes referred to as "status mobility" which is influenced by both state policies and the behavior of migrants over time and space' (McIlwaine 2014: 3).

We now explore its dynamics. Legalization occurs in three main ways. The first concerns access to the status of legal resident through amnesties or other regularization procedures. This occurs in several countries, such as France, through demonstration of socio-cultural integration into the country following long residence or a stable relationship with a legal resident or an active economic role. In Italy, as elsewhere, the emphasis is on work and the intermediation of an employer as factors justifying eligibility in repeated amnesties.

The second way to acquire legal status is legalization due to particular biographical conditions, usually evaluated at entry: for example, this is the case of unaccompanied minors, or the children of irregular immigrants. A similar measure of humanitarian admission applies to pregnant women and sick people. Here human rights, in democratic regimes, bend the principle of national sovereignty and force governments not only to tolerate unwanted immigrants but also to take charge of subjects recognized as deserving protection by granting them appropriate hospitality, education, and health care. In regard to the humanitarian acceptance of sick people, Fassin (2005) has spoken of 'biolegitimacy', i.e. access to rights by virtue of the suffering body. According to Fassin, in France today it is easier to be accepted as sick than as a refugee. Asylum gives way to compassion: biology has become more important than biography. The sick body unable to work, which in the past was subject to refoulement, has now become a resource. Despite the pessimism, this argument confirms that biographical conditions trigger the protection of human rights, and they open the way to acceptance, even if it is sluggish and reluctant.

Quite similar is the more controversial case of regularization by marriage (e.g. Engbersen 2001; Van Meeteren 2010): here, liberal principles, such as the freedom of marriage and the right of spouses to live together in the same country, supersede any condition of irregularity. However, the suspicion that fraudulent use is made of marriage has prompted restrictions, more controls, and long delays before rights can be exercised. Precisely because human rights can open windows of opportunity, many governments try to close them in advance.

The third form of legalization is the recognition of dangerous situations or a serious violation of fundamental human rights (Anderson 2008). This applies to migrants able to demonstrate that they crossed the national border not by choice, but because they were compelled to do so by external circumstances. This is the case of 'forced migrants' compelled to flee their country, or deceived or coerced by traffickers and exploiters. It is also the case of women who have escaped from prostitution, or workers in conditions close to slavery. This differs from the previous case because here legalization is not an almost automatic result of objective biographical conditions (minority age, pregnancy, illness, marriage). On the contrary, this third way to legalization occurs after a complex procedure in which migrants must prove they are in danger, or that they had no other option.

On the basis of these forms of legalization, we can now identify three basic devices with which to achieve regularity, or at least temporary tolerance.

The first is deservingness (Chauvin and Garcés-Mascareñas 2014). The irregular migrants can prove that they deserve a residence permit because they have a permanent job or because they are culturally embedded. The formal exclusion can be overcome by demonstrating a *de facto* inclusion: this is a crucial point, which shows how rules can be subverted and redefined by individual initiative. At the same time, the acknowledgement of deservingness (implicitly or explicitly) involves the distinction, sometimes the opposition, between unauthorized and undeserving immigrants (Nicholls 2013). It is also subject to conditions that are not always within the reach of the subjects concerned, can discriminate among the fates of immigrants in similar situations, or may give rise to forms of blackmail and circumvention. In Italy an immigrant must find not only a stable job but also an employer willing to carry out the regularization procedure. Hence, the costs are often borne by the worker, or the formal and the real employer do not always correspond. There are immigrants who have jobs but are unable to acquire a legal status; others who do not have stable jobs but manage to regularize their position. Finally, others have been regularized in situations different from those in which they should be entitled: for instance, construction workers regularized as domestic workers.

The second device is 'liberal legalization'. In this case, the applicant appeals not to subjective merits but to the humanitarian principles of the host country, on the basis of an objective state of fragility. The political intent to close borders may clash with fundamental ethical values often enshrined in constitutions and international conventions. Governments seek to resolve this contradiction by restricting the forms and times of acceptance, or, in the case of unaccompanied minors, by stating that 'for their own good' they must be returned to the family home, if they can find it. Highly controversial, and in some ways dramatic, is the case of children who have entered the United States illegally: until they reach majority age, they are admitted into the school system and acquire a commitment to education and civic values; however, once they turn 18 they become irregular immigrants and must learn to survive on the margins of the system. They pass from protection to lack of protection, from inclusion to exclusion, from a condition of *de facto* legality to a condition of illegality (Gonzales 2011).

The third device is connected to the previous one, but it can be better described as victimization. In this case, in order to access humanitarian protection, migrants must prove that they are victims of processes that have uprooted them, forced them to migrate, or involved them, against their will, in situations that offend human rights. In other words, in order to be believed, immigrants must behave like victims, recounting stories able to arouse compassion. They must prove their victimhood to the authorities. As noted by Anderson (2008), irregular migrants are considered to be either villains or victims: not to fall into the former category, they must be able to enter the latter. In democratic countries, the counterweight to restrictions on voluntary human mobility is a certain openness to forced mobility. However, since the authorities suspect that migrants use it as a strategy to circumvent access restrictions, the focus moves to assessment of the validity and credibility of each case (Kneebone *et al.* 2014).

Table 5.2 summarizes the transition processes considered, adding a further element: the spaces for initiative by migrants within the mesh of entry control policies. If migrants intend to claim deservingness, they must demonstrate that they have found a stable job, or that they have established social and affective relations. When they appeal to liberal principles, they must overcome the difficulties of travel and access to receiving countries that, in this case, often represent the most severe obstacles. When they come before the authorities in the receiving country, they must demonstrate that they fulfil the requirements for protection. These requirements, however, are 'objective' and verifiable: minor age, illness, pregnancy, and to a lesser extent marriage.

In the case of victimization, access to protection instead requires a more complicated and challenging process. Not only must migrants be able to reach a country in which to apply for asylum, they must also pass the filters ascertaining the validity of their claims. They must convincingly demonstrate that they are the victims of forced mobility (Jubany 2011).

Table 5.2 Transition towards legal status

Legalization forms	Admission devices	Possibilities for initiative by immigrants
Regularization procedures, amnesties	Deservingness	Demonstrate integration into the labour market or social relationships
Assessment of particular biographical conditions	Liberal protection	Demonstrate possession of the right requirements
Recognition of a condition of danger or abuse	Victimization	Demonstrate real victimhood

Intermediaries of tolerance and legalization

The management of irregular migration and regularization processes depends largely on the action of a number of intermediaries, often well established and publicly recognized. Thanks to these intermediaries, the opaque and hidden world of irregular migration is intertwined with society's formal institutions (Engbersen and Broeders 2009). Table 5.3 presents the main categories. Described in what follows are the functions performed and the forms of action taken.

First, some of the entries by new immigrants (but only a minority in Europe: see Düvell 2006; Triandafyllidou and Maroukis 2012) are favoured by a particular class of intermediaries, namely smugglers. Growing restrictions in immigration policies have fostered the development of what has been called the 'migration business' or 'migration industry' (Salt and Stein 1997; Koser 2010). Fabrication of fake documents, provision of invitations, corruption of public officials, organization of trips and border crossings by sea or by land, are some of the services provided by smugglers. Research on this topic has shown that smugglers can have very different organizational profiles, ranging from single smugglers operating in proximity of borders, through networks of co-ethnics, to more complex criminal organizations (Heckmann 2004). Much public discourse mixes up smuggling with trafficking and presents smugglers as dangerous criminals, even when they carry asylum seekers to safe countries. The reality is more complex and diverse: most 'clients' of smugglers want to cross borders and they voluntarily purchase the smugglers' services (Koser 2010), and only a part of the smuggling is connected with other illegal activities and managed by organized crime. Smuggling can evolve into the trafficking and exploitation of immigrants, or it

Table 5.3 Types of intermediaries and functions performed

Types of intermediaries	Functions performed	Beneficiaries
Smugglers	Organizing unauthorized entrance into receiving societies through various strategies	Aspiring immigrants without other entry channels
Co-ethnic brokers	Matching labour demand and supply; patronage and guarantees to employers	Fellow job-seekers and native employers
Employers	Provision of employment opportunities; access to regularization procedures	Immigrant workers
NGOs	Provision of services, often compensating for the closure of public institutions	Migrants with special needs for a structured supply (language, health care, food, paperwork)
Ordinary (native) citizens	Provision of immediate aid, with low organizational complexity	Especially immigrants in need and personally known
Civil servants	Benevolent interpretation of the rules, information and guidance, abstention from controls	Immigrants judged deserving, not dangerous or annoying

can put the lives of clients at risk, also in consequence of the growing criminalization of this activity. But in other cases it is a kind of provision of services not available in the formal market of border crossing (Sanches 2014 for Arizona; Van Liempt 2007 for the Netherlands). Moreover, smuggling can be seen as a by-product of mobility regimes with their social and political stratification of mobility rights (Faist 2013).

A second major category of intermediaries consists of co-ethnic brokers (see Bashi 2007; Faist 2014): those that connect employers with job-seeking immigrants but without the necessary documents. Their function is crucial and delicate, because those migrants who cannot enter the formal labour market and perhaps do not know the language of the host country depend more on co-nationals able to help them find a job (Bloch *et al.* 2014). At the same time, such intermediation takes place on the margins of the law. Nonetheless, brokers are vital for the functioning of the informal labour market, and they are actively sought by employers in need of labour. From agriculture to construction, from domestic and care services to restaurants, supply and demand are matched by the brokers of 'black labor': 'doubly black', one might say, in terms of legal status and contractual position. Moreover, intermediation is not furnished for free. For those who engage in it, labour brokerage entails moral rewards in terms of reputation and prestige, but often economic rewards as well (Vianello 2013).

Third, I have already mentioned the role of employers, who in Italy and elsewhere in effect perform the role of *gatekeepers*: they can decide whether an immigrant without a residence permit deserves first to work and to remain in the host country, and then to acquire legal status. In this regard, I would emphasize various aspects. The large participation of employers in amnesties confounds stereotypes of the relationship between the economies of the receiving countries and irregular immigrant workers. It is true that markets (and families) need flexible, cheap and compliant labour (Düvell 2006; Van der Leun and Ilies 2012). Hence, they derive profit from illegal immigration. Less convincing is the idea of a hidden and astute political project, as well as an undeclared agreement between governments and economic actors, to let foreign workers without permits, and hence rights, into the country in order to exploit them. In this way, such large participation by employers in amnesties cannot be explained. Why should employers give up exploiting undocumented workers, after they have been trained, if they have pursued a clear strategy of taking advantage from their legal status? In fact, expediency, the fear of workplace accidents, complaints or inspections, as well as the interpersonal relationships established – especially in households and small enterprises – matter.

A fourth type of intermediary consists of individuals engaged in voluntary and solidarity activities. I refer to the more formal and organized activities carried out by NGOs and other civil society actors (see, for the USA, Hagan 2008; Eastman 2012; for Italy, Ambrosini 2013b). These activities are related to the provision of services of a certain complexity, ranging from medical care to hot meals, from language courses to support with regularization procedures. Their support is necessary for immigrants who cannot access public services. I will discuss this topic in the next section.

It is also interesting to consider another type of aid, more informal and spontaneous, which can be related to a fifth class of intermediaries. Involved in this case are neighbours, passers-by and ordinary citizens: the very people who often appear politically receptive to xenophobic campaigns. Here the difference between 'abstract immigration', shadowy and menacing, and real people with names, faces and evident needs, becomes crucial. Many citizens demanding more drastic measures against immigration are not insensitive to the insistence of a flower-seller, are willing to help an acquaintance access regularization, and to send email messages to their contacts to help a woman who has lost her job to find another one. Irregular immigrants try to make themselves invisible to the institutions, but they are often integrated into the neighbourhood where they live and into a network of social relations (McIlwaine 2014). By contrast, it is precisely the lack of, or expulsion from, a supporting network, co-ethnic but also native, that make them vulnerable, marginalized, possibly deportable.

A sixth class of intermediaries consists of civil servants, not necessarily social service workers, who interpret the rules in different ways, help to process the paperwork, give information, and refer applicants to the services of NGOs if they cannot by law provide certain kinds of support; or they simply 'turn a blind eye' when they are confronted by an irregular immigrant. These are the so-called 'street level bureaucrats', discussed below.

NGOs and irregular immigration

Restrictions in immigration policies increase the role of civil society actors: the distance between official policies and social reality is managed through the intervention of NGOs and other non-public actors (religious institutions, trade unions, social movements).

Although the public authorities in some countries have sought to restrict the action of NGOs in favour of irregular immigrants (see for example Van der Leun and Bouter 2015), in several other countries benign tolerance or some forms of cooperation between local authorities and NGOs allow access to certain services also to migrants with irregular or uncertain status (basic healthcare, shelters, language courses, etc.). Hence the enforcement of basic human rights is often secured by non-public actors.

According to critics, however, service-oriented NGOs can also be viewed as functional to the system. Good intentions notwithstanding, they enable politicians to continue to use a rhetoric of closure without having to face accusations of inhumanity. From this standpoint, NGOs can be depicted as co-opted in 'hegemonic neoliberalism, despite their façade of opposition' (Castañeda 2007: 20). Their activities may even create consensus on exclusionary policies by preventing highly visible human rights infringements that might backfire (Castañeda 2007: 20).

Civil society's services evidently soften many aspects of restrictive formal immigration policies, but one can ask whether irregular immigrants would be better off without the support of NGOs when they have to deal with practical issues such as basic healthcare because they are excluded from public services. Moreover, in the Italian case as in others, NGOs have acted to support regularizations and consequently full access to formal institutions. Their action as providers of alternative services is particularly salient in the twilight zone between the informal insertion of immigrants in paid employment and official recognition of them as sojourners.

Beyond this general consideration, I shall identify the main forms of support provided by NGOs and other civil society actors in favour of irregular immigrants. The first type of activity occurs in the area of *regularization of legal status* and involves two levels of action. At the political level, trade unions, religious institutions, voluntary associations demand amnesties for irregular immigrants. In Italy, also thanks to the influence of these organizations, seven major amnesties were granted between 1987 and 2012, besides other undeclared or minor interventions. Another form of support in this area is bureaucratic assistance, case by case, in accessing regularization, provided mainly by trade unions and some national associations.

A second type of activity is the *provision of services*. In Italy this mainly concerns language courses (irregular immigrants are excluded from public schools), basic health services (irregular immigrants are entitled to receive only urgent and necessary care in hospitals), soup kitchens for people devoid of resources, and in some towns a limited availability of shelters. Volunteer work, private donations, support from other social institutions (in Italy, mainly run by the Catholic Church and trade unions) are key aspects of the everyday activity of non-public providers. Overall, these services grant basic protection to many immigrants in the intermediate period between entrance and acquisition of legal status.

The third type of activity is the *legal advocacy* provided by some associations of lawyers for free, often in connection with other civil society actors. Also in the case of irregular immigrants, these associations have won important victories, like the judicial ruling on the admission of children of unauthorized sojourners to nursery schools in the city of Milan.

Last but not least, I would also mention the *political and cultural activity of opposition* against the criminalization of irregular immigrants, protests against local policies of exclusion or against restrictions in healthcare, the defence of asylum seekers, the promotion of views alternative to dominant representations of the issue. By adopting a frame of the victimization of irregular immigrants, or emphasizing the link between poverty and emigration, civil society actors often play a role in the cultural struggle on immigration, in some way countervailing the political exploitation of anxieties in receiving societies. Moral choices and political militancy, humanitarian values and religious convictions fuel active forms of citizenship and social commitment in this field.

Apply or interpret the rules: the spaces of discretion available to street level bureaucracies

A crucial linkage between the social recognition of irregular immigrants and public institutions – on which many aspects of social life depend – is constituted by civil servants. As said, their intermediation takes place at different levels. I now provide details by drawing primarily on research on the subject by Campomori (2007, 2008), Chauvin and Garcés-Mascareñas (2012), Van der Leun (2006), and Zincone (1999).

First to be distinguished is resistance to the application of restrictive rules considered to conflict with professional ethics. This dynamic regards operators belonging to professional groups with greater autonomy, awareness, and internalized and consolidated professional ethics. As noted by Van der Leun (2006), when the Dutch government introduced more stringent criteria for access to welfare services, doctors and teachers resisted more strongly than mere employees.

A second case concerns the abstention from controls potentially threatening for immigrants without documents authorizing residence or work, or the use of selective and targeted controls. In this case, the police are mainly involved. The reluctance to check the documents of immigrants depends on several factors. One of them is the perception that numerous irregular immigrants are non-threatening, and perhaps deserving, such as the already mentioned women working in care activities. In this respect, social recognition also affects the work of public institutions and their staff, influencing the effective application of rules. Another reason is the perception by many services and their operators, including those responsible for the maintenance of public order, that their mission and their priorities are different: devoting time and energy to checking the documents of foreigners means taking time away from more socially and professionally rewarding activities, or at least more closely related to their institutional tasks (Vogel 2000). Also important is the simple knowledge that there are insufficient resources to identify and deport unauthorized immigrants. Therefore the final outcome is the focus on more labelled immigrants, on those who disturb or react badly, on the contexts in which residents, the media and politicians call for more controls.

A third function is referral to private social services accessible to irregular immigrants: employees who know that they cannot provide a benefit or service to immigrants (for example, enrolment on an Italian language course) because they do not have a valid residence permit, can just send them away, or direct them to an association that offers Italian free classes. At local level, informal networks between public services and civil society organizations (Ambrosini 2006) thrive, with mutual referrals of cases, helped by the fact that volunteers are not infrequently civil servants who dedicate free time to volunteering, or retired civil servants, or in the example of Italian courses, teachers or former teachers.

A fourth interesting feature is that of providing advice and practical help in understanding procedures and correctly compiling the forms necessary to access services. Once again, the operator can send away an immigrant unable to fill out a form without giving adequate information, can receive the form but delete it if it is incomplete or contains errors, or can help the applicant compile it correctly. This feature probably concerns legal immigrants, who have access to many social services, more than irregular immigrants. However, in regard to the latter it has to do with a decisive procedure: the acceptance and assessment of applications for regularization. Given the myriad grey and doubtful situations, or also the fact that some services are available even for irregular immigrants (emergency medical care and education for children, legal aid), the magnitude of the phenomenon expands.

Civil servants also have a certain power to interpret the rules and procedures when it comes to applying them to specific cases. Here the possibility of extensive and generous interpretations arises in dealing with the complex situations, obvious needs, and sometimes dramatic human cases that immigrants present. Street-level bureaucrats can then 'honestly cheat' the legislator, whose rules they should apply (Zincone 1999) by giving access to certain benefits and services also to irregular immigrants not entitled to them. For instance, municipal offices may give residency rights to foreigners even if they live in precarious shelters that do not fulfil habitability standards: in this way the immigrants can obtain connections to electricity, gas and water supplies. Or, they may admit also undocumented immigrants to night shelters. In healthcare, treatment may be considered 'necessary and urgent' even if it is not (Pasini 2011) in order to treat the care needs of unauthorized immigrants. Or they may 'turn a blind eye' if an employer asks for a medical prescription for herself when it is instead intended for a care-worker not entitled to it because she does not have a residence permit. The active intermediation of employers and Italian acquaintances is a crucial factor explaining the willingness of civil servants to accept exceptions, replacements of people, and the bending of the rules.

The final feature is the corruption of public officials, a device sometimes used to obtain illicit support by immigrants often willing to do anything to regularize their position. A large amount of discretion on the one hand, and political weakness on the other, as well as the need for and maybe even the customariness of such practices, represent fertile ground for frauds and abuses.

Conclusion: the actual governance of irregular migration

In this chapter I have shown how the fight against illegal immigration proclaimed by governments is counteracted by diverse interests and social representations of the phenomenon that tend to redefine it selectively. In practice, despite the supposed universality of the rules, their effective implementation is rigid with some individuals and rather lax with others. The rhetoric of closure, undoubtedly exacerbated in recent years, is contradicted by the silent tolerance of various forms of irregular migration. On the other hand, the allegation of 'crimmigration' (Coutin 2011), or the increasing criminalization of immigration, should be made more nuanced and differentiated: it matters more in declared than in actual policies; more in legislation that in everyday governance; more for certain categories of migrants, and in some circumstances, less for others and in different circumstances.

Second, immigration defined by the rules as 'illegal' should be understood in dynamic terms, not as an indelible stigma. The history of irregular immigration in democratic countries since this definition emerged at the political level has largely been a story of 'survival in the shadows' and then emergence and gradual legalization (Sciortino 2011). It is a story of suffering and injustice, but also of tenacious resistance and hard-won victories. In recent years, both survival and emergence have become more difficult and complicated, but they are not impossible. The walls of nation-states have breaches and open passages through them; the means necessary to remove all those who violate the rules far exceed the resources available. In Europe, only some of the transgressors are caught up by the interception system and are effectively punished, detained and eventually deported.

I have then identified some devices that allow transition to legal status, or at least to tolerance. Hence, the exclusion of irregular immigrants is not absolute and without appeal; marginalization and the deprivation of rights are severe but not insurmountable difficulties. In the effective management of irregular migration, of tolerance practices and emersion processes, a diversified and often unsuspected set of intermediaries comes into play. Indeed, irregular immigrants could not be accommodated and could not settle in the host country without receiving some forms of support from insiders.

Again, the idea that the host society rejects illegal immigration is dominated by fear of it, and seeks to repel it with all possible means, must be calibrated. Hostility in principle, especially in politics, is a matter different from the management of specific cases. State institutions are not solely hostile forces; in certain circumstances they show little interest in the actual enforcement of strict controls, exercise some kind of tolerance, and sometimes create opportunities to settle in the host country (Chauvin and Garcés-Mascareñas 2012). Several civil society actors, in turn, act to protect, support and if possible legalize irregular immigrants. Employers portrayed as the wicked exploiters of immigrants vulnerable because of their irregular status in Italy, Southern Europe and elsewhere are often households with elderly members requiring care, and they are sooner or later willing to respond to their employees' demands for regularization. And when they are businesspeople, in many cases they are willing to apply for an amnesty. In their turn, neighbours, the parents of classmates, and local authorities may sympathize with immigrants threatened with expulsion (Ellermann 2006).

Overall, if the phenomenon is analysed from a bottom-up point of view, the governance of irregular immigration appears to be rather different from what is stated in the rules and proclaimed at political rallies.

Notes

1 With some irony, the author entitled her study *Who Cleans the Welfare State?* to castigate Swedish society's self-perception as being free from irregular immigration and irregular employment.
2 In 2011, in all the southern Italian regions the Italian government discovered 361 migrant workers without residence permits (the report of the Ministry speaks hastily of 'clandestine foreign workers': Ministero del Lavoro 2012: 30): thus, either there are no irregular immigrants working in Southern Italy, or public institutions are not bothering to track down and punish employers.

References

Ambrosini, M., ed. 2006. *Costruttori di integrazione. Gli operatori dei servizi per gli immigrati*. Osservatorio regionale per l'immigrazione e la multietnicità, Milano: Regione Lombardia-Fondazione Ismu.

Ambrosini, M. 2011. *Sociologia delle migrazioni*. Bologna: Il Mulino.

Ambrosini, M. 2013a. *Irregular Migration and Invisible Welfare*. Basingstoke: Palgrave Macmillan.

Ambrosini, M. 2013b. 'Fighting discrimination and exclusion: civil society and immigration policies in Italy'. *Migration Letters*, 10(3): 313–23.

Ambrosini, M. 2014. 'Irregular but tolerated: unauthorized immigration, elderly care recipients, and invisible welfare'. *Migration Studies*. First published online 11 October, doi:10.1093/migration/mnu042.

Ambrosini, M. and Cominelli, C., eds. 2005. *Un'assistenza senza confini. Welfare 'leggero', famiglie in affanno, aiutanti domiciliari immigrate*. Osservatorio regionale per l'integrazione e la multietnicità, Milano: Regione Lombardia-Fondazione Ismu.

Ambrosini, M. and Tosi, A., eds. 2007. *Vivere ai margini. Un'indagine sugli insediamenti rom e sinti in Lombardia*. Osservatorio regionale per l'integrazione e la multietnicità, Milano: ISMU-Regione Lombardia.

Ambrosini, M. and Tosi, A., eds. 2008. *Favelas di Lombardia. La seconda indagine sugli insediamenti rom e sinti*. Osservatorio regionale per l'integrazione e la multi etnicità, Milano: ISMU-Regione Lombardia.

Anderson, B. 2008. *'Illegal Immigrant': Victim or Villain?* COMPAS, Working Paper No. 64, University of Oxford (WP-08-64).

Anderson, B. 2011. 'Us and them, or one of the family? Migrant domestic workers in private households'. Paper presented at the conference *Making Connections: Migration, Gender and Care Labour in Transnational Context*, University of Oxford, Oxford, 14/15 April.

Bashi, V. F. 2007. *Survival of the Knitted: Immigrant Social Networks in a Stratified World*. Stanford: Stanford University Press.

Bloch, A., Sigona, N. and Zetter, R. 2014. *Sans papiers*. London: Pluto Press.

Boccagni, P. and Ambrosini, M. 2012. *Cercando il benessere nelle migrazioni. L'esperienza delle assistenti familiari straniere in Trentino*. Milano: FrancoAngeli.

Calavita, K. 2005. *Immigrants at the Margins: Law, Race and Exclusion in Southern Europe*. Cambridge: Cambridge University Press.

Campomori, F. 2007. 'Il ruolo di policy making svolto dagli operatori dei servizi per gli immigrati'. *Mondi migranti* 1(3): 83–106.

Campomori, F. 2008. *Immigrazione e cittadinanza locale. La governance dell'integrazione in Italia*. Roma: Carocci.

Castañeda, H. 2007. 'Paradoxes of providing aid: NGOs, medicine, and undocumented migration in Berlin, Germany'. PhD dissertation, University of Arizona Graduate College.

Catanzaro, R. and Colombo, A., eds. 2009. *Badanti & Co. Il lavoro domestico straniero in Italia*. Bologna: Il Mulino.

Chauvin, S. and Garcés-Mascareñas, B. 2012. 'Beyond informal citizenship: the new moral economy of migrant illegality.' *International Political Sociology* 6(3): 241–59.

Chauvin, S. and Garcés-Mascareñas, B. 2014. 'Becoming less illegal: deservingness frames and undocumented migrant incorporation'. *Sociology Compass* 8(4): 422–32.

Coutin, S. B. 2011. 'The rights of noncitizens in the United States'. *Annual Review of Law and Social Science* 7: 289–308.

Datta, K., McIlwaine, C., Evans, Y., Herbert, J., May, J. and Wills, J. 2007. 'From coping strategies to tactics: London's low-pay economy and migrant labour'. *British Journal of Industrial Relations* 45(2): 404–32.

De Genova, N. 2002. 'Migrant illegality and deportability in everyday life'. *Annual Review of Anthropology* 31: 419–47.

Düvell, F. 2006. *Illegal Immigration in Europe: Beyond Control?* Basingstoke: Palgrave Macmillan.

Eastman, C. L. S. 2012. *Shaping the Immigration Debate: Contending Civil Societies on the US-Mexico Border*. Boulder, CO: FirstForum Press.

Ellermann, A. 2006. 'Street-level democracy: how immigration bureaucrats manage public opposition'. *West European Politics* 29(2): 293–309.

Engbersen, G. 2001. 'The unanticipated consequences of panopticon Europe: residence strategies of illegal immigrants'. In V. Guiraudon and C. Joppke, eds, *Controlling a New Migration World*, 222–46. London: Routledge,

Engbersen, G. and Broeders, D. 2009. 'The state versus the alien: immigration control and strategies of irregular immigrants'. *West European Politics* 32(5): 867–85.

Faist, T. 2013. 'The mobility turn: a new paradigm for the social sciences?' *Ethnic and Racial Studies* 36 (11): 1637–46.

Faist, T. 2014. 'Brokerage in cross-border mobility: social mechanisms and the (re) production of social inequalities'. *Social Inclusion* 2(4): 38–52.

Fassin, D. 2005. 'Compassion and repression: the moral economy of immigration policies in France'. *Cultural Anthropology* 20(3): 362–87.

Gavanas, A. 2010. *Who Cleans the Welfare State? Migration, Informalization, Social Exclusion and Domestic Services in Stockholm*. Research Report 2010/3. Stockholm: Institute for Future Studies.

Glytsos, N. P. 2005. 'Stepping from illegality to legality and advancing towards integration: the case of immigrants in Greece'. *International Migration Review* 39(4): 819–40.

Gonzales, R. G. 2011. 'Learning to be illegal: undocumented youth and shifting legal contexts in the transition to adulthood'. *American Sociological Review* 76(4): 602–19.

Hagan, J. M. 2008. *Migration Miracle: Faith, Hope and Meaning on the Undocumented Journey*. Cambridge, MA: Harvard University Press.

Heckford, F. 2004. 'Illegal migration: what can we know and what can we explain? The case of Germany'. *International Migration Review* 38(3): 1103–25.

Jubany, O. 2011. 'Constructing truths in a culture of disbelief: understanding asylum from within'. *International Sociology* 26: 74–94.

Kneebone, S., Stevens, D. and Baldassar, L., eds. 2014. *Conflicting Identities: Refugee Protection and the Role of Law*. London: Routledge.

Koser, K. 2010. 'Dimensions and dynamics of irregular migration'. *Population, Space and Place* 16: 181–93.

Lipsky, M. 1980. *Street-Level Bureaucracy: Dilemmas of the Individual in Public Services*. New York: Russell Sage.

Lutz, H. and Palenga-Möllenbeck, E. 2010. 'Care work migration in Germany: semi-compliance and complicity'. *Social Policy & Society* 9(3): 419–30.

McIlwaine, C. 2014. 'Legal Latins: creating webs and practices of immigration status among Latin American migrants in London'. *Journal of Ethnic and Migration Studies*, doi: 10.1080/1369183X.2014.931803 (accessed 7 July 2014).

Menjívar, C. 2006. 'Liminal legality: Salvadoran and Guatemalan immigrants' lives in the United States'. *American Journal of Sociology* 111(4): 999–1037.

Ministero del lavoro e delle politiche sociali. 2012. *Secondo Rapporto annuale sul mercato del lavoro degli immigrati*, Roma. www.lavoro.gov.it.

Nicholls, W. J. 2013. 'Fragmenting citizenship: dynamics of cooperation and conflict in France's immigrant rights movement'. *Ethnic and Racial Studies* 36(4): 611–31.

Pasini, N., ed. 2011. *Confini irregolari. Cittadinanza sanitaria in prospettiva comparata e multilivello*. Milano: FrancoAngeli-Fondazione Ismu.

Salt, J. and Stein, J. 1997. 'Migration as a business: the case of trafficking'. *International Migration* 35(4): 467–91.

Sanches, G. 2014. *Human Smuggling and Border Crossing*. London: Routledge.

Sassen, S. 2008. 'Nuove politiche di appartenenza'. *Mondi migranti* 2(3): 7–29.

Sciortino, G. 2011. 'Regolarizzazioni: introduzione'. *Mondi migranti* 5(1): 27–36.

Sciortino, G. 2012. 'The regulation of undocumented migration'. In M. Martiniello and J. Rath, eds, *An Introduction to International Migration Studies: European Perspectives*, 349–75. Amsterdam: Amsterdam University Press.

Tognetti Bordogna, M. 2010. 'Le badanti e la rete delle risorse di cura'. *Autonomie locali e servizi sociali* 25(1): 61–77.

Triandafyllidou, A., ed. 2010. *Irregular Migration in Europe: Myths and Realities*. Farnham: Ashgate.

Triandafyllidou, A. and Maroukis, T. 2012. *Migrant Smuggling: Irregular Migration from Asia and Africa to Europe*. Basingstoke: Palgrave Macmillan.

Van der Leun, J. 2006. 'Excluding illegal migrants in The Netherlands: between national policies and local implementation'. *West European Politics* 29(2): 310–26.

Van der Leun, J. and Ilies, M. 2012. 'Undocumented migration: an explanatory framework'. In M. Martiniello and J. Rath, eds, *An Introduction to International Migration Studies: European Perspectives*, 303–24. Amsterdam: Amsterdam University Press.

Van der Leun, J. and Bouter, H. 2015. 'Gimme shelter: inclusion and exclusion of irregular immigrants in Dutch civil society'. *Journal of Immigrant and Refugee Studies* 13(2): 135–55.

Van Liempt, I. 2007. *Navigating Borders: Inside Perspectives on the Process of Human Smuggling into the Netherlands*. Amsterdam: Amsterdam University Press.

Van Meeteren, M. 2010. *Life Without Papers: Aspirations, incorporation and transnational activities of irregular migrants in the Low Countries*. Rotterdam: Erasmus Universiteit.

Vianello, F. A. 2013. 'A transnational double presence: circular migration between Ukraine and Italy'. In A. Triandafyllidou, ed., *Circular Migration between Europe and its Neighbourhood: Choice or Necessity?*, 187–211. Oxford: Oxford University Press.

Vogel, D. 2000. 'Migration control in Germany and the United States'. *International Migration Review* 34(2): 390–422.

Vogel, D., Kovacheva, V. and Prescott, H. 2011. 'The size of the irregular migrant population in the European Union – counting the uncountable?' *International Migration* 49(5): 78–96.

Wihtol de Wenden, C. 2010. *La question migratoire au XXIe siècle. Migrants, réfugiés et relations internationales*. Paris: Presses de la Fondation Nationale des Sciences Politiques.

Zincone, G. 1999. 'Illegality, enlightenment and ambiguity: a hot Italian recipe'. In M. Baldwin-Edwards and J. Arango, eds, *Immigrants and the Informal Economy in Southern Europe*, 43–82. London: Frank Cass.

6 The securitization of the EU external borders and the rise of human smuggling along the Eastern Mediterranean route

The case of Afghan unaccompanied minors

Enza Roberta Petrillo

Introduction

This chapter investigates the relation between the strengthening of the EU's external border control initiated since the 1990s, and the increase in migrant smuggling along the Eastern Mediterranean route (EMR). Starting from the fact that two decades of growing investment into border controls by the EU has not stopped migration, but rather has increased the vulnerability of migrants and their reliance on smuggling, this research raises a number of questions about the functions and the implications of the EU's borders control and presents a series of prospective political, geopolitical and humanitarian criticalities regarding the paradigmatic case of unaccompanied Afghan minors (UAMs) smuggled along the EMR.

The research will advance these arguments in the following order. First, following a wide-ranging analysis of the EU's border controls deployed along the EMR, it describes the latest developments from the route and the unintended effects of border control, such as the smuggling of human beings, the violations of human rights related to the externalization of migration control, and the displacement of smuggling routes. Following, it scrutinizes the case of the smuggled UAMs, by critically examining the main push factors behind the UAMs' mobility, the major issues they experience along their smuggled path and the human rights violations faced in the transit countries before they manage to enter the EU. The chapter concludes by providing conclusions regarding priority areas in the field of migration management where further policy action is needed to overcome the identified gaps.

The methodology for this study comprises a theory-based analysis of academic literature and secondary materials, including EU reports and statistics along with reports by international organizations and NGOs. Additionally, insights and extra information were collected through a number of semi-structured interviews with key informants working with international organizations and NGOs, as well as informal conversations with young smuggled Afghans meeting in Italy. Notes from the semi-structured interviews and from the informal talks were transcribed during and after each conversation, and all data material was analysed qualitatively.

Irregular migratory trends along the Eastern Mediterranean route

Providing an overview of the developments in the field of irregular migration and human smuggling along the EMR is challenging, as it is extremely difficult find reliable quantitative and qualitative information on the extent, patterns, routes and modus operandi of irregular migration along the EMR. When this data was collected, classification and methodology differed from one country to another, and even among services within a single country, thus jeopardizing many potential comparisons. Against this background, this and the following sections rely substantially on data supplied by Frontex, as well as government agencies, international organizations and NGOs. As the various agencies collect slightly different data and use a range of classifications to track rates of human smuggling, journalistic accounts and previous case studies were used as an additional source of qualitative data in order to add knowledge about smuggled victims and smugglers' modus operandi.

In 2014, the Eastern Mediterranean route was the second largest area for detection of irregular border-crossing in the European Union: almost twice as much as in 2013 (Frontex 2014). In the general context of smuggling routes into Europe mapped out by Frontex, the most common path taken by irregular migrants moves from Central Asia and sub-Saharan countries, transits through Iran and Turkey[1] and enters the EU through eastern Greece, southern Bulgaria or Cyprus. According to the Greek authorities,[2] in 2014 alone, more than 14,000 people, more than 90 per cent of them from Syria, have tried to reach Greece by sailing from the Aegean islands.

The first quantitative information released by Frontex on the irregular migratory flows along the EMR at the EU's external borders (Greece, Bulgaria, Cyprus) refers to 2008–09, when the number of apprehensions surpassed more than 40,000 per year. This accounted for approximately 40 per cent of all irregular migrants, consisting primarily of Afghans, Iraqi Kurds, Pakistanis and, more recently, Syrians, detected at the external borders of the European Union. Usually migrants moved on to Athens, and from there spread to urban and rural centres in search of jobs, or to the harbours of Patras and Igoumenitsa to embark towards Italy. These kinds of trans-border movements increased in summer 2010, when detections of irregular migration across the land border between Greece and Turkey saw a sudden surge of smuggled migrants, mostly from Afghanistan and Iraq.

Due to a variety of factors, from the increased surveillance at sea by Greek coastguards supported by Frontex, through to the completion of the demining operations on the Greek side of the land border, together with the lowering of the smuggling prices at that entry point, made it convenient for migrants to cross on foot from Turkey along the River Evros at the north-east corner of Greece.

Numbers peaked further in October 2010 when approximately 300 people crossed the border near Orestiada each day. The shift of arrivals was accompanied by a significant influx in arrivals that once more caught the Greek state unprepared. A large group of irregular migrants detected on the borders were arrested and detained with little screening or access to asylum. 2010 marks the turning point in Greece's migration management policy, as the country accounted for 90 per cent of all arrests of irregular migrants entering the EU (FRA 2011: 12). In this year, the sea border was steadily being abandoned for the land border: fewer than 5 per cent of all apprehensions for the year took place at Greek–Turkish sea borders, compared to nearly 21 per cent in 2008.[3] As the overall apprehensions that year peaked at 55,700 (Frontex 2011a) on 24 October 2010, Greece submitted an official request for further assistance followed by the six-month deployment of the EU joint Rapid Border Intervention Teams.

However, after an initial drop in the migratory pressure, numbers climbed again in 2011 with a total of 57,000 illegal border crossings along the Turkish frontier. In 2012, sustained by the EU, Greece tightened border controls through Operation Aspida, involving the transfer of 1,800 border guards along the Greek–Turkish land border, and the construction of a border fence across the 12.5km land stretch used as the main entry point in the region of Evros. At the national level, Greece launched a range of 'securitized' internal measures, increased passport controls and provided technological upgrades to the harbours of Patras and Igoumenitsa to target migrants seeking to leave for Italy by ferryboat. In parallel, Operation Xenios Zeus, an internal policy of apprehension and detention based on daily police patrols, was launched. The strengthening of border surveillance through the combination of Operation Aspida and inland measures led to a reduction from a peak of 57,025 detections in 2011 down to 37,214 in 2012 and 24,799 in 2013 (Frontex 2013: 22).

Since 2012, the tightening of controls along the land border with Turkey through Operation Aspida caused a gradual shifting of the route to less patrolled areas. These include the Aegean Sea borders and the Turkish–Bulgarian land border, and where border agencies accounted an increase of migrants attempting to cross directly from Turkey.

According to the Greek police,[4] the number of migrants apprehended crossing the land border dropped from 15,877 in the first five months of 2012 to 336 in the same period in 2013; conversely, apprehensions on the Greek islands or in the Aegean rose from 169 in 2012 to 3,265 in 2013 (see Figures 6.1 and 6.2).

As noted by Amnesty International, 'this shift is claiming lives. Since August 2012, 101 individuals – mostly Syrians and Afghans, among them children and pregnant women – have lost their lives in at least six known incidents in this stretch of water' (2013: 7).

Additionally, the curbing in land detections was accompanied by systematic violations of human rights and the progressive criminalization of irregular migrants, reinforced through an extensive detention policy in overcrowded detention centres for those overstaying their visas or apprehended on the external borders. The Fundamental Rights Agency (FRA 2011: 18–19) also reported that

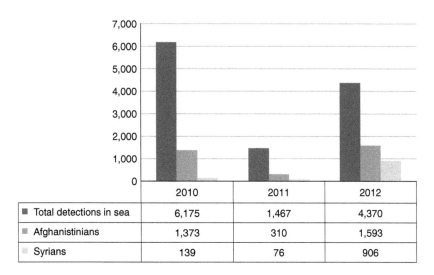

	2010	2011	2012
■ Total detections in sea	6,175	1,467	4,370
■ Afghanistinians	1,373	310	1,593
Syrians	139	76	906

Figure 6.1 Top nationalities detected along the Eastern Mediterranean route (sea)

Source: Elaboration on Frontex data

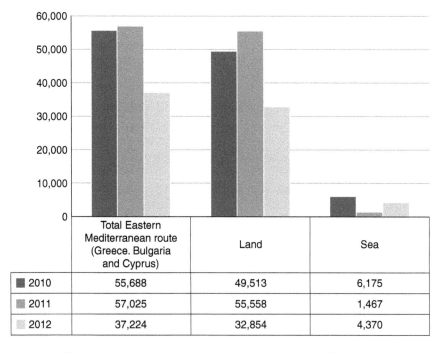

	Total Eastern Mediterranean route (Greece. Bulgaria and Cyprus)	Land	Sea
■ 2010	55,688	49,513	6,175
■ 2011	57,025	55,558	1,467
2012	37,224	32,854	4,370

Figure 6.2 Total detections along the Eastern Mediterranean Route (land and sea)

Source: Elaboration on Frontex data

informal push-backs to Turkey took place at the land border as well as along the Evros river. This situation was worsened by the fact 'that Frontex's border guards were also assigned the task of "screeners" responsible for conducting interviews with migrants documenting their identity and channelling them to the migration or asylum procedure' (Triandafyllidou and Dimitriadi 2013: 612).

Following the enforcement of migration control along the Greek–Turkish border, also the number of people crossing the Bulgarian border irregularly rose from 2,332 in September 2013 to 3,626 in October 2013 (Frontex 2013). To stop the flows, the Bulgarian Council of Ministers adopted a 'containment plan',[5] designed to reduce 'the number of illegal immigrants entering and residing illegally in Bulgarian territory and the number of persons seeking protection in the territory of Bulgaria'.[6] This initiative was flanked by the construction of a 30km 'barrier wall along the most sensitive sections of the 274-kilometer State border'[7] with Turkey. Human Rights Watch (HRW 2014) claims in a recent report on Bulgaria that, according to interviews with several refugees, Bulgarian police officers prevented people from crossing the border by pushing them back by force into Turkish territory without giving the migrants the opportunity to ask for asylum.

Inside the unintended effects of border control: an analysis of the Afghan minors smuggled along the EMR

To date, the real magnitude of the number of UAMs arriving in the EU is difficult to establish. The cases annually reported by the EU member states mainly concern UAMs claiming asylum. Additionally, as in many EU countries border control officers deliver the UAMs' identification to other national authorities, it is not known how many of the migrants identified are in reality UAMs.[8]

Figure 6.3 The Eastern Mediterranean route

Furthermore, in different transiting countries, inland detection of undocumented UAMs is made by the police, who do not necessarily inform border control authorities of these cases.

Aspects relating to the transnational mobility of UAMs remain understudied by scholars, who have mainly investigated the final stage of their migration paths in EU host countries (Valtolina 2014; Campani *et al.* 2002).

Against this paucity of information, the next section analyses the experiences of UAMs through their irregular transnational mobility towards Europe, looking in depth at the smuggling practices and the related counter-smuggling policies displaced in the transit hubs along the Eastern Mediterranean route, such Pakistan, Iran and Turkey; in the peripheral EU member states like Greece, Bulgaria and Italy; and in the Balkans states along the EMR sub-route.

'Exit or violence': the push factors behind the flow of Afghan UAMs

Since the mid-2000s, Afghanistan has been the main country of origin for the UAMs transiting along the EMR and arriving in different EU countries. Eurostat[9] reports that in 2014 there were 5,790 Afghan UAMs in the EU countries out of a total of 22,855 minors. This trend has grown over the past two years, mainly due to the withdrawal of NATO security forces in 2014 (Gall 2013). In general, the need to seek humanitarian protection and the desire for better life conditions and economic opportunities have combined to shape the root causes of UAMs' irregular mobility from Afghanistan to Europe.

The Human Development Report of 2013 (UNDP 2014) put the Afghanistan Human Development Index at 0.468, positioning it at 169 out of 187 countries.[10] Additionally, a report on the human rights dimension of poverty in Afghanistan (United Nations Secretary General 2010) noted that poverty affects more than two-thirds of the Afghan population. It also refers to the way in which widespread insecurity, whether associated with local disputes resulting in violence or military operations associated with the insurgency, have profound impact on the lives of Afghans (Tober 2007; Rodan and Lange 2008). This exacerbates feelings of insecurity and nourishes a permissive environment for the abuse of power, to the detriment of the most vulnerable. Migration is among the few coping mechanisms that exist in Afghanistan to face this socio-economic and institutional weakness that, as argued by Monsutti, is part of the Afghan social and cultural landscape (2007: 167).

The number of Afghans currently living outside their country is a matter of some debate. According to the National Risk and Vulnerability Assessment (NRVA) 2011–12 published by the Afghan Central Statistics Organization, 'Emigration is dominated by young adult men, most of whom move to Iran (76 percent), with smaller numbers going to Pakistan (13 percent) and the Gulf states (8 percent) alongside other countries' (2014: xvii). However, this characterization does not shed light on the composite push factors that nourish these migratory flows, nor does it indicate whether immigration to Iran and Pakistan represents the end of the migratory route or if they are a transit point along the general route toward the EU.

The current Afghan population who face serious poverty daily is very young. According to the NRVA 2011–12 report, the adolescent population (aged 15–24) consists of 19 per cent, equal to 5,106,000 people out of a total population of 26,955,000 (Central Statistics Organization 2012: 10). An additional 48.4 per cent (13,048 million) are under 15 years of age, whereas elderly people aged 65 and over represent only 2.5 per cent of the total population. Afghanistan's very young society produces a situation in which a relatively small number of persons in the economically most productive age group of 15–64 have to provide for a very large number of people in the dependent ages below 15.

As an additional push factor for migration, Lee-Koo observes:

> any person under the age of 18 who has been raised in Afghanistan has been raised amid conflict. Those on the cusp of adulthood were born during the second stage of the Afghan civil war (1992–1996), and have lived through the Taliban regime (1996–2001) and the current ongoing war (2001–). Moreover, these children were raised by a generation of people who lived through the Soviet invasion of Afghanistan and the subsequent conflict (1979–1989). (2013: 475)

Additionally, the difficulty in accessing education represents an additional push factor for youth in Afghanistan. For most Afghan children, the reasons for non-attendance mainly revolve around their responsibilities to paid work (AIHRC 2008: 15). The Watch List on Children and Armed Conflict (2010: 39) recounted that in November 2009, 80 per cent of children worked, while 38 per cent of Afghan children were engaged in hard labour. For those capable of attending school on top of work, fatigue and lack of concentration contribute to their learning difficulties. Poverty itself is a factor contributing to children's non-attendance at school, with children and families unable to pay for school supplies (AIHRC 2008: 15). Insecurity and distance to schools are primary reasons for non-attendance in rural areas. No more than two in five rural households live within 2 kilometres of a primary school. Overall net primary school attendance in rural areas is 54 per cent, while in urban areas it is 78 per cent. Looking at this landscape, Matsumoto observes that:

> from January 2006 to December 2008, there were 1,153 attacks on educational establishments in Afghanistan. Furthermore, from 2006 to 2007 alone, some 230 educational-related personnel (students, teachers, etc.) died as a result of attacks on schools, according to Ministry of Education statistics. (2011: 567)

By examining this very critical context, Matsumoto argues that young Afghans 'are increasingly turning to alternative strategies that increasingly define Afghanistan's "transition": exit or violence' (2011: 567).

The current critical atmosphere in Afghanistan is one where security deteriorates day by day (Tamang 2009); promises of post-conflict developments but have not materialized in any substantive way for the majority of Afghans. This has a devastating impact, especially upon the lives of children and youth.

> As in all migratory movements, the decision for an Afghan child to leave for Europe has two elements: a context and a trigger. The general context in Afghanistan is well known: widespread poverty, economic hardship, political instability, physical insecurity, poor educational prospects and rapidly declining hope for a brighter future. (UNHCR 2010: 14)

Additionally, a significant factor contributing to the irregular mobility of UAMs is the fact that Afghanistan does not have sufficient institutional capacities and legal tools or mechanisms to fight irregular migration. Most of the efforts to raise knowledge about the risk of relying on smugglers to enter the EU are made at the donor level, which support awareness campaigns on the risks related to the phenomenon of irregular migration. In addition, Afghanistan currently does not have a domestic legislation that specifically addresses the smuggling of migrants. In this regard, there also appears to be confusion in terminology, as the same term in Dari, one of the official languages in Afghanistan, is used to refer to irregular migration, human trafficking and migrant smuggling. Additionally, government officials, law enforcement officers and other stakeholders in Afghanistan generally have a limited understanding of these crimes due to this linguistic confusion (US Department of State 2013: 66).

According to a recent UNICEF report (2010), when deciding to send their child to Europe, families often hire a broker to engage a smuggler, who then holds a so-called 'handshake agreement' with them. However, the destination country is not always defined before leaving Afghanistan, and may change along the journey due to different factors, often linked to the border policing deployed by enforcement authorities along the route. The costs of the smugglers' services are usually described as high and, in reported cases, smugglers have demanded a great deal of financial indebtedness from UAMs' families. This places them at high risk of becoming victims of labour exploitation in order to pay off their debt.

The transiting corridors: Pakistan, Iran and Turkey

There is a marked contrast between the quantity of literature available on the migratory patterns and the routes followed by Afghan UAMs in Western Europe and that concerning Eastern Europe and Central Asia, two regions predominantly used as migration corridors. This lack of analysis requires careful integration that takes into account the varied experiences of smuggled migrants along the different frontiers that they cross. To date, little attention has been paid to the stops experienced by UAMs at each of the border crossed, while the majority of the literature focuses on the typology of smuggling organizations and border management issues. In particular, the first stages of a UAM's long journey through Europe are particularly under-researched.

Due to geographical, social and cultural proximity, Pakistan and Iran are the main target destinations for Afghan migration in terms of cross-border migrants, refugees and asylum seekers, as well as seasonal migration (ICMPD 2013: 26). Pakistan is a key transit country for Afghans. Historically, Afghans represent the largest group of foreigners in Pakistan, as they have been immigrating since the late 1970s and 1980s due to armed conflict and political instability. According to UNODC, as of 1 July 2013, Pakistan has a total of 2.7 million irregular migrants who originated from Afghanistan (UNODC 2013b: 20). However, Pakistan's economic and political circumstances limit its appeal as a destination country for Afghans, who use Pakistan as a transit country to reach the Gulf States, Europe and Australia. However, currently there are no statistics on how many other foreign nationals use Pakistan as a transit country for onward migration.

Currently a large majority of them (76 per cent according to the last Afghan NRVA) depart for Iran. This is due to Pakistan's recent policy shift that restricts Afghan citizens from entering and residing in the country (Central Statistics Organization 2012: 19):

> Pakistan terminated access to education and destroyed the camps. Those who already held refugee status were invited, in 2007, to receive a new registration card that would allow them three-year stay at the end of which they would return to Afghanistan. In parallel, new arrivals were perceived and treated as irregular. It simultaneously proceeded to close the border with Afghanistan, increase controls and deportations of irregular Afghans. (Dimitriadi 2013: 28)

In mid-2009, a daily average of 40,000 persons transited official crossing points into Pakistan in either direction with minimal, if any, formal processing. In addition, it is estimated that over 4,000 Afghans cross daily into Iran (ICMPD 2013: 18). These cross-border movements have historically involved a mix of motivations, including opportunities for employment and small-scale trade, either licit or illicit. According to various sources, the flow is so historically funded that the current Afghan–Pakistani border is perceived as an artificial crossing dividing two major tribes that live along the border region on both sides (Adelkhah and Olszewska 2007). This mindset helps to explain the reluctance of the population to accept the official state line.

According to Koser, 'nobody is willing to even "guestimate" how many Afghans have been smuggled out of Pakistan in the last 20 years' (2008: 8). It is estimated that nearly a million Afghan migrants live in Pakistan without any legal documentation, 400,000 of whom in Peshawar alone. Afghan irregular migrants generally work as unskilled manual labourers in low-paid sectors, such as in construction, brick-making, stone-cutting and the agriculture sector. In this context, the border crossings of Chaman (Pak–Afghan border), Taftan (Pak–Iran border) and Mand (Pak–Iran border) represented the most used crossing points by UAMs who start their irregular path through the EMR. The Wikipedia article on

Taftan, Pakistan's only official border crossing into Iran, claims that it is 'famed by locals as the *"road to London"* because it is a famous smuggling route'.

Information available online[11] reveals a heavy trend of smuggling of Afghan and Pakistani nationals across Pak–Afghan/Pak–Iran border and into European countries. However, heretofore no official assessment has ever been carried out by Pakistan or by Iran on these border crossing points with regard to the irregular flows of migrants, including UAMs. What is known is mainly reported by the smuggled people transited there. Monsutti (2007: 173) reports that the border crossing at Taftan, used to enter irregularly into Iran 'was the trickiest moment for migrants, and it was here that they turned to the services of professional smugglers'.

Reports indicate that those who can afford to pay large amounts, some ranging up to $20,000, try to get smuggled from Taftan to western countries in Europe, among other destinations. Meanwhile, those who can afford to pay only a few hundred dollars try to get smuggled from Pakistan to Iran.[12]

Whereas in the past Pakistan was the most important destination for Afghan migrants, now the large majority of emigrants (76 per cent) leave for Iran (Central Statistics Organization 2014; Courau 2003). Causes of this shift likely include Pakistan's recent policy implementation that restricts Afghan citizens entering and residing in the country. However, also in Iran, the situation for undocumented minors is also fraught with difficulties and dangers, as resulted by the informal interviews with smuggled Afghans collected in Italy. While Iran has been a long-standing destination of preference for male Afghan migrant workers, since 2007, over a million undocumented Afghans have been deported from Iran to their country of origin (Abbasi-Shavazi and Glazebrook 2006), a development that has stark implications for the way that refugees in Iran, both registered and unregistered, perceive their future.[13]

In an effort to 'push' Afghans towards return, Iran has developed restrictive policies, significantly changing the reception and settlement framework and harshening the registration methods of refugees.

> The refugee population now had to pay for each renewal card in conjunction with a range of taxation services and goods. Thirty districts became inaccessible for Afghans, forcing those already living in them to become internally displaced. Access to employment became even more difficult, while the regularisation of irregular migrants in 2011 was set up in such a way as to record an 'invisible' until then population but also facilitate future deportation proceedings. (Dimitriadi 2013: 27)

For many of the young Afghans in Italy who had lived in Iran prior to departure for Europe, the triggers for departure were related to these general difficulties. Some young children, almost exclusively males, decided to leave after being deported to Afghanistan as irregular workers, concluding that since opportunities for finding work were even poorer there, their only choice was to head for Europe.

Often UAMs coming from the western provinces of Heart, Farah and Nimruz in Afghanistan reach Iran directly after crossing several deserts and marshlands on their own, only paying for smuggling facilitation to cross the international border with Iran. Once there, migrants generally travel in buses or vans from Bandar-e-Abbas to Tehran, where they join nationals from Pakistan and Afghanistan arriving from the east. From Tehran, different groups of facilitators offer options with prices arranged accordingly: those who continue without documents can be transported to Urmia, the capital of West Azerbaijan province which borders Turkey, or travel to the city of Orumiye, a major hub on the Iranian–Turkish border. They can travel openly towards the city of Van with counterfeit Iranian travel documents, at least to Turkey, because Iranian nationals do not need a visa to enter Turkey. An assessment dedicated to the flows of UAMs transiting towards Europe, reported:

> Afghans and Iranians also travel in small groups from 5 to 10, accompanied by adults. They might stay a certain period of time in Iran to earn some money to pay the facilitation networks (if not, they mostly pay for the smuggling by carrying goods (such as oil, drugs, cigarettes, arms, etc.) over the Turkish border in Van). From Tehran the migrants were transported to Urmia, the capital of West Azerbaijan Province which borders Turkey. From there they crossed the Iranian-Turkish border in large groups of up to 1,000 migrants heading towards the Turkish city of Van. In Van migrants were given false Turkish documents and used public transport to Istanbul. From Istanbul facilitators transported them to the River Evros or alternative routes to cross into Greece. When crossing the River Evros migrants tended to travel at night in small groups and used small-size inflatable boats propelled by oars. (Frontex 2010: 18)

According to UNODC (2013b), it is in Van that facilitator experts in the counterfeiting of documents sell false Turkish documents to UAMs, while offering the use of public transport to Istanbul. The routes and the strategies adopted by UAMs are the same of those followed by the adult nationals. Information collected directly from UAMs in Italy indicates that Turkey is a key transit country in the migratory experience of smuggled UAMs. Young Afghans rely on small criminal groups involved in the smuggling of migrants and human trafficking, organized both within Turkey and transnationally. They work to move individuals efficiently over long distances, and make use of resources such as local citizens in border areas in order to facilitate border crossings into Turkey with the objective of reaching Europe. The extended and rocky terrain renders the border difficult to monitor, creating opportunities for migrants to cross undetected (Kaya 2013).

An Afghan national interviewed by a Turkish journal that works with Afghan smugglers reported that often the migrants are recruited in Afghanistan, corroborating similar reports by several UAMs smuggled into Italy. 'They take them up through Iran and into Istanbul. They then house them [in Istanbul] for a few days before taking them to Izmir where they cross on boat' (Nielsen 2013). For the whole trip from Kabul to Athens, the estimated price is from 5,000 to 8,500 euros, depending on the quality of the services and whether obstacles arise along the way. The Afghan migrants pay 20 per cent up-front in Istanbul and the rest when they reach their final destination. Those who run out of money in Istanbul try to raise extra funds by doing cash-in-hand low-skilled labour (Nielsen 2013).

Faced with few prospects for normalization of their status in Turkey or of resettlement in Europe or further afield, many Afghans who successfully enter the country are clustered in Istanbul's Zeytinburnu neighbourhood, by 'kacakci', what the locals call the smugglers. A large number of kacakci are believed to be in operation in Turkey. They are predominantly of Turkish, Iraqi, Iranian, Afghani or Pakistani nationality, often with a common ethnic and linguistic background (Galeotti 1998). They also operate separate departments, each of which specializes in a specific illicit activity, so that groups never mix. Kacakci cells hand the people from one cell to the next at each stage, using disposable mobile phones to coordinate the operation. Travelling migrants hand over cash at the beginning of each new stage. Sometimes, they may have to pay a percentage, such as half the total, up-front with the rest due on arrival (Nielsen 2013).

In 2008, criminals from 64 different countries operating in conjunction with Turkish crime groups were arrested in Turkey. Many of these worked in drug trafficking, but their networks were also used to smuggle human beings (Shelley 2014).

According to Triandafyllidou and Maroukis (2012), there is no evidence linking organized groups like the mafia to the smugglers. Smuggling rings are loose operations run by people of the same ethnicity as the people they smuggle. Media outlets have reported that families are organized like an army with a godfather-type figure, called a 'baba', at the top of the structure. They do not work directly on smuggling operations, but they help host and oversee them. They also provide the local knowledge, contacts and infrastructure to help people move around (Nielsen 2013). Looking at the evolution of smuggling in the Middle East region, Içduygu and Toktas (2002) wrote that smuggling of people through Turkey is operated mainly by small groups of smugglers operating as networks of local agents without strong transnational criminal relations. Often these small criminal groups are characterized by ethno-national interpersonal relations that enforce the mutual trust between smugglers and those smuggled. Young smuggled Afghans have also referred to the specific functional organizations of these smuggling groups. They reported that within each group are actors specialized in different tasks: the boss, the recruiter of migrants; the transporters, responsible for the hosting facilities in the transiting countries; and often an intermediary figure who, if necessary, works to bribe officials. Recently, media outlets reported that the growth of social media represents a versatile tool in the hands of migrants and smugglers. Many smugglers use Facebook accounts to share information about how to enter the EU illegally and elude authorities once inside.[14]

According to Europol (2013), traffickers have access to transportation services in key hubs such as Istanbul. The business of trafficking is closely integrated not only with transportation and logistical businesses but also with tourist agencies, hotels and taxi services, both in Turkey and elsewhere. Europol notes that a strong link exists between networks facilitating irregular migration and the nationality of the migrants involved in the irregular movements, a factor that is believed to explain the wide variety of organized crime groups involved in the smuggling of migrants.

Once in Istanbul, UAMs typically travel towards the Greek–Turkish land border or to a lesser extent towards the western coast of Turkey by car (Antonopoulos and Winterdyk 2006). The journey from Turkey to Greece is often extremely dangerous:

> The boat journey from Turkey to Greece is one of the most traumatic experiences for Afghan children who are on their way to Europe. Most of the boys interviewed were herded into small inflatable rubber craft that were built to carry a much smaller number of people, and pushed off into the night to make the short but dangerous crossing to the Greek islands of Samos or Lesbos. (UNHCR 2010: 19)

In this context the low level of Turkish institutional and police reaction to the phenomenon represents a further element of criticality. While article 79 of the Turkish Criminal Code punishes the smuggling of Turkish citizens or foreigners abroad with three to eight years' imprisonment and a punitive fine up to 10,000 euros, this provision is rarely applied. Additionally, while Turkey and Greece signed a Joint Declaration on Enhancing Cooperation in the Field of Illegal Migration and Readmission[15] in March 2013, efforts to stem the flow of irregular migrants across Turkey's border with Greece have been only relatively successful. This is demonstrated by the displacement of the routes from land to sea that followed Operation Aspida in August 2012.

The effectiveness of the externalization of migration control through bilateral agreement is controversial. While the agreement between Turkey and the EU on readmission was signed on 16 December 2003, it has not yet been ratified. As Içduygu notes, perhaps it is due to the concerns that with the EU–Turkey readmission agreement, Turkey will become a 'buffer zone' between irregular immigrant-targeted countries of Western Europe and their origin countries in the East and the South. Against this background, Içduygu states that 'the question of [whether] a possible readmission agreement between the EU and Turkey will work effectively or not' still remains unanswered. The other questions, such as 'whether or not readmission agreement, as it operates and manages the return of irregular migrants to their home countries, will discourage the potential irregular migrants and then will cause the decline in the similar irregular flows' is also unanswered (Içduygu 2004: 15).

As described earlier, the unprecedented addition of police officers deployed along Greece's border with Turkey since 2012 resulted in a drastic drop in irregular migrant land crossings. However, in response to the difficulty of crossing the land border between Turkey and Greece, detections of attempted crossings in the Aegean Sea increased 912 per cent in 2012 (Frontex 2013). The number of detected migrants travelling with fraudulent documents on flights from Turkey to the EU nearly doubled during the same period, indicating that irregular migrants and their facilitators respond quickly to changes in border control measures and identify new avenues to exploit. It is evident that for UAMs attempting to cross Turkish land, there are several viable options.

Land crossings from Turkey to Greece or Bulgaria typically take place at night. Irregular crossings usually occur relatively close to the road networks on both sides of the border so that facilitators easily drop off migrants with minimum cost and time. This also allows migrants the choice to continue their journey further into the EU on their own or to be picked up by facilitators. The size of groups varies from a few people to large groups of about 50. Facilitators usually arrange the last leg of the trip to the Balkans by boat or by car/lorry respectively, making irregular border crossing very hazardous (Frontex 2012). Smuggling groups operating directly on the border crossing points are primarily made up of Afghan and Iranian nationals and appear to be completely independent or only loosely connected (UNODC 2013a).

Frontex's apprehension data, albeit inconclusive, reveals that the chief nationality of apprehended migrants at the Greek–Turkish sea borders in recent years (2007–09) was Afghan. However:

> There is no record of the total number of unaccompanied minors, even though we know they are more than the 350 available positions in reception centers for minors. In fact, Afghan minors form a group for which we have the least knowledge. On the other hand, it is unclear to what extent the minors are 'unaccompanied' throughout, i.e. to what an extent some beginning migration with the family which they lose on the way or are left behind. (Dimitriadi 2013: 22)

While disaggregate data on UAMs are not available, in informal interviews different minors have described their experience in Greece as traumatic. This is confirmed by UNHCR: 'many of the young Afghans interviewed in Greece were self-financing and had run out of money, had spent weeks or months in detention, and/or had made a number of unsuccessful attempts to reach Italy and were unable or unwilling to go any further' (2010: 11). This strongly affects the perception of UAMs who might consider staying in the transit country of Greece. Settlement in the country is seen as difficult, due to existing policies in place: the absence of legalization measures; 'sweep' operations like Xenios Zeus; the fragmented asylum system; and racist violence, social exclusion and an economic crisis that is raising migrant unemployment rates (Dimitriadi 2013: 28). For the majority of UAMs transiting towards Greece, the goal is to move on to Italy and beyond. Most find their way to the port of Patras, where they try to hide in trucks that take them to ferries bound for Bari, Ancona or Venice.

The sub-routes (Italy and Western Balkans)

During the 2000s, the sea route to southern Italy was the most travelled by UAMs. Until 2012, Afghans comprised one of the principal nationalities attempting to cross, hidden in trucks and cars, at the ports across from Italy, mainly Patras and Igoumenitsa. Many UAMs have reported the difficulty of hiding in a truck bound for Italy, many having attempted multiple times, sometimes incurring serious injury as they fell, or were pushed from, moving vehicles. For those who do eventually reach Italy, apart from the difficult living conditions experienced by many children, the journey itself appears to be quick and relatively problem-free compared with the previous leg of the journey. As for UAMs leaving Greece, this is consistently becoming harder, with intensification of checks at major ports like Patras and Igoumenitsa and constantly changing routes, as evidenced by the decrease in UAMs detected in Italy in the last two years.

Current evidence from Frontex and Europol report an increase of UAMs transiting along the Western Balkans region. These secondary movements from Greece are characterized by the attempt to re-enter the Schengen through Hungary or Slovenia in order to reach Northern Europe. In 2010, Frontex found that taxi services for migrants operated openly from Macedonia to the Serbian border. This border experienced the largest number of movements, again with Afghans as the most detected nationality, representing 45 per cent of the total population. In 2011, Slovenian authorities reported an increase in the detection of Afghans who tried to illegally enter the EU after claiming asylum in Croatia. In 2012, the Slovenian–Croatian border reported a 95 per cent increase in detections, the highest increase in the region (Frontex 2013). Afghans continued to dominate the nationalities detected. The increase was significant enough for the Slovenian Ministry of Interior to issue a public warning, calling on its citizens to report sightings of irregular migrants.

In recent years, according to information collected in Serbia in 2013, irregular migrants were detected close to the border area between Romania, Hungary and Serbia, displaced from the main Serbian–Hungarian route where additional border control measures made crossings more difficult. Serbia was deeply affected by the phenomenon. According to statistics from the Serbian Interior Ministry, during the first ten months of 2012 the largest number of detained foreign nationals was from Afghanistan (718). While no data shows the prominence of UAMs inside this group, officers from different NGOs reported that these migrants are often minors without any specific protection provided to them. Human Rights Watch (2015) has recently documented that Afghan migrants in Serbia are being harassed and abused at the hands of Serbian police.

Aalem, a 16-year-old Afghan boy, said that twice in November police forced him and three of his friends – ages 12, 13, and 15 – back to Macedonia. They succeeded in applying for asylum in Serbia after their third attempt. Four adults said the border police in southern and eastern Serbia told them to hand over money to avoid being pushed back to Macedonia and released them after they did.

Summary returns of unaccompanied children, without procedural safeguards or the opportunity to lodge asylum claims, shape the essence of border control set out by the Serbian government to curb the flow of migrants entering the Schengen area. This border practice is in opposition to Serbia's obligations under national and international law. The Convention on the Rights of the Child, to which Serbia is a state party, obligates Serbia not to summarily return unaccompanied children unless their claim has been fairly determined. Two Afghan UAMs told Human Rights Watch that Serbian police pushed them back to Macedonia without adequate assessment of their individual need for protection. They said Serbian border police apprehended them on Serbian soil, took them to the border and ordered them to walk in the direction of Macedonia. In some cases, the police beat or otherwise mistreated them (HRW 2015). For this reason, similarly to what was observed in Greece and Italy, UAMs seek to rest invisibly until they reach the northern EU countries.

Conclusion

This research has analysed the relation between the strengthening of the EU's external border control and the increase in migrant smuggling along the Eastern Mediterranean route, focusing on the transnational irregular mobility of Afghan unaccompanied minors. Contrasting with the humanitarian needs presented by this forced migratory flow, the EU approach has emphasized policing, defence and pushing migrants back into third countries over a human rights-based approach, predominantly focusing on the 'securitised' aspects, such as cooperation agreements on 'illegal' immigration, external border controls through logistical and surveillance technologies and capacity-building in third countries designed to stop irregular migration. However, the analysed case study has demonstrated that these efforts to prevent migrants from entering Europe have not stopped most of them from doing so. In addition, these measures have had a series of unintended effects.

First, as demonstrated by the systematic rise of alternative routes opened to avoid the policing deployed on the controlled routes, border securitization has only stimulated the rise of new smuggling routes, mainly traversed by vulnerable migrants who have no other choice but to migrate. Second, border policing has exposed vulnerable migrants at risk and death:

> For the period 1993 and 2008, 92 people died trying to cross the Greek-Turkish land border, and 45 people died from the cold trying to reach Greece from the mountains at the Greek-Bulgarian and Greek-Turkish Borders. During the 1994–2009, around 1333 people drowned in an attempt to cross the Greek-Turkish sea border. Seven people have died in their attempts to board ferry boats connecting the Greek port of Patras with Italy. (Triandafyllidou and Maroukis 2012: 108)

These tragic data are a further proof of the ineffectiveness and mortality linked to the EU approach to migration control, for those vulnerable migrants like UAMs. No one knows exactly how many Afghan UAMs have made it to Europe, as the only available numbers are Eurostat statistics about the countries of origin of UAMs applying for asylum. Despite this, in 2013 Afghans were the most populous group of UAMs requesting asylum, accounting for 3,295 applications, the highest in all of Europe.[16]

The examination of the main push factors behind UAM mobility shows how the current EU approach, which emphasizes border policing and the externalization of migration control, falls short in addressing the serious criticalities experienced by UAMs along their smuggled path, including the human rights violations they face in the transit countries until they enter the EU.

In the face of this phenomenon, the EU member states have shown themselves unprepared and short-sighted. As a further proof of this, it is useful to consider how the EU only began examining the topic in 2010, through the Action Plan on Unaccompanied Minors. Two years later, the EU recognized 'that the arrival of unaccompanied minors is not a temporary phenomenon, but a long-term feature of migration into the EU, and that there is the need for a common approach by the EU to this group of migrants'.[17] However, UAMs' rights are not always respected as they are often dealt with as adult irregular migrants, not taking into account their specific vulnerabilities, needs and rights. The absence of a coordinated approach designed for all the EU countries, together with the lack of specific policies addressing this kind of mobility, call for rapid and specific policy action that takes into account the transnational dimension of UAMs' mobility. The transnational lens is crucial for the development of targeted policies aiming at enhancing a rights-based approach able to ensure the protection of migrants in irregular situations. This is fundamental when considering that proper identification and detection mechanisms of minors smuggled is largely missing in almost all the EU's entry points.

The enhancement of the protection of EU external borders has had an impact on the rise of new illegal markets in EU neighbouring countries. Improved political dialogue is needed among countries along the EMR in order to launch a comprehensive solution to address the challenges posed by the growing smuggling networks operating along the route. In particular, addressing the root causes of migration, including push factors in the countries of origin, as well as pull factors in countries of destination, such as those related to humanitarian protection, must be included both in the EU and the governmental response in each country along the route.

Last but not least, the phenomenon of Afghan UAMs smuggled along the EMR, as suggested by UNHCR (2010), must be viewed in a broader context. Even if it has increased in scale in recent years, the number of UAMs involved in this movement remains very small in relation to the size of the Afghan population as a whole and to the number of Afghan refugees and displaced people in the sub-region. Compared to the 3.7 million Afghans who have either moved permanently to neighbouring countries like Iran and Pakistan, migration to EU countries remains relatively limited.

More relevantly, as UAMs are not the only unaccompanied minors moving transnationally to seek protection or work, they represent a paradigmatic case to launch a new season of policy to protect the most vulnerable.

Notes

1 Currently, in Turkey, the EMR divides into two sub-routes: the maritime route, pointing to Italy, and land route through the Balkans, pointing to Northern European countries.
2 See 'Greece turns its back on those who have nowhere to go'. *Protothema News*, 4 December 2014: http://en.protothema.gr/greece-turns-its-back-on-those-who-have-nowhere-to-go/.
3 See: www.resettlement-observatory.eu/documents/greece/outputs/countryprofile/country profile.pdf.
4 See statistics available on the website for the Greek Police: www.astynomia.gr/index.php? option=ozo_content&perform=view&id=24727&Itemid=73&lang=EN; www.astynomia.gr/ images/stories//2013/statistics13/stat_allod/etsynora.JPG.
5 Bulgarian Council of Ministers, 'Plan for the containment of the crisis resulting from stronger migration pressure on the Bulgarian border'. Sofia, Bulgaria, 6 November 2013.
6 See Human Rights Watch Report: www.hrw.org/news/2014/09/17/bulgaria-upr-submission-september-2014.
7 See 'Facing refugee influx, Bulgaria to build 30km fence on Turkish border'. *Sofia Globe*: http://sofiaglobe.com/2013/10/16/bulgarias-cabinet-to-hold-special-meeting-on-refugee-issue/.
8 For instance, both border officers interviewed during two field missions in Serbia and Germania, then civil servants interviewed in Italy have noted that sometimes those claiming to be minors mislead the authorities regarding their age.
9 See: http://appsso.eurostat.ec.europa.eu/nui/submitViewTableAction.do.
10 See: http://countryeconomy.com/hdi/afghanistan.
11 See: www.geocurrents.info/geopolitics/the-iran-pakistan-border-barrier#ixzz3X4ZeN76g.
12 See 'Afghan asylum bids at 10-year high, human smuggling rife as troops begin to leave', *Associated Press*, 24 January 2012: www.unhcr.org/cgi-bin/texis/vtx/refdaily? pass=463ef21123&id=4f1fa6645.
13 Afghanistan says 760,000 refugees risk deportation from Iran: www.reuters.com/ article/2014/12/03/us-afghanistan-iran-idUSKCN0JH1CM20141203.
14 See *Hurriyet Daily News*, 'Gangs from Turkey benefit from human smuggling in Mediterranean: EU': www.hurriyetdailynews.com/gangs-from-turkey-benefit-from-human-smuggling-in-mediterranean-eu.aspx?pageID=238&nID=76871&NewsCat ID=509; and *Daily Mail*: www.dailymail.co.uk/news/article-2906317/Internet-heart-new-tactics-Med-people-smugglers.html.
15 Republic of Turkey, Ministry of National Defence, 'Joint Declaration between the Government of the Hellenic Republic and the Government of the Republic of Turkey', 6 March 2013: www.avramopoulos.gr/en/content/joint-declaration-between-government-hellenic-republic-and-government-republic-turkey.
16 http://ec.europa.eu/dgs/home-affairs/what-we-do/policies/asylum/uam/uam_ infographic_a4_en.pdf.
17 European Commission 2012, 'Mid-term report on the implementation of the Action Plan on Unaccompanied Minors', http://ec.europa.eu/dgs/home-affairs/e-library/docs/ uam/uam_report_20120928_en.pdf.

References

Abbasi-Shavazi, M. J. and Glazebrook, D. 2006. *Continued Protection, Sustainable Reintegration: Afghan Refugees and Migrants in Iran*. AREU. www.areu.org.af/ Uploads/EditionPdfs/614E-Continued%20Protection-BP-web.pdf.

Adelkhah, F. and Olszewska, Z. 2007. 'The Iranian Afghans'. *Iranian Studies* 40: 137–65.

'Affected by armed conflict in Afghanistan'. 2010. http://watchlist.org/reports/pdf/Afghanistanpercent20Reportpercent202010.pdf.

AIHRC (Afghanistan Independent Human Rights Commission). 2008. 'The General Situation of Children in Afghanistan.' www.unhcr.org/refworld/topic,4565c2252f,4565c25f3d1,483bedd22,0,AIHRC,,AFG.html.

Amnesty International. 2013. *Frontiers Europe*.

Antonopoulos, G. and Winterdyk, J. 2006. 'The smuggling of migrants in Greece: an examination of its social organisation'. *European Journal of Criminology* 3(4).

Campani, G., Lapov, Z. and Carchedi, T. 2002. *Le Esperienze Ignorate: Giovani Migranti Tra Accoglienza, Indifferenza, Ostilità*. Milan: Franco Angeli.

Central Statistics Organisation. 2014. *National Risk and Vulnerability Assessment 2011–12*. Afghanistan Living Condition Survey. Kabul, CSO.

Courau, H. 2003. 'Tomorrow inch Allah, chance! People smuggler networks in Sangatte'. *Immigrants and Minorities* 22(2–3).

Dimitriadi, A. 2013. 'Migration from Afghanistan to third countries and Greece'. Hellenic Foundation for European and Foreign Policy (ELIAMEP). www.eliamep.gr/wp-content/uploads/2013/09/IRMA-Background-Report-AFGHANISTAN_EN-1.pdf.

Europol. 2013. 'EU serious and organized crime threat assessment'. www.europol.europa.eu/sites/default/files/publications/socta2013.pdf.

Eurostat. 2011. 'Statistics: asylum applicants considered to be unaccompanied minors by citizenship, age and sex: annual data'. Luxembourg: Publications Office. http://epp.eurostat.ec.europa.eu.

Frontex. 2010. 'Unaccompanied minors in the migration process'. Warsaw. http://frontex.europa.eu/assets/Attachments_News/unaccompanied_minors_public_5_dec.pdf.

Frontex. 2011a. 'Annual risk analysis'.

Frontex. 2011b. 'Situational overview on trafficking in human beings'. Warsaw.

Frontex. 2012. 'Annual risk analysis'. http://frontex.europa.eu/assets/Publications/Risk_Analysis/FRAN_Q3_2012.pdf.

Frontex. 2013. 'Annual risk analysis'.

Frontex. 2014. 'Annual risk analysis'. http://frontex.europa.eu/assets/Publications/Risk_Analysis/Annual_Risk_Analysis_2014.pdf.

FRA (European Union Agency for Fundamental Rights). 2011. Coping with a fundamental rights emergency: the situation of persons crossing the Greek land border in an irregular manner. http://fra.europa.eu/sites/default/files/fra_uploads/1500-Greek-border-situation-report2011_EN.pdf.

Galeotti, M. 1998. 'Turkish organized crime: where state, crime and rebellion conspire'. *Transnational Organized Crime* 4(1).

Gall, S. 2013. *War Against the Taliban: Why It All Went Wrong in Afghanistan*. London: A and C Black.

HRW (Human Rights Watch). 2014. 'Containment plan: Bulgaria's pushbacks and detention of Syrian and other asylum seekers and migrants'. www.hrw.org/sites/default/files/reports/bulgaria0414_ForUpload_0_0.pdf.

HRW. 2015. 'Serbia: police abusing migrants and asylum seekers'. www.hrw.org/news/2015/04/15/serbia-police-abusing-migrants-asylum-seekers.

Huysmans, J. 2006. *The Politics of Insecurity: Fear, Migration and Asylum in the EU*. London: Routledge.

Içduygu, A. 2004. 'Transborder crime between Turkey and Greece: human smuggling and its regional consequences'. *Southeast European and Black Sea Studies* 4(2).

Içduygu, A. 2011. 'The irregular migration corridor between the EU and Turkey: is it possible to block it with a readmission agreement?' *Migration Policy Institute*. http://cadmus.eui.eu/bitstream/handle/1814/17844/EUUSpercent20Immigrationpercent20Systemspercent202011_14.pdf?sequence=1.

Içduygu, A. and Toktas, S. 2002. 'How do smuggling and trafficking operate via irregular border crossings in the Middle East? Evidence from fieldwork in Turkey'. *International Migration* 40(6): 25–52.

ICMPD. 2013. 'A Silk Routes partnership for migration, Afghanistan, migration country report'. *Budapest Process*. www.imap-migration.org/fileadmin/i-map-logos/Budapest_Process/Afghanistan_Migration_Country_Report.pdf.

Kaya, K. 2013. 'Turkey's role in Afghanistan and Afghan stabilisation'. *Military Review*. http://usacac.army.mil/CAC2/MilitaryReview/Archives/English/MilitaryReview_20130831_art007.pdf.

Koser, K. 2008. 'Why migrant smuggling pays'. *International Migration* 46(2): 3–26.

Koser, K. 2009. 'The migration-displacement nexus in Afghanistan'. Brookings Institute. www.brookings.edu/research/opinions/2009/05/04-afghanistan-koser.

Lee-Koo, K. 2013. 'Not suitable for children: the politicization of conflict-affected children in post-2001 Afghanistan'. *Australian Journal of International Affairs* 67(4): 475–90.

Matsumoto, Y. 2011. 'Young Afghans in "transition": towards Afghanization, exit or violence?' *Conflict, Security and Development* 11(5): 555–78.

Monsutti, A. 2007. 'Migration as a rite of passage: young Afghans building masculinity and adulthood in Iran'. *Iranian Studies* 40(2): 167–85.

Nielsen, N. 2013. 'Istanbul: smuggler capital for EU-bound migrants'. Last updated July 2014. https://euobserver.com/fortress-eu/118377.

Protothema News. 2014. 'Greece turns its back on those who have nowhere to go'. Last updated 4 December 2014. http://en.protothema.gr/greece-turns-its-back-on-those-who-have-nowhere-to-go/.

Ritendra, T. 2009. 'Afghan forced migration: reaffirmation, redefinition, and the politics of aid'. *Asian Social Science* 5(1).

Rodan, D. and Lange, C. 2008. 'Going overboard? Representing Hazara Afghan refugees as just like us'. *Journal of Intercultural Studies* 29(2): 153–69.

Shelley, L. 2014. *Human Smuggling and Trafficking in Europe: A Comparative Perspective*. Washington, DC: Migration Policy Institute.

Tamang, R. 2009. 'Afghan forced migration: reaffirmation, redefinition, and the politics of aid'. *Asian Social Science* 5(1): 3–12.

Tober, D. 2007. 'Introduction: Afghan refugees and returnees'. *Iranian Studies* 40(2): 263–85.

Triandafyllidou, A. 2010. *Irregular Migration in Europe: Myths and Realities*. Aldershot: Ashgate.

Triandafyllidou, A. 2014. 'Greek migration policy in the 2010s: Europeanization tensions at a time of crisis'. *Journal of European Integration* 36(4): 409–25.

Triandafyllidou, A. and Dimitriadi, A. 2013. 'Migration management at the outposts of the European Union'. *Griffith Law Review* 22(3): 598–618.

Triandafyllidou, A. and Maroukis, T. 2012. *Migrant Smuggling: Irregular Migration from Asia and Africa to Europe*. London: Palgrave.

Triandafyllidou, A., Vogel, D. and Duvell, F. 2011. 'Irregular migration from a European perspective: an introduction'. *International Migration* 49(5): 58–63.

UNDP. 2014. *Human Development Report 2014*. http://hdr.undp.org/sites/default/files/hdr14-report-en-1.pdf.

UNHCR. 2010. 'Human Rights Dimension of Poverty in Afghanistan'.

UNICEF. 2010. 'Children on the Move: A Report on Children of Afghan Origin Moving to Western Countries'. www.unicef.org/infobycountry/files/Book_children_on_the_move.pdf.

United Nations Secretary General. 2010. *The Situation in Afghanistan and its Implications for International Peace and Security*. New York: UN General Assembly Security Council.

UNODC. 2011. 'Smuggling of migrants by sea'. www.unodc.org/documents/human-trafficking/Migrant-Smuggling/Issue-Papers/Issue_Paper_-_Smuggling_of_Migrants_by_Sea.pdf.

UNODC. 2012. 'Pakistan, human trafficking and migrant smuggling routes from Pakistan to neighbouring and distant countries'. Last updated November 2012.

UNODC. 2013a. 'Comparative research on financial flows within migrant smuggling from Asia to Europe'.

UNODC. 2013b. 'Recent trends on human trafficking and migrant smuggling to and from Pakistan'.

US Department of State. 2013. 'Trafficking in Persons Report'. www.state.gov/documents/organization/210738.pdf.

Valtolina, G. G. 2014. *Unaccompanied Minors in Italy. Challenges and Way Ahead*. Milan: McGraw Hill.

Watch List on Children and Armed Conflict. 2010. 'Setting the right priorities: protecting children affected by armed conflict in Afghanistan'. Last updated June 2010. http://watchlist.org/reports/pdf/Afghanistanpercent20Reportpercent202010.pdf.

7 Gender and borders in a comparative perspective

Sub-Saharan migrant women facing Fortress Europe: the cases of Italy, Greece and Turkey

Giovanna Campani and Zoran Lapov

Introduction

Despite predictions of a borderless world through globalization, nations keep being divided. In other words, *'Toujours plus de murs dans un «monde sans frontières,'* as remarked by the title of a map in the *Atlas des migrants en Europe.*[1] Barriers separate India from Pakistan (Kashmir), Israel from Palestine, Greece from Turkey (Evros), and 25 years after the fall of the Berlin Wall, border barriers – far from being relics of the past[2] – are given a renewed vigour.

Barriers, fences, walls dividing regions, peoples and cultures are not only a consequence of border disputes or conflictual relationships between states: too often, they are moulded by socio-economic inequalities as a selection mechanism to split between 'legitimate' and 'illegitimate', granting thus differing rights: whereas 'rich' people are considered to be legitimate travellers, migrant job-seekers in 'rich' countries are illegitimate 'trespassers', and borders are meant to keep 'unwanted' migrants away. It is about separating different segments of humankind, which makes borders a symbol of the gap between rich and poor. As such, border areas have been progressively militarized, entailing both financial and human costs. Accordingly, crossing borders has become a dangerous step, costing yearly thousands of lives. At long last, the phenomenon has caused migration to become a security issue.

While exploring the gender dimension in the process of border crossing, this chapter focuses on the case of sub-Saharan African women crossing borders in three Mediterranean countries. In this comparison, Turkey is outside the EU border, while Greece and Italy, though within the EU borders, are still separated from the 'mainland Europe'.

Research in this field proves to be fragmented, often addressing local contexts, hence ignoring a broader 'frontier perspective'. Meanwhile, newly securitized spaces are emerging (e.g. the Mediterranean) and reshaping large regions, frontier societies and border communities. To boot, the 'border of Europe', perceived as such by migrants attempting to reach the promised continent (King *et al.* 1999), involves several frontier levels: it is, at the same time, the border of the EU, and the border of different states enjoying different socio-economic conditions. Single states, whose differences in economic prosperity have increased over the last years, are also playing different roles within the EU border system: furthermore, their conditions are interrelated with different migration histories, and – under the common Schengen rules – different asylum policies. Besides, research work on border crossings encounters several difficulties, especially in relation to departure areas. Last but not least, gender dimension is little developed, which is due to a dominant idea that most of irregular border-crossers are men. Migrant women's voices in the process of border-crossing, or in their precarious settlements in Europe, are commonly heard only when tragic events occur. Yet, though being inferior to that of men, the number of female border-crossers is growing worldwide.

The contents of this chapter rest in part upon findings emerged from the European Project *Learning for Female African Migrants' Solidarity: Help-Desks for Female African Migrants in the Eastern Mediterranean Region* (LeFamSol). In the framework of the Lifelong Learning Programme, the project involved three partner countries: Italy, Greece and Turkey. As suggested by its title, the project's objective is to pave the way for a community self-help service to be run by network facilitators coming from the concerned communities. The idea of producing a community self-help desk channelled the project's actions pursued with women native to sub-Saharan Africa, including methodologies and concomitant activities (research, focus groups, life stories, workshops, training, etc.), which produced information in the form of research reports and deliverables.

Security-based responses: processes of enclosure and mobility

The policies that have brought about the hardening of borders and the Fortress Europe date back to the 1990s, beginning from the Schengen Agreement (signed in 1985, but effective from 1995) which was supposed to lead to the creation of Europe's borderless Schengen Area. Yet, the process of confining and militarizing border areas has never ceased, being further reinforced in the last decade.

In this sense, the southern border of the European Union is another area where the 'North' and the 'South' meet as problematic border regions. With the goal of keeping migrants away, the Mediterranean Sea, as a border basin between Europe and Africa, has been militarized. In addition, fences were built in Ceuta and Melilla, European enclaves in Africa, as well as at the mainland border shared by Greece and Turkey, Evros. The product of militarization and fence-building is Fortress Europe, a definition that is nowadays shared by scholars, experts and organizations working on EU migration policies and denouncing concomitant human costs. In a recent report, Amnesty International (2014a) denounced how EU policy puts refugees and migrants at risk by preventing them from seeking asylum; it said that this pushes refugees to take perilous risks to reach Europe.

As a matter of fact, the European Union, focusing on the issue of security, deals with the Mediterranean border according to a logic that aims to lock it.

The main tool of such a security-based policy is Frontex,[3] a border agency set up in 2004 to help control the external EU borders from irregular migration. As stressed by some authors,[4] Frontex employs novel military equipment and other costly instruments for reaching its goals.[5] Needless to say, the operation demands a high budget, which has been increasingly multiplied over the years.

In parallel, the existence of Frontex boosted the emergence of processes that had found their place inside and outside the European Union. Among other outcomes, construction of detention centres for migrants, and even walls in some cases, has become a reality. And already diffused xenophobia has been further intensified and used for political goals (Rodier 2012).

The hardening and militarization of the borders have been justified with security discourse. And, justifying the entire process with security issues, governments neglect the fact that the exclusion and violence necessary to prevent border-crossing undermine the very ideals of freedom and democracy that European countries claim to represent.

Finally, undocumented migrants are being depicted as a bulk of threatening characters acting 'illegally' and becoming themselves 'illegal'. Such a menacing representation of border-crossers is reflected in young males taking any risks to reach the promised land – which is pushing women to the background.

How many borders for Europe?

Geographically speaking, the southern border of Europe[6] is the Mediterranean Sea. As a result of history, a few islands – Malta (former British colony) or the Italian Lampedusa (territorially closer to North Africa than to continental Europe) – act as European territories in the midst of the sea. Besides, legacy of the colonial past on the Moroccan coasts, Ceuta and Melilla, represent European enclaves in the African continent. The land borders of Europe are in the East: between Greece, Bulgaria and Turkey, as well as between Finland, Baltic countries, Poland, Slovakia, Hungary, Romania, and the heirs of the former Soviet Union. Finally, an internal border divides the Greek and the Turkish parts of the island of Cyprus.

The European border system is shaped by both EU common policy and national contexts of single member states. The whole system is further underpinned by the scheme of the EU border policies aimed at containing immigration. The Schengen Agreement establishes common rules with respect to external border controls, internal free movement, and migration/asylum policies. In practice, Schengen means a sum of rules that tend to hinder newcomers (be they asylum seekers or migrants) in the countries or specific areas of their arrival, irrespective of their aspirations and the presence of family members or networks in other European regions. To this effect, Frontex constitutes a Europeanized version of a national border guard that actually reinforces the national ones.

As a consequence, this system produces a huge impact on migration processes and regions touched by them, granting Frontex a crucial role in (re)directing migration flows: being concerned by border policies, migration routes are constantly reorganized in response to stricter controls or open spaces that appear here and there. On the other hand, while being particularly important in some border areas (e.g. Greece and Italy) within the EU, border policies extend – in some cases – beyond its geographical demarcations (e.g. Turkey, Morocco). This is due to the process of 'externalization' of the borders towards non-EU countries: the said process is implemented by both European and national policies, and combined with a sort of border 'internalization' in specific EU areas (e.g. Italy and Greece).

Migration and border control policies enacted by the EU, along with the shift of Turkey from a sending to a transit/receiving country, are interrelated phenomena making Italy, Greece and Turkey main migration channels to Europe. The situation is being exacerbated by a socio-economic and political instability reigning over the region of Southern Europe. Besides, North European countries neglect the fact that Italy, Greece or Spain are the borders of Europe, and not of individual member states; they further ignore that most migrants want to go north, not being interested in staying in the South European countries where they first arrive.

To boot, the Mediterranean has been marked by a series of tragic events in the form of fatal shipwrecks, occurring mostly off the Italian island of Lampedusa situated between Malta and Tunisia. In the panorama of Africa-to-Europe migrations, the island has become a symbolic place of the European frontier as it annually receives a great deal of arrivals (numbers peak at a thousand persons per day). According to the International Organization for Migration (2011), the situation has been critical for years now: with a permanent population of 5,000 people, the island can accommodate 800 refugees at most. In order to prevent the situation from descending into chaos, Italy launched a mission known as Mare Nostrum[7] (October 2013–October 2014): this rescue operation, facing a constant emergency and a series of difficulties, aroused controversies and fuelled new political arguments at both national and European levels.

Establishing a database of crossings, and making estimations of those who die and those who succeed in landing, is mainly a job done by NGOs (e.g. UNITED[8]) and the UNHCR, rather than official institutions. According to the figures offered by various reports, it is reckoned that 623,118 refugees and irregular migrants reached the EU coasts in the 1998–2013 period (Kiggundu and De Vries 2014: 14) – meaning an average of almost 40,000 people a year. UNHCR said in 2014 that almost 3,500 people died, and more than 200,000 were rescued while trying to cross the Mediterranean Sea to reach Europe.[9]

The catastrophe is not only due to shipwrecks and drownings, but also to hunger, cold, choking, assassination, suicide, immolation and hunger strike, turning the Mediterranean into the biggest sea cemetery in the world. According to various reports by Amnesty International (2014a, 2014b, 2015), since the late 1980s some 23,000 people are estimated to have lost their lives in the Mediterranean while trying to reach Europe. And, while documenting deaths, UNITED remarks how the phenomenon did not awaken Europe's conscience.

Sub-Saharan Africans heading for Europe: shifting borders, shifting trends

Despite a growing rate of risk, Africa-to-Europe flows prove to be on a constant increase. What is pushing those migrants to cross the Sea instead of undertaking other possible routes? To answer such a question, migration phenomena are being analysed through the prism of policies and actions migrants are targeted by, along with socio-economic and political conditions in both sending and receiving countries as crucial aspects affecting migration trends and routes. And the reasons of their departures are multiple, including:

- escalating crises;
- economic and political insecurity causing deprivations of the same nature;
- persecutions and violations of human rights;
- conflicts in the Near East, Middle East and Africa;
- Arab Spring (2010);[10]
- crisis and civil wars in some of the border countries (especially Libya and Syria).

On the EU side, the reasons that have boosted changing migration trends and routes include border control policies implemented by the EU as a major factor, and, more specifically, the closing of land borders in the South-eastern Europe.

Some of the said causes have been particularly important in producing shifts in borders and migration trends, namely the crisis, armed conflicts especially in Libya and Syria, the Frontex operation, and border controls in the Greek region of Evros.

In the scope of recent crises and conflicts in some Mediterranean regions, the cases of Libya and Syria are all-important. For many years, both countries used to be the destination or transit points for migrants coming from Asia and Africa. Libya was a place of both permanent and temporary settlements for sub-Saharan Africans. In recent years, the civil war that struck Libya has forced migrants to leave the country, where they could – though in a precarious condition – stay. As a result, the border between Algeria and Libya was reinforced, producing a strong impact on migration flows. The Syrian civil war has been another crucial factor in this arena that has brought about rapidly growing numbers of refugees.

In 2010, the number of entries is likely to drop: it is clear that the closure of other routes to Europe (West Africa to Spain, Libya to Italy/Malta) has made Greece the last remaining gateway to the European South, turning it into an embattled ground where the EU is decisively intervening. Due to a stronger surveillance of the EU land borders, crossings by land diminished, whereas those by sea increased. Such an outcome is one of the direct consequences of the EU policies that are handling the borders with a security logic, and through its main instrument, Frontex (e.g. in Evros).

But, who are the border-crossers we are talking about? And what are their pathways before reaching the Mediterranean coasts, and their further destinations? Although being the departure continent for a number of nationalities, for the most part recent arrivals from Africa are native to the sub-Saharan region (above all Somalia and Eritrea), and Asia (mostly the Near and Middle East, above all Syria and Afghanistan). Along with these, many other national groups (from Egypt, Nigeria, Libya, Tunisia, Morocco, Palestine, Sudan, Mali, for example) find their place among the people trying to reach Europe through the Mediterranean. Observing the conditions in their homelands, many of them are basically refugees. Following the Arab Spring, hundreds of thousands of refugees and economic migrants native to the Near East and North Africa have attempted to enter Europe by crossing the Mediterranean Sea, increasing thus the pressure upon the southern European and especially Italian coasts.

Sub-Saharan Africans represent an important part of these flows. Economic and political insecurity, along with widespread violence and civil wars, are pushing thousands of people from diverse sub-Saharan realities to embark on dangerous routes across deserts and seas.

In order to reach the southern European coasts, either as their final destination or as a door to the EU, the exodus of sub-Saharan migrants – men and women – has to cross the Sahara Desert, the region of North Africa (both sending and transit region), and the Mediterranean Sea. There are several main migration routes in this scenario.

First is the *Western African–Mediterranean* route: migrants, mostly coming from Western and Central Africa (the Gulf of Guinea), trying to reach the western Mediterranean, follow the path through Mauritania and the western Sahara to Morocco, or across Mali and/or Niger to Algeria and Morocco, and from there to Spain or France.

Second is the *Central African–Mediterranean* route: this path crosses Niger (occasionally Chad) to Algeria or rather Libya and Tunisia, moving therefrom to Italy and/or Malta. In these routes, important crossing points are at Tessalit (Mali), Arlit (Niger), Tamanrasset (Algeria) and Ghadames (Libya). Finally, boats departing from the ports of Zuwarah, Zlitan and Benghazi (Libya) try to reach various points on the opposite bank of the Mediterranean (Lampedusa, Sicily, Malta, Sardinia).

A third, the *Eastern African–Mediterranean* route, is rather diverse: migrants native to the Horn of Africa go across Sudan to Egypt, and therefrom to Greece or even Italy, or through the Near East to Turkey; some go through Sudan (and Egypt) to Libya and Tunisia, wherefrom they attempt their final step to Italy and/ or Malta (this route proves to be the most opted one); another possibility takes them to move across Arab countries and the Near East to Turkey, and finally to Greece and Bulgaria.

Another important route is the *Eastern Mediterranean* one coming from Asia and involving a part of African migration flows: Asian flows depart from the Near and Middle East (mainly Afghanistan and Pakistan), pass over Iran to reach Turkey, from where migrants attempt their passage to Europe by crossing Greece, Cyprus and/or Bulgaria; this route has been the main transit channel for Syrian refugees too.[11]

The outlined routes have been continuously affected by diverse processes. Western and central Mediterranean routes (Italy, Spain, Malta) were predominantly used over more than two decades, while its eastern channels (Greece, Cyprus, Turkey) have become increasingly important, particularly in the last decade. In this landscape, Italy protrudes out towards the south Mediterranean coasts acting as a springboard for migrants coming through the region of North Africa, mostly Libya and Tunisia, but also Egypt, or even Turkey and Greece. Other flows are trying to enter Europe by going through Greece and Turkey, especially since some North African routes have been hindered by local conflicts (Libya) and border controls (Tunisia).

All told, information on gender ratio in the process of crossing borders are far from accurate, as a demographic profile of migrant women is often missing. Meanwhile, qualitative studies exploring the situation of migrants staying at the external borders of Europe, especially in Turkey and Morocco,[12] show that there is a growing number of women.

In this respect, the LeFamSol Project is a pioneering study, certainly in Turkey and Greece, and to a certain degree in Italy. The project represents an opportunity to shed light on diverse issues, starting from the narratives collected among women native to the sub-Saharan Africa who experienced long trips through the Sahara Desert and the Mediterranean. By way of illustration, the following is a fragment of the life story of a young Somali woman (Florence, 26):

> I left Somalia with my sister when I was 18. Step by step, we were moving from Somalia to Ethiopia, Sudan, Libya, and finally Italy. In Somalia and Ethiopia, we were moving by bus or other means. In Sudan, instead, you must walk for 9–10 hours at night through the desert, and always in group, 27–30 people. In the desert between Sudan and Libya, they [traffickers] left while we were sleeping. Then, we walked for some 2 days ... two young men died. We arrived at an oil refinery in the desert, where we were assisted. Police was called, and we ended up in jail for 4 months ... the prettiest girls used to be taken away and raped. A guy bought us, as you're not in jail for a crime. After that, he asked for money to release us ... It took us a lot of time to get from South to North Libya ... We had to wait for the sea to calm down, and we – men and women – had been locked in a house for almost a year ... you couldn't go out for fear of going to jail. Then, we were put into a container, and asked not to make noise. No one saw us landing, we arrived in a city, in Sicily, police arrived and took us to a reception centre in Trapani where we stayed for 20 days. As soon as we got our residence permits, they let us out of the door at 5 in the morning without knowing a word of Italian, with nothing, no money ... We walked to the station, and took a random train without knowing where we would arrive, and we got to Palermo ... After some two days, we left for Florence – a youngster fetched us at the station, and hosted us at his place in Signa. After four days, he said we had to leave ... We didn't know where to go, and he introduced us to a Somali girl ...

Sub-Saharan migrant women: a heterogeneous community

The LeFamSol target group are migrant women native to the sub-Saharan African region. The project considered two sub-Saharan communities, the former consisting of Nigerian women, the latter of female migrants native to the Horn of Africa. Such a rationale rests on the fact that the most significant population of African migrants, especially women, residing in the countries covered by the project, are Nigerians; the second most important community of sub-Saharan migrant women is the one coming from the Horn of Africa. By country, the picture is the following: Italy – Somalis, Nigerians, Eritreans; Turkey – Nigerians, Somalis; Greece – Nigerians, Ethiopians. The named are also among the most represented communities within the totality of African migrants in Italy, Turkey and Greece. Finally, the main target group has been added by other sub-Saharan nationalities in the last stages of the project.

The cluster of variables that should be taken into account while depicting the target group displays ample contours, both shared and unshared. In the set of shared features applying to the LeFamSol target group, the most transversal one is that they are *women*: thereby, it is essential to see how gender affects their condition in their native countries, communities, migration projects, etc. To be more precise, it is a matter of *African migrant women*: beyond its mere geographic demarcation, this characterization proves to be highly generic. Only if taken in some specific aspects and analysed more in detail, the *sub-Saharan African* denominator offers a set of intersection points: the target group is coming from unstable countries sharing certain historical and political circumstances (with inner differences); many (especially in the last decades) are fleeing from economic instability, socio-political insecurity, and, not seldom, armed conflicts.

Thereby, African migrants in Italy, Greece and Turkey are not a monolithic but *heterogeneous* community presenting a variety of *origins* and *backgrounds* (life conditions and socio-cultural aspects in their native contexts: social strata, religion, language skills, education, professional background, etc.), along with diverse *migration patterns* (push and pull factors). They are also variously distributed in the territories of their new settlement, being mostly represented in large urban centres. Depending on the context, their *condition in hosting societies* (mechanisms of exclusion/inclusion, especially labour and social integration) may or may not be shared by the LeFamSol target groups.

Receiving contexts vs sub-Saharan African migrants[13]

It is important to reckon the characteristics of receiving countries in relation to migration processes. According to the goals of the project, it was particularly relevant to analyse recent migrations to Italy, Greece and Turkey, female migrations, and flows coming from the sub-Saharan region, giving emphasis to the specificities of the target group.

Considering potential differences, it is important to understand what are the *push and pull factors* of sub-Saharan female migrations heading for Italy, Greece and Turkey, as well as for the rest of Europe. This implies an analysis of their migration projects and underlying reasons (socio-economic, cultural, study, family reunification, asylum/refugees, politics, war, trafficking, genital mutilation, etc.).

Each of the involved realities has a different migration profile, thus making it not conducive to adopt a unifying approach to the issue. To start, the statistics of the LeFamSol partners offer different national outcomes: broadly speaking, migrant women native to sub-Saharan Africa represent a relatively small but significant component of the flows moving towards South Europe. In this panorama, African and sub-Saharan migrant groups display a higher demographic significance in Italy for various reasons, including Italy's colonial past in Somalia and Eritrea; on the other hand, African migration is a relatively recent phenomenon in Greece and Turkey, hence the available data are less eloquent than in Italy. While Italy has a longer presence of African migrants (since the 1980s), recent shifts in migration trends in the Mediterranean have implied a growing number of African migrants in Greece and Turkey too.

Once in South Europe, African migrants may be given a different *status*: while women coming from the Horn of Africa can receive a refugee status, for Nigerian women this is more complicated, which is relevant for their social and economic integration. Besides, the Italian legal peculiarity, that does not seem to apply neither in Greece nor Turkey, distinguishes between residence and work permits. Those lacking in legal status have meagre chances of accessing health services (for example, being victims of trafficking particularly vulnerable to STDs – a condition particularly observed in Greece and Turkey). Along with that, their condition makes female African migrants susceptible to *exploitation* in terms of physical and sexual abuse, even by their employers and landlords (as observed by the Turkish partner).

Mechanisms of integration (exclusion/inclusion) into the receiving societies, especially in terms of *employment*, differ from one country to another too. Hence, the conditions they are facing (legal status, health condition, motherhood, etc.), particularly their social and professional integration in hosting societies, present several divergences that are best seen in the field of their labour integration.

African migrants have not many *employment opportunities* in Southern European countries: in fact, many of them are employed in the informal economy, which is actually an extremely visible phenomenon (peddling, selling umbrellas, water bottles or other goods), including the phenomenon of occupational 'ethnic niches' (e.g. the Senegalese in peddling). Other segments of African migrants, being mostly hired for low-skilled or unskilled jobs, are found in the service industry, agriculture, trade, and other sectors; the paper produced by Turkish partners speaks about Nigerians (in general) working in the garment industry in some regions of the country. Sub-Saharan migrant women share the same conditions. In the LeFamSol countries, their employment opportunities prove to be rather scarce. Unskilled jobs predominate, along with some *occupational niches*: some are engaged in domestic service and care work (e.g. Eritrean women working as maids and care-givers in Italian families) or in the entertainment sector (e.g. Nigerian women, some of whom are victims of trafficking).

Typologies of labour integration of sub-Saharan African women in the host countries are interrelated with their *in/visibility*. Broadly speaking, the reality of migrant women is defined as a 'triple oppression: social, economic and cultural' (Campani 2007: 5–6), which is due to their general condition in emigration, their employment in the private (domestic) sector, and absence from the public sphere. Female African migrants are simultaneously depicted as the most visible and invisible group of migrant women, and intersectionally vulnerable group, hence deserving special attention (Turkish report). To boot, the perception of *racism* in combination with their visibility is quite pronounced in all the partner countries, even if the Greek and Turkish cases present additional challenges. Such a situation is mainly due to their somatic visibility or to particular socio-economic niches some are involved in. Thereby, African women face various difficulties in the host societies ranging from regularization procedures to employment, housing, health service and discrimination.

In conclusion, the *level of social integration* is strongly dependent on the cluster of actions promoted by organizations (associations, NGOs, political groups) active in anti-racism and implementing activities aimed at vulnerable people, along with solidarity and mutual support networks made up by migrants themselves or along with other groups.

Sub-Saharan Africans in Turkey: from transit migration to precarious settlement[14]

Its geostrategic position makes Turkey an ideal transit country. As a relatively new phenomenon, African transit migration to Turkey has not received the necessary attention so far, given the fact that it is rather small compared to other forms of migration. Still, with the reinforcement of Fortress Europe and the closing of the border in Evros, it has also become a country of settlement for Asian and African migrants. Besides, Turkey has been touched by an increasing number of women among transit migrants, including Africans.

The irregular nature of transit migrations pushes African migrants into invisibility, thus decreasing their traceability, and making it difficult to gather specific data and statistics on the issue. Thereby, researches and surveys, reaching only a limited number of African migrants, are far from reflecting their demographic reality. As for the LeFamSol target group, Nigerians and Somalis have been among the most represented within the totality of African migrants in Turkey in the last decade.

The 1995 IOM Report speaks about 2,000 African transit migrants by the mid-1990s; in this scope, 380 African asylum seekers, native to Ethiopia, Ghana, Nigeria and Somalia, were registered in Turkey in the 1983–91 period. The results of the survey indicate that Africans left their countries due to economic (56 per cent) and political (56 per cent) reasons, and the risk of war (46 per cent). The 2003 IOM Report enumerates 704 asylum seekers from both Africa and Asia in 2001. This time, grounds for leaving Africa were: political reasons (significantly increased, 97.1 per cent), followed by social, cultural, religious motivations

(66.7 per cent), and armed conflict (66.7 per cent). Reasons for coming to Turkey were instead: 45.5 per cent by error, and 30 per cent the low costs of living in Turkey (İçduygu 2003; İçduygu and Aksel 2012).

A survey by Yükseker and Brewer (2005) on African migrants in Istanbul shows that most of them entered Turkey illegally: while 66 per cent of African migrants participating in the survey stated that they had entered Turkey illegally (the majority of Somalis, Mauritanians, Eritreans and Ethiopians), 34 per cent of them declared that they had entered the country by legal means (the majority of Nigerians, Congolese and Kenyans). The way of entering the country also varied by nationality: Nigerians (45.7 per cent) were the biggest group to arrive by air, followed by the Congolese (19.6 per cent) and Kenyans (10.9 per cent); the majority of Africans reaching Turkey by boat or by foot were Somalis, Eritreans and Burundis, with a remarkable percentage of Ethiopians arriving by foot (37.5 per cent). A large number of respondents (40.8 per cent) claimed that they came to Turkey as they were 'told they would be taken to Greece but were left in Turkey', which was especially the case for Somalis and Mauritanians (80 per cent of them), and for more than a half of Eritreans. As for their gender distribution, 41.3 per cent of the respondents were female; though being a minority in most of the African groups, women were the majority among Somalian, Eritrean and Ethiopian migrants.

The report *Apprehended Irregular Migrants by Nationality* (produced by the Bureau for Foreigners, Borders and Asylum at the Directorate of General Security, Ministry of Interior) provides information on irregular migration to Turkey. According to the statistics from 2003 to 2011, Somalis are the most apprehended African migrant group, followed by Mauritanians and Eritreans; Nigerians present quite small and decreasing numbers. And while the number of apprehended Somalis and Mauritanians has significantly decreased over the last years, the number of Eritreans has increased since 2007, up to 1.308 Eritreans in 2012 as the largest apprehended African group, followed by Somalis (677) (İçduygu 2003; İçduygu and Aksel 2012).

Another important source to measure African migration to Turkey are asylum applications. The UNHCR data (Ankara Office) show that Somalis (2,385) and Sudanese (334) were the largest asylum-seeker groups from Africa in the 1995–2009 period. The number of Somali refugees and asylum seekers increased in the last five years. According to the *Active Caseload Breakdown by Gender and Age* (UNHCR Turkey 2013), Somali refugees, as for April 2013, formed 8 per cent of all refugees (1,757 people), and 3 per cent of all asylum seekers (413 people). While examining these data, it is important to know that many Africans, once apprehended, declare themselves to be Somalis so as to have a higher probability of getting asylum. In addition, 58 per cent of refugees and 63 per cent of asylum seekers were in the 18–59 age group, while 50 per cent of refugees and 43 per cent of asylum seekers were women.

Despite relatively small numbers of African migrants in Turkey, their presence gives us information on the relationship between the nature of transit migration, security concerns and human rights. The main problems faced by African migrants are the following: lack of access to legal work permits, implying the lack of income and involvement in the illegal labour market; no access to social and humanitarian assistance; exploitation and extreme poverty; racial discrimination, accompanied by the trend to be stereotyped as criminals (drug dealers or stolen-item sellers), both by the media and state officials; a clear prejudice translated into different forms of physical or symbolic violence (glimpses, verbal insults, sexually offensive behaviour, mistreatment); rather than being a focus of curiosity, their skin makes them a target for various forms of harassment perpetuated by the police (scrutiny, robbery, beatings, threats of detention and deportation) – the existing idea associates dark skin, i.e. the African migrant in Turkey, with irregular status, and hence a lack of rights.

African migrants in Turkey lack solidarity and social networks. West Africans, such as Ghanaians and Nigerians, are the only ones to have strong social networks organized through churches. There are very few places where migrants may seek assistance in Turkey. These include a limited number of Christian churches, refugee support programmes, the UNHCR, human rights associations, and solidarity networks. These organizations provide legal aid, refugee advocacy, counselling, medical assistance, assistance to migrant women with small children and pregnant women, material support when needed (food, clothing), etc.

For many other Africans, racial discrimination, exploitation, extreme poverty, no healthcare, along with the lack of solidarity and social networks, is the reality that puts them in a particularly vulnerable position by exposing them to the risk of hunger, disease and abuse. Along with the lack of legal long-term stay possibility in Turkey, these conditions push many of them to continue their journey to the EU.

African women constitute, simultaneously, the most visible and invisible group of migrant women in Turkey. African migration to Turkey being relatively new, their (somatic) visibility attracts a certain attention and curiosity; still, they are socially very isolated, mostly because of their irregular status in the country. The discrimination they are affected by is not based on their race and gender only: African migrant women are very vulnerable to the potential risks and human rights violations caused by the precarious nature of transit migration and lack of rights, creating unsafe working and living conditions. Studies on Somali and Ethiopian migrants indicates that many African women encounter problems such as robbery, physical violence and sexual abuse during their stay in Turkey.

As an intersectional group, African migrant women need to be provided with accessible and affordable health services irrespective of their legal status in order to lessen their vulnerability. The lack of legal status increases their risks of violence and sexual assault; besides, their social invisibility, produced by their irregular status, reduces their access to the necessary healthcare (e.g. maternal health care, contraceptive services, safe abortion).

According to Turkish legislation, irregular migrants and asylum seekers are not granted a work permit. The lack of regular job opportunities reduces their access to public benefits, and forces migrant women into the informal labour market, including prostitution, which increases their vulnerability to exploitation.

The most common work among irregular migrant women is domestic work providing care services. Still, this sector is dominated by migrant women from ex-Soviet countries. Irregularity, which equates to lack of rights in Turkey, puts these women in a very vulnerable position with their employers: working with no social benefits or security, their salary is susceptible to manipulation and exploitation.

Sub-Saharan Africans in economically afflicted Greece[15]

Deeply affected by the economic and political crisis that produced massive unemployment and poverty, especially since 2010, Greece has concurrently turned into a main gateway for migrants on their way to Europe. In the last years, the Turkish–Greek border has become particularly 'popular' due to the Syrian civil war and the crisis in Libya. In response to an increasing number of attempts to cross the frontier, Greek border guards started being supported by the EU Frontex Agency. The reinforcement of controls at the land borders, particularly in Evros, forced migrants to try out novel – and risky – routes from Turkey to Bulgaria, or by sea crossing the Bosporus, or directly to the Greek islands of Kos, Kios and Samos.

What happens at the Evros border was denounced in 2011 by the organization Human Rights Watch in a report entitled *Greece: The EU's Dirty Hands*. Abuses of migrants, and especially women, in Greek asylum and detention centres are described in the report: Europe's border police has been knowingly aiding the serial abuse of migrants during its first major deployment on the EU frontiers. 'Frontex has become a partner in exposing migrants to treatment that it knows is absolutely prohibited under human rights law,' said Bill Frelick, Refugee Program director at Human Rights Watch (2011, web press). The report highlighted alarming conditions in detention centres in north-eastern Greece close to the Turkish border, with men and women herded together in overcrowded cells, allegations of rape, and unaccompanied minors dumped in packed 'cages' with adult males.

In 2011, the European Court of Human Rights found Greece guilty of breaking the European Convention on Human Rights, and also ruled that any EU state sending illegal immigrants to Greece had 'knowingly exposed [them] to conditions of detention and living conditions that amounted to degrading treatment' (Human Rights Watch 2011: 47).

In this context, African/sub-Saharan migrants are facing huge difficulties in a country that was thought by many of them to be a transit one. Their major problems are related to acquisition and retention of residence permits; unemployment; housing; social integration; citizenship rights; acquisition of Greek language skills; lack of bureaucratic orientation; racism, and especially institutional racism within the Greek state.

Among various African communities, Nigerians and Ethiopians are the only sizeable groups in Greece. The vast majority of sub-Saharan Africans are concentrated in the Athens region (92.2 per cent) and especially at the centre of Athens.

In such a scenario, networks and associations founded by African/sub-Saharan migrants are a recent phenomenon, being basically concentrated in Athens: 57 per cent of associations are founded after 2005, while 92 per cent of sub-Saharan African associations (51) are based in Athens, especially in the city centre.

As far as employment is concerned, the large majority of Ethiopians, Senegalese, Nigerians and Ghanaians are employed in Greece; this is not the case for Somalis, which is probably connected to their short average stay in the country. Some groups are represented in particular occupational niches: thus, Ethiopians and Senegalese work as street vendors, while employees are more likely to be Nigerians and Ghanaians. On the whole, African men and women are largely represented in unskilled and manual labour, African women being much more represented in unskilled labour, as well as in services.

According to the 2011 data, 7,609 African women were present in Greece. The majority of them were Egyptians (2,411 women), followed by Nigerians and Ethiopians, as the only national groups counting more than 1,000 women. As far as the LeFamSol target group is concerned, Nigerians were 1,196, Ethiopians 1,164, Somalis 196 and Eritreans 144 (Census 2011). However, statistical data on this migrant group are particularly unreliable, offering mostly 'trends' rather than a basis for a policy development.

According to the Greek reports, Nigerians constitute a major part of sub-Saharan African women in Greece, hence their larger visibility and participation in African women's associations. Though being an organized community, many (usually underage girls) are victims of trafficking being used for the purposes of drug dealing and working in the sex market. As for Somali women, they are difficult to approach, theirs being a closed community having meagre contacts with other African communities or autochthonous population. Yet, some changes in attitudes have been observed in young generations (especially those under 20). Somalis view their stay in Greece as a transit point on their northward route, with the usual destination being Sweden which hosts a much bigger Somali community.

Domestic services are dominated by migrant women, who constitute one of the most vulnerable groups as their work is often undervalued. Thereby, they are often exempted from health insurance. Similarly, women asylum seekers are often denied female interpreters, medical assistance and gynaecological care. Besides, migrant women may be subject to sex and gender-based discrimination, such as mandatory HIV or other testing without their consent, as well as sexual and physical abuse by agents or escorts during transit. Accordingly, the main conclusion of the CEDAW report on Greece (United Nations 2013) is that migrant women are exposed to specific challenges in the field of health.

Sub-Saharan Africans in Italy: community organization and commitment[16]

The reality of African migration is not a new phenomenon in Italy: it particularly applies to the Horn of Africa, Senegal, Morocco, Egypt, Nigeria, and other nationalities whose citizens have been migrating to Italy since the 1970/1980s. Despite specificities of single communities, there is a certain level of social mobilization (associations, NGOs, parties) in Italy. Several African national groups have been making attempts at organizing themselves since the very beginning of their migration experience in Italy. Amid various forms of community organization, associations have constituted a useful resource to provide solidarity and support networks among African migrants. Though being present all over the Italian territory, the bulk of African migrants is settled in larger urban centres, especially in the centre and north of the country, where they are socio-culturally and politically organized.

The will to be organized has led African migrants to create their own associations, parties, networks, founded on various grounds: community, ethnic, national; inter-ethnic, multinational, i.e. mixed-African (e.g. *Associazione Donne dell'Africa Subsahariana* in Milan – the Sub-Saharan African Women's Association (ADAS)); international, i.e. mixed with other migrant groups; mixed with Italian citizens. These structures are further defined by their affiliation (associations/ networks made up of students, youth, workers, professional groupings, etc.), and commitment (socio-cultural promotion, voluntary work, struggle for rights and equality, etc.). From a gender perspective, male, female and mixed-gender organizations are all found in this arena. Finally, religious aggregation with churches, having main centres in Rome, is another pattern of community organization (particularly Eritrean, Ethiopian and Nigerian communities).

Some organizations are established on rather informal grounds; this is often the case for associations acting as an inner tool of community organizing and governing. In other cases, African migrants have been organized so as to create a national level of community networking, for example the *Ass. Donne somale in Italia* (Somali Women's Association in Italy), or *Comunità Eritrea in Italia* (Eritrean Community in Italy), with the possibility of local branches, for example the *Comunità Eritrea in Toscana* (Eritrean Community in Tuscany), *Comunità Somala in Toscana* (Somali Community in Tuscany), Nigerian Citizen's Community (Tuscany) – or, more generally, the *Federazione Africana in Toscana* (African Federation in Tuscany).

In this panorama, organizations and support networks among African women have not been missing either. Broadly speaking, migrant women organizations tend to reproduce the specific migration history of single national groups (associations of women native to Cape Verde and the Horn of Africa have existed since the 1980s), and to reflect the degree of group cohesion and inner gender relationships (female or mixed-gender associations). Migrant women are frequently gathered on a gender basis in multi-ethnic associations, often including Italian members, with the goal of supporting migrant women in achieving their rights, and developing specific skills in providing welfare services to the migrant population. Women native to sub-Saharan regions (e.g. Somalia, Eritrea, Nigeria) count experiences in this sector as well: whether they are involved with female, community, national, mixed, or other sort of associations, they play a key role in the socio-cultural life of their communities, and beyond.

Regarding the scope of action, the situation is rather varied. As already mentioned, the profiles of African associations are variously defined – they can be national, African or mixed; male, female or mixed; in relation to Italian territory, they reach local, regional, interregional or national level. Some of them rely on other structures (authorities, NGOs, associations, churches, etc.) operating in the field, making common efforts in presenting themselves and their activities (e.g. information, press, public presentations, conferences).

Accordingly, community cohesion is defined by the same set of factors and priorities dictating the scope of action that a single organization or a group of organizations may cover. On these grounds, their activities will be further diversified, meaning that associations organized at the national level (for instance) have different prospects of action in comparison with locally contextualized structures; the same can be said for mixed and nation (community) based associations. Starting from the cluster of *priority needs*, the activities of African communities are aimed at promoting inner cohesion and solidarity; cooperation with the surrounding social context; socio-cultural activities; communication, information and exchange activities; educational activities; struggle for peace; struggle for rights and equality.

Frequently organizations develop contacts and relationships, even if only temporarily, with each other, often in the frames of specific projects and programmes. The group of female African migrants involved with the LeFamSol Project in Italy are chiefly active on a local (city, municipality, province, regional) level. As for the stakeholders involved, many of them have a larger action history – on the same grounds, some of the female African migrants have experienced involvement in activities of a greater extent as members of particular structures operating in the field. In this sense, some African associations have been rather active, as well as some mixed organizations involving (in various ways and to various extents) female African migrants into their activities (projects, programmes, cooperation, campaigns etc.).

As envisaged by the LeFamSol Project, women native to Nigeria, Somalia and Eritrea, as well as other countries such as Senegal, Mali, Burkina Faso, Ivory Coast and Cameroon, were involved into the project activities (meetings, interviews, informal talks, focus groups, training, conferences) that provided important information on the topic. Accordingly, we conclude this chapter by presenting some findings in the form of observations and remarks as expressed by the contacted women. The aspects that have been remarkably stressed by them are the following:

- *Visibility and participation*: though being in continuous growth, African and generally migrant associations have a little weight in policy-making and decision-making in Italy; as for Greece and Turkey, such structures are in a rather initial stage of their life. These variables often preclude African migrants, especially women, from reaching an adequate social visibility and active participation, which in turn deepens their exposure to vulnerability. Finally, their condition makes women susceptible to trafficking, exploitation and abuse, putting them in a particularly vulnerable position.

- *Specific needs of female African migrants*: activities promoted by African associations and related organizations are linked to specific requirements based on the needs claimed by the community of sub-Saharan migrant women in relation to the context of their host societies, namely particular attention to female segments of African communities; reception and protection; attention to their specific needs and rights; attention to specific sectors where they can be exploited as women; specific healthcare; legal assistance.
- *Sustainability and continuity*: what was pointed out as a fleeting aspect in research and action projects (in general) is a meagre potential of their sustainability and continuity, hence the need for sustainable cooperation between all social actors in order to provide more effective services to the community of female African migrants.
- *Remarks to ethnic/nation-based networks*: some women expressed their remarks regarding ethnic and/or nation-based networks: they agree that this form of networking may bring people together, yet it entails risks of reducing a person to 'her/his' ethnic and/or national space, and may imply risks for some individuals, women included, who have escaped from hostile conditions in their countries, or have suffered particular migration experiences.
- *Self-help desk as a good practice*: women stated that a self-help desk could be a useful tool of guidance and positioning: while solidarity networks, information points and reception centres are not a novelty in the Italian context (though they are in Greece and Turkey), the idea of creating a self-help desk for female African migrants with particular migration experiences and needs is generally judged as a good practice.
- *Employment*: regarding the need of a job, in combination with other hardships faced by migrants, in particular female African migrants, women contacted by the University of Florence team stated that they were quite happy with the reception and guidance they were given in Italy (this is not the case for Greece and Turkey). Still, the economic crisis brings a number of difficulties, the situation being even harder for newly arrived migrants, especially female African migrants: language barriers (at least initially) coupled with xenophobia take them to unemployment or employment in the irregular market. In the light of difficulties finding a long-term job, some women – especially those involved in various forms of social work – expressed their doubts regarding the sustainability of mediation and guidance activities.
- *Pending difficulties and issues*: many African migrants experience difficulties in interacting with the host society, constantly facing pending issues that range from race-based discriminatory attitudes to labour exploitation; some encounter difficulties in approaching services dealing with healthcare, housing and refugee/asylum status.

Conclusion

In the border cases touched on in this chapter, migrant women's testimonies show how processes of enclosure and mobility intersect and produce continuous violations of basic human rights. Risk of death and violence at border crossings are followed by risks and instability both at external (Turkey) and internal borders (Italy and Greece).

Research conducted in the frames of the LeFamSol Project, addressing female migration from sub-Saharan Africa, has brought about conceptualizing the idea of the European border as consisting of multiple borders: in practical terms, it is about the external border whose management is assured by the non-EU states in agreement with the EU member states, and an internal border dividing the North and the South of Europe, the latter being represented by the Mediterranean countries where migrants first arrive. Moreover, the 'internal border' implies the existence of specific forms of detention centres and precarious settlements that can last from a few months to several years, producing – in some cases – niches of survival.

And, this is the limbo that sub-Saharan African women find themselves trapped in after risking their lives by crossing the Sahara Desert and the Mediterranean Sea. Only a radical improvement in living standards of many sub-Saharan countries would stem the flow of desperate people heading from Africa to Europe. Yet, this is not likely to happen in the near future: Africa is strewn with conflicts, unstable situations, socio-economic and political crises, while Europe has a crisis feeding the rise of populist anti-immigration parties and xenophobia across the Continent.

Characteristics of single communities, combined with the specificities emerging from their migration experience, are to be taken into account: an analysis of their migration experience (including concomitant effects in receiving societies) gives an idea of their coping strategies in emigration contexts. In this perspective, the existence of solidarity networks and the engagement of associations can be viewed through the prism of survival strategies.

Such a state of affairs leaves little opportunity for change. What it is possible to do with and for a specific group – sub-Saharan African women in a migration context – is to develop, as predicted by the LeFamSol methodology, a particular survival strategy, namely networking competence in a gender-aware perspective with a network facilitator as a key social actor.

Notes

1 A map by Nicolas Lambert; see Migreurop (2012: 144).
2 Human history has been marked by walls: from the Great Wall of China to the Antonine Wall and Hadrian's Wall, built in the northern portion of Roman Britain to strengthen the Roman defences; more recently, from the Berlin Wall to the one dividing Cyprus in Greek and Turkish parts.
3 See: http://frontex.europa.eu/.
4 Jean Ziegler, for example, qualified Frontex as '*organisation militaire quasi-clandestine*' (see Ziegler 2008, quoted therefrom by a number of organizations e.g. UNHCR, Migreurop, BugBrother).
5 See: http://frontex.europa.eu/partners/third-countries.
6 The notion of Europe and the EU differ from each other: whereas Europe is a geographical area, the EU constitutes a political and institutional structure.
7 *Mare nostrum*, lit. 'Our Sea', as called by Romans.

8 See: UNITED for Intercultural Action, European Network against nationalism, racism, fascism and in support of migrants and refugees (www.unitedagainstracism.org/campaigns/refugee-campaign/fortress-europe/). UNITED is observing the phenomenon near Lampedusa, Malta and the Greek islands of Kos, Kios and Samos, as well as at the junction between the Bosporus and the Black Sea, and other localities.

9 See: UNHCR (www.unhcr.org).

10 The Arab Spring, or *Ar-rabī⁽ al-⁽arabī* in Arabic, is a revolutionary movement that has hit the Arab world in the last years. The phenomenon commenced in Tunisia in 2010 (18 December), and spread throughout the countries of North Africa and South-west Asia in the form of demonstrations and protests (both non-violent and violent), riots, unrests and civil wars; followed by a series of reforms in some places. While it is generally deemed to have ended by mid-2012, the ongoing conflicts in the Middle East and North Africa are regarded as a continuation of the Arab Spring, at times referred to as the Arab Winter – i.e. the aftermath of revolutions and civil wars.

11 Before the conflicts and destabilization of the region, migration routes used to cross Iraq and Syria too.

12 African migrants, choosing Morocco as their destination or point of transit, are mainly native to Central and Western Africa (less to other regions). As regards the female portion, several reports state that most African migrant women in Morocco are citizens of Nigeria and the Democratic Republic of Congo, followed by women from Angola, Cameroon, Congo-Brazzaville, Ivory Coast, Mali and Niger. In recent years, a certain concentration of African migrants, especially women, has been observed in the North, chiefly in the region of Tangier. Various local, national and international organisms, NGOs and associations, are active in the sector with particular attention to the reality of Tangier: they offer their contribution in form of research, assistance, expertise or other support. Nonetheless, the condition of African migrants continues to be precarious, and tensions (also linked to racist attitudes) are also present (see Cherti and Grant 2013; De Haas 2005, 2014; Lahlou 2005; Amnesty International 2006; Women's Link Worldwide 2012; Human Rights Watch 2005; Caminando Fronteras/Walking Borders, web).

13 This section is based on the LeFamSol reports by Lapov (Del. 2.2, 8 June 2014), and LeFamSol Consortium (Del. 2.1, 26 May 2014).

14 This section is based on the LeFamSol report by LeFamSol Consortium (Del. 2.1, 26 May 2014).

15 This section is based on the LeFamSol report by LeFamSol Consortium (Del. 2.1, 26 May 2014).

16 This section is based on the LeFamSol reports by Lapov (Del. 2.7, 30 June 2014; Del. 4.3, 30 September 2014; Del. 4.4, 30 September 2014).

Bibliography

ACODI. 2009. *Shedding Light on the Invisible / Los derechos de las mujeres migrantes: una realidad invisible* (Report). Action Against Discrimination Project (ACODI) by Open Society Justice Initiative, SOS Racismo Madrid, and Women's Link Worldwide.

Aden Sheikh, M. and Petrucci, P. 1991. *Arrivederci a Mogadiscio*. Roma: Edizioni Associate.

Baldwin-Edwards, M. 2006. 'Between a rock and a hard place: North Africa as a region of emigration, immigration and transit migration'. *Review of African Political Economy* 33(108): 311–24.

Baldwin-Edwards, M. and Zampagni, F. 2014. *Regularisations and Employment in Italy*. REGANE Assessment Report. Vienna: ICMPD.

Bonanni, G., ed. 2014. *Migranti - Il Vademecum*. XIV Ed. Comune di Firenze.

Campani, G. 2007. *Gender and Migration in Italy: State of the Art*. Working Paper No. 6 – WP4. FeMiPol Project. Frankfurt: University of Frankfurt.

Carchedi, F. 2004. 'Immigrazione e riduzione in schiavitù'. In P. Cendon, ed., *Diritti della persona. Tutela civile, politica*, Vol. 1, 485–92. Roma: Utet.

Carchedi, F. *et al.*, eds. 2000. *I colori della notte: migrazioni, sfruttamento sessuale, esperienze di intervento sociale*. Milano: FrancoAngeli.

Censis. 2013. *Immigrazione e presenza straniera in Italia*. Rapporto Sopemi Italia 2012–2013. Roma.

Census of Greece. 2011. Athens: Government of Greece.

Ceschi, S. and Lulli, F. 2012. 'Migrazioni femminili dall'Africa. Percorsi di inserimento e dinamiche identitarie'. In S. Ceschi, ed., *Movimenti migratori e percorsi di cooperazione. L'esperienza di co-sviluppo di Fondazioni4Africa-Senegal*. Roma: Carocci.

CeSPI. 2009. *L'Africa in Italia tra integrazione e co-sviluppo. Verso il I Forum della diaspora africana*. Documenti dei Workshop: Sociale-associativo, Economico, Politico e Culturale. Roma: Provincia di Roma/CeSPI.

Cherti, M. 2013. 'British stories of Nigerian Cinderellas are no fairy tale'. *The Independent*.

Cherti, M. and Grant, P. 2013. *The Myth of Transit, Sub-Saharan Migration in Morocco*. London: Institute for Public Policy Research.

Cole, J. 2006. 'Society reducing the damage: dilemmas of anti-trafficking efforts among Nigerian prostitutes in Palermo'. *Anthropologica* 48(2): 217–28.

Council of Europe. 2008. *Immigration from Sub-Saharan Africa*. Council of Europe Parliamentary Assembly, 11 February 2008.

Farah, N. 2003. *Rifugiati: Voci dalla Diaspora Somala*. Roma: Meltemi.

Fernández Rodríguez de Liévana, G., Montañez, P. S. *et al.*, eds. 2014. *La trata de mujeres y niñas nigerianas: esclavitud entre fronteras y prejuicios*. Women's Link Worldwide.

Fullin, G. 2012. 'Per un'etnicizzazione degli studi sul mercato del lavoro italiano. Alcuni esempi in tema di disoccupazione e segregazione occupazionale'. *Sociologia del lavoro* 126: 53–70.

Ghidei Biidu, D. and Hagos, E. 2010. 'Io noi voi intervista a donne della diaspora eritrea nell'Italia postcoloniale'. *Zapruder. Storie in movimento* 23: 144–52.

Human Rights Watch. 2011. *Greece: The EU's Dirty Hands. Frontex Involvement in Ill-Treatment of Migrant Detainees in Greece*. New York.

İçduygu, A. 2003. *Irregular Migration in Turkey*. IOM Migration Research Series. Ankara: Bilkent University.

İçduygu, A. 2005. *Transit Migration in Turkey: Trends, Patterns and Issues*. CARIM-RR, Robert Schuman Centre for Advanced Studies. San Domenico di Fiesole (FI): European University Institute.

İçduygu, A. and Aksel, D. B. 2012. *Irregular Migration in Turkey*. Ankara: IOM in Turkey.

İçduygu, A. and Yükseker, D. 2012. 'Rethinking transit migration in Turkey: reality and re-presentation in the creation of a migratory phenomenon'. *Population, Space and Place* 18(4): 441–56.

Istat. 2011a. *Grado di istruzione della popolazione straniera*. Roma.

Istat. 2011b. *Italy's Resident Foreign Population*. Roma.

Istat. 2014. *Employment and Unemployment (provisional estimates)*. Roma.

Kastner, K. 2013. 'Nigerian border crossers: women travelling to Europe by land'. In A. Triulzi and R. McKenzie, eds, *Long Journeys: African Migrants on the Road*, 25–44. Leiden: Brill.

Kiggundu, I. E. S. and De Vries, G. 2014. *Strengthening Multilateral Cooperation in the Era of Globalization*. European Council Study Guide. UNISAMUN – University of Salerno Model United Nations.

King, R., ed. 2001. *The Mediterranean Passage: Migration and New Cultural Encounters in Southern Europe*. Liverpool University Press.

King, R., Lazaridis, G. and Tsardanidis, C. G., eds. 1999. *Eldorado or Fortress? Migration in Southern Europe*. London: Palgrave Macmillan.

Lahlou, M. 2005. *Migrations irrégulières transméditerranéennes et relations et Maroc - Union européenne*, XXVe Congrès international de la population, 18–23 July 2005. Tours.

Marchetti, S. 2011. *Le ragazze di Asmara. Lavoro domestico e migrazione postcoloniale*, Roma: Ediesse.

Médicos sin Fronteras (MSF). 2010. *Violencia Sexual y Migración. La realidad oculta de las mujeres subsaharianas atrapadas en Marruecos de camino a Europa*. MSF.

Mezzetti, P., Guglielmo, M. 2010. 'Somali organisations in Italy'. In A. Warnecke, ed., *Diasporas and Peace*, 16–31. Bonn: BICC.

Migreurop. 2012. *Atlas des migrants en Europe. Géographie critique des politiques migratoires*. Paris: Armand Colin.

Nanni, M. P. 2010. 'I migranti africani nel mondo del lavoro dipendente italiano. Un quadro di insieme'. In *Africa-Italia. Scenari Migratori*, CARITAS. Roma: Idos.

OECD. 2013. *International Migration Outlook 2013*. OECD Publishing.

Petrini, B. 2009. *Comunità nigeriana e organizzazione dello spazio-tempo a Roma*. Roma: Aracne.

Primi, M., Bavar, N. and Picchi, G. 2006. *Nuova cittadinanza. Mappa per turisti molto speciali: i passeggeri, gli ospiti e gli abitanti della città – Guida aggiornata al dicembre 2006*. Firenze: Edizioni Polistampa.

Pugliese, E. 2011. 'The Mediterranean model of immigration'. *Academicus – International Scientific Journal* 3: 96–107.

RMMS. 2013. *Migrant Smuggling in the Horn of Africa & Yemen: The Political Economy and Protection Risks*. Mixed Migration Research Series, Study 1. RMMS (Regional Mixed Migration Secretariat).

Rodier, C. 2012. *Xenophobie Business*. Paris: La Découverte.

Toma, S. and Vause, S. 2010. 'Gender differences in the role of migrant networks in Congolese and Senegalese international migration'. African Migrations Workshop, The Contribution of African Research to Migration Theory, 16–19 November 2010. Dakar.

Triandafyllidou, A. and Maroukis, T. 2012. *Migrant Smuggling: Irregular Migration from Asia and Africa to Europe*. London: Palgrave Macmillan.

United Nations. 2013. 'Concluding observations on the seventh periodic report of Greece adopted by the Committee at its fifty fourth session (11 February–1 March 2013)'. Convention on the Elimination of All Forms of Discrimination against Women (CEDAW). Committee on the Elimination of Discrimination against Women.

Warnecke, A., ed. 2010. *Diasporas and Peace: A Comparative Assessment of Somali and Ethiopian Communities in Europe*. Bonn: BICC.

Women's Link Worldwide. 2012. *Migrant Women in Hiding: Clandestine Abortion in Morocco / Mujeres migrantes en la clandestinidad: El aborto en Marruecos*. WLW.

Yükseker, D. and Brewer, K. T. 2005. *A Survey on African Migrants and Asylum Seekers in Istanbul*. MiReKoc Research Projects 2005–2006. Istanbul.

Ziegler, J. 2008. 'Réfugiés de la faim'. *Le Monde diplomatique*, Mars 2008.

LeFamSol reports and deliverables

Lapov, Z. *A Focus Group Delineation Strategy for a Female African Migrants' Curriculum* (Del. 2.2, 8 June 2014).

Lapov, Z. *National Focus Groups Delineation Progress Reports – Italy* (Del. 2.7, 30 June 2014).

Lapov, Z. *National Stakeholders' Networks Outreach Assessment – Italy* (Del. 4.3, 30 September 2014).

Lapov, Z. *National FAM Networks Outreach Assessment – Italy* (Del. 4.4, 30 September 2014).

LeFamSol Consortium. *Summary Report based on National Reflection Papers*, including *National Reports and relevant Literature Review* (Del. 2.1, 26 May 2014).

Online sources

Amnesty International. 2006. *Spain and Morocco: Failure to Protect the Rights of Migrants in Ceuta and Melilla One Year On*, 25 October. www.amnesty.org/en/library/asset/EUR41/009/2006/en/6bad2145-d3e6-11dd-8743-d305bea2b2c7/eur410092006en.html.

Amnesty International. 2014a. *The Human Cost of Fortress Europe: Human Rights Violations against Migrants and Refugees at Europe's Borders*, 9 July, London. www.amnesty.org/en/documents/EUR05/001/2014/en/.

Amnesty International. 2014b. *Vite alla deriva: Rifugiati e migranti a rischio nel Mediterraneo centrale*, Rome. www.amnesty.it/flex/FixedPages/pdf/Vite_alla_deriva_ita_summary.pdf.

Amnesty International. 2015. *Search and Rescue Operations in the Central Mediterranean: Facts and Figures*, September. www.amnesty.org/en/articles/news/2014/09/search-and-rescue-operations-central-mediterranean-facts-and-figures/.

BBC News. 2007. *Key Facts: Africa to Europe Migration*, July. http://news.bbc.co.uk/2/hi/europe/6228236.stm.

BBC News. 2014. *Mapping Mediterranean Migration*, September. www.bbc.com/news/world-europe-24521614.

Choe, J. 2007. *African Migration to Europe*. Council on Foreign Relations (CFR), 10 July. www.cfr.org/world/african-migration-europe/p13726.

Countryeconomy.com. 2014. *Greece Unemployment Rate*, December. http://countryeconomy.com/unemployment/greece.

De Haas, H. 2005. *Morocco: From Emigration Country to Africa's Migration Passage to Europe*, PROFILE, October. www.migrationpolicy.org/article/morocco-emigration-country-africas-migration-passage-europe.

De Haas, H. 2014. *Morocco: Setting the Stage for Becoming a Migration Transition Country?*, PROFILE, March. www.migrationpolicy.org/article/morocco-setting-stage-becoming-migration-transition-country.

Dore, G. M. D. 2014. 'Huddled masses yearning – Europe's immigration crisis'. *The American Interest*, 5 September. www.the-american-interest.com/2014/09/05/europes-immigration-crisis/.

Frenzen, N. 2015. 'Very few migrants reaching Italy apply for asylum'. *Migrants at Sea* (blog), January. http://migrantsatsea.org/.

Frenzen, N. 2015. 'Turkish coast guard reports intercepting 12,872 migrants in Aegean Sea in 2014'. *Migrants at Sea* (blog), January. http://migrantsatsea.org/.

Frenzen, N. 2015. 'Some migrants pushed-back into Turkish territorial waters'. *Migrants at Sea* (blog), January. http://migrantsatsea.org/.

Frenzen, N. 2015. 'Frontex: preliminary figures indicate 270,000 irregular migrants and asylum seekers reached EU in 2104 – double previous record set in 2011'. *Migrants at Sea* (blog), January. http://migrantsatsea.org/.

Frenzen, N. 2015. 'UNHCR: urgent European action needed in Mediterranean'. *Migrants at Sea* (blog), January. http://migrantsatsea.org/.

Human Rights Watch. 2005. *Spain: Deportations to Morocco Put Migrants at Risk. Violence against Migrants in Ceuta and Melilla Requires Independent Investigation*, October. www.hrw.org/en/news/2005/10/12/spain-deportations-morocco-put-migrants-risk.

Human Rights Watch. 2011. *EU: Border Agency Exposes Migrants to Abusive Conditions. Frontex Sends Migrants to Inhuman and Degrading Treatment in Greek Detention Centers*, 21 September. www.hrw.org/news/2011/09/21/eu-border-agency-exposes-migrants-abusive-conditions.

Inequality Watch. *Poverty in Europe: The Current Situation* (2010 data), Inequality Watch – the European observatory of inequality. www.inequalitywatch.eu/spip.php?article99&lang=en.

International Organization for Migration. 2011. *Situation in Over-crowded Reception Centre on Lampedusa Remains Difficult*, 15 February, IOM Rome. www.iom.ch/cms/en/sites/iom/home/news-and-views/press-briefing-notes/pbn-2011/pbn-listing/situation-in-overcrowded-reception-cent.html.

UNHCR. *Asylum and Migration – All in the same boat: The challenges of mixed migration.* www.unhcr.org/pages/4a1d406060.html.

UNHCR. 2013. *UNHCR Turkey Newsletter*, April 2013. www.unhcr.org.tr/uploads/root/unhcr_turkey_newsletter_april2013.pdf.

UNHCR. 2015. *UNHCR Subregional Operations Profile – Northern, Western, Central and Southern Europe.* www.unhcr.org/pages/49e48e996.html.

Welcome to Europe. 2010. *Frontex in the Aegean*, July. http://w2eu.net/frontex/frontex-in-the-aegean/. See blog of the antiracist network *Welcome to Europe* (http://w2eu.net/).

8 The European convergence towards civic integration

Angela Paparusso

Introduction

With the expression *civic integration*, we generally refer to those policies requiring migrants to learn the language, the civic values and the culture of the residence country. Civic integration policies often force[1] migrants, through the signature of an 'integration agreement' or an 'integration contract', to take language and civic courses immediately after their entry into the new country of residence, in order to ask for a residence permit or to apply for the citizenship. Sometimes courses are organized in origin countries, in order to facilitate the so-called 'integration process from abroad' or, more likely, to prevent or limit the entry of those migrants who are considered particularly difficult to integrate. The success of migrants in civic integration courses results in the issue or the renewal of residence permits and the granting of naturalization, while failure means the denial or the non-renewal of residence permits and naturalization (Joppke 2007a). However, civic integration can also include 'civic participation' (Gsir 2014; Vogel and Triandafyllidou 2005) and, therefore, the active engaging of migrants in political parties, labour unions, ethnic associations and migrant organizations in destination countries, and the local vote. The local vote has been defined by Bauböck (2006: 24) as a 'residential citizenship that is disconnected by the nation-state membership': currently, it is granted by 15 of the 28 European Union (EU) member states to third-country nationals (TCNs) (Groenendijk 2014). Anti-discrimination policies, that is, actions aimed at preventing episodes of discrimination and xenophobia towards migrants and their descendants in hosting societies and at ensuring basic civil and social rights, such as healthcare, housing and public schooling for their children, are considered forms of civic integration as well. In particular, the transmission of the language and the culture of the country of settlement to migrants' children, and the socialization with natives, are seen as functional to the integration process of the entire migrant family.

A series of events such as the 9/11 terroristic attacks in New York City and Washington, DC, the political rise and murder of Pim Fortuyn in 2002 in the Netherlands, the attacks of 11 March 2004 in Madrid and 7 July 2005 in London, the murder of the film director Theo van Gogh in November 2004 in Amsterdam and the 2005 Paris riots have highlighted the lack of integration and the socio-economic marginalization of populations with immigrant background, especially those with Muslim origins. This has led hosting countries to reassess their integration policies, emphasizing the need of improving migrants' socio-economic integration, through the knowledge of the language of the hosting society, the respect of the national identity, the promotion of the culture and values of the hosting society among newcomers. For this reason, it has been argued that European countries have converged towards civic integration policies (Joppke 2007b; Zincone 2011).

Regardless of their capacity to promote migrants' socio-economic integration and to foster social cohesion in the hosting society, civic integration policies seem to favour 'a certain degree of socio-cultural assimilation' (Sciortino 2014: 261) and to contribute to the decline of multiculturalism as integration philosophy (Joppke and Morawska 2003; Joppke 2004); on the contrary, the 'category of practice' (Sciortino 2003: 276) of multiculturalism appears to remain at the core of the social relationship between migrant and hosting society in almost all liberal states, with hosting countries being more heterogeneous than their policies state 'on paper'.[2] However, I argue that the grade of socio-cultural assimilation produced by civic integration policies, as well as the coercive nature of their programmes, can vary geographically, as a result of countries' immigration experience and of their so-called 'national models of migrant integration'.

In light of these considerations, this chapter aims to offer an overview of civic integration programmes adopted by European countries over time, in order to shed light on their main features and, in particular, on the rationale that is behind the European convergence towards civic integration. My hypothesis is that a philosophy based on migration control and selection underpins this convergence. This philosophy is coherent with the EU policy ideology, which appears to be marked by a 'securitization' approach towards migration. The European debate on the 'civic direction' (Joppke 2004: 253) undertaken by integration policies in the last decade is mainly focused on 'old' European immigration countries. 'New' immigration countries appear to be involved in the European convergence towards civic integration as well, but generally remain excluded from this debate. Therefore, I choose to focus on Italy as one of the Southern European countries with the largest migration inflows. The chapter comprises the following sections: an analysis of the EU framework on migrants' integration; a discussion of the traditional national models of migrant integration; an explanation of the data and method used; a description of various civic integration programmes; a focus on the civic integration programmes in Italy. The chapter ends with a discussion of these programmes in the final section.

The EU framework on migrant integration

Although often seen as a sort of 'pendulum' between actions aimed at protecting the EU from unwanted immigration and measures on the admission and the settlement of migrants in its member states, the existence of a common EU migration and asylum policy is now almost beyond doubt (e.g. Boswell and Geddes 2011;

Faist and Ette 2007). With the increase of migration inflows, the EU migration and asylum policy has become progressively more restrictive over the years: it appears to be marked by a 'securitization' approach (Bonjour 2011; Carling 2002; Geddes 2003), both at the level of policy measures and at the level of public debate. Moreover, with the effort of policy harmonization, the 'securitization' approach has affected the EU member states' migration measures as well. Strict border controls, stringent visa requirements, draconian asylum procedures and demanding administrative measures have made migration and residence in the EU more complicated. For this reason, it can be argued that 'under control' (Bendel 2007) has become one of the distinctive features of the EU migration and asylum policy. The Treaty of Amsterdam is considered a very important starting point of this policy since in 1999 it transferred asylum and immigration policies in a new Title IV of the Treaty dealing with free movement, migration and asylum. In particular, the Treaty of Amsterdam provided for the European competences on external border controls; reception of asylum seekers; conditions of entry and residence for TCNs and fight against illegal migration. The entry into force of the Lisbon Treaty in December 2009 marked a further step towards a real communitarization (Geddes 2003), by transferring more powers to the EU institutions. Starting from Amsterdam, three five-year work plans have been organized, with the aim of monitoring and actualizing treaties' provisions on migration and asylum (Boswell and Geddes 2011). The Tampere Programme covered the period 1999–2004, with the agenda of enhancing cooperation with third countries, promoting fair treatment of TCNs regularly residing in the EU member states, establishing a European Asylum System and controlling irregular migration. The Hague Programme (2005–09) intended to create a common asylum area and reinforce measures to contrast illegal migration, trafficking and smuggling. Finally, the Stockholm Programme (2010–14) tried to counterbalance the goal of promoting the socio-economic development of migrants' origin countries on the one hand, by incrementing the protection of the 'Area of Freedom, Security and Justice' on the other hand (Kostakopoulou 2012).

Conversely, a similar consensus on the existence of a common EU migrant integration policy, does not exist. Integration became a topic for the EU institutions in the 1990s, as a result of the increasing immigrant population residing in European countries. In particular, considering that what 'happens after' the entry (Favell 2003: 14) often reflects what happens at the entry, and that could be defined an 'immigration-integration nexus' perspective (Pastore and Sciortino 2001; Penninx 2003), the Tampere Programme in 1999 established an EU cooperation on the integration of non-EU nationals, thus including the integration issues in EU competencies. The Thessaloniki summit of June 2003 and the consequent publication of the *Communication on Immigration, Integration and Employment* confirmed EU interest in migrant integration. The 2004 *Common Basic Principles for immigrant integration policies in the EU* set out the importance of developing goals and indicators to implement policies and evaluate the national efforts and actions on integration. In 2007, the *Handbook on Integration* was produced by the European Commission with the aim of promoting the exchange of good practices among policy-makers and experts across Europe. The *Common Basic Principles* were also adopted in Malmo in 2009. Four core areas – employment, education, social inclusion and active citizenship – and 14 core indicators were set out in that occasion. The 2010 Zaragoza Ministerial Conference Member States established a set of core outcome indicators, which are now considered some of the most important sources of integration indicators at European level. However, in the 2011 *European Agenda for the Integration of Third Country Nationals*, the EU's role was limited to the establishment of common standards for integration measures, to the exchange of best practices and successful models of integration and to support integration strategies in the EU member states. Therefore, it can be concluded that the EU contributes almost exclusively to orientate and coordinate states' integration policies. In particular, it acts as a framework of standards and recommendations and as a forum of dialogue and information exchange (Bosswick and Heckmann 2006) for the development of integration strategies, rather than as a policy-maker. For this reason, it can be argued that a common EU migrant integration policy does not exist (yet). Nevertheless, it is incontrovertible that the EU principles and guidelines are able to influence the formulation and the implementation of integration policies at national level and can help in producing a harmonization and a convergence of integration measures across Europe.

While the term and the meaning of integration can be understood differently among the EU member states, mainly depending on the timing when they experienced their first mass immigration and on the level of institutionalization of such a phenomenon (Freeman 1995), the EU generally considers integration as a 'dynamic, two-way process of mutual accommodation by all immigrants and residents of Member States' (Justice and Common Affairs Council 2004). From this perspective, migrants *have to* demonstrate their willingness to be integrated into the host society and to respect its rules and values. On the other hand, the host societies *have to* answer to migrants' needs and make efforts to grant and preserve their culture and origins. Since the integration process takes place primarily at local level (Penninx 2004; Penninx *et al.* 2004), with cities and municipalities as the places where migrants are received and natives encounter new cultures and identities, the EU argues that integration policies should be developed primarily at local level. According to the principle of subsidiarity, the local level appears closer to migrants in providing services they need and, at the same time, more apt in managing their interaction with natives. Nevertheless, a strong coordination between all the actors involved in the integration process, therefore the European institutions, the EU member states, the national, regional and local authorities, as well as NGOs and migrant organizations, is considered necessary in order to produce consistent and effective integration policies.

The traditional national models of migrant integration

The academic literature generally distinguishes between three traditional national models of migrant integration: the exclusionist model, the assimilationist model and the multiculturalist or pluralist model (e.g. Castles 1995; Koopmans and Statham

1999). This kind of categorization reflects the fact that the debates on integration and integration policies have been historically mainly focused on the so-called 'old' immigration countries. Nevertheless, if the 'new' immigration countries (Freeman 1995) are taken into consideration, this categorization becomes incomplete. Therefore, I suggest that the Southern European model also be considered (e.g. Peixoto *et al.* 2012), when referring to traditional national models of migrant integration.

The exclusionist model of integration (Germany (pre-2000), Austria and Belgium-Flanders) considers migration as a temporary and functional phenomenon: a means to meet short-term labour demands. Migrants are expected to return home rather than permanently settle in the host country. Consequently, the residence permit is often linked to the job contract: the expiration of the job contract means the loss of the right to live in the host country. Migrants are well integrated into the labour market, but not in the social and political community (they are generally excluded from welfare systems, citizenship rights and political participation). Countries fitting this model are quite reluctant to permanent settlement, family reunification and migrants' naturalization. Citizenship rights are based on 'ethno-cultural belonging to nationhood' (Koopmans and Statham 1999: 660) and therefore mainly on the principle of *ius sanguinis*.

According to the assimilationist model (France), migrants are expected to be fully incorporated in the host country as individuals: they have to accept and internalize both the values and the culture of the country of settlement. The existence and maintenance of ethnic communities is prevented since these are seen as a sign of incomplete assimilation. As a consequence, the naturalization is relatively easy, since it is essentially based on civic territorial criteria and, therefore, on *ius soli*. However, it is noteworthy, for instance, that France evolved towards more pluralist policy measures over the years, with a mixture of *ius sanguinis* and *ius soli*.

According to the multiculturalist or pluralist model (Britain, the Netherlands and Sweden), migrants' culture and origins should be granted, preserved and enhanced, 'as positive marks of a diverse heritage' (Simon 2012: 3). Hosting societies that adopt multiculturalist or pluralist models of migrant integration generally show a strong willingness to include ethnic minorities into their community, respecting their language and their cultural and religious differences. Although migrants do not always have the benefit of full social and political rights, ethnic communities are officially accepted, forms of ethnic entrepreneurship are encouraged and quotas of social benefits and facilities are reserved to them. Nevertheless, the academic literature has recently questioned the validity of such a model (Duyvendak and Scholten 2011; Poppelaars and Scholten 2008) and the capacity of multiculturalism to grant migrants equality and emancipation (Koopmans 2010).

The last model of integration is that of the 'new' immigration countries or the Southern European model (Italy, Greece, Portugal and Spain). As pointed out by Freeman, only a few years ago these countries were characterized by 'the near complete absence of any institutional mechanisms or administrative experience as to planning and regulating immigration' (1995: 894). As a consequence, these countries do not have a strong integration ideology and integration practices are still embryonic and spontaneous, although rather inclusive. For instance, the expression 'implicit model of integration' or 'subordinate integration' has been coined for Italy (Ambrosini 2001, 2005), in order to denote an unintended and unsystematic way of integrating migrants which tends to privilege the economic inclusion (therefore, into the labour market), with forms of over-qualification and labour 'ethnicization' (Ambrosini 2013: 183), rather than the full political participation of migrants. This *de facto* integration process is to some extent similar to the so-called 'differential exclusion model' described by Castles (1995: 294), according to which certain dimensions of integration are favoured, such as the socio-economic dimension.

I believe that the European convergence towards civic integration is not necessarily competing with the traditional national models of migrant integration. In other words, the civic integration convergence does not mark a decline of the traditional national models of migrant integration. On the contrary, these models remain and can represent useful interpretative criteria of civic integration programmes adopted by European countries over the years. Nevertheless, though the usefulness of models in reducing the complexity of the issue of the migrant integration, explaining and taking into account the national differences and making international comparisons, has been largely demonstrated by the numerous classifications of integration policies available in the academic literature (e.g. Brubaker 1992; Favell 1998; Castles and Miller 2009), models should not be considered as static and immutable identities able to perfectly explain the social processes, that is, the relationship between migrant and hosting society (Bertossi 2011; Bertossi and Duyvendak 2012). Sometimes this relationship can diverge from the dominant policy model and conceptualization, taking forms that often do not correspond to the alleged national models of migrant integration. As already stressed (e.g. Cento Bull 2010; Czaika and de Haas 2013), a gap between the normative model (policy discourse), the policy practices (policy outcomes) and, finally, the social processes, may exist. Several reasons can produce this gap: at national level, electoral needs and economic interests can lead policy-makers to implement measures that can contradict the policy discourse; at the public opinion level, terroristic and tragic events need strong policy actions to reassure the public opinion; at international level, the states' obligations to participate in supranational bodies, for instance the EU, can orient national policy strategies and contribute to produce a 'convergence of specific policy measures' (Finotelli and Michalowski 2012: 234). Therefore, it is important to keep in mind these considerations when interpreting the civic integration programmes and their rationale.

Data and methods

In order to provide an overview of the civic integration programmes adopted in Europe, I made a systematic review of actual legal texts and academic literature. I found civic integration policies in 14 European countries: Austria, Belgium, Denmark, Estonia, Finland, France, Germany, Greece, Italy, Latvia, Poland, Spain, the Netherlands and the United Kingdom. As shown in Table 8.1,

Table 8.1 Overview of the civic integration policies in Europe

Country	Year	Policy	Target group	Civic course	Integration test	Integration from abroad	Local vote
The Netherlands	1998	Newcomer integration Law	Non-EU permanent residents and citizenship	600 hours of language, civic and labour market courses	Yes	Yes, for family and long-term migrants	Yes
Denmark	1999	Danish Integration Act: A. Integration Program; B. Contract of Integration and Declaration on Integration and Active	A. Permanent residents; B. Family migrants and refugees	The Danish culture and history, social conditions in Denmark, the functioning of the labour market, the welfare system, the schooling and housing system	No	No	Yes
Estonia	2000	A. Integration in Estonia Society B. Adaptation Programs	A. 'Russophone' migrants; B. Recommended to those migrants who work in the service sector	Estonian language, life, culture and values to migrants.	No	No	No
Germany	2001	Integration courses	Permanent residents and citizenship applicants	600 hours of language course and 30 hours of civic course	Yes	Yes, for ethnic and family migrants	No
Spain	2001	Integration Plans	Not specified	Orientation, juridical guidance, education and language courses	No	No	Yes
United Kingdom	2002	Nationality, Immigration and Asylum Act	Long-term residents and residents seeking British citizenship	English for Speakers of Other Languages (ESOL) and citizenship classes	Yes	No	Yes
France	2003	Contrat d'accueil et de l'integration	Migrants with long term visa or a temporary permit of stay for work, study or family reasons, migrants with a residence card or CE long term residence card	A 6 hours civic course; a course which can ranges from 1 to 6 hours for the learning of the access to the public services and the everyday life in France; a 400 hours French language course	Yes, for the delivering of the language certificate	No	No

(Continued)

Table 8.1 Overview of the civic integration policies in Europe (Continued)

Country	Policy	Year	Target group	Civic course	Integration test	Integration from abroad	Local vote
Austria	Integration Contracts	2003	Non-EU newcomers arrived after 1998, who asked the issue (or the renewal) of the resident permit	Language and social, economic and cultural aspects of life in Austria	No	No	No
Belgium	Citizenization policy and integration Programs	2004	Third-country nationals registered in the National Register and holding a first residence permit of more than three months		No	No	Yes
Latvia	Immigration Law	2005	Migrants applying for a temporary residence permit	Language, traditions and culture courses	No	No	
Greece	Integration Agreement	2006	Migrants who ask for a long-term residence permit	Language and civic courses	Yes	No	No
Finland	Personal Integration Plan	2011	All the migrants residing in Finland, over 18 years and unemployed	Language courses, information on the labour market, education, schooling for children and health care system	No	No	Yes
Poland	Integration Programs	2012	Refugees, repatriates and their familiars	Language instruction, vocational training and subsistence support	No	No	No
Italy	Integration Agreement	2012	Migrants who want to obtain or renew their permit of stay	Civic values and civil life sessions + Italian language: level A2	Yes	No	No

I categorized civic integration programmes according to the policy name, the year of implementation, the target groups, whether or not civic courses are organized, whether or not language or civic tests have to be passed by migrants, whether or not integration from abroad is practised, and whether or not local voting rights are granted to migrants. In the next section, I present the civic integration programmes in a chronological order, in other words, according to their year of implementation.

Civic integration programmes across Europe

The Netherlands has been the pioneer in the civic integration, introducing the Newcomer Integration Law in 1998, which obliged most non-EU migrants to attend a 12-month integration course, consisting in 600 hours of language, civic and labour market courses. Both the state and the municipalities organized courses. The law was revised in 2006 introducing a series of more draconian amendments (Fischler 2014). In particular, all migrants from outside the EU and Switzerland applying for a residence permit for an indefinite period were required to attend an integration course and to pay for it; the issue of the permanent residence permits and the grant of the naturalization was linked to success in passing an integration test; family migrants and other migrants who asked for a long-term residence permit were asked to take an integration test at the Dutch Embassy or Consulate in their origin country or in the country where they were residing from at least three months; courses had to be organized by private organizations in each municipality rather than by the state, as in the past (Bruquetas-Callejo *et al.* 2011; Fischler 2014; Joppke 2007b). Migrants who failed in the compliance of the integration test were not granted the residence permit. However, while compliance with the test did not imply the issue of the residence permit, eventually a permit/special visa would be issued, only for one year. This special document subsequently allowed the application for the residence permit. Since 1 January 2013 all migrants, including asylum seekers, are required to pay for both the integration course and the integration exam. Moreover, starting from January 2014 the Participation Agreement has been introduced by municipalities with the aim of teaching migrants the fundamental norms and principles of Dutch society. This agreement is targeted especially to family migrants, refugees, EU work migrants and migrants from Turkey and former Antilles (Fischler 2014).

In 1999 Denmark introduced the Danish Integration Act, with the aim to teach migrants the core values and norms of Danish society. The implementation of the Danish Integration Act takes place at local level with municipalities primarily responsible for providing migrants with the 'Integration Program'. In particular, migrants are asked to be enrolled in an Integration Program in order to learn about Danish culture and history, social conditions in Denmark, the functioning of the labour market, the welfare system, the schooling and housing system. Participation in the Integration Program is needed to obtain a permanent residence permit and to be eligible for social benefits. Migrants are expected to become economically active and culturally integrated into the hosting society, and thus to be suitable to receive social rights and benefits (Mouritsen and Jensen 2014). Moreover, refugees and reunified families are asked to sign a compulsory 'Contract of Integration' and a 'Declaration on Integration and Active Citizenship'. The Danish language, the respect of democratic principles, values of liberty, freedom of speech, gender equality are required to be observed by such migrants, which are considered particularly difficult to integrate. Sanctions are imposed in the case of migrants refusing to sign both the 'Contract of Integration' and the 'Declaration on Integration and Active Citizenship'.

The 'Integration in Estonia Society 2000–2007' and the 'Integration in Estonia Society 2008–2013' strategies both focused on civic integration, and thus on the understanding of Estonian language, values and norms. The main target group of civic integration policies in Estonia are the 'Russophone' migrants – those who have migrated from other parts of the Soviet Union before Estonia's independence. Nevertheless, the integration measures are not compulsory although they are strongly recommended for migrants working in the service sector (Jakobson 2014).

In 2001 Germany introduced the *Integrationskurse* ('Integration courses'), funded by the Federal Government. It consisted of 600 hours of a language course and 30 hours of a civic course (Joopke 2007b). The 2004 Immigration Law made conditions for such courses stricter, since the non-compliance of the courses meant the non-renewal of the temporary residence permit and the denial of the permanent residence permit. Moreover, sanctions such as the reduction of welfare benefits were introduced for those migrants refusing to participate in courses. Family migrants were asked to prove their language skills before migrating. Since 2005, integration courses have been organized at local level (Borkert and Bosswick 2011). In 2006, attendance on civic integration courses and the successful completion of the language test became required also for naturalization (Joppke 2007b). In 2007, the Directive Implementation Act for EU Directives on Residence and Asylum Issues stated, among other things, the necessary evidence of basic German skills for spouses, through pre-entry tests. The rationale for this provision was to avoid forced marriages and to hinder as much as possible the integration process (Borkert and Bosswick 2011).

In Spain the autonomous communities are responsible for the migrant integration programmes. A series of 'Integration Plans' have been implemented by Cataluña, Madrid and Andalucía since 2001, with the aim of promoting the principles of equal treatment, respect for multiculturalism and the protection of cultural plurality. These mainly concern orientation, juridical guidance, education and language courses (Carrera 2006). Two 'Strategic Plans for Citizenship and Integration' were approved for the periods 2007–10 and 2011–14. Language courses are among the measures recommended by such plans (Pasetti 2014).

In United Kingdom the 2002 Nationality, Immigration and Asylum Act asks long-term residents and residents applying for citizenship to follow English for Speakers of Other Languages (ESOL) classes and citizenship courses.

In 2003, under the Raffarin government, France implemented the *Contrat d'accueil et de l'integration* (CAI) programme ('Integration contract'), consisting in one day of civic instructions and 500 hours of language course. Then, the First Sarkozy Law of 2003 imposed the knowledge of the French language and the fundamental values of the French Republic as prerequisite to renewing the residence permit and to obtain both the ten-year residence permit and legal permanent residence. Moreover, the Law stated that family members were entitled to receive only a one-year residence permit; then, after two years, they could apply for the ten-year residence permit. The rationale behind this provision was to avoid the increase of ethnic marriages, or at least to oblige family migrants to learn French language and values. However, the *Contrat d'accueil et de l'integration* was made compulsory only starting from 1 January 2007, after the entry into force of the 2006 Law of Immigration and Integration, also known as the Second Sarkozy Law. Migrants eligible and thus obliged to sign the 'Integration contract' are those who intend to permanently reside in France and thus hold a long-term visa or a temporary permit of stay for work, study or family reasons, as well as a residence card and the CE long-term residence card. Seasonal workers, researchers and highly skilled migrants (in other words, those in possession of the so-called *Carte d'Entrée et de Séjour Compétences et Talents* (Wihtol de Wenden 2011)), including their families, are exempted from the 'Integration contract'. The signature of the 'Integration contract' includes commitment to a six-hour civic course concerning the fundamental values of the French Republic and the functioning of the state; a course which can range from one to six hours on access to public services and everyday life in France; and a 400-hour French language class for those migrants whose French is considered insufficient. The course is followed by a final exam issuing the language certificate.

In Austria the Settlement and Residence Act establishes the 'Integration Agreement'. It consists of two modules: the first deals with literacy and the second focuses on language, social, economic and cultural aspects of life in Austria (Carrera 2006).

In Belgium, integration has been a community competence since the 1980s. Therefore policies are different between Wallonia, Flanders and the Region of Brussels. In the last ten years, Flanders have been developing civic integration policies with the *Inburgering* ('Citizenization') policy which, through an 'Integration Programme' encourages the learning of the Flemish language, values and norms among migrants. 'Integration Programmes' are compulsory for TCNs of 18 years and over who are registered in the National Register, are living in a Flemish city and hold a first residence permit of more than three months. The 'Citizenization' policy also includes a mandatory 'Integration Contract', which allows the migrant to understand the content and structure of the 'Integration Programme'. According to the 'Integration Contract', knowledge of the official language is compulsory, as well as the internalization of values, norms and institutions of the Flemish society (Mandin 2014).

In Latvia, the 2005 Immigration Law has introduced language, tradition and culture courses for migrants applying for a permanent residence permit (Carrera 2006).

In Greece, starting from 2006 migrants asking for a long-term residence permit need to earn an annual income of 8,500 euros (15 per cent more for each additional family member), to own a healthcare insurance and to pass a language and culture test (D'Angelo 2006).

In Finland, starting from 2011 the migrant integration policy has been oriented towards the improvement of migrants' inclusion into the labour market and the civic integration actions are seen as a tool to achieve this goal. The 'Personal Integration Plan' has been introduced. It represents an 'agreement' between the migrant and Finland and it includes language courses, and information on the labour market, education, schooling for children and the healthcare system. All migrants residing in Finland aged over 18 years and unemployed are eligible and thus obliged to follow the 'Personal Integration Plan' (Koskela 2014).

In Poland 'Integration Programmes' are targeted only to refugees and repatriates and their familiars. They consist of Polish language instruction, vocational training and subsistence support (Stefańska 2015).

Civic integration in Italy

Traditionally an emigration country, Italy turned into an immigration country from the late 1970s onwards. Due to its geographical position at the southern border of Europe, Italy is one of the most important access points and one of the major migrant destinations in the European Union. The foreign resident population amounted to 5.2 million individuals at 1 January 2015 (Istat online database) and it represents around 8.2 per cent of the total population. This number rises to 6 million (around 10 per cent of the total population), when considering non-resident regular and irregular migrants (ISMU 2011).

As in other 'new' immigration countries, the acceptance of the existence of the immigration phenomenon has been late and the first law of immigration was introduced not until 1986 (Einaudi 2007; Zincone 1998). As a consequence, the issue of migrant integration has been formally taken into account and introduced in the Italian legislation only with the Single Act of Immigration Law (Law n. 40/1998), also known as the Turco-Napolitano Law. The Turco-Napolitano Law was based on four pillars (Zincone and Caponio 2004: 4): (1) the prevention of and fight against illegal entries; (2) the regulation of new arrivals of foreign workers through annual quotas of workers and the introduction of the so-called 'sponsor system', a special settlement permit that allowed foreigners to enter Italy to look for a job if they were sponsored by an Italian or a foreigner legally resident in Italy who was financially able to do that; (3) the granting of basic human rights to illegal migrants, such as basic healthcare; (4) the promotion of the integration of migrants already resident in Italy through the creation of a 'National Integration Fund' dedicated to finance multicultural activities. These four aims corresponded to four basic elements of the so-called 'model of reasonable integration', 'a model which is not too rigid, not too ideological, not too pretentious' (Zincone 2000: 959). The four basic elements were: (1) interaction based on security; (2) full integrity for legal immigrants; (3) integrity of human rights for illegal immigrants; (4) interaction based on pluralism and communication (Zincone 2000). The rationale behind the Turco-Napolitano Law lies in the concept that migrants should benefit of the same civil, and in part social, rights of nationals. Finally, the Turco-Napolitano Law (art. 42) established a 'multilevel governance' with local authorities in charge of developing and implementing integration actions for their immigrant populations.

The centre-right government coalition reformed the Single Act of 1998 through the introduction of the Bossi-Fini Law in 2002. In particular, the Bossi-Fini Law modified the first two pillars of the Single Act of Immigration Law, making residence permits and illegal entries more restrictive. In particular, to discourage permanent settlement of migrants, a series of measures were introduced. The sponsor system was abolished, the validity period of the residence permit was reduced and the permit of stay was linked to the job contract (the so-called 'residence contract'), according to an exclusionist interpretation of migrant integration. An amnesty was established by the Bossi-Fini Law for those non-EU foreigners who had been working irregularly in Italy for at least three months before the law became effective (July 2002). It was the biggest amnesty ever given in Europe: 646,000 migrants were regularized under this law (Italian Ministry of Interior). Therefore, the Bossi-Fini Law emphasized the temporary nature of immigration and the economic dimension of integration and this trend was maintained over the years. In 2009 a new amnesty was introduced and it was addressed to domestic care-workers. The reason behind this amnesty was that despite the economic crisis the domestic worker sector continued to grow and, therefore, to demand foreign workforce (Ambrosini 2013). Finally, the amnesty of 2012 was addressed to irregular non-EU workers and in particular to full-time workers and domestic workers, employed at least 20 hours per week.

However, a turn towards the social and cultural dimension of integration has occurred also in Italy, as reaction to the above-mentioned international events which have reopened the debate on assimilation and multiculturalism in Europe. The *Carta dei valori della cittadinanza e dell'integrazione* ('Charter of the values of citizenship and integration'), introduced by the Home Affairs Minister Giuliano Amato during the II Prodi Government in 2006, the Security Package (Law 94/2009), approved by the IV Silvio Berlusconi Government in July 2009, the 2010 *Piano per l'integrazione nella sicurezza. Identità e incontro* ('Plan for integration in secure environment. Identity and encounter') and the *Patto per l'integrazione* ('Integration agreement'), approved by the same government coalition in 2009, but entered into force in March 2012, proclaimed the importance of learning the Italian language and about Italian history and culture as prerequisite for a positive and active inclusion of newcomers into Italian society. In particular, the 'Integration Agreement' defined integration as 'a process designed to promote the coexistence of Italian citizens and foreign nationals legally residing in the country, and based on mutual commitment to participate in the economic, social and cultural life, under the values enshrined in the Italian Constitution' (Italian Ministry of Interior). Within these considerations, the 'Integration Agreement' asked newcomers to learn the Italian language (level A2); to learn the fundamental principles of the Italian Constitution and institutions; to learn about civic life, the functioning of the health sector, the education and social services sectors, the labour market and related fiscal obligations; and, last but not least, to respect the rule according to which children have to attend school up to 16 years old (Caponio and Zincone 2011). At the moment of the signing the contract, migrants receive 16 credits, but then have to score 30 credits within two years by attending free courses on civic values (Caneva 2014). The non-attendance at these sessions results in the loss of 15 credits. If the number of credits acquired is more than zero but less than 30, or the knowledge of the Italian language, civic culture and civil life cannot be sufficiently proved by the migrant, the agreement can be extended for one more year. A number of credits equivalent to zero or less than zero means the denial or the non-renewal of the residence permit and expulsion from Italian territory. Finally, if the number of credits acquired is 40 or more, additional cultural and formative activities are offered to migrants. A number of non-profit organizations and institutions organize free languages courses for migrants.

Concluding this section, the Italian centre-left coalition approach towards migration appears traditionally quite inclusive and multiculturalist. It tries to equalize as much as possible migrants to Italians as far as social rights are concerned. On the contrary, the Italian centre-right coalition considers migrants as functional to the national economy, and therefore mainly as manpower to be employed in those sectors that native workers usually refuse (Ambrosini 2013). Furthermore, the Italian centre-right coalition perceives migrants as a threat when issues of public order, national identity and culture are debated (e.g. Geddes 2008; Salis 2012). Therefore, from this point of view, civic integration has succeeded in conciliating these divergent approaches to migration, since the knowledge of the Italian language and values has been considered crucial for the process of migrants' socio-economic integration by both government coalitions in the last years. In other words, the above-mentioned policy measures have aligned the two Italian political coalitions, as well as the Italian debate on migrant integration to the ongoing European convergence.

Discussion and conclusion

This chapter has focused on the civic integration programmes adopted by European countries in recent years. The aim has been to shed light on their main features and on the rationale behind the European convergence towards civic integration. I responded to these research questions by a systematic review of actual legal texts and academic literature on 14 European countries. The comparative analysis of the civic integration programmes adopted by European countries covered by my study highlights: the use of mandatory 'integration contracts' for migrants who ask for a permanent residence permit or apply for the citizenship; the obligatory participation in language and civic courses, especially for refugees and family migrants; the necessity to pass a final exam and the almost total exemption of highly skilled and temporary migrants from civic integration programmes. Regarding the so-called 'integration from abroad' or 'integration at distance', comparative analysis has shown that only two countries, namely the Netherlands and Germany, ask family migrants to follow civic courses in their origin country. Finally, eight of the 14 countries analysed grant local voting rights to migrants.

Refugees and family migrants are considered particularly difficult to integrate and they are perceived as a treat for European societies. Regardless of their national integration philosophies, more draconian measures for granting residence permits and citizenship rights have been endorsed by European countries to discourage the entry and settlement of such migrants. Taken for granted that language skills are considered fundamental to enhance social mobility and the integration of migrants into the labour market of the hosting country – recent studies have shed light on the positive relationship between socio-economic integration and language proficiency (e.g. Di Bartolomeo and Strozza 2014) – empirical evidence shows that policies based on civic requirements have a weak impact on socio-economic and political integration of migrants (Wallace Goodman and Wright 2015). On the contrary, civic integration policies appear to produce a 'stratification' of the immigrant population in hosting societies. In particular, by building up different integration regimes, civic integration tends to intensify the gap between low-skilled and high-skilled migrants or between undesirable and desirable migrants.

For this reason, it can be concluded that the European convergence towards civic integration is underpinned by a philosophy based on migration control and selection. This philosophy is coherent with EU migration policy ideology, which is marked by a 'securitization' approach towards migration, as explained at the beginning of this chapter. Policy restrictiveness and an idea of *immigration choisie*, with language and civic skills as criteria of selection, appear to be at the core of European civic integration convergence. Several studies have shown the limited success of policy restrictiveness (e.g. Castles 2004a, 2004b; Cornelius 2005; Vogel 2000). Measures aimed to restrict and select migration are generally ineffective, since the factors determining and nurturing migration processes are very complex and deep-rooted in both origin and destination areas (e.g. de Haas 2010). Moreover, policy restrictiveness contributes to changing the routes and channels through which people migrate, increasing illegal entries (Cornelius 2001; de Haas 2011). Finally, since it hinders circulation and mobility (Massey *et al.* 2014; Wihtol de Wenden 1999), policy restrictiveness makes more precarious the residence of migrants and fosters their irregularity. Irregular migration and the political rhetoric on irregular migration produce feelings of anxiety and fear against migrants in hosting societies; this undermines the social cohesion and may discourage newcomers to adopt and internalize civic values. This vicious circle provides evidence not only for the existence of a nexus between immigration and integration policies, as stressed before, but also for the fact that restrictive immigration policies and effective integration policies based on civic values cannot easily coexist.

However, active civic participation and anti-discrimination policies are not covered by my analysis, and therefore this work may appear biased and the analysis on the aim and scope of civic integration programmes adopted in Europe may be viewed as partial. Moreover, it has been argued that a divergence between national policy-making and local policy implementation may exist when integration policies are concerned (Jørgensen 2012; Poppelaars and Scholten 2008). Due to 'different institutional logics' (Poppelaars and Scholten 2008: 3) and divergent policy needs, civic integration programmes may not actually be developed or implemented at local level. Therefore, further research is needed in order to gain more insight to these aspects.

Notes

1 Several doubts about the coherence between the compulsory nature of these courses and liberal principles have been raised (Joppke 2004, 2007a, 2007b, 2012).
2 The case of France is illustrative. As stressed by Simon (2012), although multiculturalism in France is still rather rejected by both political and public debate, France is multicultural, since its population is largely and increasingly diverse. Minority identities are not necessarily conflicting with the sense of belonging and assimilation to France; migrants are transnational beings, who live constantly a sort of 'double presence' in both the origin and the destination country, and therefore they can be integrated or 'assimilated' in the host society without renouncing to their identity.

References

Ambrosini, M. 2001. *La Fatica di Integrarsi. Immigrati e Lavoro in Italia* [Struggling for Being Integrated. Immigrants and Work in Italy]. Bologna: Il Mulino.
Ambrosini, M. 2005. *Sociologia delle Migrazioni* [Sociology of Migration]. Bologna: Il Mulino.
Ambrosini, M. 2013. 'Immigration in Italy: between economic acceptance and political rejection'. *Journal of International Migration and Integration* 14(1): 175–94.
Andersson, R. 2014. *Integration Policies. Sweden Country Report*. INTERACT Research Report No. 2014/14. Florence: European University Institute and Robert Schuman Centre for Advanced Studies.
Bauböck, R., ed. 2006. *Migration and Citizenship: Legal Status, Rights and Political Participation*. IMISCOE Report Series. Amsterdam: Amsterdam University Press.
Bendel, P. 2007. 'Everything under control? The European Union's policies and politics of immigration'. In T. Faist and A. Ette, eds, *The Europeanization of National Policies and Politics of Immigration*, 32–48. Basingstoke: Palgrave Macmillan.
Bertossi, C. 2011. 'National models of integration in Europe: a comparative and critical analysis'. *American Behavioral Scientist* 20: 1–20.
Bertossi, C. and Duyvendak, J. W. 2012. 'National models of immigrant integration: the costs for comparative research'. *Comparative European Politics* 10: 237–47.
Bonjour, S. 2011. 'The power and moral of policy makers: reassessing the control gap debate'. *International Migration Review* 45: 89–122.
Borkert, M. and Bosswick, W. 2011. 'The case of Germany'. In G. Zincone, R. Penninx and M. Borket, eds, *Migration Policymaking in Europe: The Dynamics of Actors and Contexts in Past and Present*, 95–127. Amsterdam: Amsterdam University Press.
Bosswick, W. and Heckmann, F. 2006. *Integration of Migrants: Contribution of Local and Regional Authorities*. Dublin: European Foundation for the Improvement of Living and Working Conditions.

Boswell, C. and Geddes, A. 2011. *Migration and Mobility in the European Union.* Basingstoke: Palgrave Macmillan.

Brubaker, R. 1992. *Citizenship and Nationhood in France and Germany.* Cambridge, MA: Harvard University Press.

Bruquetas-Callejo, M., Garcés-Mascareñas, B., Penninx, R. and Scholten, P. 2011. 'The case of the Netherlands'. In G. Zincone, R. Penninx and M. Borket, eds, *Migration Policymaking in Europe: The Dynamics of Actors and Contexts in Past and Present,* 129–63. Amsterdam: Amsterdam University Press.

Caneva, E. 2014. *The Integration of Migrants in Italy: An Overview of Policy Instruments and Actors.* INTERACT Research Report No. 2014/05. Florence: European University Institute and Robert Schuman Centre for Advanced Studies.

Caponio, T. and Zincone, G. 2011. *The National Policy Frame for the Integration of Newcomers in Italy.* PROSINT Country Report WP2.

Carling, J. 2002. 'Migration in the age of involuntary immobility: theoretical reflections and Cape Verdean experiences'. *Journal of Ethnic and Migration Studies* 28: 5–42.

Carrera, S. 2006. *A Comparison of Integration Programmes in the EU.* Challenge Papers No. 1. Brussels: Centre for European Policy Studies.

Castles, S. 1995. 'How nation-states respond to immigration and ethnic diversity'. *Journal of Ethnic and Migration Studies* 21(3): 293–308.

Castles, S. 2004a. 'The factors that make and unmake migration policies'. *International Migration Review* 38(3): 852–84.

Castles, S. 2004b. 'Why migration policies fail'. *Ethnic and Racial Studies* 27(2): 205–27.

Castles, S. and Miller, M. J. 2009. *The Age of Migration: International Population Movements in the Modern World,* 4th edn. Basingstoke: Palgrave Macmillan.

Cento Bull, A. 2010. 'Addressing contradictory needs: the Lega Nord and Italian immigration policy'. *Patterns of Prejudice* 44(5): 411–31.

Colombo, A. and Sciortino, G. 2004. *Gli Immigrati in Italia* [Immigrants in Italy]. Bologna: Il Mulino.

Cornelius, W. A. 2001. 'Death at the border: efficacy and unintended consequences of US immigration control policy'. *Population and Development Review* 27(4): 661–85.

Cornelius, W. A. 2005. 'Controlling "unwanted" immigration: lessons from the United States, 1993–2004'. *Journal of Ethnic and Migration Studies* 31(4): 775–94.

Czaika, M. and de Haas, H. 2013. 'The effectiveness of immigration policies'. *Population and Development Review* 39(3): 487–508.

D'Angelo, A. 2006. 'L'Immigrazione nell'Unione Europea a 25'. In Caritas and Migrantes, eds, *Immigrazione. Dossier Statistico 2006,* 39–48. Roma: Idos.

De Haas, H. 2010 'The internal dynamics of migration processes: a theoretical inquiry'. *Journal of Ethnic and Migration Studies* 36(10): 1587–617.

De Haas, H. 2011. 'Mediterranean migration futures: patterns, drivers and scenarios'. *Global Environmental Change.* doi: 10.1016/j.gloenvcha.2011.09.003.

Di Bartolomeo, A. and Strozza, S. 2014. 'L'Integrazione degli Immigrati nei Paesi dell'Ue15: Riscontri Empirici per Istruzione e Mercato del Lavoro [The integration of immigrants in the EU15: empirical findings in the education system and labour market]'. In P. Donadio, G. Gabrielli and M. Massari, eds, *Uno Come Te. Europei e Nuovi Europei nei Percorsi di Integrazione,* 37–50. Milan: FrancoAngeli.

Duyvendak, J. W. and Scholten, P. 2011. 'Beyond the Dutch "multicultural model": the coproduction of integration policy frames in the Netherlands'. *Journal of International Migration and Integration* 12: 331–48.

Einaudi, L. 2007. *Le Politiche dell'Immigrazione in Italia dall'Unità ad Oggi* [Immigration Policies in Italy from the Unification to Nowadays]. Roma–Bari: Editori Laterza.

Faist, T. and Ette, A., eds. 2007. *The Europeanization of National Policies and Politics of Immigration*. Basingstoke: Palgrave Macmillan.

Favell, A. 1998. *Philosophies of Integration: Immigration and the Idea of Citizenship in France and Britain*. London: Macmillan.

Favell, A. 2003. 'Integration nation: the nation state and research on immigrants in Western Europe'. *Comparative Social Research* 22: 13–42.

Finotelli, C. and Michalowski, I. 2012. 'The heuristic potential of models of citizenship and immigrant integration reviewed'. *Journal of Immigrant and Refugee Studies* 10(3): 231–40.

Fischler, F. 2014. *Integration Policy. Netherlands Country Report*. INTERACT Research Report No. 2014/15. Florence: European University Institute and Robert Schuman Centre for Advanced Studies.

Freeman, G. P. 1995. 'Modes of immigration politics in liberal democratic states'. *International Migration Review* 29(4): 881–902.

Geddes, A. 2003. *The Politics of Migration and Immigration in Europe*. London: Sage.

Geddes, A. 2008. 'Il rombo dei cannoni? Immigration and the centre-right in Italy'. *Journal of European Public Policy* 15(3): 349–66.

Groenendijk, K. 2014. *Voting Rights and Political Participation of Non-National Immigrants*. MIGRATION Focus Policy Brief No. 26. Osnabrück: Institute for Migration Research and Intercultural Studies (IMIS).

Gsir, S. 2014. *Civic Participation and Integration: A Country of Origin Perspective*. INTERACT Research Report No. 2014/03. Florence: European University Institute and Robert Schuman Centre for Advanced Studies.

Guiraudon, V. 2014. 'Economic crisis and institutional resilience: the political economy of migrant incorporation'. *West European Politics* 37(6): 1297–313.

ISMU. 2011. *XVII Rapporto sulle Migrazioni in Italia* [XVII Report on Migration in Italy]. Milano: Franco Angeli.

Istat online database. http://demo.istat.it. Accessed 26 January 2015.

Italian Ministry of Interior. www.interno.gov.it/mininterno/export/sites/default/it/sezioni/ministero/dipartimenti/dip_politiche_personale/statistiche/scheda_15929.html. Accessed 19 January 2015.

Jakobson, M.-L. 2014. *Integration Policy Instruments in Estonia*. INTERACT Research Report No. 2014/21. Florence: European University Institute and Robert Schuman Centre for Advanced Studies.

Joppke, C. 2004. 'The retreat of multiculturalism in the liberal state: theory and policy'. *British Journal of Sociology* 55(2): 237–57.

Joppke, C. 2007a. 'Beyond national models: civic integration policies for immigrants in Western Europe'. *West European Politics* 30(1): 1–22.

Joppke, C. 2007b. 'Transformation of immigrant integration: civic integration and antidiscrimination in the Netherlands, France, and Germany'. *World Politics* 59(2): 243–73.

Joppke, C. 2012. *The Role of the State in Cultural Integration: Trends, Challenges, and Ways Ahead*. Washington DC: Migration Policy Institute working paper.

Joppke, C. and Morawska, E., eds. 2003. *Toward Assimilation and Citizenship: Immigrants in Liberal Nation-States*. London: Palgrave Macmillan.

Jørgensen, M. B. 2012. 'The diverging logics of integration policy making at national and city level'. *International Migration Review* 46(1): 244–78.

Justice and Home Affairs Council. 2004. *The Common Basic Principles for Immigrant Integration Policies in the EU*. www.consilium.europa.eu/ueDocs/cms_Data/docs/pressData/en/jha/82745.pdf.

Koopmans, R. 2010. 'Trade-offs between equality and difference: immigrant integration, multiculturalism and the welfare state in cross-national perspective'. *Journal of Ethnic and Migration Studies* 36(1): 1–26.

Koopmans, R. and Statham, P. 1999. 'Challenging the liberal nation-state? Post-nationalism, multiculturalism and the collective claims making of migrants and ethnic minorities in Britain and Germany'. *American Journal of Sociology* 105(3): 652–96.

Koskela, K. 2014. *Integration Policies. Finland Country Report*. INTERACT Research Report No. 2014/29. Florence: European University Institute and Robert Schuman Centre for Advanced Studies.

Kostakopoulou, D. 2012. 'The evolving area of freedom, security and justice: taking stock and thinking ahead'. In M. Okólski, ed., *European Immigrations Trends, Structures and Policy Implications* IMISCOE Research, 259–67. Amsterdam: Amsterdam University Press.

Mandin, J. 2014. *An Overview of Integration Policies in Belgium*. INTERACT Research Report No. 2014/20. Florence: European University Institute and Robert Schuman Centre for Advanced Studies.

Massey, D. S., Durand, J. and Pren, K. A. 2014. 'Border enforcement and return migration by documented and undocumented Mexicans'. *Journal of Ethnic and Migration Studies*. doi: 10.1080/1369183X.2014.986079.

Mouritsen, P. and Jensen, C. H. 2014. *Integration Policies in Denmark*. INTERACT Research Report No. 2014/06. Florence: European University Institute and Robert Schuman Centre for Advanced Studies.

Pasetti, F. 2014. *Country Report. Integration Policies in Spain*. INTERACT Research Report No. 2014/30. Florence: European University Institute and Robert Schuman Centre for Advanced Studies.

Pastore, F. and Sciortino, G. 2011. *Tutori Lontani. Il Ruolo degli Stati d'Origine nel Processo di Integrazione degli Immigrati*. [Far Guardians. The Role of States of Origin in the Process of Integration of Immigrants]. Report for the Commission for Integration Policies (Ministry of Labour and Social Affairs).

Peixoto, J., Arango, J., Bonifazi, C., Finotelli, C., Sabino, C., Strozza, S. and Triandafyllidou, A. 2012. 'Immigrants, markets and policies in Southern Europe: the making of an immigration model?' In M. Okólski, ed., *European Immigrations: Trends, Structures and Policy Implications* IMISCOE Research, 107–47. Amsterdam: Amsterdam University Press.

Penninx, R. 2003. *Integration: The Role of Communities, Institutions, and the State*. Migration Information Source. Washington, DC: Migration Policy Institute.

Penninx, R. 2004. 'Integration Processes of Migrants in the European Union and Policies Relating to Integration'. Presentation for the Conference on Population Challenges, International Migration and Reproductive Health in Turkey and the European Union: Issues and Policy Implications, Istanbul, 11/12 October. www.esiweb.org/pdf/turkeynetherlands/RinnusPenninx.pdf.

Penninx, R., Kraal, K., Martiniello, M. and Vertovec, S., eds. 2004. *Citizenship in European Cities: Immigrants, Local Politics and Integration Policies*. Aldershot: Ashgate.

Poppelaars, C. and Scholten, P. 2008. 'Two worlds apart: the divergence of national and local integration policies in the Netherlands'. *Administration and Society* 40(4): 335–57.

Salis, E. 2012. *Labour Migration Governance in Contemporary Europe. The Case of Italy.* FIERI Working Paper – Project Lab-Mig-Gov. Turin: FIERI.

Sciortino, G. 2003. 'From homogeneity to difference? Comparing multiculturalism as a description and a field for claim-making'. *Comparative Social Research* 22: 263–85.

Sciortino, G. 2014. 'A European sociology of migration? Not yet, not quite'. In S. Koniordos, ed., *Routledge Handbook of European Sociology*, 252–67. London: Routledge.

Simon, P. 2012. *French National Identity: Who Belongs to the National Community?* Washington, DC: Migration Policy Institute.

Stefańska, R. 2015. *Integration Policy and Activities in Poland.* INTERACT Research Report No. 2015/07. Florence: European University Institute and Robert Schuman Centre for Advanced Studies.

Vogel, D. 2000. 'Migration control in Germany and the United States'. *International Migration Review* 34(2): 390–422.

Vogel, D. and Triandafyllidou, A. 2005. *Civic Activation of Immigrants – An Introduction to Conceptual and Theoretical Issues.* POLITIS Working Paper No. 1. Oldenburg: POLITIS (Interdisciplinary Center for Education and Communication in Migration Processes).

Wallace Goodman, S. and Wright, M. 2015. 'Does mandatory integration matter? Effects of civic requirements on immigrant socio-economic and political outcomes'. *Journal of Ethnic and Migration Studies.* DOI: 10.1080/1369183X.2015.1042434.

Wihtol de Wenden, C. 1999. *Faut-il Ouvrir les Frontières?* Paris: Presse de SciencesPo.

Wihtol de Wenden, C. 2011. 'The case of France'. In G. Zincone, R. Penninx and M. Borket, eds, *Migration Policymaking in Europe: The Dynamics of Actors and Contexts in Past and Present*, 61–92. Amsterdam: Amsterdam University Press.

Zincone, G. 1998. 'Illegality, enlightenment and ambiguity: a hot Italian recipe'. *South European Society and Politics* 3(3): 45–82.

Zincone, G. 2000. 'A model of "reasonable integration": summary of the first report on the integration of immigrants in Italy'. *International Migration Review* 34(3): 956–68.

Zincone, G. 2011. 'The case of Italy'. In G. Zincone, R. Penninx and M. Borket, eds, *Migration Policymaking in Europe: The Dynamics of Actors and Contexts in Past and Present*, 247–90. Amsterdam: Amsterdam University Press.

Zincone, G. and Caponio, T. 2004. *Immigrant and Immigration Policy-Making: The Case of Italy.* IMISCOE Working Paper Country Report. Amsterdam: IMISCOE.

Part 3

Mobility, migration and transnationalism in the Mediterranean region

9 The forms and determinants of public transnationalism

A North African comparison

Thomas Lacroix and Guillaume Le Roux

The majority of transnational practices take place within the private sphere of families, under the form of long-distance contacts or remittances. But a growing body of research has started to investigate the far-reaching impacts of migrants' associational and political cross-border engagements. Public transnationalism (as opposed to private transnational practices occurring in the private sphere of the family) can take a variety of forms, from interest in the political life of the origin country, the use of online and offline media, to the participation in political or associational activities. Research highlights the impacts they may have on sending countries in the social, development and political domains. They may take a dramatic dimension, as shown by the transnational social mobilization that formed during the 2010 Arab Spring.

And yet, existing theories accounting for cross-border transfers focus either on remittances only (Taylor 1999; Carling 2014) or on private transnationalism (Carling 2008; Basch *et al.* 1994). They fall short of taking the measure of the importance of these public practices and fail to explain the relationships existing between the different forms of engagement (Boccagni 2010). This chapter paves the way for a more comprehensive understanding of transnational engagements by comparing two major immigrant groups in France: Moroccans and Algerians.

Based on the statistical analysis of the INED[1] survey *Trajectoires et Origines* (TeO) and on field research,[2] this chapter seeks to understand the respective determinants and driving forces of the passage from private to public transnationalism. The analysis pays attention to two broad series of explaining factors: the integration trajectory of migrant groups, including their migration trajectory, integration characteristics and family networks. The comparative approach provides the possibility to appraise the sway of the policy context framing people's practices. Both states have designed and undertaken active policies towards their expatriates. But while Morocco has encouraged associational engagement into development activities, Algeria has striven to support the investment initiatives of highly skilled expatriates and the cultural and political link to the homeland. Specific attention will be paid to the importance of the right to vote in homeland elections (present in the Algerian case, but not in the Moroccan one) on public transnational practices. The influence of the French 'assimilationist' context is also addressed. Indeed, a body of work argues that the French model based on easy access to nationality and the discouragement of the expression of cultural identities in the public sphere impedes the embedding of homeland orientations over time (Koopmans and Statham 2003). The TeO dataset brings new insights invalidating this assumption.

The chapter opens with an overall presentation of private and public patterns of Algerian and Moroccan transnationalisms. It includes a quantitative measurement of the different forms of practices displayed by Moroccan and Algerian immigrants. Then follows an analysis of the variables underpinning the various forms of transnational engagements. A focus is given on the individual features characterizing the integration profiles and migration trajectories of immigrants, as well as on the context factors that may hold sway over their behaviours. The chapter ends with a broad discussion of the results in relation and points to new theoretical pathways that would complement existing theories.

The forms and patterns of transnationalism among Moroccans and Algerians in France

The INED survey *Trajectoires et Origines* was carried out in 2008 and 2009 with a panel of 22,000 respondents (Beauchemin *et al.* 2010). The present analysis focuses on Moroccan and Algerian immigrants (N=891 and N=822 respectively). The questionnaire included a range of questions on transnational practices. We have identified five of them that account for both *private* ('contacts with family and friends abroad', 'remit money to people abroad') and *public* transnationalism; these in turn were subdivided into *civic*, which is 'participation in a collective project in the sending country' and 'read/watch media from the sending country', and *political*, which is 'interest in homeland politics', 'vote in sending country elections since the arrival in France', transnationalism.

The first part of this study draws an overview of the different forms of transnational engagements. It measures the proportion of migrants concerned with different forms of activities. It is a three-step analysis that addresses transnational patterns as a four-level pyramid: the first and broadest one includes the whole immigrant population; the second one those who maintain any type of cross-border linkage (whether private or public), among the latter; the third takes only into account those who practise public (that is, either political or civic) activities; and the last group gathers those who show interest or are engaged in sending country politics.

Step 1: What is the proportion of migrants engaged in transnational activities?

Both groups appear to be strongly connected with their sending country: 86 per cent of Moroccans and of Algerians maintain transnational relations, which is slightly above the average observed among other immigrant groups in France

Table 9.1 Private, public and political transnationalism among North Africans

		Moroccans	*Algerians*	*Other immigrants*
Any transnational practice (public+private)	No	13.9%	14.4%	15.9%
	Yes	86.1%	85.6%	84.1%
		N=891	N=822	
Public practices	No	10.4%	9.7%	13.0%
	Yes	89.6%	90.3%	87.0%
		N=778	N=708	
Political practices	No	78.1%	51.1%	59.7%
	Yes	21.9%	48.9%	49.3%
		N=699	N=643	

Source: *Survey Trajectoires et Origines*, 2008–09

(84 per cent[3]). Among them, 62 per cent of Moroccans and 58 per cent of Algerians maintain private sphere relations in the sending country.

Step 2: Among 'connected' migrants, what is the share of those committed to public cross-border practices?

The second step of the analysis looks into those who are engaged in 'public' transnational practices, that is to say, those who participate in transnational civic activities, keep informed about homeland public affairs or participate in homeland elections.

As shown by the survey, transnational activities beyond the family sphere are still very common among both groups: more than nine out of ten migrants who maintain private relations also connect with the public sphere through politics, media or 'philanthropy'. Once again, the figures are within the range of what is observed among migrants at large (87 per cent).

Step 3: Among those engaged in public transnationalism, how many of them show an interest in politics?

The third stage focuses on political transnationalism: those who show strong interest/participate in homeland politics with regard to those who take part in public transnationalism at large.

The passage from public to political transnationalism reveals an important gap. Half of Algerians still partake in political transnationalism (48.9 per cent of those who engage in public transnationalism, a figure roughly similar of the average observed among immigrants), compared to one-fifth of Moroccans (21.9 per cent).

Figure 9.1 synthesizes the share and forms taken by Moroccan and Algerian transnationalism.

The first observation that can be made is that the TeO survey contradicts other studies, assuming that the assimilationist French context does not favour the

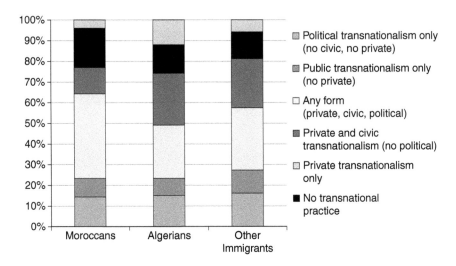

Figure 9.1 Patterns of transnational practices among North Africans

Source: *Survey Trajectoires et Origines*, 2008–09

transnational engagements of immigrants. In average, 84 per cent of immigrants do maintain ties with abroad. This percentage is almost identical between the two North African groups. The political context of the host country does not seem to affect migrant transnationalism. A wealth of studies documents the multiple facets of French transnationalism (also called migratory circulation) for the last 30 years (Simon 1979; De Tapia 1996; Gonin 1997; Charef 1999; Arab 2009). This scholarship, mostly written in French, remains largely overlooked by international authors. This erroneous assumption may also be explained by the conception of the assimilationist model narrowly defined in normative terms (access to citizenship, membership rights, pattern of insertion into the political field) and overlook the historical and post-colonial predicaments on which this model is based. Indeed, the French integration framework is highly racialized one that, far from being the commonly assumed colour-blind approach, applies differently with regard to the origin of immigrant groups. The management of religion (Catani and Palidda 1987) is historically taken charge of by origin countries. The French state has actively supported since the 1980s former colonies in preserving long-distance cultural and political linkages with a view to enhancing the propensity to return of African populations. For instance, over 20,000 pupils receive Arabic courses in French state schools (Souiah 2014: 405). The formation of ethnic enclaves is driven by administrative practices of attribution of public social housing according to ethnic criteria (Simon 2003). There are many reasons to believe that the French integration model directly or indirectly encourages rather than discourages transnational engagements of immigrant groups from former colonies.

The second finding that can be drawn from Figure 9.1 is that 'private' transnationalism does not usually come alone. Transnational activism exclusively confined to the family and friendship sphere only applies to 9 per cent of the North African population. In other words, interpersonal relations are most of the time associated with, at least, a strong interest in sending country public affairs.

However, the patterns of transnational engagements vary a great deal between both North African groups: public Moroccan transnationalism is more imbued with civic participation, while the Algerian one tilts towards political transnationalism, Moroccans are much more likely to be engaged in private and civic practices than Algerians. Conversely, Algerians are far more active in the political sphere. Moroccan associational transnationalism in France is amply documented (Lacroix 2003; Dumont 2008; Arab 2009). The literature highlights the developmentalist turn taken by the Moroccan volunteer sector abroad. Today, half of the associations created by Moroccan immigrants living in France are development associations (Lacroix 2013). This trend has been encouraged by the liberalization of the governance of rural development in Morocco. This new governance was initiated by two laws of decentralization, adopted in 1992, which granted to local authorities more responsibilities in local development, but with no additional financial resources to carry them out (Smires 2001: 351). In this context, the government encouraged the participation of NGOs, civic society and migrant organizations in local development projects. In the competition to get access to national and international funding, the link with migrant organizations became a strategic asset. The Moroccan state enforced a series of co-funding schemes in the mid-1990s meant to support partnerships between migrant NGOs and village associations: in 1995, the *Programme National de Construction de Routes Rurales* (Rural Roads National Building Programme, PNCRR); in 1997, the *Programme d'Electrification Rurale Généralisée* (Rural Electrification Programme, PERG); in 1998 the *Programme d'Approvisionnement Groupé en Eau Potable en Milieu Rural* (Grouped Potable Water Provision in Rural Area Programme, PAGER). More recently, semi-private organizations operating at the regional level, the so-called local development agencies, were created (the Social Development Agency (2001), South Development Agency (2002), the Development Agency of the Oriental (2006) and the North Development Agency (1996)) in order to direct external funding (including those coming from migrant associations) to local development projects.

In Europe, this evolution has been supported by co-development policies that provided to migrant organizations additional funding opportunities to carry out development projects (Lacroix 2008). An example is provided by the creation of the *Forum des Organisations de Solidarité Internationale de Migrants* (Forum of Migrant International Solidarity Organisations) in 2001, which provides every year a series of grants to migrant NGOs.

This has not been the case in Algeria, where the reform of local development governance has been far more limited in scope. The decentralization laws of 1984 increased the number of municipalities from 703 to 1,541, but the *wilaya* (province) remains the key administrative level. In 1988, in the wake of mass demonstrations against government policies, the state authorities put an end to the one-party system and liberalized the right to association, thereby giving birth to contemporary Algerian civic society. But the government never created conditions for the connection between the migrant volunteer sector and local development. In 1989, the government solicited 1,500 village *tajmaat*[4] of the Tizi-Ouzou wilaya to relay the development needs of each *douar*. This census was supposed to be followed by a large co-funding programme in which village populations (including emigrants) and public and private funders were to participate. But the programme was given up in 1990 despite massive social mobilization. The civil war that broke out in 1992 stopped any follow-up. The relationships with Algerians abroad do not rank high on the governmental agenda. The gas industry has always provided enough foreign currency and no need was felt to encourage immigrant transfers (Scagnetti 2014: 155). The tight control on exchange rates remains an obstacle to remittances. In the early 2000s, President Bouteflika put the emphasis on the relationships maintained with the Algerian elite of businessmen and highly skilled workers living abroad (the so-called *Compétences Nationales à l'Etranger*). A series of summer and winter schools and forums were organized between 2009 and 2011 and a website including a database of available skills was set up in 2013 (Souiah 2014: 403). But these short-lived measures have never been sustained long enough to leave a durable imprint on the migrant volunteer sector. The latter, which is historically dense and wide-reaching (Direche-Slimani 1997), remains mostly geared towards the local needs of the immigrant population. Homeland-oriented development or civic initiatives have not reached the level of systematization observed in the Moroccan case. For example, FORIM, a platform of migrant organizations based in Paris, lists only four Algerian organizations (against 28 Moroccan), including one that is not exclusively focused on Algeria but has a broader North African outreach. In addition to the absence of voluntary governmental policy, the Algerian civil society in France weakened its capacity of mobilization during the decade-long civil war (Silverstein 2004: 220; Collyer 2008). The inflows of refugees imported into France the factional conflicts fracturing the Algerian political arena. The politicization of the Algerian associational field during this period did not provide a favourable terrain for an efficient coordination of transnational activities.

Conversely, the Algerian political field is more open insofar as emigrants enjoy a parliamentary representation in Algiers. External voting is a widespread and entrenched practice. It was granted in 1976 by President Houari Boumedienne. The governmental aim was to bolster the regime's legitimacy by soliciting the allegiance of expatriates (Brand 2010). The absence of effective opposition movement in France facilitated this move. Political parties (Front de Libération Nationale, Rassemblement Culture et Démocratie, Front des Forces Socialistes, etc.) are historically well established in France. The right to vote from abroad and the presence of Algerian political structures in France encourage political transnationalism to a level unseen among Moroccans. As for the latter, they are to go back to their area of origin if they want to participate in local or national elections. In consequence, interest in political matters appears to be rather low (4 per cent of Moroccans in France are involved in political transnationalism only, against 12 per cent of Algerians). A parliamentary representation of expatriates has been a central claim of immigrant organizations for years. This right has been added to the Moroccan constitution in 2012, but not yet enforced. Their engagement in developmental practices seems to act as a substitute, a compensation for the absence of political recognition (Lacroix and Dumont 2015).

However, beyond the policy factors, we also have to take into account the effects of migration trajectories and integration.

The individual drivers for transnational engagement: length of stay and integration

The assimilationist hypothesis argues in favour of a weakening of transnational orientations in relation with the integration in the host country (Bommes 2005). For Carling, it is less integration than the presence of kin abroad that matters as, over time, interpersonal relations tend to wane or disappear (Carling 2008). In contrast, transnational scholars argue that one observes not a weakening but a mutation of transnational practices as integration gives access to resources for new forms of engagements. For Valentina Mazzucato (2005), migrants engage in more complex cross-border endeavours once they stabilize their legal and economic situation in the host country. Likewise, Guarnizo *et al.* (2003) argue that associational leaders as well as entrepreneurs who partake in transnational activities display a higher level of integration. Time may disrupt interpersonal relations, but immigrant incorporation opens up new avenues of engagement. Henceforth, one can hypothesize a shift from private to more public forms of transnationalism over time.

Time matters: the influence of the length of stay on transnational activities

The analysis shown in Figures 9.2 and 9.3 validates this hypothesis. One observes a growing proportion of migrants that do not partake in any form of cross-border activity (from 4 per cent in the first years of settlement to 18 to 20 per cent after 20 years of presence in France). But one also notes a transfer from private to public sphere. The private and civic activities of Moroccans tend to resist pretty well (above 50 per cent until 19 years of presence). But this transfer is outstanding among Algerians who tend to invest the political sphere in proportion with the duration of their migration: nearly 50 per cent of Algerians living in France for more than 20 years declare either voting and/or showing interest in Algerian politics.

The influence of individual integration …

The last phase of this analysis seeks to identify the characteristics of individuals engaged in private and public activities abroad. It is based on a combination of

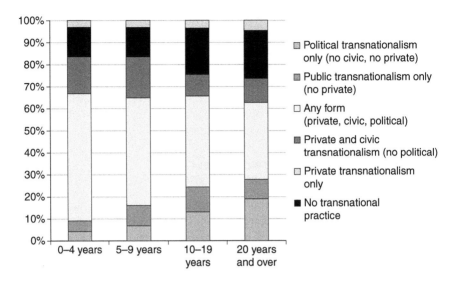

Figure 9.2 Evolution of transnational practices with regard to the time spent abroad (Moroccans)

Source: *Survey Trajectoires et Origines*, 2008–09

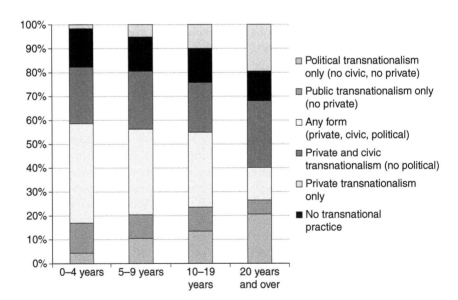

Figure 9.3 Evolution of transnational practices with regard to the time spent abroad (Algerians)

Source: *Survey Trajectoires et Origines*, 2008–09

two methods. In the first place, decision trees[5] are used to examine a set of characteristics: individual (age, sex, education, occupation status, socio-professional category, level of household income, marital status, parenthood); family and social network (immigrant origin of friends, having parents or children abroad); migration trajectory (migration status at arrival in France, length of stay in France, length of stay in the country of birth, age of departure, age of arrival, intention to return); and socio-political (membership to a union or association, command of French, interest in local politics, interest in national politics). The decision trees are helpful to establish a hierarchy of factors discriminating among the different forms of engagements. The problem of this method is to gloss over key variables that are correlated with the one highlighted by the tree. A regression analysis of the same battery of integration indicators complements and fine-tunes the decision tree-based analysis. The combination of the two methods provides the possibility not only to rank the drivers for transnationalism, but also to unfold the integration dynamics at play behind these key drivers (see Table 9.2).

... on private transnationalism

The first decision tree (Figures 9.4 and 9.5) highlights the characteristics of those who maintain private cross-border ties (within each cell, the first line refers to the percentage of those who do display private ties, while the second one, those who do not).

This first stage highlights temporal characteristics of the migration trajectory: the age of departure (for Algerians); the presence of a parent in the sending country (for Moroccans). Both criteria are tightly correlated. The time spent in the sending country prior to migration conditions the pattern of socialization and sense of belonging of individuals. As hypothesized by Carling, the other key driver for private transnationalism is the presence of family abroad (1,6 to twice more chance to practise private remittances than those who do not have any parent abroad). Likewise, having no child abroad reduces the odd of private transnationalism (among Algerians). They are adults, between 18 and 45 (for Algerians), and in general not retired (for Moroccans). Immigrant students who leave their household to continue their training in France are good candidates for private transnationalism (odds ratio 1.9 for Algerian students). Conversely, the so-called 1.5 generation who came with their parents at young age, and older people (retirees) who have lost their contact abroad, are less likely to partake in private (or public) transnationalism.

Another finding of this analysis is the ambiguous role played by socio-economic characteristics. Results are not fully conclusive. None of these criteria has been highlighted by decision trees. There seems to be a class factor in the maintaining of private sphere overseas activities. The regressive analysis shows that household members with a revenue above 2,700 euros per month display a higher odds ratio (among Moroccans), and so are people working as middle managers and semi-skilled workers. Conversely, employees have a lower

Table 9.2 Integration drivers of private, public and political remittances: a logistic regression

Variable (reference)/odd ratio		Private practices Moroccans	Private practices Algerians	Civic practices Moroccans	Civic practices Algerians	Political practices Moroccans	Political practices Algerians
Sex (Men)	Women	1.033807	1.372588	0.8330776	1.033694	0.5809278*	1.587175**
Private practices (no)	yes	–	–	2.71378***	2.820658***	2.183319***	1.813241***
Age group (26–35)	18 to 25	1.952945	3.197079***	0.8230957	0.5582193	1.04067	0.4512228
	36–45	0.8345872	1.984843**	1.294376	0.3254221***	2.193909**	0.8616053
	46 and over	1.005344	1.570945	1.088737	0.283583***	2.72287**	1.076016
Marital status (single)	Married	1.495605	2.869475	0.9283	1.165499	1.008356	0.6293635
	Widowed	1.063123	2.385747	0.4224441	2.482303	2.177101	0.5579939
	Divorced	0.764116	1.267629	0.3064018***	1.13799	0.6781331	0.414917**
Household income (€0–1300)	€1301–1900	1.115254	1.094351	0.9161085	0.9557281	1.16064	0.7401952
	€1901–2700	1.757116	0.7461009	1.273537	1.895435**	0.8780999	0.768547
	€2701 and over	2.665333***	0.8019395	1.528048	0.6552631	1.344104	0.5674589*
Education (secondary)	Primary	0.7611831	1.422962	1.408887	0.8483538	1.25177	0.8116569
	High school	1.399704	0.9614638	0.8445578	1.004145	0.6538035	0.6210364*
	University	1.057507	0.757819	0.7370856	1.154574	0.8891968	0.7618162
Child living abroad (yes)	No	0.1572977	0.4576987*	1.574645	2.070789	1.820728	0.7429431
Parent living abroad (no)	Yes	1.997607***	1.633946**	0.4768689***	0.6717946	0.8969162	0.795006
Having at least a child (no)	Yes	0.803868	0.7951546	1.285391	2.675336***	1.457595	1.745137*
Majority of friends are of the same origin (no)	Yes	1.472739*	1.154571	1.93348***	1.74367*	1.322071	1.176307
Status at arrival (family reunification)	Student	1.186938	2.022096*	0.5406471	1.4437	0.7208573	1.06259
	Labour	1.633642	1.675822	0.6559816	0.8212853	0.3299135***	1.970761**
	Spouse of French national	0.9559625	1.337658	0.4598162**	1.24198	0.7775165	1.08241
	Other	0.8306367	0.8007058	0.7047578	0.9680173	0.9463357	0.9867156

Employment (unemployed)	Farmer, merchant, entrepreneur	1.219753	1.346314	0.4009853*	0.7949034	0.1873624**	0.7613148
	Manager, skilled	0.6778316	1.016721	0.5125365	0.6011534	0.5179278	3.199704**
	Middle manager, semi-skilled	0.908979	2.303338**	0.747087	0.5202117	0.327135**	1.049655
	Employee	0.6077161*	1.099545	0.8361042	0.882787	1.041538	0.9268571
	Worker	0.8175051	1.199279	0.8193375	0.559389**	1.071126	1.288707
	Retired	0.3012668*	1.65858	2.142054	1.732842	0.5421626	1.475308
	Student	0.6283613	0.9086916	0.7149704	0.6372943	0.3471858	0.611947
Fluency in french (very good)	Good	0.632383*	1.098955	1.952265**	2.209507***	1.093589	1.433894
	A bit	1.219419	0.7024135	0.8107169	5.03992***	0.2457372***	1.035567
	Not at all	0.1298845**	(omitted)	(omitted)	(omitted)	0.8061934	(omitted)
Duration of stay in France (over 20 years)	0 to 4 years	1.279346	2.244915*	4.620037**	0.9238139	2.767842	0.3763117*
	5 to 9 years	1.35483	1.857517	2.200183**	0.9298449	3.654254***	0.3534121**
	10 to 19 years	0.8849337	1.121378	1.328516	1.058653	1.138125	0.5485078*
Age of departure (18 to 29)	0 to 5	0.3378943**	0.6502286	0.5438519	0.4156586**	0.5247553	0.4105577
	6 to 17	0.6313922*	0.7110298	0.4293828***	0.6516937	0.5676014	1.167898
	30 and above	1.28893	0.548669*	0.8047158	0.8942465	0.955419	1.155772
Interest in local politics	Yes	1.158001	0.8139932	1.379559	1.417507	1.786815**	0.8601756
Interest in national politics	Yes	0.7517787	1.100765	0.9321572	1.456635*	4.062119***	2.746103***

Note: *if $0.5 < (P > t) < 0.1$; **if $0.01 < (P > t) < 0.05$ and ***if $(P > t) < 0.01$

Source: *Survey Trajectoires et Origines*, 2008–09

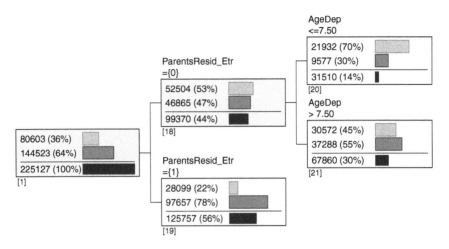

Figure 9.4 Private transnationalism (Moroccans)

Source: *Survey Trajectoires et Origines*, 2008–09

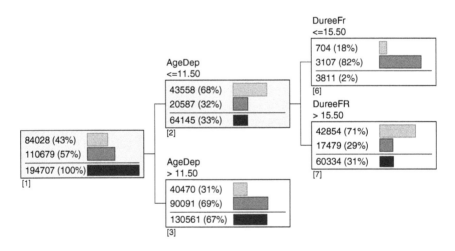

Figure 9.5 Private transnationalism (Algerians)

Source: *Survey Trajectoires et Origines*, 2008–09

propensity to private transnationalism (among Moroccans). This might hint at a relation between transnational practices and a certain level of professional stability in line with Mazzucato's hypothesis.

Indicators pertaining to social relations do not come up[6] at this stage. There is no contradiction between social embedding in France and everyday, family transnationalism.

... on civic transnationalism

The second series of decision trees (Figures 9.6 and 9.7) focuses on civic practices, either under the guise of collective charitable undertakings or interest in sending country public affairs.

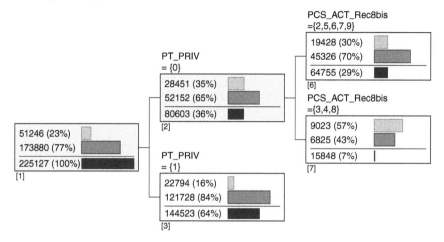

Figure 9.6 Civic transnationalism (Moroccans)

Source: *Survey Trajectoires et Origines*, 2008–09

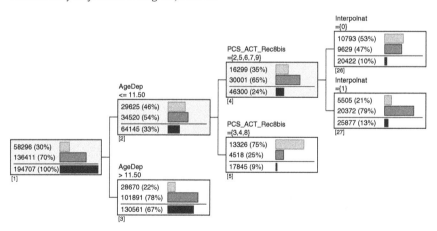

Figure 9.7 Civic transnationalism (Algerians)

Source: *Survey Trajectoires et Origines*, 2008–09

Note: ParentsResid_Etr = one parent live abroad (0 : No; 1 : Yes), AgeDep = age of departure from the country of origin, DureeFr = duration of living in France, PT_PRIV = have private transnational practices (0 : No; 1 : Yes), PCS_ACT_Rec8bis = socio-professional category (0 : Missing, 1 : Farmers; 2 : Artisans, merchants and entrepreneurs; 3 : Executives and higher intellectual professions; 4 : Intermediary professions; 5 : Employees; 6 : Laborers; 7 : Retired; 8 : Students; 9 : Other inactive person professional), Interpolnat = interest in national politics (0 : No; 1 : Yes), Interpolloc = interest in local politics (0 : No; 1 : Yes), ConditionArr2 = resident permit on first arrival in France (1 : Refugee; 2 : Student; 3 : Worker; 4 = Married to a French; 5 : Family reunion; 6 : Other).

There is a strong overlap between private and public transnationalism, at least in its civic, everyday form. This finding of the first part of the investigation (see Figure 9.6) is confirmed by the decision trees. This is particularly so for Moroccans, as highlighted by the decision tree, but it is equally strong among Algerians: those committed to private transnational activities have 2,8 more chance to partake in civic activities than those who have no family commitment. This strong correlation also explains why the 1.5 generation show a lesser inclination towards public transnationalism. Both the decision tree (for Algerians) and the regression (for Moroccans) confirms a negative relationship between civic practices and a departure during childhood.

Interestingly, socio-economic factors come up to characterize those who do not have any private commitment (among Moroccans) and '1.5' individuals (among Algerians): two groups, as mentioned above, that strongly overlap. In both cases, it turns out that upper-level managers and skilled workers (engineers, academics), middle managers and semi-skilled workers, but also students, display a lesser inclination to civic participation (and conversely for entrepreneurs, workers, employees, retirees or unemployed). This observation is somehow at odds with the drivers for private transnationalism (which seems more common among middle to upper classes). But this is not the only discrepancy with regard to private sphere engagement.

Among Moroccans, the findings are seemingly contradictory. In fact, they appear to point to the existence of two distinct profiles of actors. The first is made up of individuals arrived recently (less than nine years), and who keep a civic interest in their sending area. The second profile is more complex. It shows signs of embedding in French society. It comprises individuals who are at ease with spoken French. In the same vein, the presence of parents abroad is negatively associated with public transnationalism. But at the same time, a community-oriented embedding (friendship network of the same origin country, a foreign national spouse) into the host society is a positive factor. It is worth noting the importance of the family environment: divorcees have a lower odds ratio. This ambivalent pattern of integration (relative socio-economic integration and mixed social integration) may favour participation in collective and associational transnationalism.

Algerians display similar characteristics as the one committed to private activities. Civic participation tends to erode with age (over 35), but is bolstered by a community-oriented social incorporation (immigrant friendship circles, limited fluency in French). At the same time, other indicators plead in favour of a positive relation between civic participation and integration: a relative economic stability (household revenue over 1,900 euros) and a good proficiency in French. Likewise, workers appear to be less attracted by this pattern of engagement (odds ratio 0,5 compared to unemployed people).

At first sight, the overlap between private and civic transnationalism points to similar profiles of actors (recent migrants who grew up in the sending country). But the discrepancies and contradiction found in the analysis show that there is a plurality of profile and therefore of way of engaging into civic endeavours. It appears as an unstable, polymorphous and transitory form of engagement that leans towards a politicization of practices. Among Algerians, the oldest of North African

immigrant groups, interest in national politics appears as a key driver for civic transnationalism. We will see below that the latter is a key driver for political transnationalism. This variable does not come up in the Moroccan case. The difference observed
between the two groups may pertain to the distinctive patterns of public transnationalism displayed: political on the one hand, associational on the other.

... *on political transnationalism*

The final part of the analysis addresses political activities, namely the effective
participation in origin country election and the broader interest in homeland
politics (see Figures 9.8 and 9.9).

The characteristics associated with political involvement among Algerians and
Moroccans are markedly different. This difference, before being qualitative, is
quantitative: only one-fifth of Moroccans either vote or show interest in Moroccan
politics, half the proportion of Algerians (43 per cent). Moroccan expatriates do
not have the possibility to vote from abroad. In addition, the transposition onto
European soil of rivalries between pro- and anti-regime rivalries has, for a long
time, fed into a climate of distrust towards politics (Daoud 2002). On the
contrary, the Algerians strongly encourage expatriates to vote in order to muster
political and symbolic support. For both groups, interest in host country politics,
and therefore some sort of political education, turns out to be the key driver for
political transnationalism. Interestingly, in the Moroccan case, the variable
highlighted by the decision tree is interest in *local* politics, while in the Algerian
case it is interest in *national* politics. There are reasons to believe that the former
is associated with associational activism. The difference observed between the

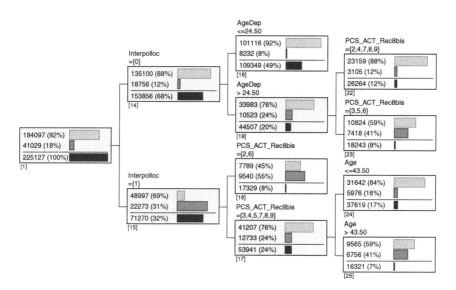

Figure 9.8 Political transnationalism (Moroccans)

Source: *Survey Trajectoires et Origines*, 2008–09

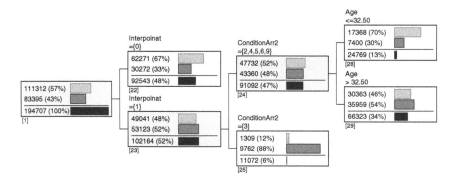

Figure 9.9 Political transnationalism (Algerians)

Source: *Survey Trajectoires et Origines*, 2008–09

two groups may pertain to the distinctive patterns of public transnationalism displayed: political on the one hand, associational on the other. The regression confirms the primary importance of political education: the odds ratio for interest in national politics is markedly stronger in both cases, and for local politics in the Moroccan case only.

As for civic practices, there is a strong correlation between private and political transnationalism. But this correlation is less strong, with lower odds ratio (1,8 to 2,1 more chance to partake in political practices, compared to 2,7 to 2,8. In addition, having parents abroad and the composition of friendship networks do not appear as relevant drivers any more. If private sphere activities are an early form of transnationalism unwritten by a vivid cross-border social field, political transnationalism is promoted by older migrants who are influenced by their socialization in the host country. Age is highlighted by the two decision trees: politically active migrants are at least in their late thirties, or early forties. This is consistent with the findings of the first part that show that the proportion of political practices increases with the duration of settlement.

Among Algerians, this link between settlement, time and politics is particularly strong. Individuals who have a stable family situation, having a child and not being divorced are more prone to engage in political remittances. This might also explain why women are positively associated with this form of commitment compared to men (odds ratio 1.5) (but this remains to be confirmed). Algerian political transnationalism is a generational phenomenon: those arrived as labour immigrants, a profile that characterized pre- and post-independence Algerian migration, is a positive driver that appears both in the tree and the regression. And yet the profile of politically active people is not limited to low-skilled migrants of the 1960s and 1970s: being a manager or a skilled worker increases the likelihood of partaking in host country politics. And conversely, wealthier households (over 2,700 euros) and people with high-school level education have a lower odds ratio than reference groups.

For Moroccans, the situation is very different. The decision tree and regression highlight a mix of temporal and socio-economic indicators. Politically active people tend to be older; but, unlike in the Algerian case, social aspects (marital situation) are not brought to the fore. But the overall picture is much more complex than in the Algerian case. When it comes to socio-economic variables, the findings are self-contradicting. Entrepreneurs and workers seem to be more active in the decision tree, but they display a lower odds ratio in the regression. So are semi-skilled/executive managers. Recently arrived migrants (fewer than nine years of settlement) are more prone to be committed to political remittances, but those who only speak a bit of French are four times less likely than the reference group in language proficiency. This points to a variety of profiles of politically active emigrants: older migrants who arrived recently and keep on moving back and forth to vote in Moroccan elections, more established immigrants who may be entrepreneurs or highly skilled workers, etc. Once again more investigation is required to unravel the Moroccan transnational conundrum.

Conclusion

This comparative investigation of Algerian and Moroccan transnationalisms reveals common drivers and specific factors.

It is first interesting to note that transnationalism, at large, is common among both groups, with over 90 per cent of positive responses. The so-called 'French assimilationist context' does not appear to impede the maintaining of long-distance linkages. However, between both groups, the patterns of behaviours display strong discrepancies. Algerian transnationalism is generally more politicized, while Moroccans tend to privilege private and civic practices. In order to understand this, we have taken into account a series of factors: context factors (institutional and civic society frameworks), the temporality of migration trajectories (length of stay in countries of departure and arrival), and integration variables.

The first conclusion drawn from the study is that, more than money, family or friendship, it is *time* that matters most. One observes two parallel trends that accelerate with the lengthening of the stay abroad: the weakening of transnational connections on the one hand, a shift from private to public transnationalism on the other. Conversely, private transnationalism through remittances and family connections prevails during the first years of establishment in France. Besides, temporality conditions are a key driver for private remittances, namely the maintaining of interpersonal relationships in the sending country: having parents or children abroad, having grown up in the sending country. The temporal dimension rules out two distinct populations: the so-called 1.5 who have not been socialized in the sending country and older (retired) emigrants who have lost these personal ties.

Second, the transnational institutional framework is also important. The right to vote to national elections from abroad turns out to be a key incentive. It explains the stronger political involvement of emigrants in Algerian politics.

But it also explains the resilience of Algerian transnationalism over time, with the possibility for emigrants to transfer their engagement from the private to the public sphere. However, the data analysis shows a dividing line between an older generation that has lived in the colonial and post-independence period and a younger generation that does not show the same level of confidence in political institutions. The younger generation of immigrants do not show the same inclination. This confirms findings of studies showing the feeling of distrust towards sending country institutions that characterize recent Algerian immigration. Increasingly, international mobility, whether legal or clandestine, is regarded as a form of exit. These elements announce the growing disaffection that can be observed among emigrants. There has been a sharp drop in political participation since the 2010 Arab Spring that is not captured by the TeO survey (the data collection was carried out in 2008–09). At the 2012 general elections, the turnout reached only 14 per cent and in 2014, for the presidential elections, just 12 per cent. The political life in Algeria with its perceived corruption and factional rivalries, aggravated by the candidacy of Bouteflika reduced to impotence by a heart attack, diverted Algerian emigrants from the political life of their origin country. The possibility to vote, on its own, does not suffice to foster participation.

Among Moroccans, the absence of an institutional channel is partly offset by the stronger involvement in associational activities. The lively Moroccan volunteer sector in France has thrived over the last two decades, providing a vehicle for civic transnationalism. But in the longer run, development cannot be a substitute for political citizenship. The right to vote from abroad was written into the kingdom's constitution in 2012, but not yet enforced. The absence of political recognition of the place of emigrants in Moroccan society may be conducive to a widening gap between the sending country and its expatriates in years to come.

Third, one can highlight some general trends associated with each form of transnationalism. Private transnationalism is an early migration phenomenon sustained by cross-border social relations. The passage to civic transnationalism appears as a transitory state, with a strong continuity between private and public sphere engagements, but, simultaneously, a greater importance granted to host country social networks favouring collective engagements. Political transnationalism, by contrast, is bolstered by maturing transborder socialities. The lesser importance of overseas interpersonal relations and a greater focus on family and political incorporation characterize this dynamics.

In this process, the bearing of socio-economic stability on transnationalism is the most difficult to grasp. Socio-economic variables gain in importance for civic and political practices, but they never stand out as key drivers. They seem to appear when social and interpersonal relations fade out. For civic practices, they characterize small subgroups (1.5 generation and those who do not engage in private sphere transnationalism). Beyond these general observations, it is difficult to draw any conclusive assertion with regard to economic integration. The analysis does not reveal any clear class or professional group that is more prone than another to sustain transnational activities, nor is there any clear positive or negative relation between transnationalism and economic incorporation. More investigation is required at this level.

By and large, this study brings about new insights that may feed into the debate on public transnationalism. The proposed typology (private, civic, political) offers a framework of analysis that may orient future research in this domain. It highlights a shift between the forms of transnationalism, the importance of social networks and the secondary role played by human or economic 'capitals'. This issue has remained a void of transnational theory. The different theories usually focus on individual characteristics of actors (their integration, social networks). Stated differently, they focus on the agentic possibilities of migrants. The present study brings to the fore the institutional and social contexts at large and more specifically to mid-range social institutions in which individuals are socialized: the families that are the crucible for private transnationalism during the first years of migration. As they wane over time, one observes the growing importance of associations, friendship circles and political parties, which may favour and orient the political education actors. The political framework in itself does not suffice to spur or discourage political remittances. The analysis highlights the influence of the structuring of migrant communities, their diversification and settlement over time over their engagement. This calls for a new theory of transnational engagement that would be based not only on actor-centred sociology but on a broader structure and agency theoretical framework (Lacroix 2014).

Notes

1 Institut National des Etudes Démographiques, Paris.
2 This research has benefited from the support of the ANR programme Global Governance of Mobility (Mobglob).
3 Beauchemin *et al.* (2011) used the same panel data with the same purpose, namely to measure the transnational engagement of immigrants. Their findings slightly differ from ours insofar as they endorse a much broader definition of transnationalism. These authors include 11 indicators broken down into four domains: economic, political, symbolic and social transnational orientations. If we prefer to restrict transnationalism to actual practices in a social constructionist perspective (see Portes *et al.* 1999; D'Amato and Fibbi 2008; and also Brubaker 2005), Beauchemin *et al.* also include 'symbolic' indicators such as the 'wish to be buried in a foreign country', a 'desire for return' that hints at some sort of prospective transnationalism, and indicators that point to past occurrence of transnational engagement that could no longer reflect the current reality (have acquired a business or a house, have returned to the origin country). Based on this broad definition, Beauchemin *et al.* find slightly superior results with an average of nine immigrants out of ten engaging in at least one form of transnationalism, which does not contradict our own conclusion, in fact quite the contrary.
4 By contrast with the *commune rurale* (rural municipality) whose constituency includes several villages (or, in Arabic, *douar*), it has no legal existence. Like in Morocco, *tajmaat(s)* are increasingly coupled with village associations that serve as an official facade acting on its behalf as a project manager.
5 C-RT Algorithm (Breiman *et al.* 1984). Learning sample (50 per cent of observations), used in the expansion phase of the tree; pruning sample (30 per cent) for post-pruning (reduction of the tree); test sample (20 per cent), used for the evaluation of the model.

6 Apart from an ambivalent result regarding the proficiency in French: it seems that those having a very good command of French have a higher tendency to be committed to private long distance relations.

References

Arab, C. 2009. *Les Aït Ayad: La Circulation Migratoire Des Marocains Entre La France, l'Espagne et l'Italie*. Géographie Sociale. Rennes: Presses Universitaires de Rennes.

Basch, L., Glick Schiller, N. and Szanton Blanc, C. 1994. *Nations Unbound: Transnational Projects, Postcolonial Predicaments and Deterritorialized Nations States*. New York: Gordon and Breach.

Beauchemin, C., Lagrange, H. and Safi, M. 2011. 'Transnationalism and immigrant assimilation in France: between here and there?' *Document de Travail* 172: 42.

Beauchemin, C., Hamel, C. and Simon, P. 2010. *Trajectoires et Origines. Enquête sur la Diversité des Populations en France*. Documents de Travail. Paris: INED. teo.site.ined.fr.

Boccagni, P. 2010. 'Private, public or both? On the scope and impact of transnationalism in immigrants' everyday lives'. In T. Faist and R. Bauböck, eds, *Diaspora and Transnationalism: Concepts, Theories and Methods*, 185–203. Amsterdam: Amsterdam University Press.

Bommes, M. 2005. 'Transnationalism or assimilation?' *Journal of Social Science Education* 1. www.jsse.org/2005/2005-1/transnationalism-assimilation-bommes.htm.

Brand, L. A. 2010. 'Authoritarian states and voting from abroad: North African experiences'. *Comparative Politics* 43(1): 81–99.

Breiman, L., Friedman, J. H., Olshen, R. A. and Stone, C. J. 1984. *Classification and Regression Trees*. Monterey, CA: Wadsworth.

Brubaker, R. 2005. 'The "diaspora" diaspora'. *Ethnic and Racial Studies* 28: 1–19.

Carling, J. 2008. 'The human dynamics of migrant transnationalism'. *Ethnic and Racial Studies* 31: 1452–77.

Carling, J. 2014. 'Scripting remittances: making sense of money transfers in transnational relationships'. *International Migration Review* 48 (September): S218–S262. doi:10.1111/imre.12143.

Catani, M. and Palidda, S. 1987. *Le Rôle du Mouvement Associatif dans l'évolution des Communautés Immigrées*. Paris: Fas, Ministère des Affaires Sociales.

Charef, M. 1999. *La Circulation Migratoire Marocaine un Pont Entre Deux Rives*. Rabat: Edition Sud Contact.

Collyer, M. 2008. 'The reinvention of political community in a transnational setting: framing the Kabyle citizens' movement'. *Ethnic and Racial Studies* 31: 687–707.

D'Amato, G. and Fibbi, R. 2008. 'Transnationalisme des migrants en Europe: une preuve par les faits'. *Revue Européenne des Migrations Internationales* 24: 7–22.

Daoud, Z. 2002. *De L'immigration à la Citoyenneté, Itinéraire d'une Association Maghrébine en France: l'ATMF (1960–2003)*. Houilles: Mémoire de la Méditerranée.

De Tapia, S. 1996. 'Echanges, transports et communications: circulation et champs migratoires turcs'. *Revue Européenne des Migrations Internationales* 12: 45–71.

Direche-Slimani, K. 1997. *Histoire de l'émigration Kabyle en France au XXe Siècle*. Paris: L'Harmattan.

Dumont, A. 2008. 'Representing voiceless migrants: Moroccan political transnationalism and Moroccan migrants' organizations in France'. *Ethnic and Racial Studies* 31(4): 792–811. doi:10.1080/01419870701784463.

Gonin, P. 1997. *D'entre Deux Territoires. Circulations Migratoires et Développement Entre Le Bassin du Fleuve Sénégal et La France.* HDR, Lille: Université des sciences et techniques.

Guarnizo, L., Portes, P. and Haller, W. 2003. 'Assimilation and transnationalism: determinants of transnational political action among contemporary migrants'. *American Journal of Sociology* 108: 1211–48.

Koopmans, R. and Statham, P. 2003. 'How national citizenship shapes transnationalism: migrant and minority claims-making in Germany, Great Britain and the Netherlands'. In C. Joppke and E. Morawska, eds, *Towards Assimilation and Citizenship: Immigrants in Liberal Nation-States*, 195–238. Basingstoke: Palgrave Macmillan.

Lacroix, T. 2003. 'Les réseaux marocains d'aide au développement'. *Hommes & Migrations* 1242: 121–28.

Lacroix, T. 2008. 'Politiques de codéveloppement et le champ associatif immigré africain: un panorama européen.' *The African Yearbook of International Law* 16: 79–98.

Lacroix, T. 2013. 'Deux décennies d'implication associative marocaine: continuités et changements'. *Hommes & Migrations*, 1303: 101–12.

Lacroix, T. 2014. 'Conceptualizing transnational engagements: a structure and agency perspective on (hometown) transnationalism'. *International Migration Review* 48 (3): 643–79. doi:10.1111/imre.12105.

Lacroix, T. and Dumont, A. 2015. 'Moroccans in France: their organizations and activities back home.' In *Development at a Distance: The Role of Immigrant Organizations in the Development of Sending Nations*. New York: Berghan.

Mazzucato, V. 2005. 'Ghanaian migrants' double engagement: a transnational view of development and integrating policies'. *Global Migration Perspectives* 48.

Portes, A., Guarnizo, L. E. and Landolt, P. 1999. 'The study of transnationalism: pitfalls and promise of an emergent research field'. *Ethnic and Racial Studies* 22(2): 217–37.

Scagnetti, J.-C. 2014. *La Wilaya Hexagonale: L'Algérie et son Émigration, une Histoire d'Identités (1962–1988).* Nice. www.theses.fr/2014NICE2013.

Silverstein, P. A. 2004. *Algeria in France: Transpolitics, Race and Nation.* Bloomington and Indianapolis: Indiana University Press.

Simon, G. 1979. 'L'espace des travailleurs tunisiens: structures et fonctionnements d'un champ migratoire international'. Thèse de Doctorat, Poitiers: Université de Poitiers.

Simon, P. 2003. 'Le logement social en France et la gestion des "populations à risques"'. *Hommes et Migrations* 1246: 76–91.

Smires, F. 2001. 'Centralisation et décentralisation territoriale au Maroc'. Thèse de Doctorat: Univ. Sidi Mohamed Ben Abdallah de Sciences juridiques, économiques et sociales.

Souiah, F. 2014. 'Les harraga en Algérie: émigration et contestation'. Thèse de Doctorat, Paris: Institut d'études politiques.

Taylor, E. J. 1999. 'The new economics of labour migration and the role of remittances in the migration process'. *International Migration* 37: 63–88.

10 Inventing an Egyptian transnational nation

Homeland politics in the Arab Spring uprisings between migration processes, diasporic policies and political opportunity structures

Lea Müller-Funk

Introduction

The events that shook the MENA region in the spring of 2011 not only led to a new political consciousness in Arab countries and an awakening of political participation, but also influenced the perception and the political participation of Arab communities outside their home countries. During the Arab Spring, the question of how Arab communities were involved in the uprisings was highly debated, especially in the media; but little serious academic research on the question exists so far, and this also holds true for Egypt. Exceptions are Abdelrahman (2011), Asadova (2012), El Baradei *et al.* (2012) and Severo and Zuolo (2012).

This chapter investigates so-called 'homeland politics' during and after the revolutionary upheavals in Egypt and analyses how Egyptians abroad participated in political processes between 2011 and 2013. Østergaard-Nielsen defines homeland politics as 'migrants' and refugees' political activities pertaining to the domestic or foreign policy of the homeland. That is, it means opposition to or support for the current homeland political regime and its foreign policy goals' (Østergaard-Nielsen 2003: 21). Taking Vienna and Paris as case studies, I first give a short overview of the mobilizations that took place during and after the uprising. Second, I analyse the similarities and differences between these mobilizations by looking at migration processes and the development of 'diaspora policies' (Gamlen 2008), as well as policies targeting homeland politics in the respective country of residence. When people leave their country and settle in another country, they actually start to live in multiple jurisdictions – the jurisdiction of their country of origin and the jurisdiction of the destination country. According to Østergaard-Nielsen, political identities and memberships of migrants are thus 'a result of the complex interplay between the events and policies of the country of origin, and the process of migration and settlement in the receiving country' (2003: 24). I argue that the jurisdictions of both the sending and the receiving country affect the political behaviour of migrants and their children towards their country of origin.

This chapter is based on data collected between March 2012 and July 2014. In the course of this field research, I followed what Østergaard-Nielsen has called 'transnational political networks', which tried to influence politics in the (post-) revolutionary phase in Egypt between 2011 and 2013. The networks studied varied in political orientation, size and organizational structure: some were openly political; others had no overt political agenda, but served as forums for homeland politics at a second remove. I studied these networks methodologically in two ways: first, I conducted qualitative interviews with people active in these networks, and second, I analysed how social media was used by these networks for political protest.

The Arab Spring as a moment of renewed political interest in homeland politics

The events since 2011 have massively mobilized Egyptians abroad, including people who had been disillusioned by Egyptian politics for a long time, people who had never been politically active before, and also people who had been active in oppositional politics in Egypt prior to their emigration to Europe. However, only a minority continued to participate in protests and associations in the long term. The 18 days of the revolution were lived by many as moments of a newly found sociability, a mutual discovery of Egyptians living in the same city, but also as a moment where perspectives changed and identity was re-discussed. However, later on, the revolutionary upheavals in Egypt made ideological differences visible not only in Egypt itself but also among Egyptians living abroad. To a certain degree, political evolutions were mirrored abroad: in both Vienna and Paris the reconfigurations and political mobilizations that have taken place since January 2011 have to a certain extent echoed political events in Egypt and have fragmented groups after an initial reunion.

Yet what is very interesting to note is that mobilizations in these two European capitals were very different in shape and vitality. In Paris, most of the networks that emerged were small groups mainly consisting of people born in Egypt, while the second generation was less present. Copts became mobilized only later with the rise to power of Mohammed Morsy and then (they) mostly mobilized around the topic of discrimination against Copts, while people of Jewish Egyptian origin did not become politically organized at all. After the first 18 days of the revolution in 2011 networks were founded that paralleled organizations in Egypt, sometimes even carrying the same names: The *Association des Jeunes du 25 Janvier* (Association of the Youth of the 25th of January) was established in the aftermath of the revolution to represent revolutionary Egyptian youth abroad, and initially united a broad spectrum of political ideologies, from leftist to moderate Islamist. This group later suffered internal conflicts and split into two separate associations. Later, the *April 6 France Movement* was set up. The Tamarrud Campaign in Egypt also had a counterpart in Paris. Finally, after the overthrow of Morsy's presidency in July 2013, the National Alliance to Support Legitimacy (*at-Taḥāluf al-waṭanī li-da'm aš-šar'īya*), a group supporting the return of Mohammed Morsy to power, was established in Paris.

Political divisions had already become apparent after the presidential elections in 2012 and greatly increased after July 2013, polarizing Egyptian social fields into two main camps. The divisions crystallized around the terms *inqilāb* (coup) and *aṭ-ṭawra aṭ-ṭāniya* (the second revolution), that is, around the question of how the events on 3 July 2013 should be interpreted. Additional groups emerged over the course of this development, such as the collective *Aswāṭ min Miṣr* (Voices of Egypt), which sought to raise awareness about political events in Egypt and to collect expertise about Egypt. *Mārid France* was another small association founded in 2012 to mobilize for secularity and against any form of discrimination in Egypt. Copts in Paris seldom organized politically. When they did, it was mainly in defence of the rights of Copts in Egypt – often framed more globally as a defence of human rights – and often at times when Copts in Egypt were persecuted, such as after the Alexandria bombing in January 2011 and the Maspero events in October 2011. Copts in Paris became more politically vocal when Mohammed Morsy won the presidential elections in June 2012, an event that brought Copts and Egyptian Muslims critical of Morsy's government closer to each other. *Mārid France*, for example, united Coptic and secular Muslim activists, as did the Tamarrud campaign, which formed a loose alliance between Copts and a section of Egyptian Muslims living in Paris. These new networks temporarily and partially transcended divides of class and religion, as some networks included on the one hand irregular migrants working in the building sector, and intellectuals, moderate Muslims and Copts on the other hand.

In Vienna, this was not so much the case, as mobilizations were much more small-scale and took place mainly within pre-existing Egyptian community associations, which were mostly defined by national origin and had no open political objectives as such. While the first generation initially refrained publicly from political participation within these associations, the second generation was more vocal, founding new associations and distancing itself from the associations of the older generation, which it regarded as too close to the former regime. Initially, the pre-existing associations founded by the first generation, such as the Egyptian Club (*an-Nādī al-miṣrī*) and the General Union of Egyptians in Austria (*al-Ittiḥād al-'āmm li-l-miṣriyīn bi-n-Nimsā*), tried to remain outside politics and avoid the politicization of their associations, especially on their Facebook profiles. The Egyptian Club is the oldest Egyptian association in Vienna and was founded in the 1970s when Egyptian migration to Austria began to increase. It organizes funeral services, celebrations for Islamic holidays, provides sports events, student exchanges with Egypt, family activities, and lectures on topics concerning Egypt. The much smaller General Union of Egyptians in Austria aims at representing people living in Austria who have at least one Egyptian parent. It deals with the questions and problems of Egyptians living in Austria and organizes different youth activities, especially trips to Egypt, Arabic classes, and lectures on Egyptian and Austrian politics, the economy, and science. Initially, the members of the General Union of Egyptians in Austria did not discuss their political opinions openly on social media; however, they became more openly critical about Morsy's government from October 2012 onwards. The Egyptian Club also discouraged discussions on its social media profile; nevertheless, members showed a tendency to support Morsy's government.

Youth for Egypt in Austria (*aš-Šabāb min ağl Miṣr bi-n-Nimsā*), a new association created by the second generation, was founded shortly after the revolution in January 2011 to 'support the claims of the revolution in Egypt'. The main goal of Youth for Egypt in Austria was the development of political attitudes among the second generation: 'Our goal is that Egyptian young people in Austria develop an opinion towards their country. That they have a vision for the future of Egypt. That they become aware from an early age onwards where they come from' (interview, Ḥikma, Vienna, 26 April 2014). The founding members claimed not to support a special political programme or party and saw their activism as more social than political. The group tried to invoke the revolutionary events of January 2011 as a unifying moment and a cause for pride in their country of origin.

Equally, Egyptian-Austrian Youth (*aš-Šabāb al-miṣrī an-nimsāwī*), founded in 2009, only became active after 2011. Austrian-Egyptian Youth was founded with the stated purpose of representing 'youth with an Egyptian background in Austria'. They assert that they 'are a main part of Austrian society and want to contribute their part to the development of the society with roots in Egypt living in Austria'. Their goals are the conservation of an 'Arab-Egyptian identity and a Muslim conscience, an intelligent blending of this identity with the Austrian one, the organisation of events and conferences and meetings for questions from the public and youth with an Egyptian background' (website, Ägyptisch-Österreichische Jugend). In 2011, the leaders of the group discussed political events in Egypt in their social media profile and organized events in connection with the revolution to show their solidarity with ongoing processes. During the presidential elections, the group lobbied for Mohammed Morsy and also supported Morsy's government afterwards.

The Coptic community in Austria became visible in terms of mobilization only through associations closely linked to the Coptic Orthodox Church in Vienna. As in Paris, Copts in Austria became more visible in summer 2013, when they supported the Tamarrud Campaign and supported the overthrow of Mohammed Morsy. The Coptic-Austrian Association, which was founded in 2008, and Coptic Youth organized press conferences to raise awareness about discrimination and violence against Christians in Egypt, such as the bombings in Alexandria in January 2011 and Maspero in October 2011, and supported the overthrow of Mohammed Morsy.

In general, as in Paris, it was during the presidency of Mohammed Morsy, and particularly after July and August 2013, that political divisions among Egyptians living in Vienna emerged more clearly. Faced with inner political fractures, one of the associations founded by the second generation decided to abstain from politics completely. In summer 2013, the Coordination Council of the Egyptian Community in Austria (*al-Mağlis at-tansīqī li-l-ğālīya al-miṣrīya fī n-Nimsā*) was founded and started to organize demonstrations against the ousting of

President Morsy in July 2013 and the violent breakdown of protests in Rābiʿa al-ʿAdawīya Square in August 2013.

Comparing homeland politics

Østergaard-Nielsen has argued that the political identity and the political affiliation of immigrants are not necessarily a function of integration into the receiving country, but a result of the complex interplay between the events and policies of the country of origin, and the process of migration and settlement in the receiving country (2003: 24). I will demonstrate in this section how migration processes, diasporic policies of the country of origin, and the political opportunity structure of the receiving country influence the shape and form of transnational protests. In my analysis, studying the political opportunity structure of host societies helps us to understand why networks take on different appearances across different countries. Odmalm argues that host societies contribute to the collective organization of migrants through the resources for, and models of, organizations they provide and through how they encourage or discourage collective identity and organization types around which mobilization can take place (2005: 181–2). Of course, factors other than political opportunity structures shape and influence transnational political participation. Researchers such as Beinin and Vairel (2011) propose a 'relational' perspective which makes 'interpersonal networks' central to their model of mobilization. However, I found that these interpersonal networks are heavily influenced by the experience migrants have in host countries and by the concepts host countries offer for the collective organization of migrants.

Migration flows: Egyptian migration processes to Paris and Vienna

In both case studies, the shape and nature of Egyptian migration as well as the size of the community and its inner organization played an essential role in mobilization.

In fact, Egyptian migration to Europe is atypical in two ways. First, historically, Europe was not the typical Egyptian migration destination, as Egyptian migration has been mainly directed towards oil-producing, mostly Gulf countries. Egyptian migration to Europe happened in larger numbers only during and after the 1980s. Second, Egyptian migration to Austria and France represents 'atypical' migration streams in both of these countries: it is not one of the three historical migration flows to Europe, which comprise migration with a colonial background, labour migration through recruitment agreements, and refugee migration from Eastern to Western Europe after the Second World War. Egyptian migration to Europe somehow represents the new type of migration that emerged in Europe from the 1980s onwards, when immigrants from all over the world started to come to Europe while practices of international migration became much more fluid than before with consecutive stays in different countries and the alternation of residence between countries.

In general, Egyptian migration in Austria and France differs greatly in – unofficial – numbers. The problem of diverging statistics between the country of origin and the country of destination has been widely discussed in migration studies. One reason for this gap is that Egypt continues to count children and grandchildren of (one or two) citizens born in another country as citizens. This explains the often huge discrepancy between statistics from receiving countries and consulates: for example, figures for Egyptian citizens living abroad from consulates and receiving countries differ from each other by +246 per cent (Fargues and Le Bras 2009: 9). In the French case, numbers for Egyptian migrants vary between 160,000 (Egyptian MFA 2009) and 36,000 (French statistics 2013).

In contrast, Egyptian migration to Austria is on a much smaller scale; according to Austrian statistics, 13,000 people born in Egypt live in Austria (Austrian statistics, 2011), while Egyptian statistics estimate that around 25,000 Egyptians live in Austria (Egyptian consulate estimations, 2014). Historically, migration flows were quite similar: both countries witnessed small inflows of Egyptians from the 1950s onwards, motivated by political, educational and professional choices. In both countries, migration flows started to increase in the 1980s when temporary labour migration to the Arab oil-producing countries declined. However, France has witnessed a high increase in irregular migration flows since the 2000s, which Austria has not. Today, a second generation exists in both countries; however, in France it is proportionally much smaller than the numbers of newly arriving migrants.

Egyptian migration to France can principally be divided into three streams. The first marginal stream included wealthy Egyptians fleeing Nasser's nationalization programmes, as well as political opponents, and an educational elite who migrated to France to continue their academic education. These included around 10,000 Egyptian Jews who left Egypt for France up to 1967 (Beinin 1992: 73–94; 1998). However, slowly, with the economic problems present in the country, the migration profile has changed considerably: the second – much more significant – migration to France and Paris started in the 1980s. Lafargue's research shows that in the 1980s and 1990s Egyptian migrants mainly came to France by prolonging their education in a French university or by overstaying holiday visas, profiting from judicial gaps or regularization measures to settle down.

These migrants included Muslims and Copts; they were mostly male and young (between the ages of 30 and 40) and came to Europe in groups of friends or as isolated individuals. Before their departure, many perceived that their settlement in Europe would be long term (Lafargue 2002: 69–70). The majority of these migrants were non-francophone entrepreneurs, as well as taxi drivers and restaurant owners. This stream has increased since the 2000s and much of it is irregular.

Figures for Egyptian migrants to France have increased steadily from the 1950s onwards: in 1954, 1,686 people migrated from Egypt to France; the figure was 2,516 in 1968 and 2,615 in 1975. The period between 1982 and 1990 in particular saw an increase of Egyptian inflows. The INSEE, the French National Institute for Statistics and Economic Research, estimated the numbers of Egyptians living in

France at 8,992 in 1982, a figure that increased to 11,992 people in 1990 (Lafargue 2002: 69).

Precise figures for contemporary Egyptian migration to France are difficult to obtain due to the large shares of irregular migrants. In 1999, the French census counted 15,974 Egyptian immigrants in France, while the Egyptian government counted 50,000 in Paris and 70,000 in Marseille (Fargues and Le Bras 2009: 22). In 2013, the French government estimated the number of Egyptians in France at 36,000; while Egyptian officials in France estimated that around 300,000 Egyptians were living in France, assuming that around half of Egyptian migration to France was irregular. These figures give a better insight into the real number of Egyptian migrants in France. Egyptian migration to France has been mainly Muslim, but also includes significant numbers of Copts. Again, in this matter it is quite impossible to get reliable data on numbers, as estimates range from 60,000 to 75,000 (interview, Tādrus, Paris, 29 September 2013).

Egyptian migration to Austria is much smaller in scale and less recent than Egyptian migration to France or Great Britain, but is somewhat comparable in numbers to Egyptian migration to Germany. Austria's connection to Egypt goes back to the time of the Capitulations when the Austrian-Hungarian monarchy became the protector of the Coptic-Catholic Church in Egypt (1899) and the Jewish community in Alexandria (1854) (Agstner 1993: 12–13). Up to the 1960s, Egyptian migration to Austria was limited in size and was mainly motivated by education: the first migration streams to Austria happened in the form of student missions organized under Muḥammad 'Ali in 1829, 1845, 1849 and 1857 (Agstner 1993: 11). After the Second World War, this trend of educational migration continued, as it did in the 1950s and 1960s, when Egyptian students continued to come in small numbers to Austria.[1] In 1934, only 75 persons with Egyptian nationality were registered in Austria; in 1961, this figure had increased to 554.

In the 1960s, Austria did not sign a labour recruitment agreement with Egypt, as it did with Turkey (1964) or Yugoslavia (1966). Still, from the 1980s onwards, the numbers of Egyptian migrants to Austria started to increase, as in other European countries: the figure increased to 1,574 in 1981 and to 4,509 in 1991.[2] During the 1980s, Egyptian migrants often entered Austria with a tourist visa and prolonged their visa when they found employment. In the 1980s, newspaper selling in Vienna became the classic entry-level job for Egyptian migrants, because practically no German language knowledge was required, and because many Austrian employees had left this job due to its precariousness. Aberer *et al.* (2006) analysed how Egyptian migrants established a security net between relatives in Egypt and social networks in Austria: Egyptian migration networks were set up which facilitated – mostly male – migration to Austria through personal relations. Newspaper selling thus became a classic migrant network, characterized by close social and family relations, one that was known prior to departure from Egypt. In 1987, the dominance of Egyptians in newspaper selling in Vienna even led to a freeze in hiring Egyptians because employers feared that they would organize too well (Aberer *et al.* 2006: 99). Today, this sector has been overtaken by Pakistani and Indian migrants, while many Egyptian migrants who came to Austria in the 1980s have moved over to the restaurant industry, particularly pizzerias, or have become taxi drivers; others have built up their own businesses (interview, Luṭfī, Vienna, 4 June 2014).

Egyptian migration to Austria has been mainly male; however, between 1991 and 2011, figures for men and women with Egyptian nationality almost aligned due to family reunification. In 2001, 9,168 people born in Egypt lived in Austria, of whom 4,818 had acquired Austrian nationality. In 2011, this figure had increased to 12,715, of whom 8,178 had acquired Austrian nationality. In Austria, as in France, official data on a second generation does not exist. Yet estimates from the General Union of Egyptians in Austria indicate that around 25,000 people with a so-called Egyptian migration background live in Austria (Medienservicestelle 2013). According to the Egyptian consulate in Vienna, irregular Egyptian migration to Austria is not comparable in numbers to that to France or Italy (interview, ʿUmar Maḥmūd, Egyptian Consulate Austria, Vienna, 14 April 2014).

In both countries, the size of the community heavily influenced the degree and the kind of political participation: in general, the larger the migrant group, the more active its participation was in homeland politics. In both cases, the time spent in the country played a role in mobilization: in Paris, where protests were much bigger, they were mostly led by first-generation migrants – including irregular migrants – who had only recently moved to France and who had been interested in Egyptian politics prior to 2011. In Vienna, where protests were much smaller, mobilizations were mostly led by the second generation. In summary, the question of the participation of the first and second generation was more one of how and not if: in Paris, political activists framed themselves as being a part of the Egyptian revolutionaries, but sojourning abroad, while in Vienna, second-generation activists framed their political action more as an expression of their renegotiated identity. For them, homeland politics constituted a way to reconstruct their relationship to their parents' country of origin.

Diasporic policies: from diaspora building to diaspora consolidation

In both cities, the change of Egyptian *diasporic policies*, and especially the lobbying for access to political rights of Egyptian citizens abroad, was a major mobilizing issue for transnational political networks shortly after the uprising in Egypt in 2011. The subsequent granting of voting rights to Egyptian citizens abroad was an incentive for many political mobilizations which took place overseas.

Today, emigrants have – at least economically speaking – become important actors of labour-exporting states. Thus, most sending states do not passively watch their citizens leave and immerse themselves into another country's society, but actively try to influence their behaviour and attachment to their home country. Most states have progressively conceded rights to their citizens abroad, including political rights. In academia, emigration policies and diasporic policies have only recently received some small scholarly attention, as research has often been focused on immigration and not emigration policies. Several researchers have lately started to study policies targeting citizens abroad (Choate 2008; Dufoix *et al.* 2010; Gamlen 2008; Green and Weil 2006; Smith 2003a, 2003b; Shefer 2003; Levitt and de la Dehesa 2003; Østergaard-Nielsen 2003; Green 2005; Lafleur 2013).

Egypt is one of the largest emigration countries in the world today. During the twentieth century, Egypt gradually changed from an educationally driven, restrictive emigration policy under Nasser to one exporting labour from the 1970s onwards as part of Sadat's *infitāḥ* policy. Under Nasser, emigration was handled restrictively and was punished with the loss of citizenship: the Nationality Law of 1952 still required a strong territorial attachment to Egypt (continued residence from 1900 regardless of Ottoman nationality), and stipulated that nationals who left the country for six months with no intention to return lost their Egyptian nationality automatically. With the establishment of the right to leave with the Constitution of 1971, nationality legislation also became more relaxed in terms of accepting dual nationality and retaining Egyptian nationality after emigration: the Nationality Law of 1975 no longer punished Egyptians for leaving the country with the loss of nationality. In fact, under Law 26/75, Egyptian nationality was now passed on by descent even outside the country (so-called 'perpetual nationality'). This meant that children born to Egyptian parents outside the country could still claim Egyptian nationality. With the emergence of emigration as a social phenomenon, Egyptian nationality thus started to include children born to Egyptian parents (or rather, fathers) abroad, hence introducing a *ius sanguinis* valid outside Egyptian territory. Slowly, the strong link between Egyptian territory and Egyptian nationality – which had been extremely important for the foundation of the concept of Egyptian nationality at the beginning of the century – started to weaken.

Especially in the 1980s under Mubarak's government and with ongoing economic problems in the country, emigration came to be progressively perceived as a development strategy and tool by the state. At the beginning of its emigration experience, Egypt perceived migration merely as a temporary change of residence and place of work for a limited period of time and defined itself as a 'guest worker' or 'rotation' model. With the persistence of emigration and increasing numbers of nationals abroad, Egypt gradually transformed and specified its diasporic policies. With the acceleration of migration flows to Western countries (US, Canada, Australia and Europe) since the 1980s and 1990s, perceived by the Egyptian state as permanent, in contrast to Egyptian migration to the Gulf perceived as temporary, the Egyptian state has increasingly developed policies dealing with its communities abroad.

In Egyptian governmental discourse, the central term for emigration is *hiǧra*, thus 'emigration' or 'departure'. The Constitution of 1971 was the first to mention the right to emigrate, in Arabic, *hiǧra*; however, it did not specify in more detail how the state designated emigrants. Interestingly, the Arabic language does not distinguish between emigration and immigration, the word *hiǧra* being used for both terms. With the emergence of institutions dealing with emigration in the 1980s and especially with Emigration Law 111/1983, Egyptian emigrants were designated *al-miṣrīyūn fī-l-ḫāriǧ* ('Egyptians abroad'). The second term used throughout the law is *muhāǧirūn*, thus 'emigrants'. The Arabic verb *hāǧara* denotes the act of emigrating; however, it also includes the meaning of refraining or keeping away from something, and thus includes the idea of a later return, adding to the imagery of a temporary departure. These terms continue to be used in legislation, so the Constitution of 2011 refers to *al-miṣrīyūn fī-l-ḫāriǧ* (art. 56), while the Constitution of 2014 talks about *al-miṣrīyūn al-muqīmūn fī-l-ḫāriǧ*. *Muqīm* means 'sojourning', or 'residing' in English, but also refers to the idea that a return is somewhat possible.

Neither the Egyptian constitutions nor the main law dealing with emigration in Egypt refer to a 'community' or a 'diaspora' abroad: that is, terms associated with a permanent residence. Terms such as diaspora (*šatāt*) or even community (*ǧālīya*) do not appear in legal texts dealing with emigration. On the contrary, Law 111/1983 refers to the new generations (*aǧyāl*) born abroad (art. 2) and the children of emigrants (*abnā' al-muhāǧirīn*). The word *ǧāliya* stems from the Arabic root *ǧ-l-w* which means 'to exile or remove someone'; *ǧāliya* itself refers to 'people who emigrated from their homeland and live in a foreign – and also strange – country' or the 'colony of foreigners in one country'. Equally, government officials dealing with Egyptians abroad in embassies, consulates or cultural offices do not use the terminology 'diaspora' (*šatāt*). The common terms to refer to Egyptians abroad, including the second and third generation, are *il-muwāṭinīn bi-l-ḫārig* ('the citizens abroad') or *el-ǧālya el-maṣriyya bi-l-ḫārig* ('the Egyptian community abroad') to refer to Egyptian expatriate communities in one particular country. All these terms used in governmental discourse suggest the construction of emigration imagined as temporary, while emigrants and their descendants remain an inseparable part of the Egyptian nation.

In terms of *diaspora building* – that is, cultivating and recognizing a diaspora in the theoretical sense (Gamlen 2008) – Egypt has undertaken efforts to build a 'diaspora' since the 1980s. In the 1980s and 1990s, the Egyptian state established bureaucratic structures dealing with emigration and Egyptians abroad, such as the Ministry of Emigration Affairs 1981, the promulgation of the Emigration Law 1983, the Migration Sector in the Ministry of Manpower and Emigration in 1996 and the implementation of the Supreme Committee of Emigration in 1997, an inter-ministerial committee dealing with matters of emigration.

With regard to dual citizenship in Egypt, since the Constitution of 1971 the trend has been towards accepting it, and, since the Nationality Law in 1975, towards imposing it: the Migration Law of 1983 repeated the right to dual citizenship and strengthened the principle of *ius sanguinis* for Egyptians migrating abroad and their children. In 1986, dual citizenship also became favourable in terms of military service, as all holders of dual nationality were excluded from undertaking military service. Egypt continues to count its emigrants as citizens, even if they acquire the nationality of another country or give up their Egyptian nationality in order to gain another citizenship, and adds irregular migrants into its statistics of Egyptians living abroad.

Law 111/1983 introduced for the first time duties for the state in terms of protection of its citizens abroad and maintenance of contact with them, especially regarding permanent emigrants, and set up a registration system for Egyptian emigrants. The law did not mention any political rights of emigrants, but only stipulated that the state should protect and maintain contact with its citizens living abroad and establish institutions to link Egyptians abroad to each other and the Egyptian state. Article 2 encourages the establishment of unions and clubs in the countries of emigration with the aim of establishing strong Egyptian assemblages (*taǧammuʿāt miṣrīya qawīya*). It also stipulated the preservation of the Arabic language and culture, and spiritual links among emigrants and their children, the establishment of Arab cultural centres, the organization of conferences and seminars dealing with Egypt and the facilitation of visits to Egypt.

In the context of the revolutionary upheavals after 2011, some Egyptian Cultural Offices became venues for political confrontation, even when directors tried to prevent the politicization of their centres. However, the choice of who to invite and who not to invite – thus, the question of who was considered a symbol of Egyptian culture and allowed to represent it – was highly contested in the post-revolutionary context and led to demonstrations and unrest during cultural events in cultural offices. For example, the visit of ʿAlāʾ al-Aswānī in October 2013 in Paris led to protests and virulent discussions because he was known to be an open critic of the Muslim Brotherhood and a supporter of the events following 30 June 2013.

As for political rights and *diaspora integration*, the Egyptian state extended political rights for Egyptians abroad only after massive campaigning in 2011. After the revolutionary upheavals in 2011, most of the discourse in Egypt primarily revolved around internal politics; however, many political figures in Egypt underlined the necessity of Egyptian migrants abroad, in particular for the reconstruction and development of Egypt through migration. The policy change concerning the political participation of Egyptians living abroad happened after a massive wave of campaigning from inside and outside the country.

Before 2011, Political Rights Law No. 73/1956, which was in force before the suspension of the 1971 Constitution, codified the participation of Egyptians in elections, but did not allow Egyptians living abroad to vote in elections. Vocal calls for the right of Egyptian expats to vote started at least one year before the revolution with the National Association for Change under the leadership of Mohamed El Baradei. In March 2011, this demand was also put forward by the Union of Egyptian Expatriates. In April 2011, a ministerial committee agreed to amend the political rights law, and in May 2011, the Supreme Council of the Armed Forces (SCAF) announced the change of political rights law No. 73/1956. However, no definite political decision was taken until the end of October 2011.

Pressure groups such as the 'Right2vote' campaign emerged and demonstrations were arranged in Cairo and in North American and European cities demanding the right to vote from abroad. Finally, in November 2011, the SCAF issued a decree addressing the right of Egyptians living abroad to vote in general elections and in referendums, and recognized that Egyptians have equal access to their political rights, including the right to vote over the age of 18, no matter where they live. Since 2012, diaspora participation in elections and referendums has become a constitutional right (Constitution 2012 (art. 56), Constitution 2014 (art. 88)).

Political opportunity structure in the country of residence

In both cities, Vienna and Paris, the shape and vitality of transnational political networks were heavily influenced by the way Egyptians abroad were organized before 2011. In Vienna, associations that aimed to represent the 'Egyptian community' were already in existence before 2011, which was not so much the case in Paris. In my analysis, this was influenced by the way migrant communities are recognized as such by the respective state. Thus, differences in the approaches to incorporating migrants into society, like the access to political rights, the recognition of ethnicity and the official representation of minority religions, are decisive for the emergence of transnational political networks.

First, in both France and Austria possibilities for political participation of migrants have historically been limited because access to major political rights has been bound to citizenship. The political incorporation of migrants only began to be debated after integration became a prime topic of public policy, an event that took place earlier in France (1970s) than in Austria (1990s). Given the more generous French naturalization practice, the problem of political rights not granted to migrants is less extreme in France than in Austria. In French politics, the political inclusion of immigrants has remained at least a debated – although as yet unresolved – issue over the last 30 years because granting local voting rights to foreigners remained a cornerstone of French Socialist integration policy and was a recurrent demand of leftist associations.

In Austria, debates on granting local voting rights to foreigners have only been initiated since 2001 by the Socialist Party and by the Greens, as a result of the Maastricht Treaty of 1997 (Valchars 2007: 130). As in France, the granting of local voting rights to foreigners in Austria seems unlikely. While being excluded from participation in national, regional and local elections, foreigners in France have voting rights on a lower level, hence in employee representative bodies, bodies of social security, social housing and school councils. They have active and passive voting rights in trade unions and workers' councils; however, they possess only passive voting rights in labour courts (*Conseils deprud'hommes*). They can vote and be elected in the administration councils of social security funds and in the boards of directors of the institutions managing social housing (OPAC, OPHLM). They can also become parent representatives in schools and thus participate in pre-school, elementary school and grammar school councils. Equally, on a university level they can participate in the bodies of university management (Vie Publique 2013).

As in France, political rights of foreigners in Austria are restricted to a lower level, to the right to petition (since 1867) and political rights on the level of employee representative bodies. Until 2006, third-country nationals could not become politically active on the work level, as they had no right to passive suffrage in the Chamber of Labour (*Arbeiterkammer*) or in work councils. It was only after the European Commission asked for the law to be changed in 2004 that passive suffrage in the Chamber of Labour and in work councils was changed in 2006 (Valchars 2007: 127). Foreigners now have active as well as passive voting rights in the Chamber of Labour and work councils (if they are members). However, the Austrian Federal Economic Chamber (*Wirtschaftskammer*) limits the active voting right to EEA nationals (Thienel 2007: 123). Foreigners have also active voting rights in the Austrian Student Union (ÖH); however, passive voting rights are also restricted to EEA nationals (Österreichische HochschülerInnenschaft 2013).

Thus, in both countries, civil society has become an alternative space for political participation. Important in this respect is the right to found associations and to be a member of associations, and the right to freedom of assembly: in contrast to France, foreigners in Austria have had the right to found associations since the signing of the European Convention on Human Rights in 1958. Since the signing of this convention, fundamental rights granted in the Austrian Constitution of 1867, such as the freedom of belief, of expression, of assembly and of association, are no longer bound to citizenship. However, nation states have the right to restrict the right to associate and assemble to foreigners. Austria restricted this right insofar as non-Austrians cannot found political parties or run an assembly, or, therefore, register a demonstration.

In France, before 1981, the freedom of assembly for foreigners was also limited. A decree from 1939 insisted on the political neutrality of immigrants, born originally of the fear that Nazi and Fascist regimes might use associations of their nationals to undermine the French government, and exempted them from the right to associate (Geddes 2003: 69). However, in 1981, the legislation on the freedom of association was relaxed due to pressure groups and leftist associations, a move that finally granted freedom of association to foreigners on the same basis as French associations, i.e. via a simple declaration to the interior ministry (Odmalm 2005: 24). This reform facilitated the creation of huge numbers of immigrant-run associations (Hargreaves 1995: 358). Unlike Austria, the right to freedom of association also includes the right to register a demonstration. This legislation was crucial for many demonstrations that took place in Paris after 2011.

Second, in contrast to Austria, France does not officially recognize migrants as being distinct ethnic or religious groups, but favours an approach that aims to transform them into citizens – theoretically – without consideration for their national, religious or ethnic origin (Odmalm 2005: 23). According to Wihtol de Wenden (2011: 67), since the beginning of the Third Republic in 1875, nationality has been perceived as a potential tool for implementing assimilationist policies. Newcomers were thus considered as individuals who had to disappear into the pre-defined political model by renouncing their own attributes in the public sphere. However, despite the formal disavowal of ethnicity and ethnic minorities, Hargreaves (1995) argues that there has actually been an 'ethnicization' of

French politics with 'political behaviour conditioned to a significant degree by consciousness of ethnic difference' (Hargreaves 1995: 36). Since the 1970s, French authorities have moved from a tolerance of difference to the institutionalization and management of difference. Schain argues that this opening up to ethnic-based difference is in fact a result of the gap between official rhetoric and actual practices, and calls this the 'recognition of ethnicity in practice if not in theory' (Schain 1999: 199).

In the 1970s, state institutions began to deal with immigrants in terms of their ethnic collective identities, both as a means of channelling new forms of political action and as a measure of tolerance (Geddes 2003: 68). During the early 1980s, political activism among the second-generation North Africans became evident. This led to the consequent emergence of associations based on ethnicity as a reuniting factor. At this time, the Socialists were caught 'between a flirtation with ethnic pluralism and the assimilationist model', as Geddes argues, and changed their vocabulary from the *droit à la différence* (right to difference) to *vivre ensemble* (living together) (2003: 69).

In contrast to France, historically, Austria has recognized the concept of ethnic minorities (so-called *Volksgruppen*) in its legislation. This goes back to Austria's history as a multi-ethnic monarchy and the idea that 'ethnic peculiarities' should be protected. Rights for ethnic minorities were already established in the Austrian Constitution of 1867 and repeated in the Ethnic Groups Law of 1976. Article 19 of the 1867 Constitution stated that the 'peculiarity' of an ethnic group is formed through language, traditional dress and symbols. These groups are furthermore defined as not speaking German as their first mother tongue, as having a common folklore (*Volksgut*), sharing an awareness of being a group, holding Austrian citizenship, living on Austrian territory and stemming historically from Austrian territory (Tichy 2001: 37–8).[3] These groups are given particular rights: So-called Ethnic Groups Advisory Boards can advise the government and ministries concerned, ethnic minorities are assisted in form of cash benefits or other support measures, bilingual topographical signs have to be installed in particular settlement areas, and members of ethnic minorities have the right to use their language in certain administrative offices and public authorities (Bundeskanzleramt Österreich).

The concept of 'ethnicity' is thus an accepted category in Austrian legislation.[4] Ethnicity also played a role in how migrant communities became organized because the Austrian state officially recognized ethno-cultural difference when it implemented measures such as multilingual information and the funding of ethnic associations. However, as Hadj-Abdou (2014: 1880–1) has shown, this recognition did not mean that ethno-cultural difference was understood as a part of the urban fabric. On the contrary, it was precisely because immigrants were seen as a temporary phenomenon in the guest worker period that measures to maintain 'their difference' were introduced and policy measures were aimed instead at immigrants' reintegration into their original societies.

This emphasis on ethnicity is reflected in Austrian migrant civil society. In 2002, the vast majority of 728 migrant organizations in Vienna were founded on the basis of a common national origin (57 per cent) or religion (30 per cent). Political activities were a priority for only 14 per cent of these organizations, while the majority of them defined their task as the maintenance of cultural identity (37 per cent), religious practice (22 per cent), leisure (22 per cent), sport (15 per cent), and support in matters of integration (15 per cent) (Sohler 2007: 378–9).

The Austrian state thus indirectly encourages the establishment of associations based on ethnicity, while France – at least officially – discourages it. In Paris, no Egyptian community structures existed as such prior to 2011 and networks that emerged after 2011 were founded with a particular political goal and not with the aim of representing a specific 'Egyptian community' as such. In contrast, in Vienna, pre-existing Egyptian community associations tried to discourage their members from organizing politically within these structures.

Third, the structures set up by officially recognized religious communities in Austria provide an alternative space for political and civic participation and therefore can have a demobilizing and moderating effect, siphoning off the political participation of some of the migrants' and their children, as Sohler has shown (2007: 385). If religious incorporation is pushed more by the state, religion can become an alternative to ethnic incorporation, as stated by Glick-Schiller and Çağlar (2008).

Austria and France have different approaches to the representation of minority religions. While France emphasizes secularism when dealing with minority religions, in Austria religious communities have been institutionalized since 1874 and have the right to political representation. The French model goes back to France's particular model of secularism (*laicité*) based on the 1905 Law on Secularity, which introduced a distinction between the practice of religion and religion's social and moral dimensions.

Austria's model has its origins in the eighteenth and nineteenth centuries, when the 'Edict of Tolerance' accepted other religious confessions besides the Catholic faith, such as the Protestant and Orthodox confessions, as well as the Jewish faith. Later on, in the Constitution of 1867, all officially recognized churches and religious communities were given particular rights through article 15, such as the right to public religious practice, the autonomous management of their 'internal' affairs, the protection of their funds, foundations and institutions, the establishment of private confessional schools, and the provision of religious education in public schools financed by the Austrian state. A law in 1874 finally defined how a religious community could be legally recognized.

As of 2014, Austria has officially recognized 16 religious communities.[5] In Austria, Hanafi Sunni Islam has been officially recognized since 1912 when Bosnia and Herzegovina were part of the Austro-Hungarian Empire. After the end of the monarchy in 1918, this regulation lost its *de facto* importance because no relevant Muslim community existed in the new Austria, but it became increasingly important with growing numbers of Muslims during the 1970s.

With increasing numbers of Muslims in Austria, an official representative institution was founded in 1979 – the Islamic Community in Austria (IGGiÖ).

Since then, the IGGiÖ has played an intermediary role between Muslim organizations and the Austrian politic and played a central role in the institutional integration of religious associations and infrastructures, such as mosques. Sohler argues that as certain religious rights did not have to be fought for or were not forbidden (such as the wearing of the headscarf in schools), they were not a subject of public debate; this, ultimately, had a depoliticizing and moderating effect on organizations (2007: 385).

Such structures do not exist in the same way in France. France has managed religion and Islam in the public sphere differently from other European countries, based on its model of secularism. The 1905 Law on Secularity assured the religious neutrality of the public service on the one hand, but guaranteed the protection of religious expression through the state on the other. As a result of this legislation, Islam has no historically developed representation in France and for a long time there was no unified representation of Islam.

The topic only began to be debated in the 1980s alongside the emerging awareness of ethnicity as an organizing principle and the gap between official rhetoric and actual practice. Initially, in the 1970s and 1980s, France passed through a phase during which it marginally accommodated Islamic practice: up until the 1980s, private prayer rooms were established, while the 1980s saw the emergence of Muslim associations in France. Since around 1990, Islam has been publicly recognized in France and efforts were made to incorporate Muslims into the French political landscape until the 2000s. In 1990, the *Conseil de Réflexion sur l'Avenir de l'Islam en France* was established with the ambition of unifying the Muslim population so that the French government could benefit from a sole united interlocutor. This was a result of the increasing demand for space to exercise Muslims' right to religious practice and the simultaneous will to control the multiplicity of emerging associations (Cesari 1994: 137ff.).

However, the process leading up to the establishment of the French Council for the Muslim Faith (*Conseil Féderal du Culte Musulman*, CFCM) in 2002 was long and conflictual (Cesari 1994: 123–36, 137–58). Hence, the debate about integrating Islam in secularized French daily life has been clearly established, but there are still serious ongoing conflicts, namely about the wearing of headscarves, such as the *Affaire des Foulards* in 1989 and the law in 2004 prohibiting the wearing of larger religious symbols, or the prohibition of the Burqa in 2011.

Conclusion and analysis

Participation in homeland politics is not a constant category. Generally speaking, so-called 'ethnic incorporation' is, as Glick-Schiller and Çağlar (2008) have shown, only one pathway to migrant incorporation, and in general, only a small minority of migrants engages in this form of politics in an active way.

The changing degree of activity in homeland politics is heavily influenced by political developments in the country of origin. Revolutionary events, in particular, can be an incentive to reinvest politically in one's country of origin because revolutionary upheavals are crucial points for the experiences and identification for migrants and their children. In the case discussed, the revolution in Egypt in 2011 led to a higher interest in Egyptian politics among Egyptians living abroad, and to a renewed feeling of patriotism. People participated who had previously lost their political interest in their country of origin but then rediscovered it during the revolution, who had never been interested in politics at all, and who had been active in Egyptian (oppositional politics) before the revolution.

In many countries, the uprisings were an incentive to demand political rights for Egyptian citizens living abroad, emphasizing their rights as Egyptian citizens. For all my interviewees, the protests since 2011 have been a way of re-discussing their relationship with their home country, Egypt, and their identity. The following quotation is a representative example for this sentiment:

> My mother told me … that we need the revolution more than the revolution needs us. I don't know if this is true for people in Egypt, I can only talk about myself … Before the revolution, I felt … that I don't fit. Sometimes, I didn't want to go to Egypt because I didn't fit … I was different. After the revolution, I can talk in poetic terms, it was like an open flower, you saw so many things in it, so many colours. Which we didn't know. It took me some time to understand that I fit in and all people fit in because there is not only one way to be in Egypt, there are millions of ways to be in Egypt and they are all crazy (*laughs*) and it's good that I am crazy. (Interview, Maryam, Paris, 4 November 2013)

These observations go against the classical assimilationist hypothesis which states that the interest of migrants in their country of origin will diminish over time and expects that with the acquisition of citizenship and political rights in the country of origin, migrants will lose interest in homeland politics. However, my analysis of homeland politics during the revolutionary upheavals between 2011 and 2013 parallels new research in the US which finds that US migrants' transnational political engagement does not depend upon whether or not they have American citizenship (Guarnizo *et al.* 2003: 1229).

Yet not everything can be described in the same way. What I observed is that homeland politics can actually take several forms. Which form and shape homeland politics take is – together with other reasons – influenced by the size of the migrant community and its migration history, as well as by the interplay between the policy framework in the country of origin and the country of destination, because migrants as political actors find themselves at the intersection of two sets of policies influencing their political participation.

Thus, homeland politics can be a refuge for people who lack access to political rights in their country of residence, as in the case of Paris with high numbers of irregular migrants. It can also serve as a forum for identity politics for second-generation migrants who mainly (re)construct and re-discuss their identity through these kind of political activities, as in the case of Vienna. In some cases, participating in homeland politics can be experienced as liberating and as a way to express one's political opinion when political participation in one's country of origin is barred due to state repression, as in the case of political opponents of the regime, such as Muslim Brotherhood supporters under Mubarak and later as-Sissi. Homeland politics is often in fact as much directed towards the country of residence in order to influence its public opinion as it is towards the country of origin itself. Forms of politics that truly cross borders to influence politics using the political contexts of both the country of origin and the country of residence are mostly undertaken by people who are especially well connected in both countries and who usually have prior political experience.

Notes

1 Before 2002, no annual data existed on Egyptian migrants to Austria. Figures stem from the national censuses, which are carried out every ten years. In 2001, for the first time, they included detailed data about the country of birth of migrants who had acquired Austrian citizenship.
2 Figures from Austrian census 1934, 1951 and 1961; data from 1971 to 2011 from Statistics Austria.
3 What 'stemming from Austrian territory' means is conflictual: mostly this is interpreted as a period of three generations, thus 90–100 years.
4 Today Austria officially recognizes six ethnic groups: Slovenians, Burgenland Croats, Hungarians, Roma and Sinti, Czechs and Slovaks.
5 With the *Bekenntnisgemeinschaftsgesetz* in 1999, a two-category system was established: besides officially recognized churches and religious communities – which are corporations of public law – 'officially registered religious denominations' which have a legal personality do exist, but are not corporations of public law. After 20 years' existence (of which ten years must have been as an officially registered religious denomination), these denominations can apply to be officially recognized.

Bibliography

Abdelfattah, D. 2011. *Impact of Arab Revolts on Migration*, CARIM AS 2011/68. San Domenico di Fiesole: EUI, Robert Schuman Centre for Advanced Studies.
Abdelrahman, M. 2011. 'The transnational and the local: Egyptian activists and transnational protest networks'. *British Journal of Middle Eastern Studies* 38(3): 407–24.
Aberer, M. *et al.* 2006. *Wo bleibt heute die Zeitung? Arbeits- und Lebensbedingungen von ZeitungsausträgerInnen*. Innsbruck-Vienna-Bozen: StudienVerlag.
Agstner, R. 1993. 'Die Habsburger-Monarchie und Ägypten. Eine Bestandsaufnahme'. In Österreichisches Kulturinstitut Kairo, ed., *Österreich und Ägypten. Beiträge zur Geschichte der Beziehungen vom 18. Jahrhundert bis 1918*, 8–29. Cairo: Schriften des Österreichischen Kulturinstitutes Kairo.
Asadova, Z. 2012. *Exploring the Impact of Transnational Civil Society on the Egyptian Uprising: Has the Transnational Engagement Been a Success Story?* Masters thesis. Budapest: Central European University.
Basch, L., Glick-Schiller, N. and Szanton-Blanc, C. 1997. *Nations Unbound: Transnational Projects, Postcolonial Predicaments and Deterritorialized Nation-states*, 4th edn. Amsterdam: Gordon and Breach.
Beinin, J. 1992. 'Exile and political activism: the Egyptian-Jewish communists in Paris, 1950–59'. *Diaspora: A Journal of Transnational Studies* 2(1): 73–94.
Beinin, J. 1998. *The Dispersion of Egyptian Jewry: Culture, Politics, and the Formation of a Modern Diaspora*. Berkeley: University of California Press.

Beinin, J. and Vairel, F., eds. 2011. *Social Movements, Mobilization, and Contestation in the Middle East and North Africa*. Stanford, CA: Stanford University Press.

Cesari, J. 1994. *Être musulman en France. Associations, militants et mosques*. Paris-Aix-en-Provence: Editions Karthala & IREMAM.

Choate, M. 2008. *Emigrant Nation: The Making of Italy abroad*. Cambridge, MA and London: Harvard University Press.

Collyer, M. and Vathi, Z. 2007. *Patterns of Extra-territorial Voting*. Working paper T22. University of Sussex: Sussex Centre for Migration Research.

Dufoix, S., Guerassimoff, C. and de Tinguy, A., eds. 2010. *Loin des yeux, près du cœur. Les États et leurs expatriés*. Paris: Presses de Sciences Po.

El Baradei, L., Wafa, D. and Ghoneim, N. 2012. 'Assessing the voting experience of Egyptians abroad: post the January 25 revolution'. *Journal of US-China Public Administration* 9(11): 1223–43.

Fargues, P. and Le Bras, H. 2009. 'Migrants et migration dans le bassin de la Méditerranée'. *Les Notes IPEMED Études & Analyses* 1: 1–32.

Freeman, G. 2004. 'Immigrant incorporation in Western democracies'. *International Migration Review* 38(3): 945–69.

Gamlen, A. 2008. 'The emigration state and the modern geopolitical imagination'. *Political Geography* 27: 840–56.

Geddes, A. 2003. *The Politics of Migration and Immigration in Europe*. London: Sage.

Geisser, V. 1997. *Ethnicité républicaine. Les élites d'origine maghrébine dans le système politique français*. Paris: Presse de Sciences Po.

Glick Schiller, N. and Ça lar, A. 2008. 'Beyond methodological ethnicity'. In L. Pries, ed., *Rethinking Transnationalism: The Meso-Link of Organizations*, 40–61. London and New York: Routledge.

Green, N. 2005. 'The politics of exit: reversing the immigration paradigm'. *Journal of Modern History* 77: 263–89.

Green, N. and Weil, F. 2006. *Citoyenneté et Émigration: Les politiques du départ*. Paris: Éditions de l'École des Hautes Études en Sciences Sociales.

Guarnizo, L. E., Portes, A. and Haller, W. 2003. 'Assimilation and transnationalism: determinants of transnational political action among contemporary migrants'. *American Journal of Sociology* 108(6): 1211–48.

Hadj-Abdou, L. 2014. 'Immigrant integration and the economic competitiveness agenda: a comparison of Dublin and Vienna'. *Journal of Ethnic and Migration Studies* 40(12): 1875–94.

Hargreaves, A. 1995. *Immigration, 'Race' and Ethnicity in Contemporary France*. London: Routledge.

Kastoryano, R. 2004. 'Religion and incorporation: Islam in France and Germany'. *International Migration Review* 38(3): 1234–55.

Kepel, G. 1987. *Les Banlieues de l'Islam*. Paris: Seuil.

Kraler, A. 2011. 'The case of Austria'. In G. Zincone, R. Penninx and M. Borkert, eds, *Migration Policymaking in Europe: The Dynamics of Actors and Contexts in Past and Present*, 21–60. Amsterdam: Amsterdam University Press.

Kroißenbrunner, S. 1997. 'Soziopolitische Netzwerke türkischer MigrantInnen in Wien – eine (fast) ungeschriebene Geschichte'. *Österreichische Zeitschrift für Politikwissenschaft* 4: 453–59.

Kurnik, P. 1997. 'Österreichisches Staatsbürgerschaftsrecht. "Von der Heimatrolle zur Staatsbürgerschaftsevidenz"'. In W. Teschner, ed., *50 Jahre Fachverband der Österreichischen Standesbeamten (1947–1997). Festschrift*, 1–32. Vienna: Fachverband der Österreichischen Standesbeamten.

Lafargue, I. 2002. *Itinéraires et stratégies migratoires des Égyptiens vers la France. Vers une nouvelle définition du modèle d'émigration en Égypte*, PhD thesis. Paris: Institut d'études politiques de Paris.

Lafleur, J.-M. 2013. *Transnational Politics and the State: The External Voting Rights of Diasporas*. London: Routledge.

Laurence, J. and Vaisse, J. 2006. *Integrating Islam: Political and Religious Challenges in Contemporary France*. Washington, DC: Brookings Institute Press.

Levitt, P. and de la Dehesa, R. 2003. 'Transnational migration and the redefinition of the state: variations and explanations'. *Ethnic and Racial Studies* 26(4): 587–611.

Müller-Mahn, D. 2005. 'Transnational spaces and migrant networks: a case study of Egyptians in Paris'. *NORD-SUD aktuell*: 29–33.

Odmalm, P. 2005. *Migration Policies and Political Participation: Inclusion or Intrusion in Western Europe?* Basingstoke and New York: Palgrave Macmillan.

Østergaard-Nielsen, E. 2003. *Transnational Politics: Turks and Kurds in Germany*. London: Routledge.

Pagès-El Karoui, D. 2012. 'Egyptiens d'outre-nil: des diasporas égyptiennes'. *Tracés* 23: 89–112.

Portes, A. 1999. 'Conclusion: towards a New Model. The origins and effects of transnational activities'. *Ethnic and Racial Studies* 22(4): 463–77.

Saad, R. 2005. *Egyptian Workers in Paris: Pilot Ethnography*. Development Research Centre on Migration, Globalisation and Poverty. www.dfid.gov.uk/r4d/Output/173792/Default.aspx, access: 14/01/2014.

Schain, M. 1999. 'Minorities and immigrant incorporation in France: the state and the dynamics of multiculturalism'. In C. Joppke and S. Lukes, eds, *Multicultural Questions*, 199–223. Oxford: Oxford University Press.

Severo, M. and Zuolo, E. 2012. 'Egyptian e-diaspora: migrant websites without a network?' *Social Science Information* 51: 521–33.

Shefer, G. 2003. *Diaspora Politics: At Home Abroad*. Cambridge: Cambridge University Press.

Smith, R. C. 2003a. 'Diasporic membership in historical perspective: comparative insights from the Mexican, Italian and Polish cases'. *International Migration Review* 37(3): 724–59.

Smith, R. C. 2003b. 'Migrant membership as an instituted process: transnationalization, the state and the extra-territorial conduct of Mexican politics'. *International Migration Review* 37(3): 297–343.

Sohler, K. 2007. 'MigrantInnenorganisationen in Wien'. In H. Fassmann, ed., *2. Österreichischer Migrations- und Integrationsbericht 2001–2006. Rechtliche Rahmenbedingungen, demographische Entwicklungen, sozioökonomische Strukturen*, 377–91. Klagenfurt: Drava-Verlag.

Tarrow, S. 2005. *The New Transnational Activism*. Cambridge: Cambridge University Press.

Thienel, R. 2007. 'Integration als rechtliche Querschnittsmaterie'. In H. Fassmann, ed., *2. Österreichischer Migrations- und Integrationsbericht. Rechtliche Rahmenbedingungen, demographische Entwicklungen, sozioökonomische Strukturen*, 83–126. Klagenfurt: Drava-Verlag.

Tichy, H. 2001. 'Das Minderheitenrecht in Österreich'. *Der Donauraum* 41(3): 37–42.

Valchars, G. 2007. 'Wahlrechte von NichtstaatsbürgerInnen in Österreich'. In H. Fassmann, ed., *2. Österreichischer Migrations- und Integrationsbericht. Rechtliche Rahmenbedingungen, demographische Entwicklungen, sozioökonomische Strukturen*, 127–41. Klagenfurt: Drava-Verlag.

Wihtol de Wenden, C. 2011. 'The case of France'. In G. Zincone, R. Penninx and M. Borkert, eds, *Migration Policymaking in Europe: The Dynamics of Actors and Contexts in Past and Present*, 61–94. Amsterdam: Amsterdam University Press.

Weblinks

Brand, L. 2014. 'The stakes and symbolism of voting from abroad', *The Washington Post*. Last modified 5 June. Accessed 24 March 2015. www.washingtonpost.com/blogs/ monkey-cage/wp/2014/06/05/the-stakes-and-symbolism-of-voting-from-abroad/.
Bundeskanzleramt Österreich. 'Österreichische Rechtslage / Volksgruppengesetz'. Accessed 14 January 2015. www.bka.gv.at/site/3515/default.aspx.
Cabot, C. 2011. 'Egyptian diaspora get involved in Tahrir Square Foundation'. *Daily News*. Last modified 28 July. Accessed 14 September 2013. www.dailynewsegypt. com/2011/07/28/egyptian-diaspora-get-involved-in-tahrir-square-foundation/.
Medienservicestelle. 2013. 'ÄgypterInnen – Die größte arabische Community'. Last modified 2 July. Accessed 11 November 2013. http://medienservicestelle.at/migration_ bewegt/2013/07/02/agypter-in-osterreich/.
Österreichische HochschülerInnenschaft. 2013. 'Passives Wahlrecht für Drittstaatsangehörige'. Last modified 22 May. Accessed 19 January 2015. www.oeh.ac. at/blog/passives-wahlrecht-fuer-drittstaatsangehoerige/.
Vie Publique. 2013. 'Quels sont les droits des étrangers?' Last modified 9 October. Accessed 18 January 2014. www.vie-publique.fr/decouverte-institutions/citoyen/ citoyennete/citoyen-france/quels-sont-droits-etrangers.html.

Cited interviews

Ḥikma, *Jugend für Ägypten in Österreich*, Vienna, 26 April 2014 (name changed).
Luṭfī, *Koptisch-österreichische Organisation für Menschenrechte*, Vienna, 4 June 2014 (name changed).
Maryam, *Association des Jeunes Egyptiens du 25 Janvier à Paris, Voix d'Egypte*, Paris, 4 November 2013 (name changed).
Tādrus, priest at the Coptic church Saint Moise Deuil-la-Barre, Paris, 29 September 2013 (name changed).
ʿUmar Maḥmūd, Egyptian Consulate Austria, Vienna, 14 April 2014.

11 From a mythical country of origin to a multi-diaspora country

The case of Israel and the Moroccan Jewish diaspora

Emanuela Trevisan Semi

Introduction

The most recent studies on diasporas have focused increasingly on themes connected with issues of 'returns' to the homelands and in particular those returns from the factual 'birthplace home' to the ancestral 'ethnic home'.[1] Certain phenomena observed in the Jewish diaspora are present in other groups. One of these, for example, is the Abkhaz (including the Circassians), who left Turkey for the Caucasus and have been defined as representing a 'diaspora of the diaspora'. What occurred was that when in the 1990s the borders of the ex-Soviet union opened up, many Abkhazis left Turkey, their then current home, and returned to their ancestral homeland. The members of this diaspora who went back believed that only a return to their ancestral homeland would allow them 'a true existence of the Adgye-Abkhaz people and culture' (see Cemre Erciyes 2008: 345), a thought that had formed the basis of the ideology of return for the wide majority of the Jewish diaspora in Israel. However, many returnees, once they had indeed gone back, began to consider themselves as a 'diaspora in the homeland', in the sense that they ended up maintaining diaspora links, a collective diaspora identity and feelings of belonging to their respective diaspora communities. These are the same mechanisms that we find in the Jewish case, although here these different belongings can be multiplied since there may be more than one exile in the long history of the Jewish diaspora.

For example, the period spent in Spain, which became in turn an exile, remained solidly embedded in the Sephardic Jews' sense of identity and collective belonging. In the colonial and post-colonial period, this Sephardi identity reconciled itself with the Moroccan one, to the extent that Morocco was placed 'at the center, as the true heir to a Sephardi and especially an Andalusian past' (see Schroeter 2008: 149). The Jews hailing from Al Andalus who had emigrated to Morocco and from there to Israel, the mythical homeland, continued to retain a sense of belonging to and a sense of pride in that place they had settled more than 500 years before, even after they had been reunited with their homeland, which was enriched by their Moroccan heritage.

We believe, in fact, that the Jews belong to a number of different places and that a part of the Jewish experience, characterized by a long period of diaspora, is the chance of having a sense of belonging to places holding the twofold trait of being at once places of birth and places of exile (see Trevisan Semi 2007; Rosen-Lapidot and Goldberg 2013).

Israel as the meeting of the diasporas

Israel was constituted on the basis of a premise in an essentially Messianic key, called in Hebrew *qibbutz galuyyot*, 'the meeting of the exiled/the diasporas'. The meeting of the diasporas was supposed to be followed by the 'fusion of the diasporas', a stage that was supposed to end with the formation of a single Jewish culture, which would serve to identify the new Jew, in the conviction that the diaspora may not have disappeared but would be severely reduced. Zionism had been built around the idea of a denial of the diaspora, an idea that considered the diaspora mentality to be a sort of pathogenic agent from which one had to break free. In reality, however, Zionism had not only to accept the continuing existence of the Jewish diaspora (in some settings such as America it is actually, at least in demographic terms, larger than Israeli Jewry) but also must witness Israel being transformed into a diaspora of diasporas.

The main points of the Zionist discourse like the *qibbutz galuyyot* (meeting of diasporas) and the *mizzug galuyyot* (mixture of diasporas) has not given rise to the mixture of diasporas but to the creation of new diasporas whose members experience feelings of strong attachment to the homeland in which they were born or where the previous generation was born, which is to say the country they left behind to emigrate to the mythical homeland. The emergence of new diasporas in Israel can therefore be considered as a phenomenon that may question Israel as a homeland or as the only homeland.

Of the million Russian Jews who emigrated to Israel after the fall of the Berlin Wall, 40 per cent return every two to four years and 20 per cent work with Russians in joint-venture companies. Every year the *Bene Israel* emigrants to Israel from India organize return trips there, bearing letters and presents from friends and relatives unable to make the journey. They pray in synagogues in India, buy Indian goods and return to Israel loaded with items from their country of origin. The same happens with Jews from Ethiopia, some of whom have set up tourism companies serving Ethiopia. Others undertake journeys back to their roots or set up import-export firms, living between Ethiopia and Israel and listening to Ethiopian music. It is as if they live between two homelands. The case of 800,000 Moroccan Jews in Israel is very similar.

Moroccan Jewish migration

The mass Jewish migration from Morocco of the 1950s and 1960s (see Trevisan Semi 2010, 2012; Tzur 2001) was directed largely towards Israel but also to Canada, France and to a lesser extent to the United States. These migrations, which have seen members of extended families head towards different countries, have given rise to diaspora networks that are connected to each other and that manifest feelings of nostalgia and identification with the country left behind (see Bordes Benayoun 2012, 2013/14) and have created virtual networks in cyberspace (see Miccoli 2014; Boum 2014). In Israel, in particular, the Moroccan migrations have recreated the symbolic places and identity geography, such as pilgrimages to the tombs of saints, streets and squares named after the kings of Morocco, ethnic museums, tours of the origins in Morocco often linked to the pilgrimage to the tomb of a saint, the establishment of an Andalusian orchestra, and they have developed a surprising artistic and literary creativity.

In particular, in recent decades we are witnessing the publication of numerous autobiographical writings by the 1.5 generation (see Rubin Suleiman 2002) of those who left as children, showing strong links to the cities of origin such as Mogador/Essayira, Marrakesh, Meknes; and, in the case of second and third generations, the publication of fiction which includes autobiographical narratives that recount the lives of mothers or grandmothers in Morocco, often in the original language spoken, like Moroccan Arabic or French.

From the second half of the 1980s thousands of Israeli Jews of Moroccan origin have made organized visits to their original homes in Morocco, to the cemeteries where close and distant relatives are buried and to the tombs of saints, returning loaded with traditional Moroccan items. Indeed, they continue to feel bound to the dynasty of Morocco to the extent of keeping in their houses portraits of the King of Morocco, who in turn considers these people to be the 'ambassadors of Morocco in Israel'.

In recent decades in Israel small and large museums have grown up, a well-known post-colonial phenomenon. For example, there are four ethnic Moroccan museums (see Trevisan Semi 2013); but there are two Indian (one of the Bene Israel and of the Cochin Jews), two Yemeni, one Libyan, one Iraqi, one Italian, one Circassian (see Perry and Kark 2013). They are places of memory, some being the work of single promoters of memory who try to give a sense of the future through remembering the past, a past that was supposed to be buried under the steamroller of Zionist ideology but which appears to be as present as ever.

Jewish Moroccan autobiographies

The heritage of that past is even more pressing in the case of autobiographies written by Jewish Moroccan writers of the 1.5 generation, which have been growing greatly in number in recent decades. I prefer to define this genre as life-writing, which is more inclusive than other literary forms which do not always correspond to the category of autobiography. In particular three Jewish Moroccan writers are discussed here who emigrated to Israel as children or adolescents and who may be relevant for my analysis: Gavriel Bensimhon, Ami Bouganim and Shelomo Elbaz. The first writes in Hebrew, the other two in French. The three writers have returned once or a number of times to Morocco to visit the places of their childhood, to go on a pilgrimage to the graves of their family or of saints, for reasons of tourism or to take part in conferences; these experiences of 'return' have without doubt supported the maintaining of diaspora-type links (see Trevisan Semi and Sekkat Hatimi 2011; Trevisan Semi 2011).

David Elmoznino, an author belonging to this generation, has written:

> The Jewish Moroccan community is today scattered throughout the world and, we may be tempted to say, continues virtually to exist in cultivated and maintained memory, in the memory of women and men who, with a care to safeguarding this immense wealth, this legacy unique to itself, endeavour to keep alive this aggregation of destinies, habits and customs, traditions and ways of life, in the most diverse formats and ready to be handed down from one generation to the next. (Elmoznino 2008: 12)

That 'cultivated and maintained' memory is enriched, dissected and questioned by the fresh productions of post-colonial life-writing (see Eldridge 2012; Trevisan Semi 2104).

Differences in autobiography

From a comparative analysis I have carried out on the narrative of those writers who emigrated to Israel and others of Jewish Moroccan origin who in contrast emigrated to France, Canada or the United States, I have noted a significant difference between those who emigrated to Israel and those who did so to other countries. In particular, among the writers analysed, it is only those who emigrated to Israel who take time to recall the city or country left behind, showing intense, complex feelings of dual belonging and identity. The writers who emigrated to other countries keep a greater distance from their native country or town, often mentioning it only fleetingly or writing about it in a detached manner, offering a less rose-tinted memory compared to the reality of the surroundings they found in the new country. Otherwise they merely narrate what are essentially family memories. The detachment of their identity-giving sense of belonging and their place of origin is greater.

Hence it is more those writers who have emigrated to Israel who present attitudes harking back to feelings of a double or multiple identity of belonging, which is to say belonging to the city of their birth and development, to the country they emigrated to and sometimes to an earlier place of exile, that of Spain. That distance seems to me to be more noticeable in the life-writing texts of those who did not emigrate to Israel, as if it had turned out easier to keep a distance from the country abandoned in the case of those who had not opted for the mythical-ideological appeal of the diaspora return to the homeland. There would appear to be, therefore, an unexpected correlation between the mythical-ideological appeal of the diaspora return to the homeland and a strong retaining of the sense of belonging to the abandoned native land, forever thought of as a country of exile. This correlation might seem surprising if one believes that the fulfilment of the desire to see the end of the exile should have led to the end of the diaspora.

A Jew from Sefrou in Israel

Gavriel Bensimhon is very interesting in this regard. He was born in 1938 in Sefrou and emigrated to Israel in 1947 aboard the first ship of immigrants. The vessel was captured by the British and taken to Cyprus. In his largely autobiographical novel written in Hebrew, *Neurah be-hulzah kehullah* (The Young Girl in the Light-Blue Shirt), set in Haifa, the writer tells the story of Yonatan Marciano, the young Sefrou-born protagonist who recounts tales where the characters retain recognizable features of Bensimhon's story. In the course of the novel, 'our' city of Sefrou (see Bensimhon 2013: 12) becomes a place of reference and the fulcrum of the whole narration.

On the one hand, the protagonist would like to lay waste to the past in order to integrate all the faster into his new society, while on the other he requires that past to give a meaning to the present; this is the dilemma of a generation. The protagonist would like to be like the *sabra*, the native Israelis who, he writes, 'are afraid of nothing', but to be like them he must 'throw away the past, hide it, burn it'[2] (Bensimhon 2013: 12). However, how can the past be thrown away if Sefrou is a constant point of reference, the place to make comparison and the root of his new existence? The present seems to exist only to recall Sefrou's past, according to the same model described by André Aciman for Alexandria in Egypt:

> 'There are enormous parts of New York that do not exist for me: they don't have Egypt, they have no past, they mean nothing. Unless I can forge an Egyptian fiction around them, if only as a mood I recognize as Egyptian, they are as dead to me, as I am dead to them. Egypt is my catalyst, I break down life in Egyptian units. (Aciman 2011: 73)'

The present refers back to the past, to the *mellah* without the colour green, while the past allows the present to acquire meaning. The search for green, necessary for a boy at school in Haifa, reminds the protagonist of the lack of green in the *mellah* and the power of imagination which makes up for that lack. The protagonist recalls comparing himself and a school friend of Polish origin and that 'while Blosh was asking for charity in Warsaw, he was wandering the little streets of Sefrou looking for the colour green. In the *mellah* there grew neither trees or flowers' (Bensimhon 2013: 20); in the *mellah* colours were missing and everything was grey. However, even if green was missing, imagination made up for that. The shopkeeper in the suburban Haifa neighbourhood does not have the colour green to sell him and suggests replying with the following words to his teacher: 'Tell him that the paint shop has no green and that's the end of it! Just forget it! Everything was grey in Sefrou so we used our imagination! In Sefrou we needed a lot of imagination to make up for what we lacked' (Bensimhon 2013: 20).

A Jew from Mogador/Essaouira in Israel

Ami Bouganim, who was born in 1951 in Mogador (today Essaouira) who emigrated to Israel in 1970, has never ceased to evoke Mogador in all his tales and novels. This writer has continued to write his stories in French, the language he grew up with and the only one allowing him to tell of his exile, an exile comprising three exiles: from Jerusalem, Spain and Morocco.

Speaking of his time on returning to Mogador, he recalls having lodged in what was his (second) home, now a *riad*. The reality of Morocco is compared to that of Israel, defined as a supreme *mellah*-ghetto:

> We did not barter the dusty and worm-eaten ghettos and mellahs with a supreme ghetto-mellah where military justification matters more than reason of state and messianic unreason more than political reason, to the point that Israel has no more moral lessons to give anyone either in terms of human charity or of social justice. (Bouganim 2013: 242)

It is illuminating to read the phrases, expressed with a vein of irony and play on words, which he offers on the complex identity of the Moroccan Jew and on his own identity, in particular as a son of Mogador:

> I remained Moroccan, a son of Mogador, more Berber than Arab, with Jewish insanity. And yet in Morocco we were living as foreigners. It was not our country and could not become so. We were at one admitted and excluded, persecuted and protected, hidden and visible. We were happy and unhappy, confiding and reserved … We did not wish to bother – we maintained a prudent reserve – and we did not wish to mix – we kept our distance. We were always about to depart and had been for thousands of years, destined to a better fate. (Bouganim 2013: 44)

This living with the attitude of those always ready to depart, for more than a millennium, because destined for another place, as well as nurturing the discourse of exile, has formed a generation that did indeed depart only to find itself remembering that past they desired to leave. We find this attitude in other writers too.

Yet a return to the same place as the one left might have produced a sense of bewilderment able to evoke devastated memories where a comparison is made between native exile, Morocco, and the exile of exile, Israel:

> The first time I went back to Mogador I had the impression that strangers had worked their way into the postcard of my memories; from then on I have had the impression of being no more than a belated chronicler of a town which would awaken, transformed, from its devastated memories … a life shared between Morocco and Israel, between native exile and the exile of exile, between sobriety and intoxication, tenderness and excitement. (Bouganim 2013: 349)

It is an exile of the exile which recalls the concept of a return to the homeland as if it were a diaspora of the diaspora, as has been highlighted in the case of the Abkhazis returning to Caucasia.

A Jew from Marrakesh in Israel

Shelomo Elbaz, originally from Marrakesh, emigrated to Israel at the age of 33, and the long period he spent in Morocco is reflected in his writing and already evident in the title of his memoir: *Marrakesh-Jérusalem: Patrie de mon âme* (Marrakesh-Jerusalem: The Native Land of my Soul). Elbaz builds an interesting example of what it means to hold a complex, plural identity:

> Plural, crossbred, assimilated, impure
> Jew
> Maghreban
> Berber
> Spanish
> French
> And, in last place,
> Israeli. (Elbaz 2013: 64)

A dual or multiple belonging is claimed and highlighted:

> Who could expect that coming to Israel as an immigrant would put an end to that double personality of the Jew as an exile and to the multiplicity of his identities? In truth the result is the opposite. The proof is that in Morocco I carried three identities within myself. A (spiritual) Jewish identity, a (civic) Moroccan identity and a (cultural) French identity. Today in Israel I carry within myself a (civic) Israeli identity, a (national) Jewish identity, a (community) Oriental-Sephardic identity and that is not all. Something has remained of the cultural French identity ... (Elbaz 2013: 92)

The two cities he is linked to are equivalent and form a pair:

> These form a pair with this city of mine. One saw me born, Marrakesh; in the other, Jerusalem, I will end my days. My life, either a classic dated verse or an archaic biblical extract, will have had its two hemistiches, around the same length. (Elbaz 2013: 101–2)

The two cities are joined together by golden threads:

> Golden threads have been stretched between the town of Machrek and that of the Maghreb. Threads of gold or silk, the web of my life. In order to weave the threads which connect these two towns (M'rakch and Jerusalem) my imagination has called upon the collective memory of a community, that community over there, in the distant Marrakesh ... (Elbaz 2013: 91)

The cities mark the beginning and the end, birth and death:

> Two towns at the extremes of my life. In one I was born and in the second my life shall end. I have therefore *two* native towns and *two* loves. Marrakesh,

my native place, my 'physical homeland' we might say, which is meant to have shaped my being but nonetheless I abandoned without regret, right in the middle of my life in order to go back to another native place, that of the 'soul', which is Jerusalem, compressed into a long history, into an inexplicably vivid nostalgia. The two homelands were sharing my mental space like two hemistiches ... my origins sing with two voices. An inner duet where sometimes one and sometimes the other gets the upper hand, with the second becoming indistinct, a sort of unbroken base note. (Elbaz 2013: 220–1)

His life in any case continues to be marked by breaks and the two cities/homelands are interlaced with other places: from the Marrakesh *mellah* to the European quarter of Casablanca, from this economic metropolis to the kibbutz Dorot and finally from Neguev to Jerusalem (Elbaz 2013: 24).

Conclusion

To conclude, feelings of a double belonging to one's city or country of origin and those of immigration, as we find documented in work within the life-writing genre arise, as I have mentioned before, mainly in those who have emigrated to Israel. In other words, the furrow lying between on the one hand Jewish Moroccan culture and on the other Arab culture in general and Muslim Moroccan culture in particular, which was created by the dominant ideology in Israel, has led to devalue, to deny, to erase the culture of the past. However, in contrast with this attitude it has also led to a mechanism driving a desire to contrast, value, recover, be informed about, convey and mourn that world on the part of those who had known it previously (see Trevisan Semi 2014). This attitude was not shared by writers who emigrated to other, not mythical homelands, who expected less from a migration which was not ideologically invested and who succeeded better socially.

Notes

1 See the last issue of *Diaspora*, 17, 3 (2008) (published summer 2014).
2 The translations from Hebrew are mine.

References

Aciman, A. 2011. Alibis: *Essays on Elsewhere*. New York: Picador/Farrar, Straus and Geroux.
Bensimhon, G. 2013. *Neurah be-hulzah kehullah* (The young girl in the light-blue shirt). Tel Aviv: Yediot Ahronot Books. (Hebrew)
Bordes Benayoun, C. 2012. 'La diaspora ou l'ethnique en mouvement'. *Revue européenne des migrations internationales* 28(1): 13–31.
Bordes Benayoun, C. 2013/14. 'Introduction. Du cœur aux confins de la judéité'. *Ethnologie française* 43: 573–79.

Bouganim, A. 2013. *Es-Saouira de Mogador*. Louvain-la-neuve: Avant-propos.

Boum, A. 2014. 'The virtual Genizah: emerging North African Jewish and Muslim identities online'. *International Journal of Middle East Studies* 46: 597–601.

Cemre Erciyes, J. 2008. 'Diaspora of diaspora: Adyge-Abkhaz returnees in the ancestral homeland'. *Diaspora* 17(3): 340–61.

Elbaz, S. 2013. *Marrakesh-Jérusalem: Patrie de mon âme*. Louvain-la-neuve: Avant-propos.

Eldridge, C. 2012. 'Remembering the other: postcolonial perspectives on relationships between Jews and Muslims in French Algeria'. *Journal of Modern Jewish Studies* 11(3): 299–317.

Elmoznino, D. 2008. *Palais et Jardins*. Ashdod: Brit Kodesh (translated from Hebrew).

Miccoli, D. 2014. 'Les juifs du Maroc, internet et la construction d'une diaspora numérique'. *Expressions Maghrébines* 13(1): 75–94.

Perry, N. and Kark, R. 2014. *Muzeonim etnografiyim b-Israel* (Ethnographic Museums in Israel). Jerusalem: Aiel.

Rosen-Lapidot, E. and Goldberg, H. E. 2013. 'The triple loci of Jewish-Maghribi ethnicity: voluntary associations in Israel and in France'. *Journal of North African Studies* 18(1): 111–30.

Rubin Suleiman, S. 2002. 'The 1.5 generation: thinking about child survivors and the holocaust'. *Imago* 59: 277–95.

Schroeter, D. J. 2008. 'The shifting boundaries of Moroccan Jewish identities'. *Jewish Social Studies* 15(1): 145–64.

Trevisan Semi, E. 2007. 'La mise en scène de l'identité marocaine en Israël: un cas d'israélianité diasporique'. *A contrario* 5(1): 37–50.

Trevisan Semi, E. 2010. 'Double trauma and manifold narratives: Jews' and Muslims' representations of the departure of Moroccan Jews in the 1950s and 1960s'. *Journal of Modern Jewish Studies* 9: 107–25.

Trevisan Semi, E. 2011. 'L'année prochaine à … Ouazzan du culte d'un saint juif; des usages socio-politiques d'un saint juif'. In N. Harrami and I. Melliti, eds, *Visions du monde et modernités religieuses*, 219–27. Paris: Publisud.

Trevisan Semi, E. 2012. 'Différents récits sur le départ des juifs du Maroc dans les années 1960–1970'. In F. Abécassis, K. Dirèche and R. Aouad, eds, *La bienvenue et l'adieu. Migrants juifs et musulmans au Maghreb XV-XX siècles*, 67–97. Paris: Karthala.

Trevisan Semi, E. 2013. 'Museums of Moroccan Jews in Israel: what kind of memory?' In E. Trevisan Semi, D. Miccoli and T. Parfitt, eds, *Memory and Ethnicity: Ethnic Museums in Israel and Diaspora*, 45–75. New Castle: Cambridge Scholars Publishing.

Trevisan Semi, E, 2014. '*Maktub* di Iris Eliya-Cohen o le retour du refoulé degli scrittori della seconda generazione di immigrazione in Israele'. *Altre Modernità* 5: 77–88. Accessed 28 February 2015. riviste.unimi.it/index.php/AMonline/issue/views/547.

Trevisan Semi, E. and Sekkat Hatimi, H. 2011. *Mémoire et représentations des juifs au Maroc: les voisins absents de Meknès*. Paris: Publisud.

Tsur, Y. 2001. *Qehillah Qeruah 1943–1954* (A torn community: the Jews of Morocco and Nationalism 1943–1954). Tel Aviv: Am oved (Hebrew).

12 Beyond musallas and the veil

The second generations' religiosity: being Muslim and active citizens

Roberta Ricucci

In Europe and Italy, research and studies have focused on the growing presence of Muslims (Cesari and Pacini 2005; Bracke and Fadil 2008; Moghissi and Gorashi 2010; Open Society Institute 2011), through observations and insights carried out from different perspectives: religious beliefs and practices, hope for a certain type of society (secular vs Islamic), definition of identity (religious, Italian, cosmopolitan), orientation regarding the education of children and inter-marriage and requests made to educational institutions (recognition of holidays, religious teaching in school). In addition, attention to the religious variable has often been correlated with that dedicated to labour issues (Are Muslims discrimi-nated against in the labour market, compared to other religious affiliations?), school (Does the increasing number of Muslim students give rise to claims against secularization and changes in education?), urban schedules and spaces, with specific requests regarding nutrition, places of worship and areas for the burial of the dead. From another point of view, the terrorist attacks in Madrid and London added a further perspective to the analysis of this specific group, in an attempt to figure out if its members can become new representatives of funda-mentalism in Europe (Meer *et al.* 2012; Bowen 2010). In this way, the intertwin-ing between Islam and politics is back in the spotlight. However, it was attention directed more to the effects of 'reaction' of the immigration society and the security concerns raised rather than the internal analysis of the different commu-nities (Vertovec and Wassendorf 2010). This is also an analysis of the manage-ment of religious diversity, the result of stabilization processes of immigrant communities, which should be conducted where biographies of the characters are created and where different modes of relationship with Italian society take form (Lorentzen 2009).

The level of the city forms the scenario wherein religious identity has been questioned, where second generations grow up and develop their identities (including their religious identities) and wherein requests for representation made by Muslim communities have been widely discussed. Attention has been focused, only recently, on how local policies, from the sphere of integration to that of social cohesion, from inter-religious to urban-architectural, have developed and how they have managed the relationship with the plurality of associations that can be traced to the Muslim milieu in each local context. Recently there has come into being a further element of interest, that is to say, how the arrival on the scene of the second generation changes (by strengthening or weakening, by changing or erasing) the proceedings for recognition carried out by their fathers and mothers (Alexander 2004).

In particular, this chapter starts by addressing the general question (Are second-generation Muslims, as a group, more religious than their parents?), then highlights whether the generational shift implies a new relationship between Muslim associations and local institutions; it considers two sides of the coin: how the children of immigration's 'entrance to adulthood' will result in relationships that Islam defines with the local policy and, conversely, whether the latter modifies its attitude towards the demands and ways of interacting with Muslim associations (Saint-Blancat 2004; Granata 2010).

From these two points of view we examine the experience of the city of Turin, which – because of its history of immigration, the abundance of the Muslim presence and migration management policies – qualifies as an observatory that is privileged in understanding how the management of Islam takes place at the local level.

The chapter will use two sources. On the side of Muslims, there are qualitative interviews with parents and children of foreign origin conducted in 2012 and 2013 in the Turin area as part of research entitled 'Across the Mediterranean: a comparison between generations of Moroccans and Egyptians': 20 interviews with the first generation and 30 with young people between 18 and 24 years old (at the time of the interview) either reunited or born in Italy.[1] I used ethnographic semi-structured in-depth interviews (Boccagni 2009) and interviews with key respondents. Through the interviews I explored, from the perspective of the subjective experiences of both first and second generations, the role of Islam in their lives and how they interact with local society on religious issues.

The motivation to carry out in-depth interviews stems from my assumption that interviews allow for capturing processes such as experiences, values and the production of meaning, and self-positioning on crucial issues such as Islam in a strong Catholic country (Lobe *et al.* 2008).

The sampling was stratified according to gender, birthplace and year of arrival in Italy. Educational attainment is homogeneous: many of the interviewed migrants had completed secondary education, some are university students. As far as occupation is concerned, the first generation works in the catering and cleaning sectors and in the retail trade, while the second generation are mainly students. More than half of the total sample have Italian citizenship.

In this chapter we consider only some of the interviews conducted as part of the project: the testimonies gathered from young people are equally distributed by origin and gender. The quotations in the text indicate the gender, age and origin of the interviewee.[2] On the city side, the analysis takes into account five interviews with institutional representatives who are involved in managing both integration and youth policies and leaders of cultural services gathered and updated from 2009[3] to 2013. Exclusive attention to the aspect of how the communal institution in its various forms responds to the requests and demands of a growing proportion of residents and, at the same time, how social cohesion policies aimed at 'old residents' are built, has subsequently given way to attention towards the second generation. All of this is taking place in an increasingly intercultural context that is less tied to specific interventions, i.e. by the transition from *ad hoc* policies (also regarding inter-religious relations) to general policies with attention to the different identities of the city's fabric.[4]

Religious socialization across generations in emigration

Portraying the image of Islam in Italy is not easy. It would be more appropriate to propose a multi-faceted study. What is labelled as Islam must be divided by backgrounds, Koranic schools of belonging, practice, and relationship with society and with the state in its various forms.

If this is true for the first generation of immigrants, what happens to the second? The question of how faith, ethnicity and level of acculturation relate to each other is very relevant in the Italian context, where Catholicism continues to be the religion of reference for the majority of the population and where even among immigrants the proportion of Christians (especially Orthodox) is the largest one, followed by that of Muslims. However, while the former can count on a generally positive climate of acceptance (at least from the religious point of view), the latter face the risk, even when they become Italians, of being labelled negatively.

This is the lesson to be drawn from the experience of traditional immigration countries (Casanova 2009; Phalet *et al.* 2011). What is happening in Italy? Above all, what are Muslim believers' experiences? Are they bound to behave differently? One wonders what effects family religious socialization will have and if it can counteract the pressures towards secularization or 'do-it-yourself' religion, which seem to characterize today's youth population. Or if the processes of exclusion, marginalization and discrimination (Alba 2005), whose victims are still the youth of foreign origin who are, rightly or wrongly, defined as Muslims, will push them to react, taking refuge in so-called ethnic identity, in which religious belonging becomes paramount (Berry 2008; Tietze 2002; Frisina 2010).

Various research on Islam in Italy (Allievi 2003; Pace 2013) has gradually revealed how those who identify themselves in this religion can be placed along a route that goes from cultural proximity to active commitment in communitarian associationism, through intermediate positions such as those of individual and/or family practice and regular attendance at the mosque. Their attitude towards religion appears to be variable and not attributable to simplifications that tend to present the second religion among immigrants (not the first or the majority religion, as is often stated) as carried out by active believers, unaffected in religious belonging by the experience of migration and living in a context where the architectural structure for prayer is missing (or is reduced to environments that are not always uplifting, such as garages, warehouses in backyards) and the schedule of working, school and social life make practice difficult (IDOS-UNAR 2014).

Religion pervades the lives of immigrants even when the process of integration and the advance of the second generation lay the foundations for becoming Italian citizens. The growing presence of prayer halls, temples, ethnic chaplaincies, and the planning (and in some cases the building) of mosques reject the idea that migrants have internalized the same secular model that has marked recent decades of European society, in a sort of religious assimilation (Modood and Triandafyllidou 2012; Vertovec and Wassendorf 2005; Cesari 2013).

The relationship with the religion of the parents certainly changes: migration also intervenes in the way of living the faith, the frequency of practice (making it more or less constant), and the attendance at places of worship. The latter do not have only a religious role, but become important places offering hospitality services and a kind of social support system, both for the first migrants and for those who emigrate irregularly. In fact, the places of worship of immigrants become environments within which they take refuge (Hirschman 2004): where foreigners find priests who speak their native language, share (or include) the same cultural or ethnic background, and know the difficulties that arise from the encounter/clash between the way of living that one is used to and the demands of the host society.

Analysing whether and how the transition from the first to the second generation transforms adherence to Islam in Italy is extremely interesting, being a paradigmatic case of the relationship between faith, immigration and recognition of participation in social life. In other words, by looking at the Muslim community we can grasp the main elements of conflict between citizens and foreigners on a particular theme, which once again becomes a sensitive matter for the definition of identity as that of religious belonging. After all, it is not a coincidence that in recent years, research and studies in Europe and Italy have focused on the growing presence of Muslims (Hunter 2002; Cesari 2014). The growing presence of Muslims in Italy stresses relations with 'diversity', especially in those areas where the incidence of migrants coming from Maghreb is higher and where there is an Arabic presence visible through ethnic shops, women wearing the *chador* and men wearing long robes. In these areas, the issues of control and safety have been on the agenda for many years. Nowadays, these issues are less evident thanks to several local policies aimed at promoting intercultural dialogue. On the other hand, according to Muslim organizations there is a common interest in presenting a 'moderate Islam'. All the activities dealing with professing religion and organizing social activities are developed in collaboration with the institutions and paying attention to the neighbourhood and its perceptions. There is a specific will and interest of Muslim organizations (especially those in which second generations are involved) to demonstrate their propensity to promote integration. Results emerging from surveys on Muslims living in Turin confirm this aim: Muslims underline those aspects that could allow individual religious practice (the possibility that Islamic festivities could be recognized, that they could eat food according to the Koranic laws in public canteens, that the teaching of the Islamic religion could be guaranteed in schools, that they could have places to pray), rather than agreements that could give more legitimization to Islam on a national level. In short, the desire to keep their own religious tradition doesn't contradict their willingness to integrate and respect Italian law.

However, from another point of view, sometimes hasty tales of terrorist events bring to the fore fears and anxieties, operating simplistic reductions of reality and making young Muslims (and the second generation) representatives of extremist groups. In this way religion is intertwined with national belonging. Is the citizenship strong enough to weaken the radical pressures and make belonging a component of the identity mosaic without coming into conflict with the values of tolerance, coexistence and respect characteristic of the achievements of democratic societies? Or do the children of immigration remain, regardless of training, civic education received and the recognition of rights, deeply attached to the community of origin, limiting their relations with the reality in which they live only to some areas of life (such as work)?

The research scenario: a Catholic country where immigrant generations cohabit

Around 4.9 million migrants were registered in Italy at the beginning of 2014 (Istat 2014) – 7.4 per cent of the total resident population in the country – which outlines a complex situation, characterized by immigrant flows from more than 191 countries, especially Central and Eastern Europe, North Africa, Latin America and Southeast Asia. In this context, Italy is becoming an interesting case study. It is not only a recent immigration country, facing a growing presence of immigrants, but also this growth has taken place in a short period, compared with other traditional migration countries. Of course the migratory flows follow a growing trend, but they are characterized by internal transformations. Among them, here we recall the increasing number of foreign minors: only a sub-group is composed of second generations; others (the majority) are split into different generational categories.

As shown by the data (see Table 12.1), in the period 1996–2014 the number of minors increased at a much higher rate than immigrant residents as a whole, growing from 125,565 to over 953,785 (Città di Torino 2014). Two factors influenced this tendency: the arrival of minors from abroad and the number of births of children to foreign-born parents (Billari and Dalla Zuanna 2008).

Table 12.1 Foreign population of Italy: total, minors and second generation, 2006–14 (as of 1 January each year)

Foreign population	2006	2007	2008	2010	2014
Residents	2,670,514	3,432,651	3,891,293	4,235,059	4,922,085
Minors	665,625	767,060	862,453	932,675	1,134,936
Incidence of minors on foreign population (%)	22.6	22.3	22.2	22.0	21.7

Source: Istat.

Foreign minors include second generations in a strict sense (the children born in Italy from first-generation immigrants) as well as the '1.5' generation (Rumbaut 1997), i.e. those minors who arrived in Italy after the beginning of compulsory school age. This latter group constitutes the majority even if the rate of the second generation is increasing.

Within this context, Turin[5] represents a particularly interesting case. It is acknowledged to be among the most advanced Italian cities in the field of integration policies. It has been characterized by a high level of engagement with immigration since the 1980s: a special municipal office devoted to immigrants was established in 1982 in Turin, long before most Italian cities. Furthermore, the city has paid attention to immigrant children since the 1990s, and more recently to second generations. The goal of the last two local administrations has been that of strongly involving these young people, supporting them in being active citizens: they (and their juvenile organizations) are evaluated as potential and crucial bridges between first generations and Italian natives. In this framework, the local Muslim organization is strongly supported. Looking at what happens in Turin is therefore particularly interesting, especially as far as intercultural policies and measures addressing second generations are concerned, since these fields are governed mainly by soft laws (i.e. Circulars of Ministries, etc.) and thus the autonomous initiatives of local administrations are very relevant.

With regard to religion, Islam represented the main religious affiliation among immigrants up to 2003: since that year, the increasing arrivals from Eastern Europe have gradually changed the religious scenario. Even if Muslims now represent the second religious group among immigrants, they continue to attract the attention of the media and Italians in general.

Cultural centres and musallas are certainly a point of reference for many immigrants (especially first generation). Over the years, Turin has seen a change in the role of these places: they are now less concentrated on initial welcoming needs and more on social and cultural promotion of the community, especially its youngest members. Although, over time, meeting places to develop a multicultural interaction where both adults and children can socialize, understand and confront other cultures have been created, there is a need for entertainment and meeting places. Recently, the city has been engaged in supporting the project of building a mosque led by the Muslim communities.

Being Muslim, becoming Italian: differences between parents and children

The Islamic scenario in Turin, as in Italy as a whole, sees a prevalence of backgrounds from the Maghreb, but also from Albania, Senegal, Pakistan, and a plurality of attitudes towards religion, its practice and its relationship in general with society and the state in its various forms. Perhaps it is precisely in this differentiation of positions and this fragmentation that the weakness of the Islamic world in its ability to speak with Italian institutions lies. This is a weakness that also stems from the fact that the institutional representative bodies[6] have loose relations with those who can be defined as Muslim faithful. In addition to a few committed activists, there are those who are indifferent and those who express their belonging along a continuum ranging from cultural proximity to active religious associationism and community, through intermediate positions such as those of individual and/or family practice and regular mosque attendance.

Identity choices have long since been very heterogeneous, with ways of reflection and adaptation of values and norms to the Italian/European context. This is true even from the religious point of view. One would expect more secularized behaviour, a distancing from religion that, in a context that is still unaccustomed to interaction with Islam, continues to stigmatize those who explicitly or implicitly refer to it. In fact the positions taken on the matter of religion appear numerous.

> There are people who come here and change their religion, their life ... There are Egyptians who come here and experience only the 'bad' things in Italy, others see only the good things, others just think about money. (M, 42, Egypt)

> Before coming here, I was not even a practising Muslim in Morocco; on the other hand I noticed that there are people who become more observant once they are here. Why do they say that you need to protect your family, that you must protect your own traditions in the West ... ? They do it for their children, because they know that when you live here you get used to it in a different way and maybe you take a road that is a bit ... while if you become very religious, it is easier to go on your own way. Religion is used to justify, to give clear rules: do not do this, do this, etc. (M, 48, Morocco)

The first generation's voices testify the difficulties of being Muslim in a host (and not Muslim) country.

What happens among the younger generation? Are immigrant children who were born abroad and reunited during the period of compulsory schooling, or were born and socialized entirely in Italy, following in the footsteps of their parents, or do they share with their peers an attitude that oscillates between indifference and an autonomous mode of belief, which is often far from institutional participation?

The young interviewees can be divided into three groups. For some, religion is a key element of their identity, sometimes in contrast with the generation of parents who have attained a more private and barely visible religiosity.

> My mom does not wear the veil. I decided to wear it after a trip to Egypt. Even if we were born in Italy, we cannot deny our roots. And religion is a part of these roots. I'm not afraid to say that I come from a country that is rich in culture and important for the history of the Mediterranean. I am proud to be the daughter of Egyptians and to be a Muslim. My mom made a different choice: she decided to stop fighting. We know that Muslims did not have an

easy life here in Italy. Today, it is a little bit different. There are many of us who wear the veil in college, nobody makes jokes about us, wherever we go, to the cinema, shops, pizzeria, no one looks at us in a strange way. It was different 20 years ago. So to cut it short and to avoid being the target, my mother said: No more veil. (F, 22, Egypt)

These are tough decisions in a scenario of youth religiosity where one reasons more in terms of the weakness of faith and 'do it yourself' religion than in the recognition of mainstream religiosity.

It is up to us to prove that we are true Moroccans, true Egyptians, true Muslims, but at the same time we have to prove that we are worthy to live in Italy. Even when we have Italian citizenship, every day is a bit like being under scrutiny. It is something that you feel. Maybe it is because here it is not like in Amsterdam or London, where going around with the veil, entering a bookstore to look for books about the Koran, having world-class restaurants that pay attention to all religious diets, are not considered as something strange. Our parents had to settle for that. Could they have done something else? We must work to avoid being moulded in their image. Generally it is said that we do not want to do the work of our parents. It is not just that. We do not want to be labelled as they were. Even with regard to religion. We are different. The way of experiencing religion does not remain constant through time. Even for Italians it is not the same. Where are the processions? Where are the veiled women in the church? And do young people go to Mass like their grandparents? Like their parents? Do they observe Lent? Why do we, children of Muslims, not have the right to be different from our parents? Why are they amazed? Isn't this what Italy hoped for? Do they call us new Italians, second generation, to erase our past, perhaps? (M, 24, Morocco)

Those who are tied to religious associations are aware of the distance that separates their generation from that of their parents in the way they live and interpret their faith, as well as in their relationship with Italy and their countries of origin. The intergenerational comparison on aspects of religion highlights a deep reflective ability of young people, particularly those with higher levels of education, in understanding the challenges they face as children of immigration. This is in addition to perceiving differences with respect to the education and socialization of their parents, which took place in an environment permeated by religion and where cultural, religious and national belonging merged to become at the same time a unique, indistinctive ensemble within the local community and a distinguishing feature compared to external interactions.

Last, there is the group who believe that religion is part of their family's upbringing and little more.

To you, a Muslim is the figure of a man who always goes to the mosque, who follows only what the imam says, who observes Ramadan. To me and many of my friends, being a Muslim means coming from a family tied to Islam. Many of us, young people, only observe Ramadan and we participate in festivities, like the Feast of the Sacrifice. We are Muslims in our own way. We live here, not in Morocco or Egypt. We must try to adapt. (M, 21, Morocco)

In this third group, religion only becomes a point of reference to the family environment, to a cultural background in which one grows up, to a relationship that is more or less intense until adolescence and is then followed by detachment. In these cases, being a Muslim is a (small) piece of the identity puzzle.

My father is very religious. I had been a practising Muslim from the age of 8 to 18. I had always observed the five daily prayers, Ramadan, etc., because my father passed me down his religious fervour. Then at some point, when I started to think a little bit for myself … I don't know, going dancing or drinking alcohol became an incompatibility between belief and what I put into practice. Although I do not pray any more, I still observe Ramadan. Obviously, this displeases my father but it is my choice. It is useless to pray just to please your father. I do not observe the five daily prayers and I do not go to the mosque on Fridays, because going to school or working prevents me from doing so, unless I have a day off on Friday. Even my sisters have followed my path: one of my sisters stopped much earlier than me, another resumed after years of interruption, the other two are believers but they do not pray. However, we all observe Ramadan. In short, there are minor differences but we all chose, more or less, the same path. My father continues to go to the mosque and during Ramadan he goes there every day. For the rest of the year, since he's working, he prays at home in the evening. However, he is still a very practising Muslim. (M, 24, Morocco)

The words above are emblematic not only of how adults and young people live their relationship with religion, but also of how this relationship cuts across all backgrounds. The difference in approach that accompanies the two generations of Moroccans (and Egyptians) is the same as what we can see in many Italian families (Garelli 2011): the outcomes of religious socialization can sometimes result in a younger generation that continues the tradition of behaviour and religious practices of their parents, sometimes giving rise to processes of detachment, to independent paths of relationship with the sacred.

My parents tried to pass me down their culture and their religion, but I immediately realized it was not something for me. However, I am tied to some things and I want them to stay for a lifetime, because it is something that binds me to them and that identifies me. Even if I am not a believer, I identify myself with it and I love it. (M, 18, Egypt)

For young people, following the teachings of their parents is not easy. There are those who come here and have forgotten Islam, especially those who have married an Italian woman. Perhaps both parents are working and children hang out with their friends, so they end up not even speaking Arabic any more. Fortunately, now there are antennae that let us watch TV shows from around the world. There were none before. Now this allows children to learn more Arabic and more about religion. In our days, it all depended on us but it was not enough. Now it's easier, because there are more young Muslims. We have educated our children like us, but they have their ways. They have more Italian friends than Egyptians. When people ask me to do something about it, I just let them be, because they know their religion and they know what they can and cannot do. (M, 53, Egypt)

The interviewee emphasizes an important aspect of the relationship between young people and religion, which is 'the power of large numbers'. The increased visibility of Muslim families, the number of students at school who claim to be Muslim, the girls who wear the veil and the associative leading role linked to religion can, therefore, be a fertile ground for the emergence of latent religious identities, whose appearance was prevented by fear of stigma or discrimination. To this end, however, mosques – or rather, prayer halls, which continue to be a point of reference for the old pioneers and the new immigrants – seem to play a lesser role, carrying out functions that are typical of those religious organizations in emigration, which is not only a reference to religion but also (and especially) to identity (McKay 1982; Portes and Hao 2002).

Looking for acceptance: is it always the same story?

Children and parents, despite their different ways of maintaining ties with religion, the tools they use in order to keep in touch with the *Ummah* (the community of Muslim believers), and how they manage religious identity in everyday life, share a setting where Islam is a minority religion and requires negotiations with the local authorities. It is precisely on what to negotiate and how to manage the process of debate and discussion with the institutions that differences between the first and second generations are starting to emerge.

At the local level, the main objectives of the first generation of Muslims concerned the basic needs of expression of the religious in emigration, such as the allocation of space to devote to places of worship and some form of cultural recognition (Allievi 2009).

The associationism of the first generation of Muslims spoke with local partners to reclaim some essential requirements for the observance of religious practice (e.g. permission to open *halal* butchers or abattoirs, allocation of land to build mosques and places of worship, rules that provide areas dedicated to the burial of the dead of Muslim faith, ability to consume food in compliance with the Islamic diet in public canteens, religious assistance on the part of ministers of religion to hospitalized people, soldiers and prisoners) and only later with the central institutions of the state. In this process, associationism, which has a more significant role on the ethno-national basis than religion, has been an important point of reference, both for members of the community and for local institutions.

These requests deal with the so-called religious 'infrastructure' (Grillo 2006): mosques, schools, butcher's shops and cemeteries. These are environments and spaces that require interaction at local level, negotiation with institutions and also with neighbourhood committees, with lay or ethnic associations, tied to other origins and religions. The discussion in the public arena is not about the entente with the Italian state but how to put the right of religious freedom and its manifestations into effect (Ferrari 2008). It is a right that has to be guaranteed, starting with the recognition of places of worship because their absence makes it difficult for them to live their own religiosity and feel like a community: both generations agree on this (Granata 2010).

> Then there is also the issue of the environment, which is just different, there is no call to prayer and maybe you're the only one to pray. In Morocco, when there is a call to prayer and everyone goes to the mosque, you really feel it, while here, during the day; maybe I do not remember it either because you do not realize it is the time of prayer. And if you're on the street or at work, how do you pray? (F, 32, Morocco)

> There is no religious life here, it does not exist. If I am religious and I want to practise, I am unable to. The mosques are the ugliest places in the world ... This is the main reason why I want to go back to Egypt. Here, I cannot practise as I would like: there are no tools and structures ... The relationship with religion here is hard because you're in a different society. Islam is a religion for the whole world but if you don't have a mosque, if you suffer in the mosque because you are hot, it stinks, there are people who are packed tight in a shameful way, if they close the mosques, these reasons cause great difficulties in practising your religion and developing your religious ideas. (M, 26, Egypt)

The mosque represents, even in a relatively recent immigration country like Italy, is a need that cannot be ignored any longer. And it is the institutional level of the city to be vested with such a request: a thorny issue in which a series of heterogeneous positions intertwine and in which the issue goes beyond the boundaries of religion to become identity, socio-economic and political ones. Parents and children are in agreement with the request, but the approach and the meaning attributed are different. For children, the mosque is only a religious reference: a place of prayer, and must be considered as such even in its structure and in its decor. For fathers (mostly), it is also a place of 'status recovery' (Dassetto 1994). In the mosque, parents, who perceive themselves as being troubled in their authority with their children, who are proceeding steadily in their integration and insertion into society, seek 'to recover a status as members of the mosque and find the symbolic strength and motivation to transfer it to the bosom of the family' (Dassetto 1994: 73).

With this different approach, a logical evolution from one generation to another becomes clear: all younger interviewees confine the mosque to its purely religious function, thus creating a clear discontinuity with the first generation.

In addition to the place of worship, we can see other issues of the relationship between Islam and the local reality, in which the two generations are placed in a different (and sometimes opposite) manner. This is participation in city life and the recognition of the socio-cultural role played by the Muslim group, in the Turin context, where one-third of the population is of foreign origin. For the parents' generation, the cognitive frame within which such a relationship is placed is that of immigration, which relies on the dialectics between a community that sinks its cultural-value roots in a place that has a plurality of origins, but a unique religious reference and an adverse context where they struggle to converse. For the children, the reference to immigration and diversity must be abandoned: the relationship is equal, between (almost) citizens, among residents who are committed to the common good of the community and the city. The change of tone is significant: as claimed by Scholten (2011) and Borkert and Caponio (2010), it goes from immigrants being recipients of interventions to being co-protagonists in policy-making. In this sense, the intercultural declination, in the acceptance, as we shall see in the next section, of an 'intercultural inclusive policy', encourages the relationships between Islamic associations and local institutions to shed the immigrants vs citizens (explosive and reductive) dichotomy. Besides that, for the second generation it is no longer about presenting requests that 'confine' Islam to being a personal issue of immigrants, who look back nostalgically, but about entering the religious discourse in the most coveted debate on religious pluralism, freeing it from its ties with immigration. And this happens primarily at the local level. Energy is invested in building partnerships, in conquering spaces of reliability and recognition: in other words, to become reliable partners of institutions and schools. The new actors, in fact, often have no experience of migration, and sometimes they are Italian citizens: young people of another religion who seek space and express willingness to participate in intercultural and inter-religious policies of their city.

Local institutions and young Muslims on the mirror

How can these generational transformations fit in the political and institutional discourse with the cities? What attitude do they adopt in relation to a generation of young Muslims? The relationship between immigrant associationism and cities can be framed according to four prevailing positions (see Table 12.2).

These are positions that change as the process of integration of immigrants into the host society continues, but only in some cases do they reach active involvement in the processes of policy-making: the dynamics of involvement and partnership in the field of intercultural activities, and those of an advisory nature, as recently emphasized by the promotion of tables dedicated to inter-religious dialogue in local institutions, seem to prevail in the Italian context.

Table 12.2 Type of relationship between associationism and local institutions

	Level of involvement of immigrant associationism in city life		
	−		+
Attitude of the city/type of activities promoted	Reactive Interactive	Informative Collaborative	Advisory Decision-making

Source: Re-adaptation from Saksela-Begholm (2009).

In these dynamics, the arrival of the second generation on the public scene introduces a new element into the debate (Levitt *et al.* 2010). The recognition of immigrant children as key players in creating social cohesion and dialogue between natives and immigrants has been part of local policies for several years. In this direction, young foreigners and young people of foreign origin are supported in their activities of active citizenship, in the organization and promotion of autonomous collective activities, and even in the religious field: the association of Young Muslims in Italy, with its various local sections, is the best-known example (Frisina 2007).

The city of Turin has for a long time developed, in its immigration policy, attention to young people, children of immigration, considering them as important actors in building and strengthening processes of social cohesion, especially in areas where interaction between natives and immigrants may be more difficult and where controversies over cultural and religious diversity take place year after year, stimulated by greater visibility, continuing a process of citizenship, an increase of students in schools and by the demands of Muslim associations posed to the citizens (Ponzo and Ricucci 2011). This choice results not only in opportunities for interventions, but also in supporting the collective pivotal role, with a view to promoting and developing the idea of 'active citizenship' in which space is also given to the religious dimension. In fact, even on this matter, 'second generations have always been a challenge and an opportunity for the receiving societies', as noted by Ambrosini (2006). The challenge is represented by the relationships that develop with the parents' generation, or how they interact with the demands of 'loyalty' and conformism. The opportunity is the ability to weave values elsewhere with their own mode of action in the context in which they create biographies. Attention to the opportunities of a young generation growing up is what characterizes the city of Turin, a context wherein practices aimed at engaging immigrant (and religious) associationism have been carried out since the 1980s.

The requests made to the administration since the beginning have been for rooms, spaces to pray, meeting places. These requests were mostly made by the Moroccan community, who were often confused between requests for assistance to help newly arrived immigrants and requests to satisfy needs of a religious nature. To everyone, in fact, the place in which one prays is also the place where they meet and exchange information, which strengthens them to face the new reality. (Municipal representative)

There are no big differences between the demands of ethnic and/or religious associations: spaces, locales, grants for activities. Recently attention – from everyone – has been paid to children, to young people. Associations are concerned about the second generation, which may be 'too Italian'. Muslim communities are the best equipped for this, because the various 'mosques' offer Arabic language classes for children. In recent years, we have also had some experiments in elementary and middle schools. Muslim parents appreciate these initiatives. Indeed, in some cases they prefer Arabic to be taught in school and not in the mosque. Even this seems like a sign of the times: we are accustomed to think of all observing and practising families as being similar (even though there are also those who are critical towards the imam) in their way of managing activities within the same religious associationism. We must be careful. The city must take into account all the different spirits of Islam, like those within the Catholic and Orthodox communities. The underlying theme is that of representation, choosing the interlocutor (or interlocutors) that are truly representative of the different communities. (Councillor for integration)

However, a diachronic look serves to highlight the strengths and weaknesses of the first and second generations in their relationship with the city. In the first case, the relationship was mostly on demand: associations, weak from the organizational point of view and unprepared to interact with the government, were placed in a predominantly 'on demand' dimension (whether they were spaces or funds for small initiatives). With the younger ones, the relationship shifts to partnership: they are more prepared both linguistically and thanks to the functioning of the administration system. The new generation aims to be recognized as a partner. They aim to be present and active in the cultural events of the city, to intervene – if possible – in the processes of decision-making to reinforce the thesis that Islam is compatible with the citizen's leading role. Aspirations collide – even in a city that is an integration laboratory like Turin – with reality, which sees the associations of the second generation, although appreciated by a large part of the local political groups, but not yet able to replace the associationism of parents as representatives of the institutions. However, we must be careful not to confuse absence in the process of decision-making with absence *tout court* in the debate regarding issues of concern: the ideas of how children of immigration intend to decline Muslim belonging spreads through participation in conferences, the organization of public events and especially on the web.

Conclusion: being Muslim and active citizens

On the one hand, there are young people, and children, who are competent in Italian, present and active in civic life, connected with their peers both in the European diaspora and their countries of origin, members of Islam that is 'tempered' or 'conditioned' by the comparison with Italian reality. On the other, there are adults and parents who are anchored to the image of Islam in emigration that took refuge in the mosque, who find comfort and support in the ethno-national community and do not feel the need to become an essential and relevant partner of intercultural policies in the city (Dassetto 2004). Of course, between these two poles, there are representative associations who are working for entente at the national level. However, this, as well as the Council for Italian Islam and the definition of the Charter of Values, has little echo at the local level, where – as seen above – there are ways of coexistence and management that highlight the need for a change of gear in reflection on the relationship with Islam in Italy. And once again it is at the local level that the internal transformations of Muslim associationism are felt: the increase of youth leadership, girls' activism, promotion of interfaith events and initiatives of debate on Italian and European Islam. The revolution then comes to light – even at the religious level – dictated by the advance of the second generation and the progress of the agenda regarding the internal confrontation of associations on the theme of leadership and the role that children of immigration play in promoting recognition and appreciation of their parents' generation.

In 2012 something happened. In that year, a kind of turning point can be identified in the relations between first and second Muslim generations: for the first time young people played a pivotal role in managing a socio-cultural initiative[7] in a place where adults – that is, the first generation – take on leadership and management roles. However, the desire of some to act as leaders, offering an Islam different from that of their fathers, is not without obstacles: it is very difficult for young people to be recognized as representatives of the community, threatening to obscure figures who have been taking on roles of responsibility within the organization for a long time.

On the other hand, young people can count on the support of the local administration:[8] perhaps unconsciously, due to the fear of assimilation that affects immigrant societies, the leading role of the second generation is sought and promoted, even on the religious front. In fact, the orientation has for some time now been of an inclusive type in Turin. After the period of presentation of different cultures, religions and languages as alternative elements to the everyday life of the city, a phase began in which attention was devoted to how a person of foreign origin and a Muslim can ever be considered an Italian citizen (and a citizen of Turin), without necessarily relegating the expression of their religiosity to their private sphere. The protagonists of this period are young people, the second generation, on whom the administration has decided to focus, considering them as 'new Italians' and promoting their leading roles.

The Turin experience seems to show a change of tone and picks up signals of a breakdown in the manners and contents between first- and second-generation associationism. The instances are more general, related to their recognition as actors and a significant part of the socio-cultural context of the city. The concerns are related to awareness-raising activities and informing citizens about the development and transformations of generations taking place with the Muslim presence.[9] The ground on which we are moving seems to be more and more that of 'symbolic religiosity' (Gans 1994), in which the religious identities of the second generation are only loosely tied to beliefs and practices, rather than being held together and strengthened by belonging together to an association. Through symbolic religiosity, affiliation to Islam can result in recognition of a common Muslim identity, shared by and practised within the association's activities, but not necessarily tied to the observance of practices. Therefore, there is a dissociation between a practising Muslim and the one who recognizes a cultural reference and identity in Islam. On this distinction, new demands and new relationships (more on the side of collaboration and partnership than breaking off and contrast) with the local reality take place. The aim is not so much the outright recognition of their practices and specificity as that of the right to diversity and the promotion of intercultural policies, in which religious difference is one element of the city's social fabric and not a factor of conflict.

The match (yet to be played) refers to the ability of Islamic associationism of the second generation not to remain 'forever young' and to be able to learn how to combine the demands of neo-Italians with those of older generations. In other words, after overcoming the phase of retreat to their origins, they look towards the future: a future where becoming adults (and the assumption of new family responsibilities) is already on the horizon and the appearance of a generation of older people who will consult, once again, religious associationism, and the city, about needs that go beyond taking care of one's soul.

Notes

1 I used ethnographic semi-structured in-depth interviews (Boccagni 2009) and interviews with key respondents. Through the interviews I explored, even from the slope of the subjective experiences of both first and second generations, the role of Islam in their lives and how they interact with the local society on religious issues. The motivation to carry out in-depth interviews stems from my assumption that interviews allow for capturing processes such as experiences, values and the production of meaning, self-positioning on a crucial issue such as Islam in a strong Catholic country (Lobe *et al.* 2008). The sampling was stratified according to gender, birthplace and year of arrival in Italy. Educational attainment is homogeneous: many of the interviewed migrants had completed secondary education, some are university students. As far as occupation is concerned, the first generation works in the catering and cleaning sectors and in the retail trade, while the second generations are mainly students. Finally, more than half of the total sample have Italian citizenship. In this chapter we consider only some of the interviews conducted as part of the project: the testimonies gathered from young people are equally distributed by origin and gender. The quotations in the text indicate the gender, age and origin of the interviewee.

2 In the knowledge that the Islamic universe is heterogeneous in its origins and reference points, this exploration looks at only two of the communities mentioned, as they now represent an example not only of a complete migration cycle (Castles and Miller 1993), but also the revision of migration projects as a result of the economic downturn (particularly in the case of Morocco) and the transnational dynamics influenced by the events occurred in countries of origin. For further details on these two issues, see Ricucci (2011) and Premazzi *et al.* (2012).

3   In 2009 a study was conducted on the policies of the City of Turin with regard to Muslim communities as part of the CLIP (Cities for Local Integration Policies) international project.
4   On this issue, see Caponio *et al.* (2015) and Ponzo and Ricucci (2011).
5   Turin is located in the north-west of Italy, in the Piedmont region. The municipality had 140,138 foreign residents at the beginning of 2014, i.e. 15.4 per cent of total residents (Città di Torino 2014). The main nationalities are Romanian, Moroccan, Peruvian, Chinese, Albanian and Filipino. Every year it becomes clearer that foreigners' presence in Turin, as in the rest of Italy, is more and more a structural phenomenon. If we analyse the age structure of the immigrant population, it is composed essentially of young people, increasing year by year.
6   We recall, in particular, the UCOII (Union of Islamic Communities in Italy), the CoReis (Islamic Religious Community) and AMI (Italian Muslim Association). For further details, see Guolo (2005) and Coppi and Spreafico (2008).
7   An initiative addressing children of immigrants during summer time has been organized by a group of second-generation Muslims.
8   Among the various ways in which cities translate the invitation into the development of intercultural approaches (Zapata-Barrero 2015), the case of Turin is an example of how interculturalism has resulted in policies and programmes aimed at recognizing religious pluralism as an element of dialogue within the city.
9   In this sense, the theatrical experience developed by the Turin section of Young Muslims in Italy, *Richiami Lontani*, which aims to present Islam and the possible ways of integration and intercultural dialogue to the public, should be read.

References

Alba, R. D. 2005. 'Bright versus blurred boundaries: second-generation assimilation and exclusion in France, Germany, and the United States'. *Ethnic and Racial Studies* 28(1): 20–49.

Alexander, M. 2004. 'Comparing local policies toward migrants: an analytical framework, a typology and preliminary survey results'. In R. Penninx, K. Kraal, M. Martiniello and S. Vertovec, eds, *Citizenship in European Cities: Immigrants, Local Politics and Integration Policies*, 57–84. Aldershot: Ashgate.

Allievi, S. 2003. *Islam italiano. Viaggio nella seconda religione del paese*. Torino: Einaudi.

Allievi, S. 2009. *Conflicts over Mosques in Europe: Policy Issues and Trends*. NEF Initiative on Religion and Democracy in Europe, London: Alliance Publishing Trust.

Ambrosini, M. 2006. 'Italiani col trattino: figli dell'immigrazione in cerca di identità'. LIMES Laboratorio Immigrazioni Multiculturalismo Società Working Paper. www. socpol.unimi.it/altrisiti/limes/documenti/File/Ambrosini2G.doc.

Berry, J. W. 2008. 'Immigration, acculturation, and adaptation'. *Applied Psychology* 46(1): 5–34.

Billari, F. and Dalla Zuanna, G. 2008. *La rivoluzione nella culla. Il declino che non c'è*. Bologna: Il Mulino.

Boccagni, P. 2009. *Tracce transnazionali. Vite in Italia e proiezioni verso casa tra immigrati ecuadoriani*. Milano: Franco Angeli.

Borkert, M. and Caponio, T., eds. 2010. *The Local Dimension of Migration Policymaking*. Amsterdam: Amsterdam University Press.

Bowen, J. R. 2010. *Can Islam be French? Pluralism and Pragmatism in a Secularist State*. Princeton, NJ: Princeton University Press.

Bracke, S. and Fadil, N. 2008. 'Islam and secular modernity under western eyes: a genealogy of a constitutive relationship'. *EUI Working Papers*, RSCAS 2008/05, Mediterranean Programme Series.

Caponio, T., Ponzo, I. and Ricucci, R. 2015. 'Policy change or policy re-styling? The case of intercultural integration policy in Turin, Lisbon and Valencia'. In M. Sacco, C. Torrekens, I. Adam and F. Zibouh, eds, *Circulation des idées et des modèles: les transformations de l'action publique en question. Le cas des politiques d'intégration.* Bruxelles: Academia-Bruylant.

Casanova, J. 2009. 'Immigration and the new religious pluralism: a European Union–United States comparison'. In G. Brahm Levey and T. Modood, eds, *Secularism, Religion and Multicultural citizenship*, 139–63. Cambridge: Cambridge University Press.

Castles, S. and Miller, M. J. 1993. *The Age of Migration: International Population Movements in the Modern World.* London: Macmillan.

Cesari, J. 2013. *Why the West Fears Islam.* New York: Palgrave Macmillan.

Cesari, J. 2014. *The Handbook of European Islam.* Oxford: Oxford University Press.

Cesari, J. and Pacini, A. 2005. *Giovani musulmani in Europa.* Torino: Edizioni Fondazione Agnelli.

Città di Torino. 2014. Torino.

Coppi, A. and Spreafico, A. 2008. 'The long path from recognition to representation of Muslims in Italy'. *The International Spectator* 43(3): 101–15.

Crane, K. R. 2003. *Latino Churches: Faith, Family and Ethnicity in the Second Generation.* New York: LFB Scholarly Publishing.

Dassetto, F. 1994. *L'Islam in Europa.* Torino: Edizioni Fondazione Agnelli

Ferrari, S., ed. 2008. *Introduzione al diritto comparato delle religioni. Ebraismo, islam e induismo.* Bologna: Il Mulino.

Frisina, A. 2007. *Giovani Musulmani d'Italia.* Roma: Carocci.

Frisina, A. 2010. 'Autorappresentazioni pubbliche di giovani musulmane. La ricerca di legittimità di una nuova generazione di italiane'. *Mondi migranti* 2: 131–50.

Gans, H. G. 1994. 'Symbolic ethnicity and symbolic religiosity: towards a comparison of ethnic and religious acculturation'. *Ethnic and Racial Studies* 17(4): 577–92.

Garelli, F. 2011. *Religione all'italiana.* Bologna: Il Mulino.

Granata, A. 2010. 'Di padre in figlio, di figlio in padre. Il ruolo innovativo delle seconde generazioni nelle comunità religiose di minoranza'. *Mondi migranti* 3: 86–100.

Grillo, R. 2004. 'Islam and transnationalism'. *Journal of Ethnic and Migration Studies* 30(5): 861–78.

Guolo, R. 2005. 'Il campo religioso musulmano in Italia'. *Rassegna Italiana di Sociologia* 4: 631–57.

Hirschman, C. 2004. 'The role of religion in the origins and adaptation of immigrant groups in the United States'. *International Migration Review* 38(3): 1206–33.

Istat. 2014. *La popolazione straniera in Italia.* www.demo.istat.it.

Hunter, S. T., ed. 2002. *Islam, Europe's Second Religion: The New Social, Cultural, and Political Landscape.* Westport, CT: Praeger.

IDOS-UNAR. 2014. *Rapporto immigrazione.* Roma: IDOS.

Levitt, P., Barnett, M. and Khalil, N. 2010. 'Learning to pray: negotiating religious practice across generations and borders'. In K. Fog Olwig and M. Rytter, eds, *Mobile Bodies, Mobile Souls*, 139–59. Aarhus: Aarhus University Press.

Lobe, B., Livingstone, S., Olafsson, K. and Simoes, J. A. 2008. *Best Practice Research Guide: How to Research Children and Online Technologies in Comparative Perspective*, Deliverable D4.2. London: EU Kids Online.

Lorentzen, L. A., ed. 2009. *Religion at the Corner of Bliss and Nirvana: Politics, Identity, and Faith in New Migrant Communities*. Durham, NC: Duke University Press.

Maddanu, S. 2009. 'L'islamità dei giovani musulmani e l'ijtihad moderno: nuove pratiche per una nuova religiosità europea'. *Rassegna Italiana di Sociologia* 4: 655–80.

McKay, J. 1982. 'An exploratory synthesis of primordial and mobilizationist approaches to ethnic phenomena'. *Ethnic and Racial Studies* 5: 392–420.

Meer, N., Martineau, W. and Thompson, S. 2012. 'Misrecognizing Muslim consciousness in Europe'. *Ethnicities* 12: 131–41.

Modood T. and Triandafyllidou, A., eds. 2012. *European Multiculturalisms: Cultural, Religious and Ethnic Challenges*. Edinburgh: Edinburgh University Press.

Moghissi, H. and Gorashi, H., eds. 2010. *Muslim Diaspora in the West Negotiating Gender, Home and Belonging*. Farnham: Ashgate.

Open Society Institute. 2010. *Muslims in Europe. A Report on EU 11 Cities*. Budapest and New York: Open Society Institute.

Pace, V. 2013. *Le religioni nell'Italia che cambia*. Roma: Carocci.

Phalet, K., Güngör, D. and Fleischmann, F. 2011. 'Religious identification, beliefs, and practices among Turkish-Belgian and Moroccan-Belgian Muslims: intergenerational continuity and acculturative change'. *Journal of Cross-cultural Psychology* 42(8): 1356–74.

Ponzo, I. and Ricucci, R. 2011. 'Second-generations: a new actor on the scene of intercultural policies?' Paper presented at the annual Conference IMISCOE, Varsaw, 9/10 November.

Portes, A. and Hao, L. 2002. 'The price of uniformity: language, family and personality adjustment in the immigrant second generation', *Ethnic and Racial Studies* 25(6): 889–912.

Premazzi, V., Castagnone, E. and Cingolani, P. 2012. 'How do political changes in the country of origin affect transnational behaviors of migrants? The case of Egyptians in Turin during and after the Arab Spring'. In IOM and LAS, eds, *A Study on the Dynamics of Arab Expatriate Communities: Promoting Positive Contributions to Socioeconomic Development and Political Transitions in their Homelands*, 71–86. Cairo: IOM.

Ricucci, R. 2011. *Le famiglie straniere di fronte alla crisi. Istantanee Piemontesi*. Torino: FIERI. Rapporto di ricerca.

Rumbaut, R. G. 1997. 'Assimilation and its discontents: between rhetoric and reality.' *International Migration Review* 31(4): 923–60.

Saint-Blancat, C. 2004. 'La transmission de l'islam auprès de nouvelles générations de la diaspora'. *Social Compass* 51: 235–47.

Saksela-Bergholm, S. 2009. *Immigrant Associations in the Metropolitan Area of Finland Forms of Mobilisation, Participation and Representation*. PhD thesis. Helsinki: Swedish School of Social Science.

Scholten, P. 2011. *Framing Immigrant Integration: Dutch Research-Policy Dialogues in Comparative Perspective*. Amsterdam: Amsterdam University Press.

Tietze, N. 2002. *Jeunes musulmans de France et d'Allemagne. Les constructions subjectives de l'identit*. Paris: L'Harmattan.

Vertovec, S. and Wassendorf, S. 2005. *Migration and Cultural, Religious and Linguistic Diversity in Europe: An Overview of Issues and Trends*. Oxford: Compass.

Vertovec, S. and Wassendorf, S., eds. 2010. *The Multiculturalism Backlash: European Discourses, Policies and Practices*. New York: Routledge.

Zapata-Barrero, R., ed. 2015. *The Intercultural Turn for Cities: How to Conceptualize and Monitor It?* Cheltenham: Edward Elgar.

Conclusion

Catherine Wihtol de Wenden

The unity of the Mediterranean has been debated as a frame of thought and of research by several observers. The geographer Yves Lacoste defines it as the civilization of the olive tree and distinguishes three different spaces: Maghreb/ Europe, Balkans and the Near East, which also corresponds to various forms of migration (immigration of work and of family reunification, disentanglement of ethnic and religious belongings, refugees). The historian Fernand Braudel in his famous book *Mediterranean in the period of Philippe II* described the region as a place of crossed civilizations and ways of life led by transborder networks, due to the intensity of its shared story of conflicts and dialogues, to its demographic dynamism and to the interdependency of its economies. But he also added that with the discovery of the New World by the Spanish and Portuguese, the Mediterranean began to decline because it ceased at the end of the fifteenth century to be turned towards itself, looking at new horizons. The comparison could be extended to now, but in a reverse approach, where the globalization of migration focuses on the Mediterranean as a concentration of almost all migration situations in the world: refugees, illegals, unaccompanied minors, processes of containment and of mobility, integration dynamics and security approaches, transnationalism and diasporas, religious identities and pluralism, which are the theme of this book.

Migration in the Mediterranean is a very acute debate, due to the present refugee crisis, the consequences of Arab revolutions, its proximity with emigration and transit countries, but also the involvement of Southern European countries in the arrival of newcomers. This book focuses on a multidisciplinary approach, mostly in sociology and economy, but also in geography, political science and history, on the logics of migration movements in the region, the perverse effects of dissuasion policies of border controls and the various forms of transnational networks which are spread between countries of departure and arrival.

The analysis is comprehensive through the 12 chapters, written from a very large variety of points of view:

1   The first question raised is how far the Mediterranean as a migration space, system and regime can be a comprehensive approach to analyse the specificity of migration movements, trends and mobilities in the region.

2   The second question deals with the Mediterranean immigration model in a time of crisis: perverse effects of border closure, illegals and trafficking, women at borders, black and segmented labour markets, and unaccompanied minors, in spite of its links with European convergence for integration through integration indexes across all European immigration countries

3   The third part focuses on various forms of transnationalism, social, political and religious in several countries: Algerians and Moroccans in France, Egyptians in Paris and Vienna, second generations of Muslims in Italy, through the lens of influences of countries of origin and of settlement, voting at distance, religious networks and memory diasporas.

The originality of the approach also lies in some of its 'Italian' point of view, with an interesting analysis of former Italian female and illegal migration to Africa in the past (Chapter 2), with two various definitions on the specificity of the so-called Mediterranean model of migration (Chapters 3 and 4), with three case studies relating to the Italian migration landscape: illegals, minors and women at borders (Chapters 5, 6 and 7), with a comparative study of convergences for integration (Chapter 8), with transnationalism focused on France/Maghreb, Egypt, Israel and Italy, a perspective rarely undertaken through the choice of these countries.

To conclude, the value of this book lies in its effort to answer the questions raised from the beginning and to illustrate by numerous field studies the theoretical and analytical framework.

Index

For Product Safety Concerns and Information please contact our EU
representative GPSR@taylorandfrancis.com
Taylor & Francis Verlag GmbH, Kaufingerstraße 24, 80331 München, Germany